THE RISE OF REFORM JUDAISM

Books by W. Gunther Plaut

Mount Zion—The First Hundred Years (1956)

The Jews in Minnesota (1959)

The Book of Proverbs—A Commentary (1961)

Judaism and the Scientific Spirit (1962)

The Rise of Reform Judaism (1963)

W. GUNTHER PLAUT

THE RISE OF REFORM JUDAISM

****

A Sourcebook of its European Origins

Preface by SOLOMON B. FREEHOF

[v. 1]

WORLD UNION FOR PROGRESSIVE JUDAISM, LTD.

New York

Library of Congress Catalog Card Number: 63-13568

This volume has been published with the assistance of the Cultural Fund of the Conference on Jewish Material Claims Against Germany, Inc. *It is the first of a series of books planned for publication by the* WORLD UNION FOR PROGRESSIVE JUDAISM, LTD. *with the cooperation of the* CLAIMS CONFERENCE *and the* UNION OF AMERICAN HEBREW CONGREGATIONS.

Second Printing, 1969

For

ELIZABETH

A true liberal

Preface

✶✶

WHILE THESE LINES are being written, the "cold war" engages two gigantic forces which are working to strengthen the morale of their own camp and to weaken the resistance in the opposing camp.

This great campaign of world persuasion can be seen as a titanic psychological enterprise akin to the national advertising campaigns of mass persuasion but on a world-wide scale and for much greater stakes than the annual profits of a manufacturing firm. The campaign is, of course, psychological, but psychology is only the instrument. The various devices, the denunciations, the posters, the parades, all these are meant to inculcate certain convictions. Behind all this use of psychology there is a philosophy. What are the basic ideas that each side in this world's "cold war" contest is trying to inculcate?

First, it is a sense of idealism. Each side believes that the happiness of mankind is attainable, and that the world *is* moving to a nobler future. The doctrine of world-future translates itself into a sense of personal mission. Each man in the respective countries is being persuaded that he is on the side of history. It is strange that two opposing philosophies such as world-Communism and world-Democracy share the basic assumption that the world can be made into an Eden and that each person may further the high intention of human history. Also, it is surprising that this faith in spritual armament is still so strong in this age of advanced technology, when new weapons, each more awesome than the preceding, are being invented and the technical means for increasing the store of these weapons is at hand. Yet the fact remains that the materialism and the technical competence of the age have not to the slightest degree so mechanized the mind of world leadership that there is any loss of faith in the effectiveness of the psychological and philosophic weapon. Although new arms are being invented and stock-piled, the chief and continuous struggle of the last twenty-five years has been in the realm of the spirit—to persuade, to convince, to strengthen faith, to deepen the sense of national idealism and personal inspiration.

Of course, the materialism of the age carries with it a certain scorn for the spiritual and a certain cynicism against all idealism. This cynicism and disillusion cannot be easily overcome. Therefore, what the nations in their psychological propaganda hope to achieve is that modern cynicism should continue in the lives of their opponents but that the older idealism should be revived among their own people. Let the fashionable cynicism sap the strength of our enemies; we will use psychological means to restore the idealism of our own people.

It need not be restated that the idealism which the whole world seeks was brought into human thought by Judaism, which had reversed the ancient cyclic or catastrophic view of history and converted the vision of history into an onward march. It changed the mood of men from "Once upon a time," to "There shall come a day." This concept, which came to its brightest ancient radiance in the time of the Second Isaiah, lived as a spark in Judaism, kept alive by the breath of Messianism, often sheltered in the lantern of Cabbala, all through the Dark Ages. It came to a flame for the first time in twenty-three hundred years in the beginning of the modern era. Reform Judaism is the first flaming up of direct world-idealism in Judaism since the days of the Second Isaiah.

Among Jewish writers of the last two generations it was customary to mock at these Reformers. The first dart hurled at them was that they had lost their sense of values. They gave up the tangible for the unreal. For the sake of an imagined comradeship with the non-Jewish world they surrendered up large portions of the Jewish tradition. They made themselves un-Jewish in order to become modern. The emancipation was paid for with too great a price. To this it may be said that it was not the Reformers who consciously abandoned Jewish habits and ceremonies and ways of life. These observances and intimacies were rapidly dropping away of their own accord, unable to resist the corrosion of the modern world. The new life lured all sorts of Jews—Reformers, non-Reformers, anti-Reformers. Old Jewish habits and the knowledge of Hebrew lore dropped away from all of them alike. The process of westernizing worked among all Jews except those who were isolated in the East. But it was the Reformers who hailed the process and believed in it. If the emancipation exacted too much of a sacrifice of Jewishness it must be said that most Jews paid the price. The fault of the Reformers, if it was a fault, was that they believed that for the tangible benefits they were getting, the price was not excessive.

The second dart hurled against the Reformers was that what they got for the price paid, even though tangible, was certainly not worth paying for. The emancipation was all an illusion. Anti-Semitism was too deeply rooted in the Christian world to be wiped away by such idealism. History has now proved that the early idealism faded quickly, was soon followed by reaction, and culminated in Nazi mass-murder.

The conclusion to be derived from such jibes at the old idealism is that it was and is a mistake to believe in the future comradeship of humanity, that it is safer to doubt it because it is a delusion. Yet if it is a delusion, it is a powerful one and a necessary one, for we see today that the greatest world powers are spending countless millions to persuade their respective camps that there is a great ideal state awaiting mankind and that each human being can be a part of humanity's hopes. If this is an illusion, it is obviously one of the most precious illusions in the world.

Jews certainly should not abandon the belief in the future of mankind and in the function of the individual to be "a partner of God" in the process of the world's rebuilding. Then, surely, Jews should by now look back with great interest, if not with admiration, to a former generation of our brothers which was so greatly moved by the old Isaianic idealism that it believed that Judaism as a religious ideal could be a central force in the redemption of mankind. It is hard to see how moderns can have the heart to mock such an exalted faith, unless their mockery conceals a hidden wish that we could recover it for ourselves. If the early Reformers were mistaken, then they were *tragically* mistaken, and by mocking at them we are laughing at humanity.

We should try to revisualize those days out of historical curiosity. How could a generation have been so idealistic, so confident about mankind's future? We know what it was that they believed. Their general idealism was a composite of various attitudes, all of which we recognize as essentially Jewish. It was the belief that the pace of the world's progress had quickened, that old human hostilities were beginning to fade, that with science and knowledge the world was moving toward liberty and dignified citizenship for all, that Judaism, which created the prophetic vision, would win the respect of mankind. To attain analogous beliefs today requires tremendous international propaganda. But in those days it was a spontaneous belief that flamed suddenly in the hearts of our youth.

This spontaneous hopefulness had a special characteristic. It was religious. Surely this religious element in it was not a chance factor. It was neither natural nor easy in those days to be religious. Neither the Catholic church nor the Protestant was then in a period of great cultural influence. The various philosophies which grew dominant were as frequently non-religious or anti-religious as religious. Within Judaism itself youth was struggling against an old-fashioned Orthodoxy which in general was opposed to every modern mood. As one of the leaders of Orthodoxy said: Take it as a general rule, that whatever is new is forbidden by the Torah (by Jewish law). A whole generation had to pass by before Jewish Orthodoxy began to come to terms with modernity. For Jewish youth to participate in the exciting hopes of the new era, it was inevitable that it should rebel in some way against Judaism, which carried with it a complete reverence for the past.

With all denominational religion deprecated, with the Jewish religion representing the medieval past, the most natural reaction for the idealistic Jewish youth would be to abandon Judaism entirely. This, of course, was the path taken by many. It is, therefore, all the more remarkable that the young people who founded Reform Judaism decided early to combine the ideals of the new age with their inherited religion. If Judaism in its present appearance hardly seemed meaningful to the new generation, it was, they were sure, only because of its *outer* form. Its inner essence must surely be consonant with the noblest ideals of the time. For did not Judaism in Bible days pioneer in proclaiming the faith of a noble and brotherly human society? Judaism needs reform in its externals and then its inner grandeur would be revealed. Thus, while many young men of the time abandoned Judaism as outworn, and were cynical of religion in general as irrelevant to the needs of the time, this section of Jewish youth believed that, since Judaism had created the world-vision, it could well represent it in the modern age. Let Judaism be freed from its medieval incrustations and it would play a great role in what they were sure was the imminent search of mankind for the new future. Thus, for reasons still not clearly understood, they held to their ancient faith and combined it with their new ideals.

Historians study the forces which contributed to the general awakening in Europe of the dream of an earthly paradise. We are interested in its sudden reappearance among our own people. What made them such confident believers in Isaiah's dream? Hitherto, historians of the Reform movement recorded the first manifestation of ritual Reform, the various debates, the conferences and the synods, the founding of congregations, schools, societies, and the publication of prayer books. This book has a different and more fundamental aim. It seeks to give a living picture of the great flowering of the spirit, the sudden upsurge of hope, the meteor of idealism which led the Reform movement. All these moods and convictions will be told in the words of the dreamers themselves. This is an actual sourcebook giving the essays, the speeches, the pronunciamentos of that idealistic age. Even if theirs were a worthless dream and if the movement which they founded in Judaism had faded away, it would still be important to read the heart of those visionaries. The movement in Judaism which was created by that up-flare of idealism has grown stronger and is a powerful force in Jewish life. These dreamers were not deluded. Their path, which for a while led through darkness, will grow brighter "until the perfect dawn."

RABBI SOLOMON B. FREEHOF
President, World Union for
Progressive Judaism

Introduction

The Nature of Reform Judaism

WHAT IS REFORM?

REFORM JUDAISM is a phenomenon of man's restless spirit. At its best it is a dynamic faith—and its very dynamism makes it difficult to describe it adequately. Its traditional roots speak of yesterdays; its branches combine the ancient spirit with the special beauty of each new generation. Reform speaks of man's longing for the sure ways of his fathers and at the same time of his own surging and daring struggle for new ways. It is Jewish to the core, although occasional and temporary acceptance of the habits of changing environments may deceive the casual onlooker.

Reform Judaism has sometimes been described as constant in content, changing in form. This is only partially accurate, for Reform has also attempted to change the current content of the Jew's outlook on life. In its earlier days, for instance, it brought a broad world view, a prophetic universalism back into the narrow, parochial Judaism of its time. Further, it has affected the Jew's image of himself. In its anti-mystical and non-miraculous approach to Jewish history, it has discovered the slow and often painful growth of the people and its theology. It has been ready to accept past errors and mishaps, as well as Israel's glorious uniqueness. It has been able to make a beginning in confronting the existence of Christianity and the personality of Jesus; and it has struggled to create a sound philosophy which could deal with the rise of Zionism and of the State of Israel. Like many a revolutionary movement, it sometimes went too far and mistook contemporary opinions and habits for permanent insights and achievements. But its critical faculty kept it from petrifying these excursions into a new Orthodoxy; its inherent dynamism has remained Reform's most cherished asset.

xiii

THE HISTORIC SETTING

A movement is nurtured by many streams. It is generally said that Reform was a child of eighteenth century Enlightenment, and that is true. But Enlightenment was not one single event: it was itself a movement with many facets. The middle of the century witnessed the final breakdown of Western feudal society and the victorious emergence of the "third estate," the bourgeois middle class. It saw the ascendency of Britain, the world's new merchant nation, to a position of dominant power after her bitter struggle with France, and at the same time witnessed the spread of French language, literature, and philosophy to the courts and universities of Europe. It saw the beginnings of the Industrial Revolution, the creation of new nation-states out of disjointed small dukedoms and municipalities, the growing urbanization of Western man, and the steady flow of peoples to the New World. Ideas of man's freedom to think and to choose his own form of government found expression first in books and then in the surge of revolutions in America and France. The Jew, long a man without a country and without permanent civic rights, suddenly found the waves of equality and fraternity sweeping him forward. Mercantile and educational opportunities which had hitherto been closed to him opened and beckoned. Hesitating at first, and then with eagerness, the Western Jew left his ghetto and tried to find his place in the larger society of men. Of a sudden, his old folkways—from his dress to his personal habits—seemed at odds with his new environment, and so he began to examine what yesterday he had accepted without question. Could one continue to be a Jew and still enjoy the benefits of the great revolutions? One would have to learn German and French, study Western culture and history; one would have to adopt at least the outward ways of the world one hoped to enter. One looked to Moses Mendelssohn, who had successfully bridged the gap between the two worlds and who had remained an observant, loyal Jew. Some, as might be expected, chose this moment to escape altogether from the burden of being Jews, and for a time it appeared as if the flight might assume epidemic proportions. The need to find modern forms for the ancient faith was a significant stimulus for the rise of Reform.

Many circumstances combined to make German Jewry most responsive to the opportunities of the new times. Central and Western Germany proceeded quickly in urbanization and industrialization, and the influence of French egalitarianism persisted even after Napoleon's occupation forces had left. For French ideas were at home in Prussian lands where French was the *lingua franca* of the educated. The intellectual acceptance of

Mendelssohn, the social acceptance of a Rachel von Varnhagen, the optimism engendered by the reforms of a briefly enlightened government under the leadership of Stein and Hardenberg—all these elements combined and powerfully stimulated German Jews to join the sunlit circle of German culture and education. For these Jews felt that Germany indeed was *their* land of hope: here they had lived without interruption for many hundreds of years, and here the future seemed to beckon as it did nowhere else in Europe. British and French Jewries had only recently resettled in fair numbers and were generally slow to find a sense of complete identification with their nations. The Eastern Jew remained almost unaffected by the stirrings of the new age; and what little penetrated there of the Messianism of the French Revolution was diverted into the Messianic sweep of Hasidism. Eastern Enlightenment (Haskalah) came to a full flowering only after the first wave of Western liberalism had passed its peak. The only other countries which were caught up in the vortex of the new age were Hungary and Northern Italy, which touched upon or were part of the sprawling Austrian Empire and had come under the influence of French political and German philosophical ideas.

But where this influence ceased, Jews and their leaders were incapable of comprehending the religious stirrings among their Germanic brethren. These were condemned and anathematized. The old school had become enmeshed in a system of thought and practice which yielded less and less to the shifting demands of time and circumstance and which came to believe that the religious status quo was divinely ordained. The traditionalists proclaimed themselves as the only right-thinking, i.e., Orthodox, Jews—and by the early decades of the nineteenth century the battle lines were sharply drawn.

Of course, there were Orthodox Jews in German lands, too, but for quite some time they remained without real leadership. Not until the 1840's, when Samson Raphael Hirsch became their spokesman, were they capable of more than rigid opposition, and thereafter theirs, too, was no longer the older, East-European Orthodoxy. They, too, had made their peace with Western culture, albeit on other terms than did their Reform brethren.

THE NATURE OF THE MOVEMENT

What Dr. Freehof, in his Preface to this book, calls the great idealism of Reform Judaism, was fed by a number of subsidiary springs.

There was, first of all, the ever-present, though oft suppressed, strain of Jewish Messianism. In some ages the hope for a divinely ordered society under the leadership of God's messenger had been merely a part of the theological system of the Jew, a piously and fervently expressed wish for the ultimate realization of His Kingdom on earth. But in other ages, especially when alien oppression became insufferable, this prayerful hope had taken on more immediate significance. Would the Messiah perhaps come in *our* time? There would be signs and omens, and occasionally there were Messianic aspirants. The destruction of medieval society, the dissolution of the Universal Church in Europe, and the convulsions of the Islamic Empire in the East profoundly affected the Jews, who, in response, became receptive to the pretensions of a Sabbatai Zevi. When these were found to be hollow, the hunger for salvation found other avenues. In the East, Hasidism was one such search after the ultimate solution and (as Buber has so movingly portrayed in his *For the Sake of Heaven*) the French Revolution and the magic personality of Napoleon added powerful stimuli to the movement. In the West, Jews detected the signs of God's Kingdom all about them. Social and political idealism abounded. Whether or not God would send His special servant, it was clear that men were on their way to smooth His way. They themselves would lay the foundations for the Kingdom; they themselves would bring on the Messianic age. Men were conquering nature with new and magic inventions; the earth was becoming smaller; nations were coming closer to the vision which Israel's prophets had seen. Reform quite naturally took the prophets to heart; they expressed best the buoyant spirit of the age. Instead of Akiba and Maimonides, Reformers quoted Isaiah and Amos. Where traditional Judaism was Halakhah-oriented, Reform was prophet-directed; it was idealistic in that it believed in a world which could be shaped by man's ideas. Its Messianic sweep expressed itself in an all-pervasive optimism, a belief in the perfectibility of the human race—not in the far distant future, but here and now. Reform's Messianism had urgency; it was divinely impatient and often inaccessible to the counsels of orderly and organic progress. Like all truly revolutionary movements, it wanted salvation *now*. Once the goal was sighted, there was no halting at the post of tradition. Not until the grand burst of enthusiasm had spent its initial strength—after the failure of the 1848 revolutions—did Reform proceed with a new, slower, and more deliberate gait. Its Messianic enthusiasm had become tempered with the disappointment in quick political and social solutions.

Along with Reform's Messianic vision went its broad universalism. Here, too, Reform combined the visions of the prophets with the dreams of man's brotherhood which the American and French Revolutions had proclaimed. The prophecies of old seemed capable of realization in one's own lifetime; Christian, Mohammedan, and pagan—all became objects of human concern. Jews joined the liberal parties, rabbis entered into the political arena, and some suffered exile and incarceration for their convictions. It was natural that on occasion the sweep of this grand vision of human fulfilment should lead to a shallow and fruitless sentimentalism. Occasionally one found men loving mankind without loving their neighbors, and one could find Jews feeling little responsibility for other Jews, while lavishing their concern on Man as such. There was a distinct trend away from parochialism and from what later came to be called Jewish nationalism. The Jewish people, some Reformers averred, no longer existed; it was Judaism that formed the bond across the lands and ages. But somehow this modern Jewish universalism, not unlike its ancient inspiration, could not or would not forsake its ethnic base altogether. Some Reformers might doubt the admissibility of Jewish peoplehood as a concept, but they were in the forefront of those fighting for Jewish rights all over the world.

In fact, Reform's emphasis on man's universal aspirations was always closely linked to the role which the Jew had to play in their achievement. God's Kingdom would be realized for all men only through Judaism. To bring its truths to the world was the Jew's noblest aim; this was Israel's mission to mankind. What made the Jew capable of carrying this burden? It was a special "racial" characteristic—an inherited, innate ability to see the world in spiritual terms. No other people had been so gifted, none other had therefore been chosen. In this way Jewish particularism and Jewish universalism were combined, similar to the manner in which the prophets had taught. For let us make no mistake about it: Reform was thoroughly Jewish. Its leaders were critical of certain traditional customs and concepts, but they were also Judaism's staunchest defenders and protagonists. Where today a polite silence makes interreligious discussion nearly taboo, the Reformers confronted other religions squarely and found them wanting. They exalted Judaism's qualities with fierce pride; they scorned apostasy and weak-kneed convictions. They had studied the cultural treasures of East and West (after a while, all rabbis in Germany were expected to obtain a Ph.D.), but their frame of reference was Judaism and its sources. They were conversant with Talmud and Shulhan Arukh; they quoted freely from all Jewish sources and did so in Hebrew. They loved the holy tongue and, even though they were realists and introduced translations into the prayer book, they insisted that every Jew learn Hebrew to the limits of his ability. They believed in scholarship and formed the "Science of Judaism," discovered old sources and made an incalculable contribution to the understanding of Bible and Talmud.

Of course, there were gradations and differences. Not all Reform leaders were scholars, and Judaism meant different things to different men. Some were blandished by the glitter of European culture and were led down the path to de-Judaization and assimilation. But these were few; the mainstream of Reform stood for a strong and distinct Jewish religious identity. That, despite these efforts, assimilation made wide gains amongst all Jews testifies to the overwhelming force of social, political, and economic developments, and not to the lack of zeal on the part of Reform itself.

The widest differences existed in the area of Halakhah and custom. If the Oral Law, i.e., the Talmud and its interpretations, were human creations (and not authoritative extensions of the divine will, as Orthodoxy claimed), what was one's guide for maintaining or rejecting tradition? Some advocated total free choice on the part of each individual, without relation to precedent. The majority, however, held to gradualism and demanded that any change from the past be founded in genuine Jewish tradition. But they, too, could not solve the basic dilemma of Reform: who had the authority to change, reject, or re-form tradition? What was the basis for Jewish Halakhah if it was purely human? It was a dilemma that remained unsolved and that remains so today, over a century later. Its confrontation was then, and is today, a chief problem of the movement. There were attempts then, too, at creating guides for Reform Jews, the most notable of which was attempted by Leopold Stein, whose two-volume work was climaxed by a sort of brief Reform Shulhan Arukh.

Reform leaders were cognizant of, and participated prominently in, biblical research and higher criticism. They maintained throughout that the Bible was God-given, a divine instrument that was to guide the Jew for all time. This emphasis on the divine nature of the Bible and the human nature of later Jewish tradition created a special danger. A thousand years before, the Karaites had attempted to create a Bible-based Judaism which rejected the Talmud. They had ended by separating themselves from the main body of Jewry and had formed a new sect. Reform, too, advocated a return to the Bible and rejected the binding authority of the Talmud. There was the lurking possibility of a new sectarianism, which at this juncture of history would have proven catastrophical for Judaism as a whole.

That Reform avoided the way of Karaism is principally due to two reasons. First, the Karaites were strict legalists, no less so than the rabbinic majority. They believed in the compelling force of Halakhah, but only in so far as it was clearly based on the Bible and was not derived from later pronouncements. The modern Reformers also returned to the Bible as their primary source of authority; however, their emphasis was not on the Halakhah of the Torah. They stressed the ethical *mitzvot* of the Prophets. This shift of emphasis led to bitter struggles and to occasional accusations of apostasy—but it did not lead to a permanent break. Secondly, Karaism rejected the Talmud completely, while Reform only rejected its binding authority. Karaism attempted to reconstruct Jewish history by omitting the import of the centuries since the close of the Bible; Reform attempted no such radical move. From time to time there were extremists who saw nothing in Talmud and later tradition that could form an acceptable basis for modern Judaism, but the majority of the Reform leaders insisted that all of tradition was significant, that Reform had to grow organically from it, and that a renewal of Judaism could only come from a continuity of spiritual development. Reform did not reject the Talmud; it only approached it with a critical mind. It selected from, rather than rejected, its dicta.

THE PROGRESS OF REFORM

The development of the movement did not take place at an even rate. The first period may be dated from the time of Mendelssohn's translation of the Bible (in the latter part of the eighteenth century); the second from the appearance of the Hamburg Prayer Book and its subsequent controversies (1817-18) to the Geiger-Tiktin affair in the mid-thirties. The first period saw tentative steps toward a reform; its hopes were raised by the early idealism of the French Revolution and dashed in its defeat, raised once more by Napoleon's early broad egalitarianism and dashed once more by his dictatorship and later by the reestablishment of Bourbon reaction. It was the period of Friedländer's approach to Christianity and Jacobson's innovations; the time of the early Jewish journals and of misguided attempts to suppress (or foster, as the case might be) the stirrings of Reform with the help of governmental authority. The second period seemed to gather up the pent-up political and social emotions of

the age and yielded some fruits in England and France, where more liberal laws made their appearance. In Jewish life, too, it was as if all were
preparing for the great outburst. In this time, Zunz published his path-
breaking work on the history of the Jewish service, Mannheimer instituted reforms in Vienna, and Creizenach prepared a new generation at
the Frankfort Philanthropin.

When in 1838 Abraham Geiger was refused recognition by his senior
rabbi, Solomon Tiktin, who attempted to keep him from exercising his
rabbinical function, the history of Reform was thrust into its most ex-
plosive stage. For the next ten years the movement became revolutionary,
intensely exciting, grand in its sweep, immensely appealing in its surging
optimism and the breadth of its universalism. This third period is the
time of Reform's greatest flowering. Dedicated leaders came to the fore,
and able opponents like Michael Sachs and Samson Raphael Hirsch
constantly tested their mettle. Journals were founded; books on Reform
appeared by the score and pamphlets by the hundreds. New prayer books
made their appearance; rabbinic conferences assembled; Reform congregations were formed. This forward rush of the mid-thirties and forties
was given wings by the revolutionary enthusiaism of the age. The French
July Revolution of 1830 had proved bitterly disappointing, and in Germany and Austria the repressive policies of the Metternich age and of
the Holy Alliance provided the very fuel for rebellion. The Jews, always
bellwethers of progress, keenly felt the coming of a new time, and its
religious and its political liberalism went hand in hand.

Rarely has any brief period in Jewish history seen such an outpouring
of the spirit. Its only parallel in modern times was the time of Israel's
birth. Exactly one century separates the latter from the time when Reform's greatest spiritual expansion came to its sudden end. The initial
success of the 1848 revolutions in Germany and France and their subsequent failure coincided with the time when Reform's burst of energy
had spent itself. The collapse of political and social hopes did the rest.
Thus ended the "golden decade" of the movement.

A time of consolidation followed in Europe. To some it appeared as
a period of retreat and stagnation, which lasted well past the end of the
century. Central European Jewry had to a large degree accepted many
of the philosophical bases of Reform. With conservatism prevailing
throughout the continent, conservatism became a hallmark also of Reform. Its forms and modes began to harden; even its musical expressions
remained on the level to which Sulzer and Lewandowski had brought
it. No significant theologian appeared in the movement, which remained

mildly liberal and became highly respectable. The last major attempt to inject new life into a dying revolution came at the time when Germany achieved political unification. The underlying idea of an all-encompassing polity appealed also in the spiritual realm. Synods, i.e., representative gatherings of rabbinic and non-rabbinic leaders, were called, but the attendance fell below expectations and the issues that were debated reflected no new thinking since the pre-1848 days.

The real forward thrust came in America, where many of the Reformers had gone in the wake of the post-revolution reaction and repression. Hither they translated their enthusiasm, and here they found new and far more fertile ground for further advances. Men like Adler, Einhorn, and Samuel Hirsch, who had broken a lance for European Reform, found the new land ready for imaginative leadership. A frontier psychology prevailed everywhere; nothing was rejected until it had first been tested experimentally. In America, Reform reached new heights of spiritual force, but it also went into more blind alleys. America afforded the Jew unprecedented opportunities, and the lures of assimilation were consequently greater. Some mistook the universalistic trend of Reform for an approval of assimilation. It was an unfortunate half-truth. The impulse to assimilation did not originate with the Reform movement; it sprang from the breakdown of social barriers and the problems arising from it. Reform did acknowledge and was ready to assimilate the best in the majority culture, and it did so openly, as a matter of principle (in contrast to the Orthodox, who did the same but unofficially). What was "best" in American or European civilization was, of course, a matter of dispute, and in this area of judgment, American Jews were more prone to embrace the mores of their environment than were their European brethren. But assimilation, i.e., the conscious preference of a non-Jewish way of life, was not part of the Reform philosophy; and in the long run, the draining away of Jewish consciousness occurred more frequently among the children of Orthodoxy than among those of Reform background. The fact that foes (and often friends also) of the movement thought it to be the gateway to convenience and defection did not make it so, and, in time, the abiding qualities of Reform emerged more clearly and put the stamp of their worth upon all of modern Jewish life.

PLAN AND SCOPE OF THIS BOOK

Our book deals with the foundations of Reform in Europe, and, therefore, it limits itself to the four periods just described: the period of the precursors (1780-1817); the period of the first reforms (1817-1838); the period of the great flowering (1838-1848); the period of consolidation (1848-1871). Parallel to this last time span runs the founding of American Reform, but its social, political, and economic setting was so different that its treatment has been reserved for a later volume.[1] The same applies to East European Haskalah. It too will be presented as a separate unit later on. In any case, our book is not a historic treatise on the Reform movement; it does not seek to do the work which David Philipson and Caesar Seligmann attempted. While we begin with a historic section, we limit ourselves to presenting the high watermarks of the various periods, and we aim at significant rather than exhaustive representation.

The historical chapters are followed by a presentation of the basic philosophy of the movement and of the ideas that buttressed it. Thereafter we turn to the particulars of worship reform and then to the main practical and theoretical issues that agitated (and, in some cases, still agitate) the movement. The final chapter deals with communal problems as Reform saw and faced them. It includes a brief section, "For the Sake of Heaven," designed to give the reader an insight into the more personal, intimate attitudes of some Reformers and their opponents.

Our volume is a *sourcebook;* it lets the founders of Reform speak through their own writings. Most of these needed translations from their German, Hebrew, or French originals. Only in a few cases were existing translations utilized, and in such cases the *Notes* will supply the exact source reference and give credit to the translator. Otherwise all translations are by the author of this book. He has had the most able assistance of Mrs. Gertrude Flor (St. Paul), whose contribution is acknowledged with sincere appreciation.

A brief word is in order about the nature of our translations. We aimed at faithfulness, not at literalness. We tried to preserve the special flavor of each author's writings, a task that was rendered more difficult because much of the original German is stilted, flowery, involved, and overwritten. Where we had to make a choice, we elected understandable rather than mirror-true sentences. Also, our text selects from and often contracts the original. We have not noted this, except where such information was deemed helpful to the reader.

Nineteenth-century writers employed certain expressions which today would no longer be used. They generally said "Israelite" where we would

[1] A few exceptions have been made. For instance, Einhorn's American inaugural was in fact a summation of his European philosophy.

say "Jew"; they said "Jewish nation" where we would say "people"; and they already called Bar Mitzvah "Confirmation" at a time when confirmation in our sense was not yet in existence. In the early days they had no word for "Orthodox," and therefore used evaluative epithets to describe the opposition, like "Stillständler" (which might be rendered as "lovers of the status quo").

In every anthology the editor reveals a personal bias. For when it comes to selecting important or interesting pieces, one makes a highly individual decision. We were guided as much by the desire to represent each man's best and most significant thought, as by our aim to give the most challenging view, or views, on the subject at hand. Where several equal opportunities presented themselves, we often chose a selection from a man who otherwise might not be included. The fairly large number of authors whose contributions are rendered here is testimony to the wide front of a movement that was blessed with many devoted and immensely capable and vocal leaders.

Our main sources were books published by the Reformers. Magazines played a secondary role in our selections, for in an age when books found ready subscribers, authors usually managed to put between covers what they considered their most important thoughts. From the journals we usually chose items from their early editions, which revealed policy and direction. Other important sources were the conference and synod transcripts, prayer books, manifestos, resolutions, and appeals. A few letters were also included.

Some issues were, and still are, more important than others. For instance, the nature of the Sabbath was debated with great zeal, for the Reformers felt that they were dealing with one of our most precious possessions which they desperately tried to save. The issue remains vital and unresolved, and therefore it is more prominently treated.

We have provided brief introductions to chapters and sections, as well as to most individual selections. It is hoped that this will aid the reader in judging the significance of the selection, and will acquaint him with the fathers of Reform. Of course, only the barest minimum of biographical information is rendered, just enough to identify the author and, perchance, to whet the reader's appetite for closer acquaintance. These biographies accompany the author's first appearance in our book and in such cases the *Index* will indicate by an asterisk (*) behind the reference page where this information is to be found.

This book, like most others, wants to be read from beginning to end. In this fashion it will best supply the reader with a full view of Reform's many facets, and elucidate for him the nature of its growth, of its insights as well as its errors, its achievements and its failures, its strength and its weaknesses, and—perhaps most important—infect him with the divine enthusiasm that fed the roots of the movement.

The book may, secondly, be read by topics. The ideas and issues that agitated the movement form a fair cross-section of Jewish thought and practice, and of these much remains relevant today. The reader's own interests will be his best guide in this procedure. The detailed Table of Contents as well as the Notes and the cross-referenced Index will help his search and choice.

Finally, the reader may wish to gain an insight into the thinking of some of the individual leaders and founders of Reform. Here, the Index will be his surest resource. He will have to keep in mind, of course, that the brief selections offered in this sourcebook cannot substitute for a fuller treatment of these men—and nothing can replace a study of the original sources. These have been listed in the Notes.

Those who desire a survey of the movement may turn to a number of studies. Bernard Bamberger's *The Story of Judaism* (Union of American Hebrew Congregations, 1957) sets Reform into its historic frame. David Philipson's *The Reform Movement in Judaism* (Macmillan, 1931) remains the best treatment of the subject in English; its German counterpart is Caesar Seligmann's *Geschichte der jüdischen Reformbewegung* (Frankfort, 1922). Sylvan Schwartzman's *Reform Judaism in the Making* (Union of Am. Hebr. Cong., 1955) is a popular history of the movement.

A WORD OF THANKS

Many had a hand in the preparation of the book. I owe special thanks to Miss Donna Margette (St. Paul), Miss Margaret B. Davidson, and Mrs. Marina Cranwell (Toronto) for their technical assistance, to Mr. Ralph Davis who designed the book and guided it to publication, to Dr. Jerome H. Kanner who prepared the index, and to the library staff of Hebrew Union College–Jewish Institute of Religion in Cincinnati and New York for their generous and invaluable helpfulness.

My sincere gratitude is expressed to Rabbi Solomon B. Freehof, President of the World Union for Progressive Judaism, for guiding me with his sage and always ready advice and for providing the Preface to this book; to Dr. Jacob R. Marcus, who read the manuscript and offered many helpful suggestions, as did Rabbis Chaim Essrog and William Rosenthall. I am particularly grateful to Rabbis Hugo Gryn and Eugene Borowitz without whose imagination and constant encouragement I would never have attempted to begin this work. They set me out on an exciting adventure during which I met fascinating people of our past whose stimulating ideas remain urgent challenges for our time. It is my hope that the sustained vitality that resides in the Liberal movement may communicate itself to the reader of these selections.

W.G.P.

TORONTO, SPRING 5723–1963

Contents

�належ✳✳✳

THE RISE OF REFORM JUDAISM

CHAPTER
I

Trail Blazers

1. THE FIRST GENERATION

MODERN REFORM Judaism has its beginnings in the eighteenth century period of Enlightenment (see above, p. xiii).

For the Jew in Europe, Enlightenment went with the name of Moses Mendelssohn, the ghetto-born philosopher (1729-1786), who became the model for all those aspiring to civil and cultural equality. Mendelssohn's success amid the great of the Christian world was, for his coreligionists, a powerful stimulus to acquire a secular education, to perfect their knowledge of German and of the arts—in short, to become accepted in the larger environment. What would happen to their Judaism in this revolutionary process of breaking the ghetto's spiritual and physical walls? For some, it was a choice between Judaism and Christianity—and, therefore, most rabbis of the time saw in Mendelssohn the symbol of a future dissolution of Judaism. Mendelssohn himself rejected the necessity of such a choice and remained a staunch adherent of tradition. Yet the tension existed, and out of it a new, modern Judaism slowly began to emerge. Fifty years later, in the 1830's and 1840's, it became a torrential stream which carved out the river bed of modern Reform Judaism.

There had been many translations of the Bible before Mendelssohn's time, but none by any modern Jewish scholar. In many ways, the effort which Mendelssohn and a group of associates made became the touchstone of a new era; the cultured, scholarly Jew, using the language and tools of German scholarship, emerged onto the stage of Western culture. The introduction to the translation, of which the following is a small excerpt, is symptomatic of this new trend.

WHY A NEW TRANSLATION? (*Moses Mendelssohn*)

In 1545, the great grammarian, R. Elijah Habachur, translated the Pentateuch and the Megillot word for word into the German, and had this translation printed at Constance in Switzerland.[1] In 1679, he was followed by R. Josel Witzenhausen and R. Jekuthiel Blitz, the latter possessing approbations of the most distinguished rabbis of his time. R. Jekuthiel says in his preface, that he had seen the German translation of the Pentateuch printed at Constance, and found it so faulty and unfit that he was convinced the translation could not emanate from the celebrated German grammarian. I, the writer of this, have never seen the translation attributed to R. Elijah, as it was not to be had in our country; but I have seen that of R. Jekuthiel, and observed that he censures faults from which he himself is not free. Though his intention might have been praiseworthy, and he might perhaps on that account have obtained the approbation of contemporary rabbis, it is certain that the execution of the work is not deserving of praise; for he is quite ignorant of Hebrew, and therefore did not understand how to penetrate into the depth of the Hebrew style; but what he understood he rendered into a most corrupt language, so that one who has been accustomed to pure language feels quite disgusted with it.

Since then up to this day no one has undertaken the task of mending this fault and of rendering our Holy Writ in correct language, suitable to our age. The children of Israel who have a mind for useful studies sought the knowledge of the word of God from Christian translations; for in every age the Christians translated the Scriptures according to the variations of language and people, suitable to the wants of the time and in conformity with the correct use of the language. They did so in euphonious style—now keeping close to the word, then only rendering the sense; now word for word, then by explanatory paraphrase—in order to satisfy the desire of every learner, and in accordance with the customary language of the age. But this way, which many of our coreligionists have already adopted, leads to manifold mistakes and carries the most dangerous consequences with it. For the Christian translators, who do not recognize the traditions of our sages and do not keep the Masorah, nay more, who do not consider themselves bound by the vowel points and accents as we have them, look upon the sacred volume "as an undefended city," where everyone can go his own way and act according to his own choice. Not only as regards the vowel points and accents, but even as regards the letters and words, they allow themselves optional alterations as they think best, and therefore read in the Scriptures not that which they contain, but that which suits them.

I will not, therefore, pronounce censure on these learned authors, for what could bind them to a tradition which has not been handed down by their ancestors, or to a Masorah which has not been laid down by men who appear to them as authorities? But then, they do not consider the Torah from

[1] (Ed. note) The first edition referred to actually appeared in Venice, an error which is explained by Mendelssohn's admission that he had never seen the book.

that point of view to observe everything which is written therein; they only treat it as a historical work, containing information on the events of past times, and representing to them the divine rule and providence in every age. From this point of view there is no harm in making trifling alterations, adding or omitting a few letters or words, in the same manner as it is done with secular authors, where every editor and reviser alters the text according to his judgment.

Now, although this may be suitable to Christian authors, it cannot by any means be considered right and proper for us. To us the Torah is a heritage, not only for remembering the past, but also for attaining a knowledge of the precepts which the Eternal, our God, commanded us to learn, to teach, to observe, and to keep; it is our life, the preserver of our existence. But in order that we should not be continually in doubt, and not have to depend upon the frail reed of speculation and upon the uncertainty of hypotheses, our sages have established the Masorah, thereby erecting a fence around the law and judgment, so that we need not grope in the darkness of conjecture. From this even path we must not turn either to the right or the left. We cannot modify our texts according to the hypotheses of one or the other grammarian; we must cling to the standard which the authors of the Masorah have established for us. This is the tradition to which we must adhere. By its guidance we understand the Scriptures, search and inquire into them, often according to the simple explanation, and often according to the interpretation of our sages, for both are equally true and just, as I shall hereafter show.

THE THREE PARTS OF JUDAISM (*Moses Mendelssohn*)

Mendelssohn's theory of the nature of Judaism had a profound though strange effect on succeeding generations. Of the three parts of Judaism—doctrines, historical truths, and ceremonial laws—he considered the first two accessible to all men and not part of divine revelation. Only the ritual law was revealed especially to Israel, and since it was the distinct mark of the Jew's relationship with God, Mendelssohn saw no reason why this law should not be meticulously observed. The rationalism and universalism which pervaded his total approach to Jewish theology soon found wide acceptance; and it was not long before the ceremonial law which he had held sacrosanct was also considered subject to rational investigation and adaptation and was accorded a place inferior to the "religious" aspect of Judaism. Traditionalists, who generally anathematized Mendelssohn, approved of his acceptance of the ceremonial law as part of revelation, while Reformers looked at his basic theory and applied it to the whole body of Judaism.

I recognize no other eternal truths than those comprehensible to human reason and those provable and demonstrable through the human power to think. However, anyone who believes that I could not make such claim without deviating from the religion of my ancestors is misled by a false concept of Judaism. On the contrary, I hold this to be an essential point in the Jewish religion, and I believe that this doctrine represents a characteristic difference between the Jewish and Christian faiths. To put it briefly: I believe that Judaism recognizes no revealed religion in the sense understood by Christians. The Israelites have divine legislation, laws, commandments, ordinances, rules of life, and instruction in the will of God concerning rules of conduct which are intended to lead to earthly as well as eternal salvation. These tenets and precepts have been revealed to them by Moses in a wonderful, supernatural way; but they are neither dogmas, nor redemptive truths, nor universal propositions demonstrable by reason. At all times these latter truths are revealed to us and to all other humans by the Eternal, by nature, and by circumstance, but never by word or writing.

At this point I can briefly sum up my views on the Judaism of the past, combining them into a single viewpoint. According to its founder, Judaism consisted of, or was supposed to consist of:

1. Doctrines and precepts, or eternal truths of God and His direction and divine providence, without which man cannot be enlightened and happy. These were not forced upon our nation under the threat of eternal or earthly punishment, but rather were recommended for rational understanding according to the nature and evidence of eternal truth. They had not been inspired through direct revelation; indeed, they could not have been made known through speech and writing, which are understandable only here and now. They were revealed by the Almighty to all rational creatures through concepts and things themselves, written into the soul with a clarity that remains legible and understandable at all times and in all places.

2. Historical truths or accounts of the destinies of former ages, especially of the life of the nation's founders; their knowledge of the true God; their virtuous life before God; their own transgressions and the paternal chastisement that followed; the covenant that God had concluded with them and the promise He had so often repeated to them, to make their descendants a nation consecrated to Him in times to come. These historical accounts contained the basis for national unity, and they cannot, because of their very nature, be accepted as historical truths, other than on faith. Authority itself affords them the required evidence; besides, these accounts were confirmed to the nation through miracles and supported by an authority sufficiently strong to render the faith immune to all doubts and scruples.

3. Laws, precepts, commandments, rules of life which are this nation's own, adherence to which will achieve not only national salvation but also the attainment of personal happiness for each individual member. God was the lawgiver, not in the sense of God as creator and preserver of the universe, but rather as God, protector and confederate of their ancestors, liberator, founder

and commander-in-chief, king and sovereign of this people; and He bestowed the most solemn sanction upon His laws, publicly and in an unheard-of, wondrous way. Thus these laws were enjoined on the nation and all its descendants as an immutable responsibility and obligation. These laws were revealed, that is, they were made known by God, through words and writing. However, only the most essential part has been entrusted to writing; and even these written laws are for the most part unintelligible without the unwritten elucidations, delineations, and detailed instructions transmitted by oral and vivid instruction. They are unintelligible, or had to become so in time, since no words or scriptures can retain their meaning unchanged throughout any generation. The written as well as the unwritten laws, representing precepts of action and rules of life, regard public and private salvation as their ultimate goal. At the same time they are a part of Scripture which has meaning and importance also as ceremonial law. They guide the seeking mind to divine truths; they guide it, partly to eternal truths, partly to historical truths, on which the religion of this people was based. The ceremonial law was the link which was to connect action with contemplation, life with theory. The ceremonial law was supposed to induce personal relations and social contact between school and teacher, scholar and instructor, to stimulate and encourage competition and imitation. This purpose was actually achieved in the beginning, before the Law degenerated, and man's folly interfered once again, transforming, through misconception and mismanagement, the good into evil, the useful into abuse.

THE RIGHT TO BE DIFFERENT (*Moses Mendelssohn*)

Mendelssohn's call for religious pluralism was issued at a time when nowhere in the German realm had Jews as yet attained citizenship.

Brothers! If you care for true salvation, let us not mismanage ourselves into uniformity when obviously diversity is the plan and ultimate goal of Providence. None of us thinks and feels exactly the same as the man next to him; why, then, do we wish to deceive one another through false words? It is sad enough that we are doing this in our daily relations, in our conversations, which are of no particular significance. But why do it in matters concerning our earthly as well as our eternal welfare, indeed our entire destiny? Why make ourselves, through mummery, irrecognizable to one another in the most important matters of our very existence, since God certainly must have impressed His own image on each individual for some good reason? Were we to do that, would we not oppose destiny as much as possible and, indeed, frustrate the very purpose of creation? Would we then not wilfully act contrary to our calling, to our destiny, in this life and the life to come?

The House of Jacob can receive no better advice than precisely this: adapt yourselves to the customs and the constitution of the land in which you live; yet, at the same time, adhere firmly to the religion of your ancestors. Carry both burdens as well as you can. To be sure, on the one side, the burden of your civic life is greater because of your religion to which you remain loyal; and on the other side, the climate of the times makes the observance of your religious laws in many regards more troublesome than they actually are. Nevertheless, hold out, stand unflinching in the appointed place assigned to you by Providence, and bear everything with patience, as your Law-giver proclaimed to you long ago.

Regents of the earth! If the voice of an unimportant co-inhabitant may be granted a hearing and reach your exalted heights: do not trust the counsels who, with their smooth words, wish to induce you to such harmful undertakings. They are either blinded themselves and do not see the enemy of mankind lurking in the background, or else they seek to blind you. Were you to lend an ear to them, it would mean the destruction of our most precious gem, the freedom to think! For the sake of your happiness as well as ours, consider that a *union of religious faiths does not mean tolerance;* indeed, it is the very opposite of true tolerance! For the sake of your salvation and ours, do not use your powerful position to give an eternal truth, which has no relation to civic contentment, the force of law; do not transform a certain religious view, in which the state has no interest whatever, into a statute of the land! Insist on the conduct of men, judge it, bring it under the judgment of wise laws, and leave to us our thought and speech with which our Father has endowed us as an unalienable heritage and immutable right.

STATE OF EDUCATION AMONG THE JEWS IN THE
    EIGHTEENTH CENTURY *(Hartwig Wessely)*

Naphtali Herz (Hartwig) Wessely (1725-1805), friend of Mendelssohn, wrote in classical Hebrew about the needs of his fellow Jews. Hailed at first by the most traditional elements, he soon became persona non grata, for his ideas pointed inevitably to the need for inner regeneration. In this open letter, published at the turn of the century, he lays the blame for the depressed educational condition of the Jew at the door of his oppressors —but it remains for the Jew himself to step forward and acquire what, for centuries, has been denied him.

There is one people on the globe who do not sufficiently appreciate nonbiblical literature, and who have neglected the public instruction of their youth in the laws of morality, nature, and science—and this people are the children of Israel, scattered through the countries of Europe and settled in most of her states. In particular, the inhabitants of Germany and Poland have turned their back upon those sciences, although there are many men of great mind and talent among them. Yet all their studies and applications comprise only the divine laws and precepts, but the laws of human nature they have never heard of or learned. They are even ignorant of the rules of the holy tongue, discern not the beauties of its diction, the elevated style of its construction, and the sublimity of its poetry—the unceasing sources of wisdom and moral instruction; much less is their acquaintance with the tongues of the nations among whom they live; nay, many can neither write nor read them. The construction of the globe, the events of history, and the principles of civil law, of natural and scientific philosophy, are altogether hidden to them. And what is the cause of this ignorance? Their never having been instructed in any of these subjects, either by their fathers or by their teachers, who themselves had no acquaintance with them. Nay, even the fundamental principles of their faith were not taught according to any method, so that the youth might become systematically conversant with them, nor did they ever hear in their schools aught of ethics, of morality, or of psychology. Some of the pupils whose theological studies have been successful, with the increase of years perceive their deficiency and endeavor to amend the fault committed by their teachers, by gleaning information either from books or from conversation, "here a little and there a little"; but of what avail are all their endeavors when system is wanting? The same as a thin silken dress on a frosty day. A sound knowledge of those subjects is only to be met within individuals whose hearts have stirred them up "and made them willing," and led them to incline their ear to wisdom, and to devote their lives to science; to learn the languages of different nations, to understand their literature, thus becoming a fountain inexhaustible in its own resources, unassisted by teachers, unaided by parents or superiors, but solely springing from the native love of truth.

Let it, however, be understood that *we* ourselves are not guilty in this matter. We ourselves are not to blame, and we have no ground for self-accusation; the blame remains with those nations who have oppressed us more than a thousand years. *They* have caused our misfortunes; they have ill-treated us by the command of their kings and rulers, and with many unrighteous designs they have risen against us to annihilate us, and to humble us to the dust, for which purpose they imposed cruel restrictions upon us, tending to suppress the energy of mind among us. It is *they* who have revolted against the laws of humanity, by pressing our bodies down to the dust and depressing our souls within us.

From that time darkness clouded the hearts of our people, who grew weary with the study of human nature, seeing that they were treated with such cruelty that their oppressors considered them below the category of human beings. Then they despised all things under the sun, perceiving that they had no portion nor inheritance in all the good that the Lord had bountifully produced for all His creatures from one end of the world unto the other. In the bitterness of their hearts, they disregarded and entirely neglected the laws and sciences relating to the administration of worldly affairs; and the knowledge of the celestial and earthly bodies, as the calculations of the motions of the planets; and the sciences necessary for agriculture, navigation, architecture, and fortification; and the knowledge of the laws of nations and their governments. For they said, "What use are all those to us? The inhabitants of the country are our enemies; they will neither listen to our counsels nor notice our abilities;

and we ourselves do not possess fields or vineyards in this country. Let us leave all those sciences and give ourselves up to commerce, to keep alive our souls and maintain our little ones, for this is the only way they have left us; and even this they have meted out with a niggardly measure, and with great parsimony. But let us stay on our Father in heaven, and only regard matters which tend to eternal life, as the laws of God and His precepts, which we are commanded, and upon which the Lord has established His covenant with our ancestors."

APOSTASY IS NOT THE WAY (*David Friedländer*)

None among the disciples of Mendelssohn gave more to the cause of Jewish cultural and political emancipation than did David Friedländer (1750-1834). To make the Jew an accepted, educated, and proud member of society was his dearest wish. But when all his efforts faltered on the rock of Christian prejudice and Jewish indifference, he was moved to equate reform with emancipation and appeared willing to do anything in order to achieve political and social equality for the Jew. He even proposed a conditional merging of Judaism and Christianity, and this occasioned a public letter to him by the Rev. Teller of Berlin, who urged him to become a Christian. But while nearly all of his friends, including Mendelssohn's children, yielded to the temptation, Friedländer drew back at this point and thus saved developing reform ideas from reaching the dead end of total assimilation.

Just as we have boldly and freely described the results of our investigations concerning the Mosaic law and the fundamentals of the religion of Moses, so we must acknowledge with equal love of truth that which should already be clear from our declaration, namely, *that giving up the traditional religion of our fathers, that is, the ceremonial laws, is entirely different from accepting Christianity.*

To be sure, there is the example of a good number of members of our nation. At all times and in all countries, there have been men who left their religion (or what they thought their religion was) without any outward pressure, who did so voluntarily and converted themselves to Christianity—sometimes to Catholicism, sometimes to Protestantism. We do not wish to judge them. When predilections and sentiment are an involuntary part of the process of judgment, cold reason, which ought to be the only fit judge, can rarely give a purely unpartisan verdict. It is always possible that such men took the step to conversion (which may appear rash to us) after much thought and in full conviction of the truth of new religious teachings. We may be revolted by the tearing of all family bonds, by the renunciation of all duties toward the old religious community; to these people the sacrifice which they brought for their conviction seemed a heroic and praiseworthy act. It is also possible that these people drowned their inner excitement in the niceties of rationalization. There is no limit to human ingenuity when there is the temptation of overwhelming advantage. It is possible that they merely followed the inclination of selfishness, which speaks so loudly to ordinary people that, because of it, the voice of conscience is often not heard. As I said, we do not wish to judge these men, but they cannot be examples or guides for us.

THE NEED FOR PRAYER REFORM *(David Friedländer)*

The longing for Jerusalem and the expectation of the Messiah were strengthened and became the most fervent hope of the people through the incorporation of these hopes and desires into the prayer book. Originally Judaism did not have prayer formulae nor devotional exercises. Animal sacrifices and other offerings substituted for them. When the state was destroyed and the Jews were dispersed among the peoples, this vacuum was filled and a different worship service was arranged. The prayer formulae which were now written consisted either of singing verses from the Bible or were newly created, and in such cases they often revealed the weakness of an ageing language. They resounded with perpetually repeated complaints over the miseries which oppressed the nation, with sighs for the return to the lost land, with longing for the restoration of the Temple service. Without exception, in all these prayers, and even in the prayers of thanks for food and joy and in the blessings under the canopy, there resounds the plaintive cry of slaves who pine for redemption. There we hear the prayer for the Messiah who shall bring the dispersed remnants of Israel back to Palestine. From century to century these prayers became more and more numerous and worse and worse, the conceptions more mystical, muddied with the principles of kabbala which were in direct contradiction to the genuine spirit of Judaism. And finally, the language in which these prayers are expressed offends not only the ear, but also mocks at all logic and grammar. The larger portion of our nation understands nothing of these prayers and that is a happy circumstance, because in this way these prayers will have neither good nor bad effect on the sentiment of the worshipers.

2. THE JOURNALS

Education was the keyword of Jewish emancipation and it was natural, therefore, that the written word should become the bearer of new ideas. While pamphlets and books for some time to come retained their role as the prime medium of communication, the appearance of journals gave scholarly, literary, and political thoughts an additional range of influence. From the mid-1830's on, the battle of Reform was fought principally in the leading magazines of the time.

HA-ME'ASSEF *(The Collector)*

In 1784, in Koenigsberg, a society of the Friends of Hebrew Literature began to issue a little magazine called *Ha-Me'assef*. Leaders in the society were Isaac Euchel, Mendel Bresslau, Simon and Samuel Friedländer—all admirers and followers of Mendelssohn. The journal's title earned its supporters the name of *Me'assefim*. The magazine was written in Hebrew and represented the first successful attempt at a modern Jewish journal. It contained poetry, historical notes, philological questions, and book reviews. There was also a German supplement, from which the following book review is taken. The brief notice throws a significant light on the political and intellectual spirit of the time. The book was called *Solomon and Joseph II,* was written by Isaac Alexander, Rabbi of Regensburg, and was published in Vienna in 1782. Emperor Joseph II of Austria, with whom the book under review deals, had proclaimed a number of fairly liberal and humanitarian laws for his subjects.

A well-meaning rabbi, deeply touched by the overwhelming goodness with which the wise Joseph showered so many thousands in his realm, including the suppressed Jews, brings his small offering to the Emperor. He draws parallels between him and the former Jewish monarch, Solomon, who, in the mind of this rabbi, is doubtlessly the perfect ideal of a wise regent. We will not note here the errors which are found in the language, orthography, and the whole context of the book. We make mention of this volume only because, first of all, it is the work of the first rabbi of our time who writes in German, and second, because it is known to us that it issues from the purest sentiments for the welfare of his nation.[2] Oh, that all the rabbis would think like him!

SULAMITH

The first Jewish journal primarily published in the German language (with a few Hebrew contributions) saw the light in 1806 in Leipzig, and was edited by David Frankel and Joseph Wolf. Frankel later became head of a Jewish school in Dessau, where he continued to publish the

[2] See Introduction, above, p. xxii.

magazine. Issues appeared intermittently until 1840. The general tenor, especially of the first volumes, reflects Mendelssohn's influence which reappears later in the East European *Haskalah,* or Enlightenment. Because of this similarity in outlook and tone, the original German movement is often referred to as *Western Haskalah.*

CONTENT, PURPOSE, AND TITLE OF THIS JOURNAL (*Joseph Wolf*)

Religion is the essential intellectual and moral need of a cultured man. It is the purpose of *Sulamith* to expose this religion to the brightest light. *Sulamith* desires to arouse the nation to a respect of religion, that is, of those truths which alone are worthy of the name religion. It wants to revitalize the urgent need for religious sentiment and concepts, but at the same time it wants to point up the truth that the concepts and commands contained in the Jewish religion are in no wise harmful, either to the individual or to society. Further, it desires to bring the Jewish nation back to its native level of education. It will demonstrate thereby that this education is entirely pure and that our religious concepts and teachings, as long as they have not been disfigured through superstitious additions, would never be an obstacle to any political constitution, but would rather be part of it, and that in those countries where total integration is not taking place, at least brotherly integration is possible. Finally, *Sulamith* wants to sort out truth from falsehood, reality from illusion, the useful from the corrupt. *It wants to enlighten the Jewish nation about itself.* It wants to strike the dry and hard rock and bring forth from it a spring of goodness which will then, by its own power, flow forth in its pristine clearness and purify the sap of the tree. In no wise do we desire, by vain artifices, to graft foreign fruit upon this tree which could not grow by itself. Only in this manner do we believe that we can utilize for the best purposes the happy atmosphere which enlightenment and education have brought to the souls of men and spread blessing and well-being to the whole Jewish nation.

Therefore, we issue an invitation to all those who want to take part in the spread of useful truths, in the advancement of general human welfare, in a pleasant and tasteful conversation amongst the readers; and we hope that they will participate with fitting contributions to this magazine in a manner adequate to its plan. Every truth, every inquiry which stems from pure intention, regardless from which pen it comes, will be welcome to *Sulamith*.

RELIGION AND CEREMONY (*Anonymous*)

From the very beginning, the ceremonial law became a focal point of discussion. The influence of Mendelssohn is strongly discernible in that his distinction between religion and ceremony reappears from now on as an essential distinction between essence and form.

The following is excerpted from an article "Some Ideas about Mosaism and Judaism," and appeared in an early issue of *Sulamith*.

Just as in the world of the visible and physical, kernel and husk are intimately joined together and yet are quite different from one another, so it is also in the world of the invisible and metaphysical, in a moral and religious system.

"Religion," says a discerning author of our time, "is in the beginning the *teaching* of God—hence the high name Doctor of Divinity—but in the end it is the *blessing* of God." This teaching, therefore, is unchangeable, just as the exalted, all-inclusive term indicates. It has its foundation in the human heart. Its basic truths, upon which alone the happiness of man rests, are not buried so deep that ordinary reason, left to itself, could not glimpse it. It is not founded so shakily that it could not oppose and disprove any speculation, as long as it follows correct rules and does not lose itself in mystical dreams and doubtful hypotheses. Religion has its seat in the human spirit. There it manifests itself in, and is so intimately connected with, its character, so deeply imbedded in human nature, that one can justifiably claim: the existence of man ceases as soon as this inborn part of his soul, this pillar of his moral system, begins to waver even in the slightest degree. The nature of religion is further so determined and firmly founded that, generally speaking, it is not capable either of diminution or addition. In every land under the sun, in every age and every society, it remains unchangingly the same.

But it is altogether different when we come to ceremony, the companion of religion. However firmly they may be bound together, however much the distinctions between them may occasionally be obliterated, still they are never fully incorporated one into the other. They may never be mistaken one for the other, and therefore the weaknesses of one may not be charged to the other. Ceremony is the daughter of imagination. To it, it owes its existence. It may appear under many guises. Its form may appear holy; its external aspects may bear many marks of the exalted and the sacred. But still it is the result of fertile imagination which brought it into being. It is sanctioned by age and confirmed by usage and repetition. Outward pomp improves its reputation and elevates its indifferent character in the eyes of the people. Ceremony is distinct from religion because of its non-essentiality; through its pure splendor, the latter lets us know of its high descent and divine origin.

Ceremony is often a necessary aid in order to prevent a complete abrogation of the main laws which certain circumstances might bring about. Indeed, sensual man needs a certain environment which attracts him with its solemnity and which is capable of bringing him closer to the essence of religion. Ceremony is, therefore, a means through which the weak eyes of the large masses—who can see like moles—are alone capable of glimpsing the glory of the divine in all its purity. And from this point of view it is no less holy. Different societies need different means of firming up their faith, hence the difference of ceremonies in every independent society according to time, climate, and circumstance. To those who are near-sighted, who cannot distinguish means from essence, both must be presented as equally holy so that they would not become disrespectful of the real essence of religion by neglecting its external forms. But even he who can see clearly will for the same reason not permit himself any public transgression, at least not until the general moral enlightenment of mankind has learned to distinguish clearly between religion and ceremony.

It follows from these premises that, if one wants to analyze the inner content of ceremonies, ordinances, and customs which are found in any nation, one must go back to their origin, to the real reason upon which they are founded, to the early maxims of the founder of the religion. One must also investigate and study the circumstances and make comparisons with the contemporaneous laws of other people. The more hidden the background of such ages, the more cautiously and carefully we must proceed in our studies; the more variegated and complex they appear to us, the more attentively must we search for the thread which can lead us out of this labyrinth.

THE BIBLICAL ORIENT (*Der Bibel'sche Orient*)

This little magazine—for so it was advertised—published only two essays by an anonymous author. It is generally believed that Isaac Bernays, then a private scholar in Mayence, wrote these tracts (which appeared in 1821). They represented a considerable degree of general and Hebraic philological learning. Bernays later became the Orthodox Chief Rabbi of Hamburg and denied all connection with the *Orient,* perhaps because much in it was at variance with his later views. Bernays was born in Mayence in 1792 and died in Hamburg in 1849. His most significant disciple was Samson Raphael Hirsch.

All true religion can manifest itself only as a reforming process. There is an eternal parallel between the singular and the universal which produces this; and similarly the human individual, in the course of his development, represents in the microcosm the prototype of all humanity. At first all appears in instinctual and developmental fashion, almost blindly; later it is reproduced in full maturity when man has reached clear vision and is reformed through self-consciousness and self-knowledge. Thus, the first period of religious maturity consists of the elimination of all that is useless and excessive. This was the work of an Abram. Thereafter comes the period of positive ritual with its legislative purpose to draw the individual into the life of the state and to integrate him into it so that he may thereby become its master. This was the work of Moses.

JOURNAL FOR THE SCIENCE OF JUDAISM
 (Zeitschrift für die Wissenschaft des Judenthums)

"Science of Judaism" (meaning the scientific study of Judaism) was the magic thought which entered the arena of Jewish life in 1822, when the twenty-eight-year-old Leopold Zunz began to give literary expression to this new concept. The year before, he and some associates in Berlin had formed a Society for Jewish Culture and Science, the objectives of which were accurately reflected in its name: Judaism was to be brought from the dark realm of a hardly known faith, with many half-known antecedents, to the light of modern scientific inquiry. Zunz (1794-1886) became the father of the new science; his contributions in the field of history, literature, and particularly liturgy mark him as the nineteenth century's greatest Jewish scholar.

The magazine saw only a single year's issues, but its contributions remained landmarks for the new approach to Judaism as a religion open to and needful of objective study.

FROM THE PREFACE *(Leopold Zunz)*

In the name of the Society for Jewish Culture and Science, I herewith present to the public the first volume of the *Journal for the Science of Judaism.*

The essays which open this volume will try to indicate what such a science might mean; however, its development must be gradual and men of insight will consider our presentation as constituting only approaches and attempts in this respect. Our society can never hope to plow the many fields of our science with its own strength alone. Rather, it will greatly welcome every effort which is dedicated to scientific pursuit, and therefore will consider every suitable contribution. We will not work for any one party, and therefore those who have the will and ability should not deny their talents to this magazine.

Even as the number of our co-workers is unlimited, so is the class of our readers neither fixed nor estimated. Science may not, with flattering elegance, pay court merely to the highest level; but neither must it, with anxious efforts, debase itself and appeal to the lowest needs of the day. If moral tone and spiritual power dwell in her house, the right guests will not stay away.

I would finally express my desire that especially my own coreligionists would give some attention to our enterprise, for it is they, first and foremost, for whom the revitalization of our science should be a challenge. Even though few may have the inclination and time to help smooth the pathway to our scientific goals, nonetheless, many may help the continuation and progress of our magazine through their financial participation. For that is the way it is on earth: every lofty spirit is bound to a physical body.

From the contents of the first volume

—On the concept of a science of Judaism, by Immanuel Wolf.
—Legislation concerning the Jews in Rome according to the sources of Roman law, by Dr. Eduard Gans.
—Letters on the reading of the Holy Scriptures, with a translation of the 6th and 7th chapters of Micah, by David Friedländer.
—Lectures on the history of the Jews in northern Europe and in Slavic countries, by Dr. Eduard Gans.
—Literary critiques.
—On the belief of the Jews in the coming of the Messiah, by Lazarus Bendavid.
—Solomon ben Isaac, called Rashi, by Dr. Zunz.
—On the natural aspect of the Jewish state, by Ludwig Markus.
—Basic outlines of the Mosaic-Talmudic law of inheritance, by Dr. Eduard Gans.
—On written and oral law, by Lazarus Bendavid.
—On the empiric psychology of the Jews in the age of the Talmud, by L. Bernhardt.
—Basic outlines of a future statistic of the Jew, by Dr. Zunz.
—Correspondence.

THE SOCIETY FOR CULTURE AND THE SCIENCE OF JUDAISM TO M. M. NOAH

Noah, American entrepreneur, literateur, journalist, and government official, was then devising a scheme to create a Jewish province in upstate New York. The Society's letter to him is included because it shows that, from the first, there was an intimate connection between liberalism and social and political concern.

(Berlin, Jan 1, 1822) Dear Sir! In the midst of universal misery, which has been oppressing a large part of European Jewry for the past several years, it was a great comfort to all who are not indifferent to the fate of our brothers to hear the noble voice of an outstanding man. You have awakened the depressed minds of the members of our slighted faith, to lead them from an ungrateful, unjust country to that part of our earth which is called the New World, but should rightfully be called the Better World. You, dear sir, gave us that great comfort. Since then, a large part of European Jewry looks hopefully to the United States of America, happy to be permitted at last to exchange the misery of their homeland with the freedom that is granted there to all religions. . . .
The Society who dares to write you this letter would be guilty of neglecting

an urgent duty if it failed to recognize the full measure of your meritorious undertaking. We appoint you, therefore, to be our honorary member and general correspondent for the United States. . . .

We would be most grateful to you if you could provide us with an accurate report on the affairs of the Jew in every province of the United States. We would be even more grateful if you would suggest to us a sufficient number of people who could found a society whose special task it would be to carry on a steady correspondence on the possibilities of how to transplant a large part of European Jewry to the United States, so as to rescue them from endless slavery and oppression.

E. GANS, Dr. Jur., President
ZUNZ, Dr. Phil., Vice-President
M. MOSER, First Vice-Secretary

THE SCIENTIFIC JOURNAL FOR JEWISH THEOLOGY
(Wissenschaftliche Zeitschrift für jüdische Theologie)

This is the lead article in the new magazine which began its publications in 1835 in Frankfort. Though anonymous, the style and nature of the article reveal that Abraham Geiger was its author. On its fly leaf the journal advertises that it is edited by a "Society of Jewish Scholars," amongst whom were found Creizenach, Formstecher, Geiger, Herxheimer, Jost, Munk (Paris), Rapoport (Lemberg), and Zunz.

Geiger (1810-1874) was then in his first rabbinic post, at Wiesbaden. The publication of this journal marks the beginning of four decades of liberal leadership, and of the most prolific scholarly and popular literary production. The history of Reform Judaism is inconceivable without the embattled dominant figure of Abraham Geiger, whose radicalism was blended with a keen appreciation and knowledge of the Jewish past.

JEWISH MOVEMENTS TODAY

Religious life in a time like ours, in which ideas have gained so much power, must present the strangest appearances and configurations. A battle is in progress and is fought with all the weapons which heavily armed contestants can command. It is a battle between the elements of dissolution and destruction, guided by largely negative reasoning, over-critical judgment of all historical and speculative documents on the one hand, and the unifying, encompassing, and affirming action of reason, the deep longing of the spirit with its poetic view of religious legends, forms, and ancient prejudices, on the other.

Let us ask in which phase of the battle Judaism stands. The most likely answer must be that we have not as yet passed through the first phase. There is still all too much of a quasi-enlightenment, interested only in tearing down; others, more discriminating, have chosen searching criticism as their leader— but alas, it too leads only to a goal where everything dissolves in a vague mist. Then there are those who strive to combine existing concepts with the demands of deep thinking. But all too often the nostalgia of their religious ideas is influenced by forms and views which a pleasant pietism would like to maintain as its precious heritage from days of childhood. And finally, there is rigid, deadly prejudice which locks the door to all thought, to all independent searching and striving. To be sure, there was a time when the disciples of a Jewish science thought to greet the dawn of a more beautiful day. It was the time when, fifteen years ago, Bernays published his *Bibel'sche Orient,* when Zunz came forth with his *Zeitschrift für die Wissenschaft des Judenthums* and most recently his splendid work, *Die gottesdienstlichen Vorträge der Juden,* Jost with his historic works full of universal scholarship, Rapoport with his splendid biographies. We will strive to make such views dominant and thereby give our internal struggle greater dignity. To this purpose we want to dedicate our new journal. However, whether our efforts will soon be crowned with success is a question which we cannot answer with any degree of certainty.

THE GENERAL JOURNAL OF JUDAISM
(Die Allgemeine Zeitung des Judenthums)

The title of this magazine, which became the chief organ of German Jewish liberalism, reveals the philosophy of its editor: it was meant to be a "general," all-inclusive, non-partisan publication. If Geiger leaned toward the left, Ludwig Philippson (1811-1889) was inclined toward a moderate point of view, and in the long run it was he rather than Geiger who gave permanent direction to Reform Judaism in central Europe. He organized the first rabbinic assembly (see below, pp. 74 ff.), and set the forces in motion to found a rabbinic seminary (below, p. 232). Perhaps it was symbolic that Philippson, the father of so many liberal institutions, was born in Dessau, the birthplace of Mendelssohn.

THE PRINCIPLES OF THE EDITOR (1837)

The appearance of the *Allgemeine Zeitung des Judenthums* has aroused general public interest. Naturally, it has also found its opposition. But if we disregard all those opinions and jealous glances which have their origin either in the envy of authors or in an animosity against Judaism in general—two matters with which we cannot occupy ourselves here—there remains one other view which has manifested itself occasionally, though not generally. It deals with this question: does the appearance of a Jewish paper point to the kind of separatism which should no longer occur in these days? It is necessary to understand each other in this regard so that we may counteract superficial attitudes.

When we speak of Judaism, we must distinguish on the one hand its religious and on the other its national aspect. In its religious aspect, Judaism is and remains something individual—just like Catholicism, Protestantism, the dissenting churches, the Mennonites, etc. It will retain its individuality as long as the promised unity of mankind in faith and religion does not exist. As far as its national aspect is concerned, it is true that there is in recent days the tendency to urge its obliteration. But as long as Jews have not obtained full civil rights, as long as they are a disadvantaged portion of the population, excluded from the full enjoyment of civil rights, we Jews will retain special interests. We want to emphasize expressly and want it understood that these special interests are merely those which will aid us in obtaining equal civil status and complete civil rights, and will afford us the opportunity to amalgamate ourselves with the general population.

All churches, all parties, any group which is in pursuit of some special goal, all have their organs through which they speak to the world, express their desires, make their requests, explain their compromises. We have our goals: to expand our religion, to transplant the institutions of antiquity into the new age and to have the requirements of the new age make their voice heard vis-à-vis the institutions of antiquity. We have to break the heavy bonds of restriction, prejudice, and hatred. Will anyone find fault with us? And yet people take it amiss if we want to speak out, if we want to explain ourselves! Can it be called separatism if we want to have a magazine dedicated to these purposes? Where are reason and fairness? I think the reader will agree with us and will know how to refute those amongst the Jews and Christians who, alas, deride the most serious and sacred efforts, and take cover under the pretext of an equality which does not as yet exist and which the events of recent days have so terribly decried.

Our magazine has announced itself as a general non-partisan organ. Its columns are open on an equal basis even to those who oppose the external emancipation of the Jews, and their articles will not be rejected, even though it will remain the conviction of the editor that emancipation is both a demand of justice and also a need of our present situation. This latter view will be reflected in the articles and comments which originate with the editor. He is not disposed to discount entirely all opposing opinions in this regard, but rather believes that victory will be more precious and sacred after the battle has been fought out thoroughly. Indeed, the more violent and intense the struggle, the closer victory will be.

Beyond this external emancipation, there is the inner emancipation which will be the subject of our columns. It is our final grand goal to awaken the spirit of our Jewish coreligionists and, where it has been awakened, to uplift and ennoble it and to call it back from the pernicious ways of indifferentism. This is what we hope to achieve, and it is this which will permeate this magazine's being and aim. We, therefore, are concerned both with the faith and the morality of Judaism and its adherents.

In Judaism there are no sects, but there are parties. The one, the conservative, is in part strictly conservative and wants to maintain tradition as it is. Others are reformers in part; they want to cleanse the old and revitalize it spiritually. And then there are the radicals who want to eliminate the old entirely and replace it with something altogether new. Next to them are the indifferentists to whom religious development is of no consequence and who interest themselves in Judaism only in respect to its moral or political progress.

It may, therefore, be asked, what point of view does the editor have regarding these various factions? It is here that we will demonstrate our full nonpartisanship. Not that we ourselves are lukewarm or would try to ingratiate ourselves with every party; not that we are afraid to enter the fray! Our nonpartisanship is founded on the principle that Judaism stands immovable above all partisanship; and that it is not the participants in the struggle who are important, but the struggle itself—for that means progress. Those who will understand us properly will not accuse us of crude eclecticism, but will see the progress of humanity itself, which consumes the product of its age but in time eliminates that which it cannot use.

ARCHIVES ISRAÉLITES DE FRANCE

Samuel Cahen (1796-1862) established his monthly magazine in Paris, in 1840, and it was destined to appear for a full century and make its scholarly and liberal impact on French-speaking Jewry. Cahen was a man of wide erudition and literary capacity. His French translation of the Bible achieved great popularity.

NO SIMPLE GAZETTE

Distinguished coreligionists in government service and at the bar, various correspondents and rabbis as well, have written us in a manner so as to arouse the fondest hope that the publication of the *Archives* will respond to a real need. One distinguished coreligionist, a lawyer, writes us from a city in the south:

"I am convinced that you have in mind a journal which will aim to return Mosaism to its pure state; to assimilate our religious customs to our civilization without changing their nature; to eliminate those of our laws which have their origin in circumstances of time or place, in persecutions or other accidental causes which have no relation to the true spirit of religion, or in opinions which are more or less variable and were expounded by savants who were subject to varying influences. I hope that it will be a journal that will tend to prove that Judaism need not envy any other faith, neither as regards its dogmas nor its ethics, and certainly not as regards that charity which people are pleased to call Christian and which is believed to be a Christian attribute (which, however, existed as strongly and was practiced already as fervently in the time before Christ).

"Finally, I trust that this will be a journal which, in its historic portions, will allow us to see the ancient Israelites in their true character and the Jews of the Middle Ages in their role of great importance which they were called to fill amongst other peoples, a role which undoubtedly can be demonstrated from historic documents. Indeed, such a journal will render a true service to the Israelites and will become an object of interest for all those who occupy themselves with the sciences and with useful knowledge. In this enterprise you have our fervent good wishes, as well as our assistance."

This, in effect, is our hope. In good faith we want to contribute to the spreading of the knowledge of Judaism, to the illumination of the present through the knowledge of the past, and through our efforts always hope to merit the approval of men of good will.

In the next issue the editor reported:

The *Archives* has been received with greater favor than we had a right to expect. If there are some people who disapprove of our intentions and have not accorded us their approval, there is a larger group of others, men of high repute, and especially administrators, grand rabbis, and men of letters, who have given us such encouragement that we have the duty to thank them publicly.

We have also received criticisms and counsels. We shall listen closely to the counsels and reply to the criticisms. "You seem to have in mind," someone writes us, "a literate public, but you ought to write for the large masses." The writer suggests that we take as our model *The Christian Archives of the 19th Century*. To this we would respond: our journal addresses itself indeed to literate people and to those who want to be instructed. We do not have the intention of putting out a simple gazette. The *Christian Archives* addresses itself to one public, and our *Archives* to another. It has been suggested to us that we publish extracts from sermons. When there will really be true sermons, we will consider it, but preaching does not exist in the French synagogue—so, therefore, what sermons should we publish?

We are asked what reforms we support. Our response is: reforms of our ritual wherever it stands in contrast to our actual habits. We support reforms which our sages would have instituted were they living in 1840. Such reforms must be agreed to by a majority of the rabbis and theologians, and must have due consideration for the minority which will have the right to reject such reforms for its own adherents.

JOURNAL FOR THE RELIGIOUS INTERESTS OF JUDAISM
  (Zeitschrift für die religiösen Interessen des Judenthums)

In 1844, Zacharias Frankel (1801-1875), then Chief Rabbi of Dresden, entered the journalistic arena with an ambitious scholarly magazine. In its pages he fought his major battles against radical reform (see below, p. 80). Frankel was a recognized authority on talmudic law, and later became the head of the first modern German rabbinical seminary, in Breslau. His "moderate reform" became the forerunner of present-day Conservatism.

FROM THE PROSPECTUS

In these pages we shall emphasize the progress of Judaism. We shall conceive it to be our task to avoid the kind of negative reform which leads to complete dissolution, but instead, to show how the teachings of Judaism itself contain the possibility of progress. We need to talk and counsel together, because we share the deep sorrow over the threatening destruction of the synagogue and the undermining of its foundations. We have the sad conviction that, in dispensing with the unnecessary parts, we are also giving up too much of that which is necessary. Meanwhile, many people display nothing but a dull indifference instead of the deep religiosity of former days, and we notice that there are many who, misunderstanding the depths of Judaism, wish to dissolve it in the general mood of the modern age. The synagogue faces a crisis, but this must not dishearten us nor must we give way to doubts that it can be victorious, for the innermost content of Judaism is guaranteed both in its continued existence as well as in its latent possibilities of self-development. How such development shall take place must be determined by scientific research based on positive historical foundations. Not every point of view can predominate, not every hypothesis can succeed, but this must not discourage us from undertaking our investigations, and as long as they are begun with sincerity and dignity and are continued in a scientific manner, we may give room to the hope that even our weak attempts may lead to more mature studies and finally to results of practical utility.

For we must understand that there is nothing but disaster in that kind of absence of motion and deed behind which one looks in vain for certainties, or in that hesitance which fears to awaken new doubts or to provoke attacks upon traditions which heretofore have not been challenged. Such silence without defense encourages its opponents to make further attacks, and in its apathy there is admission of obvious weakness, which arouses doubts even amongst the neutrals.

We aim to secure that which can be maintained in our tradition, as well as to eliminate that which disfigures the purity of our faith. We want to oppose unworthy tampering with our tradition and at the same time eliminate all reasons for doing so. We want to reconfirm and reinforce; we want to alleviate all doubts. In order to do this it is our inescapable task to speak publicly, through worthy scientific study, about the nature, the eternity, and the progress of Judaism and to offer a guide for learning and further study.

Motivated by such thoughts, the editor, in cooperation with other theologians who share these convictions, has founded this monthly *Journal for the Religious Interests of Judaism.*

MODERATE REFORM (*Zacharias Frankel*)

Time hurries onward and radical reforms are demanded, but we do not want to forget that not all demands of our time are justified. But on the other hand, we cannot overlook the fact that the long-standing immobility of the past needs rectification. Until a few decades ago, Judaism had for a long period been in a state of total immobility. It satisfied the people and, therefore, their teachers did not have the right to introduce reforms even if they had been able to transcend their age. The great gap between yesterday and today has still not been bridged, and the will of our people is still firmly rooted in the past. As long as this will still pulsates strongly, we cannot and will not touch it; rather, it must be the desire of our teachers to gain the confidence of the people by leading them gently, so that ultimately they may be granted the right to reform.

Will these reforms then be valid? When the will of the people is expressed through these teachers, when they make reforms in full knowledge of their time and in the spirit of the people—what dictum, what authority could deny them this right? The will of the people, this strong power which Judaism recognizes, this will validated by history and science and represented by teachers of truth and loyalty to our faith—would not these be valid? For some time now it has been suggested that a Synod be called where theologians would agree on reforms. But a time for such a realization has not come as yet. The theologians do not express the will of the people, for they have not gained their general confidence, partly through their own fault, and partly because the popular will cannot be expressed as long as there is inner strife and as long as the struggle between the old and the new is fought so fervently. But time will heal and help to fill the gap between yesterday and today. The teachers will find in their own lack of success a new challenge to fulfil the duties which their position imposes upon them. Thus, they will become conscious of the will of the people and will become truly living representatives, and reforms will come, not out of the people's illness, but grow from living principles.

Representation of the total popular will and of science—these are the two main conditions for a reform of Judaism. Next to faith, the Jew puts his confidence in science. His whole past history of study and mental orientation guarantees that, without a genuine science of Judaism, our theologians will never have any influence upon the people. In such a science, history too will find its just tribute and due recognition.

It would be too bold to anticipate the shape of a future which perhaps is not far away, and to determine whether it will find a common way for both faith and life. But at the same time it would be a total misreading of the great ferment of our time if on one hand one criticizes the status quo and on the other the lack of definitive reform. The opposites do not as yet permit of a compromise. Either reform will break itself on the wall of opposition, or it will dissolve tradition without displacing it and will destroy it without maintaining it through progress. We aim at a worthy representation of the total will of the people and at a science of Judaism. These will lead us to our goal and aid ¹¹º to find that measure for reforms which live not only in abstraction but can be translated into reality. Our slogan is *Moderate Reform* which, properly understood, will be Judaism's saving force and will contribute to its eternal continuity.

THE MONTHLY MAGAZINE
(Monatsschrift für Geschichte und Wissenschaft des Judenthums)

The Journal for the Religious Interests of Judaism faltered after only two years, but in 1851, Frankel tried his hand once more at editing a first-rate magazine. His new attempt was crowned with success. The revolution of 1848 had failed and Reform had spent itself in its first burst of radical enthusiasm. The time was ripe for thoughtful literary and scholarly assessment. The *Monatsschrift* became, and remained, one of the world's leading Jewish publications. After more than eighty years, its existence was ended by the Nazis.

HISTORY AND SCIENCE *(Zacharias Frankel)*

Every periodical must justify itself by what it is. It must base itself on the needs of the time in which it originates. All writing in the field of Judaism must fall into one of two categories, the religious and the political. Since, in the final analysis, the separate political position of the Jew was based on his religion, the two categories largely coincided, and religious and political matters had to be considered together. But now the special treatment of the Jews in Germany has been abolished (with the exception of one state), and the Jew takes part in politics and does not have to follow special economic pursuits. To have anxiety for the Jewish future would mean to have no faith in truth and integrity. Therefore, a journal which is dedicated to Jewish matters has neither the need nor the right to draw political matters into its purview.

But even the religious area is now acquiring a wider scope. To be sure, the religious sentiment which has its source in God is in itself divine and eternal and can never disappear entirely from the heart of man. Still, the character of our time makes itself felt even here, and its manifestations become the measuring stick for religious movements. The tensions and divisions in the political arena, which had preceded the cataclysmic events of the year 1848, reflected themselves in religious matters as well, sometimes more and sometimes less, sometimes through the effect of external events and sometimes because of the ideas underlying them. We, too, were embroiled in a struggle; party stood against party, the sword was unsheathed, and even those who slept the unblessed sleep of indifference could not fail to hear the noise of battle, and, if nothing else, curiosity would make them participate or at least look on with interest. In those days, defense and battle armor were our concern. To be sure, we also thought of education, but it had to be tied to polemics, and just as it was with the builders of the Temple, "everyone with one of his hands wrought in the work, and with the other held his weapon" (Nehemiah 4:11).

But then came the reaction. In part this was due to the political changes and in part because the divine urge had been lacking in the attack, which was, therefore, unable to bring something viable, independent, and positive into being. Once the battle was no longer necessary, people turned to other interests.

But the end of the battle has brought us no pleasure; it was not accompanied by shouts of victory but only by dull silence. The battle had ceased because the interest in religious matters has almost entirely disappeared. Therefore, it must be the purpose of a journal dedicated to the interests of Judaism to make people receptive to the high and noble contents of Judaism.

For internal and external reasons, we no longer need the kind of polemic which former days demanded. Instead, we shall give more room to instructive discussion. Such discussion will be attractive and will, therefore, not be confined to abstractions, for it does not want to be a dry-as-dust teaching of religious truths. To be sure, teaching is its final aim, but it can get there only on a path which combines the pleasant with the useful. History and Science of Judaism—these seem the most effective levers which might once again move apathetic souls and elicit new interest in the higher things of life.

This is the point of view from which the undersigned proceeds. As he edits this journal he is moved by the urge to awaken a renewed interest in Judaism. Others who are suffused by the same desires have joined him. The direction of this journal has been clearly explained above, and unless sad events should force us to do otherwise, we shall aim at hewing closely to these principles.

The undersigned has yielded to the request to take over the editorship because he has the hope that an educated and scientifically oriented public will welcome the journal and that it can achieve something to further the higher interest of Judaism. He has taken on this task for two or three years only, especially since it will mean for him many inconveniences and even sacrifices. The reception which the journal will find will help him decide whether his own powers are sufficient for the task he has set himself and whether he might be able to carry on his duties beyond the time limit. For now, may God's blessing rest upon our labors, for it is in His honor that they are undertaken.

CHAPTER

II

New Temples, New Prayer Books

‥‥‥‥‥‥‥‥‥‥‥‥‥‥‥‥‥‥‥‥‥‥‥‥‥‥‥‥‥‥‥‥‥‥‥‥‥

1. SEESEN, 1810

DEDICATION OF THE TEMPLE OF JACOB

ISRAEL JACOBSON (1768-1828) is often called the father of Reform Judaism. He was a successful businessman in the little town of Seesen in central Germany, and he was the first to give the burgeoning demands for service and prayer reform the opportunity for practical expression. He founded the first modern synagogue, introduced confirmation and other reforms, and later, as the official head of Westphalian Jewry under Napoleon, saw many of his ideas accepted into law and general practice. The following description of the dedication ceremonies was written by an anonymous witness to the historic event. Jacobson's address appears here in excerpted form. Note the specific disavowal that any of his reforms might be construed as religious assimilation. But the strong universalism of Mendelssohn shines through, and this tendency remains a basis of Reform Judaism.

The many hundreds of persons who had been invited came from Brunswick, Kassel, Halberstadt, Göttingen, Goslar, Helmstädt, and all surrounding places. Most of them had arrived in Seesen on the previous day, the sixteenth day of July. Some of them lodged in the ample buildings of the president [Jacobson], and others, for whom there was not enough room, were put up in the inn, and all costs were borne by Mr. Jacobson. In the evening he entertained everyone for dinner.

On the day of the dedication itself, on the seventeenth of July, at 7:00 in the morning, lovely music resounded from the roof of the temple (which was flat like a platform) and announced to the city the approaching festivities. At 8:00, all who had come to participate in the festivities assembled in the school hall

27

of the well-known educational institution which President Jacobson had founded in Seesen. One could see persons of distinguished rank, scholars, Jewish, Protestant, and Catholic clergymen, officials, businessmen of all kinds, all walking together in complete concord, and uniform tolerance seemed to permeate all members of this numerous company. Here friends met, acquaintances and comrades from university days who had not seen each other for a long time and found each other unexpectedly here. The manifold and different groups in this large assembly were most interesting. Everyone found something to talk about.

At 9:00, the ringing of bells announced that the ceremonies would begin. Someone explained in a loud voice how the procession from the hall into the temple would take place and what the celebration itself would consist of. Thereafter, everyone began the solemn processional under the ringing of bells. The procession was led by two flags and by the students of the Jacobson Institute and the teachers. Then followed President Jacobson, the Prefect of the Department of Oker, Mr. Hanneberg, and the clerics and lay members of the Israelite Consistory from Kassel. Then came all the rabbis present, walking in pairs, in their clerical robes, and the Christian clergymen similarly. The mayor of the town and the deputy mayor came in their robes, the Count of Brabeck, public officials of the kingdom who were present, and all the other invited persons appeared in their best clothes. Finally, there came many other people from all classes and all faiths, who had come from the entire surroundings to observe the festivities. In solemn silence the long procession went from the auditorium of the school into the halls, through the doors into the street, and again through the doors of another house, and through this house into the court to the temple. Special admission cards had been printed for this festival in order to preserve order, and they had been distributed amongst all the participants in the procession.

After the procession had entered the temple proper, there came from the organ loft lovely music by sixty to seventy musicians and singers, and this put all hearts into the most solemn mood. After everyone had taken his seat, a cantata composed especially for this celebration by Dr. Heinroth, one of the teachers in the Jacobson Institute, was sung splendidly to the accompaniment of the rousing sound of the instruments.

The Jewish ritual now began, with Mr. Jacobson himself being the chief officiant and the rabbis assisting him. At the end, President Jacobson gave an address, which we print further on in excerpt. After the scrolls of the Torah, which were elaborately ornamented, had been taken from the Ark with great ceremony, they were carried around the temple seven times, preceded by boys with burning wax candles. Then several chapters of the Pentateuch were read, first in Hebrew and at once in German, publicly and with a loud voice. Mr. Schott, director of the educational institution, then mounted the rostrum and talked to the assembled multitude. Then came a chorale accompanied by organ and full orchestra, and this was sung first in Hebrew and then also in German. At the end of this song, in the singing of which the Christians and Israelites participated with deep emotion, Church Counselor Heinemann delivered an address befitting the occasion. After this address there were further songs by the choir.

The Temple was richly and tastefully illuminated. Its architectural beauty, its decorations and guilded pieces visible on all sides to the eye, the graceful columns and antique chandeliers, the flower garlands which hung everywhere, the colorful mixture of people, all this presented a most beautiful and interesting view. At the end of the service, President Jacobson elaborately entertained at a table of two hundred in the school auditorium, in adjoining rooms for his seventy musicians, and in other rooms for an additional one hundred persons. The students of the Institute ate in the open, in the courtyard.

The festivities were original and unique. Where would one have seen a similar day on which Jews and Christians celebrated together in a common service in the presence of more than forty clergymen of both religions, and then sat down to eat and rejoice together in intimate company?

DEDICATION ADDRESS *(Israel Jacobson)*

It has been left to the tolerance of our days to bring about and to make possible that which only a little while ago would have appeared impossible. In building this edifice, it has not been my intent to bring about a complete religious unification of all religions. One accomplishes nothing at all if one desires everything or too much at one time. What is needed is gradual and slow development as is demonstrated by nature itself, when it brings forth its greater spiritual and physical accomplishments. Any divergence from this wise procedure of our common mother Nature which human stubbornness or frivolity might suggest, would only be followed by failures or even by the very opposite of that which was desired. What I had in mind when I first thought about building this temple was *your* religious education, my Israelite brothers, *your* customs, *your* worship, etc. Be it far from me that I should have any secret intention to undermine the pillars of your faith, to diminish our old and honored principles through the glitter of new opinions, or that, because of some hidden vanity, I should become a traitor to both our religion and you. You know my faithful adherence to the faith of my fathers. I need not protest it. My actions will witness for me more than my words. But if I do seek here first some rapprochement between you and our Christian neighbors, I would ask more for your gratitude and honest help than for your criticism or even opposition. For your true and progressive enlightenment depends upon this rapprochement. On it depends the education of your spirit for true religiosity and, at the same time also, your future greater political welfare. Who would dare to deny that our service is sickly because of many useless things, that in part it has degenerated into a thoughtless recitation of prayers and formulae, that it kills devotion more than encourages it, and that it limits our religious principles to that fund of knowledge which for centuries has remained in our treasure houses without increase and without ennoblement. On all sides, enlightenment opens up new areas for development. Why should we alone remain behind?

Let us be honest, my brothers. Our ritual is still weighted down with religious customs which must be rightfully offensive to reason as well as to our Christian friends. It desecrates the holiness of our religion and dishonors the reasonable man to place too great a value upon such customs; and on the other hand, he is greatly honored if he can increasingly encourage himself and his friends to realize their dispensability. Our ecclesiastical office, the Israelite Consistory, is willing to help us, is greatly concerned with the improvement of our synagogues and schools, spreads more correct principles abroad, and will, without partisanship, do the best for us even if at the moment we cannot see the flowers or fruits of these efforts.

And you, my highly honored other friends, who in name and in some aspects are different from my faith, I hope I have the full agreement of your sympathetic hearts in the principles I have set forth of the intent of this temple building, and of the hope for a happier future for my compatriots. There is nothing in this intent that in any way contradicts the principles of pure religion, of the demands of general morality, of reason, or of your own humanitarian attitude. I trust, therefore, that you will be far from receiving my brothers coldly. I trust that you will not reject them, as did your forebears only too often, but rather, that you will accept them with love into the circle of your society and business; that you will solicitously stretch out your hand to us in that rapprochement which I have sketched in its ideological outline, and for the sake of which partially I have dedicated this temple. Accept, therefore, my deepest and most devoted thanks for your warm interest in this rare celebration which you have so obviously manifested for me and my friends through your precious presence and through the expression of your sentiments.

And Thou, O God, whose mighty hand has lifted up our people once again after such long debasement, just as it happened once after a long imprisonment; Thou, O God, whose goodness has made it possible to complete the work of several years and bring it to a happy ending—grant unto us further, we pray, that we might sense the glorious traces of Thy love, of Thy benevolence, of Thy protection, both in the faith of our compatriots as in the results of this temple building. But with this confidence let us not be guilty of the indolence of delay, of the embarrassment of indecisiveness, of the mystical hope of the superstitious, and merely hope for Thine assistance. May we, conscious of our dignity, never forget *man,* the high destiny of a being whom Thou hast gifted with reason and freedom, that he might think for himself, act for himself, and whom Thou didst destine not to be a soulless machine in the plan of Thy creation. Let us never despair of the good cause of religion and mankind. Let us not lose heart when new obstacles will be thrust across our path, when we find that any beginning, like the uplifting and enlightenment of a dispersed people, can proceed but slowly and with many difficulties, and can mature only after centuries. Above all, O God, make us vividly conscious that we are brothers with all the adherents of other divine teachings; that we are descendants of one humanity which adores Thee as their common Father; that we are brothers who must learn love and gentle tolerance; brothers, finally, who under Thy guidance walk toward a common goal and who, in the end, when the mist will have been dispelled from before our eyes and all the errors gone from our spirit and all doubts removed from our reason, will meet each other on one and the same road. Amen.

2. HAMBURG, 1817

Actual systematic worship reform began in Hamburg, when sixty-six members of the community, led by Israel (Eduard) Kley, Meyer Israel Bresselau, and Seckel Isaak Fränkel, founded the "New Israelitish Temple Association." Building on their antecedents in Seesen and Berlin, the reformers chose the term "Temple," because they sought to avoid all conflict with the established Hamburg synagogue, with which they continued to be affiliated. The innovations they desired were modest: German prayers, German sermon, choral singing, organ music. They quoted the Talmud to support their innovations, and they thought of themselves as upholders of a continuous Jewish tradition. The Reform movement they set in motion was for many years dominated by the principles laid down in the Association's constitution and new prayer book.

FROM THE CONSTITUTION OF THE ASSOCIATION
DATED DECEMBER 11, 1817

Since public worship has for some time been neglected by so many, because of the ever decreasing knowledge of the language in which alone it has until now been conducted, and also because of many other shortcomings which have crept in at the same time—the undersigned, convinced of the necessity to restore public worship to its deserving dignity and importance, have joined together to follow the example of several Israelitish congregations, especially the one in Berlin. They plan to arrange in this city also, for themselves as well as others who think as they do, a dignified and well-ordered ritual according to which the worship service shall be conducted on Sabbath and holy days and on other solemn occasions, and which shall be observed in their own temple, to be erected especially for this purpose. Specifically, there shall be introduced at such services a German sermon, and choral singing to the accompaniment of an organ.

Incidentally, the above-mentioned ritual shall not be confined to services in the temple; rather it shall apply to all those religious customs and acts of daily life which are sanctified by the church[1] or by their own nature. Outstanding amongst these are the entrance of the newly-born into the covenant of the

---

[1] This word, which was to convey the purely religious character of the synagogue, enjoyed limited currency for several generations.

fathers, weddings, and the like. Also, a religious ceremony shall be introduced in which the children of both sexes, after having received adequate schooling in the teachings of the faith, shall be accepted as confirmants of the Mosaic religion.

FROM THE HAMBURG PRAYER BOOK (1819)

Meyer Israel Bresselau (1785-1839) and Seckel Isaak Fränkel (1765-1835) edited this first Reform prayer book. Though they were businessmen without rabbinic degrees, they were deeply learned. Bresselau's brilliant Hebrew style (see below, p. 37) drew the admiration even of his opponents.

The prayer book is printed from left to right. Transliterations are in Sephardic. Translations are at the bottom of the page. The word *go'el* (Redeemer) is retained in the Hebrew but translated *redemption.*[2] The Kaddish has the addition *Al Yisrael.*[3] In the *Musaf* prayer the Orthodox petition reads: "May it be Thy will, O Lord, our God, and God of our fathers, to lead us up in joy unto our land and to plant us within our borders where we will prepare unto Thee the offerings that are obligatory for us, the continual offerings according to their order, and the additional offerings according to their enactment. And the additional offering of this Sabbath day, we will prepare and offer up unto Thee in love according to the precept of Thy will as Thou hast prescribed for us in Thy law through the hand of Moses, Thy servant, by the mouth of Thy glory, as it is said. . . ." The Hamburg prayer book inserts the following new paragraph:

LeMoshe tsivita. At Sinai Thou didst give unto Moses the command, "Remember the Sabbath Day to observe it." Thou didst command to heighten the solemnity of this day through a special sacrifice [*Musaf*]. O God and Lord, may it be pleasing unto Thee to accept in mercy the prayers which we place before Thee in the fullness of our hearts. Instead of the *Musaf* sacrifice which Thou didst command in Thy Holy Bible, accept graciously our prayer.

IN DEFENSE OF THE HAMBURG REFORMERS (*Aaron Chorin*)

Israel Jacobson, to whom the new prayer book was dedicated, was instrumental in securing a number of rabbinic opinions in favor of the new

---

[2] The *Union Prayerbook,* following the same philosophy, also uses "redemption," but adjusts the Hebrew text accordingly to read *ge'ullah.*

[3] This too has passed into the *Union Prayerbook*—"The departed whom we now remember. . . ."

temple and its worship order. These responses appeared under the title *Nogah Tsedek* (Righteous Splendor). Leading among the respondents was the Hungarian rabbi, Aaron Chorin (1766-1844). To him belongs the distinction of having been the first of the rabbis to set down his liberal views on paper. In the accepted manner he published them in Hebrew, in the style of the *She'elot u-teshuvot* (Questions and Answers), which for centuries had been used by rabbinic authorities. Chorin was also the first to declare prayer with uncovered head permissible, and to allow riding on the Sabbath under certain conditions. The following is from Chorin's *A Word in its Time*.

For a long time now I have noticed with regret the sad situation of my core-ligionists. A portion of them have surrendered to superstition, another to un-belief. While that harmful conglomeration of pious simulators, the hasidim, spreads more and more and daily wins new supporters, another group eschews all religious obligations and declares as true only that to which the senses can witness. More on this on another occasion; presently only this "Word in its Time."

During the past year a circular letter from a greatly honored congregation in Germany informed me that about three hundred of the most highly re-spected heads of families had resolved to arrange their worship service in such a manner that it would comply with a sense of dignity, with the spirit of the age, and at the same time with the principles of Judaism, strictly interpreted in accordance with the Holy Scriptures and the Talmud. At the same time I was asked to state whether the teachings of the Talmud permit:

1. To cleanse our liturgy from later additions (Heaven only knows when and by whom they were added!) and to restore it to its pristine simplicity.

2. To say one's prayers in the understandable language of one's country, so that the heart of the worshiper may know what the lips speak.

3. To hold a service to the accompaniment of an organ, so that harmony and order, which are now lacking in our synagogues, might be reintroduced.

4. Or whether such changes are prohibited because of the rule, "The cus-toms of Israel have the force of Torah," which, therefore, may not be altered.

Frankly, I could not at first muster much courage to make a public state-ment about this. The unpleasant treatment I had received when, with the best of intentions, I published my *Rosh Amanah*,[4] made me hesitant. I knew well the yen which some zealots have for persecuting others, which does not rest until it has done harm, which is deaf to all reason, insensitive to all progress,

---

[4] "Principles of Faith," an essay published in 1803, in Prague, as the opening chapter of the work *Emek Ha-shaveh*. A German translation appeared in 1837 under the title "Hillel."

and resistant to all ennoblement. But after mature thought my reason returned. What, I thought, shall truth remain repressed because weak people dislike it? Shall the sun hide its light because the night owl cannot bear it? No, I thought, I will publicly testify to the truth and not shrink back from the hatred which would likely descend on me.

And so I issued my treatise *Kin'at Ha-emet* [Zeal for Truth, published in Dessau, 1818], in which I hoped to deal with the above-mentioned questions in simple, unambiguous terms. I stated that it was not only permissible, but obligatory, to free the worship ritual from its adhesions, to hold the service in a language understandable to the worshiper, and to accompany it with organ and song.

ORTHODOXY ATTACKS

The Hamburg experiment aroused the leaders of the old school from one end of Europe to the other. The reformers were condemned as unbelievers, the Reform service was excoriated, and the secular authorities of Hamburg were urged to forbid the new venture. When this failed, an appeal went out to the traditionally-minded rabbis of Europe to state their opinions of the Hamburg temple and its innovations. The replies were gathered into a volume *Eleh divre ha-berith* (These Are the Words of the Covenant), and its appearance may be said to mark the beginning coalescence of an Orthodox party, opposed to any and all tampering with tradition. Its stand was unequivocal and unyielding. Even as staunch a traditionalist as Heinrich Grätz considered these responses vapid, superficial, and unequal to the challenge. The conclusions were summarized in this proclamation:

It is forbidden to change anything in the order of the prayer ritual, as it has been handed down to us from days of yore.

It is forbidden, in the synagogue, to pray in any other language except the holy tongue, as it has been the usage in all Israel.

It is forbidden to play on any instrument in the synagogue, either on Sabbath or holidays, even if the playing is done by a non-Jew.

The responsa of Mordecai Benet, Rabbi of Nikolsburg, like those from Prague and Triesch (below), are characteristic of that personal invective which for many years made a reasoned exchange of opinion impossible.

... As regards the responsum of Rabbi Aaron Chorin, the Rabbi of Arad, be it far from us to accept any teaching from him concerning any kind of religious subject, for this man has only a mediocre knowledge of Talmud and commentary and usually occupies himself only with the secular sciences.

It is also rumored that an occidental Talmudist who lives in Livorno[5] has been misled to approve some innovation, but it is also said that he has already regretted this. It would be advisable to write to the Chief Rabbi of that town in order to obtain from him the truth in this matter.

From the responsum of the Beth Din of Prague, headed by Eleazer Fleckeles:

... However, these people [of the Reform Temple in Hamburg] really have no religion at all. It is their entire desire to parade before the Christians as being more learned than their brothers. Basically, they are neither Christians nor Jews.

As far as the playing of the organ on the Holy Sabbath is concerned, this is in every way contrary to Jewish law, even if it is done through a non-Jew. To be sure, here in Prague we have an old custom to observe the eve of the Sabbath with music. However, this takes place a half-hour before *Barechu,* at which time the musical instruments have to be laid aside.

As concerns the blasphemous book, *Nogah Tsedek,* printed in Dessau, it is not permitted to follow its dicta. We know of those people who, with much pomp, are being paraded in this book. The whole thing is deceit and deception and aims to mislead us through empty words.

In one word, any change in the prayers and customs which were ordered for us by our forefathers is against Jewish law.

Responsum of Rabbi Eliezer of Triesch in Moravia:

... We know this Rabbi Aaron Chorin. He is a man of only mediocre knowledge in Talmud and commentaries, and far be it from us to lean on his pronouncements. Indeed, we know this man and his character! Who can rely on this kind of a person? ...

Now, as regards the book *Nogah Tsedek,* its unreliability speaks from its own pages. Those who want to lie usually call on strange witnesses. Why should the author rely on the pronouncements of some Italian scholar and look around for a man like Aaron Chorin? Aren't there enough legitimate rabbis in Germany, Moravia, Bohemia, and Poland who have posts in rabbinical academies and congregations? Even in Hungary, aren't there highly

[5] Benet has reference to Recanati (see below, p. 165).

learned men whose pupils have greater knowledge in Talmud and commentary than this Rabbi of Arad?

. . . Go to the government and ask them to humble these wanton people so that the development of a new sect which no state should suffer be nipped in the bud. We understand that you live under a mild and just government which has always protected morality and religion. Go to them, therefore, and ask your senate that they stay the arm of the evil-doers.

One of the chief opponents of the Hamburg Temple was the renowned scholar, Moses Sofer of Pressburg. He argued that the use of an organ was inadmissible because it went back to the biblical Jubal and was, therefore, a pagan instrument. Further, music in the synagogues was prohibited because, since the destruction of the Second Temple, all joy had been banished from our services. The Hebrew language, he said, was the language of God, and a subject should speak with his king only in the king's language, even if the subject did not understand it. Therefore, one should talk with God in Hebrew whether or not one had an understanding of Hebrew.

These people [of the Hamburg Temple] really have no faith. Their main intention is to persuade Christians that they are wiser than their brothers. In reality, they are neither Jews nor Christians.[6]

Only Rabbi Jacob of Lissa gave the Orthodox opposition a theoretical foundation:

It is unquestionably true that the first element of religion rests on a foundation of faith, that is, faith in the truth of all that which our forefathers transmitted to us since ancient days. Hence, we call positive religion "Faith." In divine matters we cannot rely on our reason, for human reason is subject to error. Reason may be an aid to, and instrument of, the tradition of our forefathers, which may illuminate laws and customs which the ancients handed down to us. One may rely on reason only to the extent that it is congruous with law and tradition. "Forsake not the Torah of thy mother," we are taught by the wise Solomon. By this he understands the customs which the nation (whom he calls "mother") has accepted and introduced, even though reason may not fully approve of them. Hence the Torah teaches the unity of God by saying, "Hear, O Israel," and not "Think, O Israel." Why? Because even

---

[6] Note that this part of the response agrees almost verbatim with Fleckeles' (above, p. 35). One may suspect that Moses Sofer's opinion served as the model.

the most distinguished sages of antiquity, like Aristotle and his disciples, stumbled in their contemplation of this fundamental article of faith and were led into the paths of deception.

A REFORM REJOINDER (*Meyer Israel Bresselau*)

Bresselau replied to the attacks in classical Hebrew. His impassioned and well documented essay (which he called "The Sword which Avenges the Covenant") reassured the reformers that not only were they Jews, but that they were good Jews.

He takes up the main arguments of *Eleh Divre Ha-berith* and quotes classical sources to refute them. If his opponents were bitter he repays them in like coin. The following is an excerpt from his discussion of the admissibility of non-Hebraic prayers.

The Mishnah says (Sota IV): The following prayers may be said in any language: the Hear O Israel portion (*Shema*), the main prayer (*Tefillah*), and grace after meals.

Says the Gemara: Whence do we know this concerning the *Shema*? Because the Torah says "Hear O Israel," which means "in any language which you can hear." As to the *Tefillah*, it is merciful to receive all who come; and as to the grace after meals, it is written, "Thou shalt eat and be satisfied and praise God" —in whatever tongue you can.

Despite all this the Rabbi of Lissa has the nerve to say with Isaiah (6:9): "Hear ye indeed, but understand not," by which he means that in "Hear O Israel" the act of hearing is sufficient, even without understanding! Therefore, he says, even when it comes to hearing about God's unity, it does not say "Understand O Israel," but "Hear O Israel," which speaks only of the transmission of words. Thus his argument.

Let the heavens behold this! No wonder the rabbi's name is Jacob, for he holds on to his brother's heel twice, yea thrice, with such exegesis!

Further, the Jerusalem Talmud says: "And thou shalt praise God" in such a manner so that you know whom you are praising; and as for the *Shema*, one fulfils his duty even by saying it in a tongue other than Hebrew.

If our ancient sages were like angels, then is it not clear that the latter-day sages, the authors of *Eleh Divre Ha-berith,* are but a generation pure only in their own eyes?

Bresselau's closing appeal is couched in the same language which Orthodoxy had used.

And now, dear reader! After God has made all this known to you, is it not right and wise to see that *all the bans which these rabbis have pronounced upon us are null and void;* that their bans are as naught; that they neither stand nor persist, for they are like chaff which the wind blows away. And behold, you have not learned even one-half of the words of our teachers of truth, our rabbis—may they rest in peace—for there is much more, my son! May the words of the sages not depart from before your eyes, for they are life to those who find them. For they are right for those who understand and straight for those who seek after knowledge. "At the end of the matter all will be heard: fear God and guard His commandments, for that is the whole man." For the Lord will be God unto us and will make a covenant of peace with us. . . . Amen.

DISCOURAGEMENT (*Gotthold Salomon*)

Despite its early vigor, Reform was slow to take hold. Gotthold Salomon (1784-1862) became the preacher of the Hamburg Reform Temple. His letter is directed to a like-minded friend, Isaak Noa Mannheimer, the rabbi of the Vienna congregation (on Vienna see below, p. 42).

(Hamburg, June 1, 1830) . . . The news concerning the arrangements of the synagogue there has been a most pleasant surprise. I had read in the public press that your house of worship was one of the most imposing structures; I also knew that every fourteen days you preach, edify, inspire, and enrapture; and it did not remain unknown to me that your cantor there is a genuine delight for the musical ears of the Viennese. But that the spirit of God, the spirit of true piety had also entered your congregation's domestic and family life, that the marriage altar as well as the cradle and the grave are being sanctified and at the same time hallowed by the living word of religion, that I did not know. That German prayers were recited and German hymns introduced at your synagogue I did not suspect either. . . . And now, since things stand the way they are, you have the least cause to complain about your situation. What? You say you are standing alone? But you have a complete congregation, while here I can barely dispose over a fragment of a community. I say, barely! For there is no unity even in this fragmented group; some have their children confirmed, others are against it; marriage ceremonies occur rarely in our group; the *b'rith* for newly born boys is not the most alluring. Funeral sermons are still taboo. There is a wide divergence of views amongst the trustees; one member is for advancement, the other thinks we have already advanced so much that no congregation can follow us and that, therefore, we are standing alone. You see, dear friend! That is what I call standing alone; that is what I call piecemeal labor. But yours is truly significant and blessed. You say that we are locally victorious. God have mercy on such victory and such victors! In my opinion, the triumph awaiting you is much greater and more extensive, for as soon as the principle of reform will be recognized there, its spirit will create and enforce its proper form, and thus your synagogue will become the norm for several kingdoms. . . .

THE SECOND ROUND (*Aaron Chorin*)

Twenty-five years after the Hamburg Temple had been founded, a revised edition of its prayer book was issued. Once again there was spirited attack and defense, and once again Aaron Chorin took up the fight. His essay was part of a collection entitled *Theologische Gutachten* (Theological Opinions).

In the late evening of my life, near the goal of my pilgrimage, and near the entrance to the portal of heaven, here I am, close to passing from the battlefield of tumult and struggle to the peaceful chambers which are filled with the light of a higher clarity and the presence of pious souls who have gone to their reward. In this mood my soul finds inexpressible pleasure in looking back on the path I have walked with so many sorrows and tribulations. As I do so, I find not merely solace but complete reward for all my trouble and my work, for my zealous striving for the sake of the glorification of the holy name of God and of His Torah.

The genuine spirit of Jewish religiosity has integrity only when the soul is ever free of fetters and does not impose upon our conscience any oppressive restraint. That is the spirit and uniqueness of our sacred Torah whose "ways are ways of pleasantness and all its paths are peace" (Proverbs 3:9). And do we not see how the academies of Shammai and Hillel, which judged so obviously differently on so many subjects and concerning so many important ceremonies, commands, and prohibitions ordained by the holy Torah—how they acted in accordance with their judgment and how they issued their decrees for the Jews of their area and yet lived in mutual peace and concord (Yeb. 13 and 14). The principle of the Talmud remains as firm as ever (Gittin 4): "Even though one academy commands and the other one releases, still both teach the words of the living God," as long as they do it with pure intention and each one strives with all its power and insight to spread true religiosity and virtue and in order to formulate ceremonial laws in such a manner that they would revitalize religious and moral sentiment.

If this is the case with the ordinances, commands, and prohibitions which Moses handed down to us in the name of God, how much more shall and must we follow this subject which is in question, which concerns itself with the external form, the order of the temple, and the formulation of prayer ritual.

Each community should keep its own temple order; none of them should strive to press its opinion upon any other. Each should arrange its temple in accordance with its own taste, should formulate the prayers to assuage its own conscience—and all should treat each other as comrades of *one faith,* as coreligionists. The noble thinkers of each party shall both do *everything* that is within their might and power to remove all bitterness, all division, all hatred and discord. If only the parties would join in the spirit of the true religion of their fathers, which commands: Love God with all your heart, with all your soul, and all your might, and love your neighbor as yourself—if only this would happen, the difference of external forms would vanish and all souls would gather around the banner of the true worship of God. Until that time comes and the unessential divergencies are meliorated through progressive and true emancipation and enlightenment of the soul, we should be as one people held together through the bonds of religion, love, peace, and hope.

Because I am near my grave, I am unconcerned with most ephemeral interests but feel within me the power and the challenge to come forward with the fire of youth and to give witness: That I have not found in the prayer book which has come under attack any reason for condemning it for any believing Israelite; on the contrary, I have found in it many prayers which are worthy of general distribution.

And if the voice of a man who, like myself, has become grey in conscientious service and who has had manifold experience, if such a voice would find some attention amongst the maturing youth of our rabbinic profession, then let them heed this important caution: dialectic noise may penetrate the ear and dull the sense, but it will not assuage one's soul and hold back the pressing force of the needs of our time. May these young people never become rabbinic Karaites who exalt the rigid letter above all, and neither may they become worse than Karaites (who after all deify only the letter of the divine Torah) and become like those rabbis who ascribe divine authority even to ordinances written by men and hold on to them literally, pedantically, and without change, and think them above all criticism.

Finally, whatever means they use, may they never lose sight of the basic purpose of our holy Torah, that goal of concord and atonement for the sake of which, says the Talmud, one may even erase the sacred name of God from a sacred place (Succa 43). May the Lord give strength unto His people, may the Lord bless His people with students of the wise who shall increase peace in the world. Amen.

Arad—January 17, 1842

THE TEMPLE AND JEWISH TRADITION
(From the Introduction to Theologische Gutachten)

Our temple wants to remain within the framework of the synagogue. It has remained on a basis of positive, historic Judaism, and in this way has attempted to preserve its character in being as well as in action. It did not wish to separate itself in any way from the community. It desired to adopt the idea of progress primarily for itself, but the idea of man's gradual fulfilment of his divine potential was to become "an inheritance of the house of Jacob." The Association, therefore, accepted much which a more radical approach would have eliminated. It did this in deference to the community as a whole, hoping that this would facilitate the transition. The Association preferred to remain an integral part of, and to accommodate itself to, the whole community, rather than to satisfy completely a small broken-off segment. Practical thoughtfulness can only approve of this approach. The temple wanted no separation, least of all a schism, and it trusted much to the passage of time. It could more safely consider itself as an organic part of the synagogue, because it had the conviction that it was part of it and acted in its spirit, and that it could find historical justification for the change of forms and the formulation of certain teachings.

However, even though we declare, and actually have proved, that we consider ourselves as standing within the context of the synagogue and that we acknowledge the spirit of its teachings as valid for us too, we must also declare forthrightly that we are far from making necessary reforms dependent on the approval of every rabbinic authority. For us, the term synagogue does not mean the agglomeration of all the teachers of the synagogue, but the concrete understanding of Jewish teaching, whose progressive nature can be proved and which knows how to preserve the divine spirit of the Jewish religion throughout the course of the ages. This Synagogue of the Spirit follows principles different from those of a formal and fixed rabbinism which, happily, forms only a small fraction of our modern Judaism. In such rabbis we see a hierarchical authority which we reject as error. Hence we must hold up to obloquy all these apostles of regression. *Progress!*—that is our slogan. In Judaism we distinguish between kernel and shell, matter and form, the lasting and the ephemeral, the eternal and its temporal manifestation. This distinction is in the spirit of the synagogue, which disputes ceremonial law with Hillel but agrees with him that the whole law rests on *one* essential point. Israel needs more such teachers, and more and more of them do appear; for our time provides a natural school for such men, and in them we see the possibility and hope of complete Jewish regeneration.

Men of progress! You who are suffused with the idea of progress and would lead your fathers' religion toward its goal of universal human salvation, do not grow impatient in your efforts if our time permits only a slow development and if circumstances demand certain considerations. Do not storm recklessly forward in order to gain victory for the better cause; but neither become tired because of opposition which you will meet in varied forms. There has always been opposition to those who wanted to cleanse away abuses and advance the reign of light; still, to light will belong the victory which it will surely gain.

But you men of regression! You who are kept in bonds by the spirit of the dark ages; you who misjudge the rights of the present and who can see in us nothing but frivolous iconoclasts, in vain do you battle against the necessity of change in religious life. This necessity meets you everywhere, just as Elijah met Ahab, and you will eventually have to yield to the force of a reforming world spirit. It does not help to hold desperately fast to outmoded and petrified forms of life; life itself, unmoved, rejects them and regenerates itself like a chrysalis which sheds its covering when its time has come. Learn wisdom from the sages of former centuries who paid attention to the heartbeat of the times. But if you reject an organic change of ritual as heresy and apostasy, and declare its followers as non-Jews simply because they do not recognize all the phrases of the old rite as obligatory prayers, then, as before, you will further hasten the ruin of our fathers' religion and will force the supporters of change to abandon you altogether. They have made sacrifices to keep this from happening and, should it come to pass, they would sincerely regret it— not because of you but because of the total house of Israel which has been called to walk in the light of the Lord. Every attempt to stand in the way of, or even to suppress, progress will be no more successful than Balaam's attempt to ban and curse, which turned into blessing. In the same way the latest reaction against the temple became helpful rather than harmful, especially since the enlightened teachers in Israel had an opportunity to express themselves in favor of progress. Thereby this idea, founded deeply in Judaism and in the nature of man, has been emphasized and spread abroad. We, therefore, offer these pages of rabbinic opinions to our contemporaries and posterity as a true *monument of progress* and confidently look to the future of which it is written (Jer. 31:33f):

> But this is the covenant that I will make with the House of Israel after those days, saith the Lord, I will put my law in their inward parts and in their hearts will I write it . . . for they shall all know Me, from the least of them to the greatest of them. . . .

DR. M. FRÄNKEL,
for the editorial board of the
Temple Prayer Book

Hamburg, April 1842

3. VIENNA, 1826

FROM FAILURE TO SUCCESS (*Isaak Noa Mannheimer*)

Mannheimer (1793-1885) was just thirty-three years old when he wrote this letter. An ardent Reformer, he became, in time, the champion of Reform's conservative wing. His service in the Vienna synagogue, and the music rendered by his cantor, Solomon Sulzer (see below, p. 170), set new standards of inspiration. But the start was slow, and he wrote to Zunz:

My sphere of activity here is not what I had formerly imagined my higher calling to be.
     . . . Rebirth of a crushed, disintegrated people, reinstatement of the pure divine worship service, restoration of unity and dignity among our ignorant, neglected coreligionists—those were clearly the ideas and dreams which oc-

cupied our mind. I no longer think of them, for I must not permit myself the luxury of such thoughts if I am to accomplish any good whatever. I submit to the circle of ideas in my environment, and I do whatever my profession demands of me. My scientific efforts have also come to an end, since my duties leave me neither time nor tranquillity. I teach at school and preach —that is all. . . .

But three years later Mannheimer's pessimism and depression had yielded to exuberant optimism and self-assurance. He wrote a friend:

To restore the divine service in its purity, to win over the members of the community—all the people, women, and youth—is the one goal we wish to realize. To that end we employ the following means:

1. The simplification of the liturgy. We pray without any modification from *Adon Olam* until *Alenu,* but we leave out all *Piyutim,* except on the New Year when we use a special selection, and we use the special laments on the ninth of Ab, likewise in concise selection. . . .

2. There is strict adherence to set procedures of the service; there is order, strict punctuality, and solemnity at all functions. The chanting is most exalting, the choir consisting of twelve boys. The cantor must recite the prayers word by word and, when chanting, he must strictly observe certain melodies; more important and solemn passages are being sung in three or four voices. The cantor is assisted by two others besides the chorus. Our compositions are generally masterpieces of synagogue chant, even though I am not quite satisfied with the style. I wish for more choral singing, less figurate descant. . . .

3. To establish a close connection between the service and domestic life represents one of our most zealous endeavors. Every celebration in domestic life is being observed according to prescribed rules. I consider the so-called pastoral work my most sacred calling, and I hold it in even higher esteem than teaching and preaching. From birth to grave, religion shall accompany man, admonishing and comforting him. . . .

4. The sermon shall be the living word of God at all festive occasions; but it must always be vital. Therefore, if necessary, it may be used less often, as long as it thereby remains powerful.

. . . We have not as yet introduced German chants, though indeed we have German prayers at all solemn occasions before and after the sermon. However, these are only for the preacher and are not prayers of the congregation. The latter, too, I hope to achieve. The basic *Tefillah* as a ritual act can still remain in Hebrew. Not much will be gained by modifying the *Tefillah;* in fact, a great deal may be lost in respect to popular appeal.

In 1830, Mannheimer's conservatism begins to show. His early success made him eager to protect the status quo.

Both religion and morality are gaining scope and depth in the community, and the blindest zealots, as well as the most enlightened free-thinkers, cannot deny that in this community powerful support has arisen for Judaism. My most fervent wish and energetic effort is now directed at maintaining what we have gained, and I gladly give up all claim to any expansion and extension of our reform principles, if only I can protect securely what we have achieved so far. Therefore, during the last year, we have not modified our worship service in the least; sermon, chant, ritual, external procedures—everything is as it was years ago. . . . I have even tried to secure the status quo as much as possible through statutes which were sanctioned by the congregation and signed by each member, as in the days of Ezra.

The only thing that I would still like to add, but did not quite dare to do all on my own, is the chanting in German, particularly for the sake of the younger generation, since I find the congregation too inactive and unoccupied during the service. However, I have found out long ago that nothing is gained with superimposed reforms. Young people reject the new because only after a few years it becomes as old to them as antiquity. There has to be an inner strengthening, a strengthening of faith.

I would never figure on an organ, even if all outward objections against it were to cease. I admit that the sound of the organ, like the sound of bells, has become too much a characteristic of the Christian church, and it is, therefore, offensive to the Jew. Honestly, in the five years since I have become unaccustomed to the sound of the organ, it would no longer quite suit my own feelings. . . .

4. METZ, 1841

In France, the beginnings of Reform were repeated in that it was laymen rather than rabbis who took the lead in pressing for reforms. Metz was the first French city to see an organized attempt at breaking through the traditional policies of the Consistories, which held the reins of communal government tightly in their hands. The reforms spread until, in 1856, a half-century after the Napoleonic synod, another general French synod was called which, with rabbinic approval, recommended moderate reforms.

A PUBLIC APPEAL (*31 Jewish Householders*)

Gentlemen, the evils are many. It is time to act. The Israelite head of a family searches everywhere to create for his children a defense against the invasion of irreligion. But what does he find? Superannuated ceremonies, practices which choke the sublimity of our teaching and are entirely at odds with today's customs and habits. Everywhere there is doubt, but nowhere the means of combatting it.

The majority of our people, especially those who are alert and intelligent, see the evil in its full extent; but because of negligence or disunity we persist in our old ways.

Perhaps it is the task of our regularly instituted authorities to be the first to raise the standard of reform. In that case progress would find organizers who are ready, and none of that anarchy, which so often ensues when the old order is overturned, would succeed in interfering with these new developments.

Gentlemen, we submit to you this last consideration. Perhaps it may move you to withdraw your denunciation. Should you issue it nonetheless, remain sure that our persistence at some attempt of reform will not be diminished. Emboldened by the great progress we have already made, we shall not cease to work for the erection of an edifice which stands complete and permanent. Let us unite our desires, our sentiments, our efforts; and let us fight against the intrigue which operates in the shadows with legal action and petition. Let us organize committees; let us develop a literature which will express the spirit of our philosophy; let us reassure the one side that our aim is not to endanger the foundations of our religion, and the other that we want to harmonize our external forms and rituals with our daily customs and social duties. To all, let us say that we are determined to march forward regardless of the obstacles which our adversaries will put in our way. To persist means to succeed!

We have the honor, gentlemen, to be your respectful and devoted servants, etc.

(Signed by 31 Jewish Householders)

PROPOSAL FOR REORGANIZATION (*Gerson-Lévy*)

Art. 1. There is established hereby amongst the Israelites of Metz a Society whose aim it is to restore dignity to the Jewish service and to preserve it from that oblivion, apathy, and indifference which threaten it.

Art. 2. Founding members of the Society are those Israelites who within the three months will signify their adherence to this Constitution.

Art. 3. The Society will commence its activities as soon as thirty heads of families will join it.

Art. 4. Until such a time as a sufficient number of supporters will permit the Society to erect its own temple for the observance of day-to-day rites, the worship service will take place on Sabbaths, holidays, and anniversaries, in a hall suitable for this purpose.

Art. 5. The care for, and the supervision and direction of, such an establishment shall be entrusted to a commission of eight members who shall be elected by a plurality of votes.

Art. 6. Every year, in September, half of the commission shall be elected in a public assembly composed of all the members. The lot shall designate the first four members who will in this manner be reelected.

Art. 7. The functions of the eight members of the commission are divided as follows:

> One President
> One Vice-President
> Three Trustees
> One Treasurer
> One Financial Secretary
> One Secretary

Art. 8. It shall be the duty of the commission to supervise the finances of the organization as well as its order and discipline. It will discuss the measures which are necessary for the dignity of the service. It will draw up the outline for every holiday ritual and will arrange confirmation services for the two sexes. The commission will supervise the funeral services and the engagement of employees such as the officiant, cantor, choir members, preacher or lecturer, sexton, and beadle, and it will undertake all the steps to obtain the necessary authorizations demanded by Article 291 of the Criminal Code.

Art. 9. The Ark of the Law shall be placed at the east end of the sanctuary. Some steps shall lead up to it. On the two sides of the Ark there shall be three candelabra. In front of it shall be the pulpit of the officiating minister, the choir master, and the preacher or lecturer. The middle aisle shall be at least three feet wide and shall separate the seats on the left and the right, one side being occupied by men, the other by women. Two chandeliers of the old type shall be suspended from the middle of the hall, and religious inscriptions in Hebrew and French shall cover the walls.

Art. 10. The service shall consist of the reading of the prayers, the reading of God's word, the singing of psalms and other religious pieces, and of the explanation of our faith.

Art. 11. The Society recognizes as obligatory only those prayers attributed to the Men of the Great Assembly, which have been adopted by the three major rites, the Portuguese, German, and Polish. The Society shall also reserve for the solemn assemblies a choice of religious poetry composed by such sensitive poets of great merit as Gabirol, Ibn Ezra, Judah Halevi, etc. These poems shall be rendered by song in the same manner as are the psalms on every holiday.

Art. 12. On Sabbaths and holidays there shall be two morning services, one entirely in Hebrew for those to whom such practice is sacred. During the season this service shall begin at seven or eight o'clock. The other shall be held in French and shall begin at ten o'clock with prayers, psalms, and chants. The sermons, instructions, exhortations, and appeals to piety shall always be given at the end of the French service and may not be rendered in any other language except the national tongue. It is understood that each member may choose which of these services to attend.

Art. 13. Absolute silence and deep contemplation shall prevail during the service in the sanctuary. All conversation and other communication are strictly forbidden. Prayers and responses may be spoken aloud only by the officiant and the choir, excepting only the psalms, which are recited responsively.

Art. 14. Everyone without distinction shall be admitted to all religious services, except that the specially rented pews may be occupied only by their owners. There shall also be set aside a certain number of places of honor reserved for benefactors and for visitors of note.

5. LONDON, 1842

Reform Judaism came to England with the establishment of the West London Synagogue of British Jews, at the beginning of the 1840's. The first rabbi to serve the congregation was David Woolf Marks (1811-1909), who occupied its rabbinic office for over fifty years. The following is taken from the sermon he delivered at the dedication of the synagogue.

DEDICATION SERMON (*David W. Marks*)

The first solemn act, constituting us a "congregation of Jacob," has this day been performed. We have consecrated our synagogue to the worship of the Lord God of our fathers, to be henceforward, we trust, a beacon of light and a secure haven to the sons of Israel; and we have invoked a blessing on our house of prayer, and upon all those who, with devout and grateful hearts, approach these precincts to seek the divine protection. With these sacred sounds still in our ears, it might be well for us to retire to our homes, there to meditate on the goodness of Him, who has been with us in all our labors, suffered us to triumph over many difficulties, and permitted us to witness this day the realization of our fondest hopes. . . .

Not, then, to weaken, but to strengthen our faith; not to trespass against, but to consolidate the great principles of that law which our fathers tremblingly heard amidst the thunders of Sinai—this synagogue has been established. Our unerring guide has been, and will continue to be, the sacred volume of the Scriptures; by that *alone* have we endeavored to regulate our principles. In matters relating to public worship, we desire to reject nothing that bears the stamp of antiquity, when that stamp is genuine and in accordance with the revealed will of God; nor to condemn anything because it is new, provided the newness of the measure be consonant with the spirit of the religion given us by the Almighty through Moses; a religion so framed as to adapt itself to all our destinies, in all their various phases, whether politically glorious on the throne of David, or politically prostrate in the thral-dom of dispersion. . . .

The time appointed for divine service is such as to enable the entire congregation, men, women, and children, to assemble prior to the commencement of prayer. The prayers will be read aloud by the minister only; appropriate psalms and hymns will be chanted by the choir, and responses made by the congregation. The reading of the Law will not be interrupted by the *Aliyah,* for, as that institution has long lost its primary aim, the necessity for it no longer exists. Free-will offerings, unaccompanied by personal compliments, will be permitted in the synagogue on the three festivals of Passover, Pentecost, and Tabernacles, as well as on such other days as occasions may require, after the book of the Law shall have been returned to the Ark. It will be incumbent upon children of both sexes, connected with this synagogue, to be publicly confirmed in their faith at the age of thirteen years (if duly qualified); the catechetical exercises joined with this important ceremony will embrace the whole of the principles of the Jewish faith. As prayer will be offered up in Hebrew only, and as it is indispensable that every Israelite should perfectly understand the supplications he addresses to the Supreme Being, I confidently hope that the sacred language will be generally cultivated by both sexes of this congregation. The holy festivals will be celebrated on those days *only,* commanded by God through our legislator Moses. The days commemorative of the great events of Jewish history will be duly observed.

Let it not be supposed that this house is intended as a synagogue of ease or convenience; that it has been established as a formal place of meeting for those who set at naught the declared will of God. No, my friends, such men need not labor for improvement; they need no sacrifice of time, ease, and means, to effect ameliorations in our religious worship, since any system will please that affords them a formal connection with a nominally religious community. But for those who cherish a sincere love for their religion, who consider their well-being in this life and their immortal hopes hereafter to be indissolubly bound up in a rigid practical observance of the Mosaic Law, this synagogue has been reared.

FROM THE LONDON PRAYER BOOK

The first edition of this significant prayer book, entitled *Forms of Prayer,* called forth violent denunciation from London's orthodox leadership, who put the new congregation and its prayer book under the ban. The book, however, was very moderate in its reforms, and its philosophy quite conservative. The following is taken from the Introduction.

. . . It thus being evident that time has exerted its influence on these prayers, it is but meet that the exigencies of the time should again be consulted when we have arrived at the conviction that the house of prayer does not exercise that salutary influence over the minds and hearts of the congregants which it is intended and capable to exert. History bears us out in the assumption that it becomes a congregation of Israelites to adapt the ritual to the wants of its members; and it must be universally admitted that the present mode of worship fails to call forth the devotion so essential to the religious improvement of the people.

Two indispensable requisites of a petition with which man may approach his God are, first, that the prayer should be perfectly intelligible to the mind of the humble supplicant; and, second, that the sentiments which it expresses should be of a pure and elevating character. In our collection we have, with all solicitude, retained only those portions of the common rituals in which these essentials are to be found. We have removed those parts of the service which are deficient in devotional tendency; and have expunged the few expressions which are known to be the offspring of feelings produced by oppression, and which are universally admitted to be foreign in the heart of every true Israelite of our day.

If, however, we had satisfied ourselves with omitting only those passages which are open to the objections above referred to, the forms of service adopted by us would still have been longer than those which the following pages contain. But we are convinced that it is a requisite of public prayer, scarcely less indispensable than those already mentioned, that the service should be confined within such a period of time as to afford ground for the expectation that, from the beginning to the end, it may be able to command the constant, unwearied, and devout attention of the congregation. Such attention it is vain to hope from minds of ordinary strength, unless the duration of the service be moderate: and without such attention, the outward show of worship may remain, but the substance will be wanting; the lips may praise the Supreme, but the heart will be far from Him. Impressed with these convictions, we have, in order to reduce the forms of service in length, avoided those frequent repetitions of some of the finest prayers which seemed to us to weaken their effect; and we have for the same purpose omitted, in several instances, prayers which, although unobjectionable in themselves, appeared inferior in beauty of composition and of thought to those we have retained.

Many portions of the common ritual, by their holy and dignified tenor, afford every Israelite the opportunity of joining cordially in the worship of his brethren wherever he meets them in the house of prayer, and thus form a valuable bond of union amongst all Hebrew congregations. These sublime portions we trust we shall be found to have carefully preserved: and we hope to have strengthened rather than weakened the bond of union which they constitute, by blending in our ritual the varying form of the Portuguese and German liturgies, and striving to give, on all occasions, the preference to the superiority of intrinsic merit alone.

As the house of God is the fittest place for offering up sacrifices of thanksgivings on all occasions of life, and as no moment is so full of intense interest to the Jewish parent as that which ushers into existence a new claimant of the "inheritance of Jacob," we have supplied the deficiency of a prayer for such an occasion, by instituting a formula, the wording of which, being a faithful transcript of biblical language, cannot but convey devotion and comfort to the Hebrew mother for whom it is intended. A similar necessity has dictated the composition of some few other prayers, for which no formula has hitherto existed. With these exceptions and that of the introduction of a few additional portions of scripture, it will be seen that the service we have adopted is altogether based on the existing ritual.

In order to render the prayers at once more dignified and more generally intelligible, we have translated the Chaldaic expression into the sacred Hebrew (the language of the Law), a knowledge of which we trust it will be the pride, as it is the bounden duty, of every Israelite to attain.

In the English translation of the prayers, we have endeavored to combine correctness of diction with that fidelity which must be considered the paramount requisite in a work of this character. . . .

Such then are the motives which have influenced the execution of the present task. And if, by promulgating this improved form of the Jewish ritual, we contribute to the glorious end of endearing our holy institutions, and the pure fountain from which they flow, to the heart of every member of Israel; if, by the measures we have adopted after mature deliberation and with all the seriousness befitting our great cause, we become instrumental in attaching our rising generation to a mode of worship as impressive in its form as it is holy in its essence, we shall have ample cause for unbounded gratitude to our Heavenly Guide, for the glorification of whose name this work is wrought, and by whose omnipotent hand we humbly hope that it will be made to prosper for the peace, happiness, and salvation of Israel.

6. FRANKFORT, 1842

A DECLARATION OF PRINCIPLE (*The Society of the Friends of Reform*)

Frankfort on the Main became the breeding ground for the radical Reform movement (later it also became the center of right-wing Orthodoxy). Perhaps the presence in that city of the first modern Jewish school, the Philanthropin, had made Frankfort's Jews especially responsive to contemporary trends. From 1825 to 1842, Michael Creizenach taught in the Philanthropin; he was a learned Talmudist who, with his erudition, sought to give Reform a theoretical underpinning. In 1842, the year Creizenach died, his friends—all laymen—founded the Verein der Reformfreunde (Society of the Friends of Reform), which published the most radical program yet proposed. Its statement of principles brought forth the sharpest reactions, both from the Orthodox and from the majority of the Reform leaders.

In our day the split between the inner truth of Judaism and its external form has become especially acute. Nurtured by the intellectual culture of the age, many of those who are accounted members of the Mosaic religious community have arrived at the conviction that most of the practical commands, the observance of which constitutes the bulk of present-day Judaism, rest on human and temporary premises. They claim rightfully that this external form is for the most part without significance—yes, even unworthy of pure religion, and they draw the inner content of divine truth, which an earlier generation found in the Law, from those treasures of wisdom which alone have won over to the truth so many great spirits of all nations. Thus thousands have renounced allegiance to talmudic rabbinical Judaism and are connected outwardly with the Mosaic religious community only by habit or by the control of the state or by family ties. This condition of affairs is destructive and immoral; for as long as a man lives in a community he should not pass externally as something altogether different from what he is in thought and inner conviction. The Jew who has grown indifferent to his religion on this account must decide whether he will continue to be known merely as a Jew by birth, thus sacrificing free-will to habit and being deprived of all that outward religious association which is expressive of his inner conviction; or whether, longing for some tangible form, he will join some other religious association. . . . But those who cannot content themselves with either of these alternatives will pin their faith to the belief in the capacity of Judaism for development, and, instead of continuing in a state of indolent lethargy, will aim to harmonize their spiritual convictions with their professions. . . . Moved by these considerations, a number of German Israelites have determined to give expression to their opinions of the present conditions in Judaism through a public declaration, and to renounce formally their allegiance to all objectionable commands and to all antiquated customs, which to all intents and purposes they have rejected long ago. They disclaimed any purpose of desiring to obtain through this declaration more political rights than were accorded to the strict observers of the rabbinical code; neither did they intend to formulate any dogmas or create a sect or a schism; all that they aimed at was an open, honest statement of facts and beliefs as had obtained in Jewish life for a number of years past; and particularly did they desire to convince competent religious teachers that truth has a home in Israel, and to encourage them to support with all the weight of their learning the religious standpoint of truth-loving laymen.

Least of all is it our desire to hurt the susceptibilities of the strict adherents of rabbinical Judaism. Let us hope that success will crown this our honest endeavor, not only to give our religion a worthier form, but also to expound the pure content of Judaism, and to remove from it everything which has degraded and dishonored it in the eyes of thinking men. Every participant in this movement feels already great inner satisfaction in that he has chosen his position in accordance with the highest spiritual interests, and has paid allegiance to the truth. Let us begin bravely, then, a task, not only necessary from the civic standpoint and justified intellectually, but also highly moral and, in all truth, pleasing to God.

THE FRANKFORT PLATFORM

1. We recognize the possibility of unlimited progress in Mosaism.
2. The collection of controversies, dissertations, and prescriptions commonly designated by the name Talmud possesses for us no authority either from the dogmatic or the practical standpoint.
3. A Messiah who is to lead the Israelites back to the land of Palestine is neither expected nor desired by us; we know no fatherland except that to which we belong by birth or citizenship.

"THEY ARE SECTARIANS" (*Solomon Judah Loeb Rapoport*)

Many members of the Society considered circumcision as an outmoded barbaric rite. This attitude more than anything else caused most Reform adherents to view the Society with apprehension. The Orthodox party, led by Rabbi Solomon Trier of Frankfort, asked a number of rabbinic authorities to advise on how members of the Society ought to be treated. One of the respondents was the famed Solomon Rapoport, Rabbi of Prague (1790-1867), biographer, Hebraist, and leader of Eastern European *Haskalah* (Enlightenment). Although he held many progressive views he joined in anathematizing the Frankfort Society. (On other reactions to the question of circumcision, see below, p. 206.)

What should we do to protect ourselves against this sect? We merely have to imitate the example of our ancestors and see what they did against such sects, which had as their task and aim the annihilation of rabbinic Judaism.
   We must strictly insist and warn our coreligionists not to have any social contacts with the members of this Reform association, and especially not to enter into matrimonial union with them. That is the way it was done long ago with regard to Samaritans, Sadducees, Karaites, and Saruans.[1] This separation must be strictly maintained, for if it is not, many disadvantages arise because of our marriage laws in case we enter into matrimonial union with those who reject tradition and interpret Mosaic laws according to whim or convenience (compare the responsum of Rabbi Bezalel Ashkenazi, No. 3, which deals with Karaites. The "Friends of Reform" are even farther removed from Judaism than are the Karaites). I, therefore, ask Your Honor [Rabbi Trier] to issue a request to all rabbis:
   That, to be sure, they should not battle this sect as if it were an enemy and should not use any force against it. However, you will make public and warn all members of the congregation that in order to guard our descendants from all religious, private, and civic disadvantages, no one should enter into marriage with anyone who has joined the Reform association; further, that he

[1] Rapoport apparently means the Yudghanites or Isunians.

who, disregarding this warning, enters into such a marriage, should also be considered a member of this sect and be so treated.

"THEY DENY REVELATION!" (*Moses Gutmann*)

The Zedwitz rabbi (1805-1862) represented the majority of the Reformers who were critical of the Society. If Judaism was not revealed, what was it? And if it was "Mosaism" only, were all the intervening centuries of Jewish life since the close of the biblical canon as if they had never been? The following excerpt, part of a thorough critique of the Society, treats only the first point of the platform.

Your statement is as follows:
"We recognize the possibility of unlimited progress in Mosaism."
This sentence is put in such a way as to have the appearance of being positive. Yet, actually, it is just as negative as the other two. Human institutions are capable of unlimited progress, since they are at no time perfect, hence they are also at no time definitive. The next generation will always find something new and better which was unknown to earlier generations.

However, it is quite another matter when it comes to divine institutions, to which, above all, revealed religion belongs as it is set down in the writings of Moses and the prophets. The divine is in itself perfect and definitive and may not be submitted to the changing judgment of humans, but should rather serve them as an eternal rule for guide and conduct. Therefore, the above sentence contains the implicit assertion that Judaism is not a divine but rather a human institution, whose form and interpretation can be changed according to different notions and views existing at various times, as, for instance, the philosophical system of a Plato or an Aristotle, which are interpreted and shaped by each subsequent philosopher according to his own individual opinion. He will make use of the unlimited malleability of these systems, unless he prefers to spurn them completely and to substitute his own ideas in their place.

If anyone could have the slightest doubt as to the meaning connected with those words of your statement, one should have to seek the clue in your accompanying program. There, however, one clearly gets the viewpoint that the source of Mosaic teaching and the religion of Israel is *not a divine revelation,* but that it is rather the *reasoning spirit* (as it was manifest in Moses) which must be considered the origin of all religious truths. Therefore, the reasoning spirit, as it is manifest also in ourselves, has the right to set itself up as judge over the teachings promulgated by Moses, thus replacing with its greater insight whatever it finds to be short of perfection. Even though the entire program, if I may say so, exudes the spirit of gross rationalism (a fact which elevates reason to be the supreme judge in matters of religion, disavowing any and all supernatural divine revelation), I nevertheless wish to quote from it, but, for brevity's sake, two passages only. At the very beginning, you say:

> "Mosaism was not only the highest degree to which the power of abstraction, the reasoning spirit of those primitive people, could rise, it was a revelation of that spirit itself! Among the blurred, mystical superstitions of that time, it supplied the necessary respect for the teaching of a rational divinity; it gave the loftiest truths their rightful place by ascribing to them divine origin."

Consequently, the power of abstraction, the reasoning spirit, is the primary source from which Moses drew the highest truths, which he proclaimed to his people and indirectly to all mankind. He gave these truths their significance by *ascribing* to them divine origin. Thereby he merely played a pious trick, passing off his own teaching as a revelation received directly from God, while in reality it was the result of his own thinking, his own critical reasoning. The same is said at once also of the prophets, who, starting from the principle of Mosaism, reached the *highest possible spiritual levels of their epoch*. Thus the significance of those sentences, which to be sure are rather nebulous, becomes increasingly clear.

The second paragraph is on page 6 of the program. We find there a discussion of the religious viewpoints of people who have been nourished on, and imbued by, education and culture, those same individuals for whom you wish to found this society, whose opinions must consequently also be yours. About these people you say the following:

> "While they rightfully consider all external forms as being mostly without significance and as intellectually disqualified for, and indeed at times unworthy of, a purified morality, they now derive the inner substance, the divine truth (which an earlier generation had found in the Torah) *only from the treasures of wisdom which were gathered by so many great minds among all nations.*"

However, we do not derive *divine truth* from the works of mortal humans, no matter how outstanding and distinguished they may be, but rather from God's own revealed teachings, which He imparted to Moses and the prophets for the salvation of Israel and, through it, for the salvation of all mankind. We do not believe that man's reasoning spirit would have been able to discover on its own the eternal truths of religion. The wavering philosophical systems, with one supplanting the other, do not encourage us to hold such high opinions of those intellectual giants who, from their self-erected lofty throne, look contemptuously down on the humble children of men. Knowing their weakness, the latter confess to the need of higher guidance in order to find direction in their life. We say to you in the words of the poet:

> "There are more things in heaven and earth, Horatio, than are dreamt of in your philosophy."

Now, I am ready to respect any sincere conviction, even if it differs from my own, and therefore I also grant your rationalism, as well as any other religious viewpoint, the right to assert itself, provided it is straightforward and sincere, showing what it really stands for and fighting opposing viewpoints with honest weapons. In this regard, however, it seems to me your beginning deserves most to be censured. It would have been well had you stated directly: "We do not recognize any divine revelation; we no longer derive divine truth, as did our ancestors, from the teaching which was hitherto regarded as sacred, but rather from the writings of scholars and philosophers; from now on, critical reason and the thinking mind shall be the supreme judge in divine as well as in human matters." Instead of thus revealing your viewpoint freely and openly, you hide behind "Mosaism" and pretend to adhere to it as the foundation of your new dogma, when actually Moses and his teachings mean less to you than Plato, Aristotle, Spinoza, Hegel, and their systems, since undoubtedly you consider these latter ones more advanced in the general development of man than the former. If Mosaism with its progress, which admittedly it had achieved through the prophets, meaning through God himself, were indeed your basic premise, you should not have given expression to the wavering, actually meaningless phrase:

"We recognize the possibility of unlimited progress in Mosaism."
Instead you should have said:

"We recognize the teaching of Moses as the basis of our faith and as
the guide for our conduct in life, a teaching which we believe capable
of limitless growth."

To be sure, you would have still remained outside the sphere of belief in revealed religion, and no believer in revelation could have applauded your endeavor. But at least you would have taken the lead in something positive, and the people who share your point of view would at least have known to what banner they were rallying. But even this position appears to have been too confining for you, no matter how much latitude it might have given the reasoning spirit. You, therefore, chose to present your position in such a manner that you would not thereby be bound by any obligation or responsibility whatsoever.

What I have said so far shows clearly enough why I feel obligated to decline your request to join the Reform Society.

7. BERLIN, 1844

The spirit of the Frankfort Society found its strongest echo in Berlin. Here Sigismund Stern (1812-1867), a school teacher from Posen, delivered a series of lectures calling for the organization of all radical Reformers into a "German-Jewish Church." His ideas were met with intense interest, and soon he and his friends formed the *Genossenschaft für Reform im Judenthum* (Association for the Reform of Judaism). The Association became a fully established congregation and published a prayer book of the most extreme kind. It eliminated almost all Hebrew, it reflected the spirit of German idealism, but it did not succeed in capturing the leadership of the Reform movement. Until its dissolution in the

Nazi destruction, the Association represented Reform's most radical element, a determined but small minority among German-Jewish liberals.

"I AM NO REFORMER" (*Sigismund Stern*)

The impression which my lectures produced surprised me no less than it did my listeners. In fact, it frightened me for a moment, but I must say that it did not deceive me. I could rejoice over this impression without boasting too much about it; I could recognize it as a victory, not for myself, but for the good cause of which I had spoken. This is not proof of my personal capabilities but a sign of the times, a sign of a new life which manifests itself in Judaism, which abandons disinterested indifference for self-development; a sign that the need of which I am convinced is not unique with me but is found generally.

I am far from the conviction that in these lectures one may find excellent and new truths, and I have not attempted to proclaim myself a reformer of Judaism. The reader should only expect to find in these lectures the free and open expression of opinions by a man to whom Judaism is a precious possession and who, therefore, considers it his duty to think about the essence and significance of his faith, who believes it to be his obligation not to cover up the dichotomy which exists between its present forms and its own inner essence and all the total living needs of its adherents. These are the lectures, finally, of a man who has great hopes for the elimination of this dichotomy as a prelude for the great and universal future of Judaism.

He who looks for deep scholarship in these pages will be bitterly disappointed. I do not possess it; but even if I should possess it, I would hide it rather than display it publicly. A voice out of the people must also be a voice for the people. The needs of the time will not be known from books but from life itself. Religious convictions have their roots in the soul and not in science. He who hopes to find newness of thought and splendor of description will also search in vain, for truth is old and unchangingly the same, and it appears best in the simplest garment. Deep conviction does not need to seek for words; it finds them. And as for those who want to find the reflection of party struggle in these pages, who count on the derogation of people who think indifferently or look for a debasement of our own past—they might as well put this book aside, for they will in no wise be satisfied in their expectations. A self-conscious conviction struggles for its own recognition and not against other convictions; true religiosity honors the past and values its significance in order to assert the rights of the present; it respects the convictions of all in order to claim for itself, too, the right to freedom of conscience.

What is to be found in these lectures, then, is not scholarship, not sparkling talk, and least of all internecine struggle; instead, warmth of sentiment, sure knowledge and conviction, decisive attitudes, but above all, true and unflinching loyalty to Judaism. If these are merits, then it is these and these alone for which my lectures would claim recognition.

PROCLAMATION OF THE ASSOCIATION

Our inner faith, the religion of our hearts, is no longer in harmony with the external forms of Judaism. We want a positive religion; we want Judaism. We hold fast to the spirit of Holy Writ, which we acknowledge as a witness of divine revelation. We hold fast to everything by which God is truly honored in ways rooted in the spirit of our religion. We hold fast to the conviction that Judaism's teaching of God is eternally true; we hold fast to the promise that this teaching will some day become the possession of all mankind. But we want to understand the Sacred Scriptures according to the divine spirit, not according to the letter. We can no longer pray honestly for a Messianic kingdom on earth which shall bring us back to the homeland of our forefathers, pretending that we would return to it from a strange land—the very fatherland to which we are tied with all the bonds of love! We can no longer recognize a code as an unchangeable law-book which maintains with unbending insistence that Judaism's task is expressed by forms which originated in a time which is forever past and which will never return. We who are deeply committed to the sacred content of our religion cannot hope to sustain it in its inherited form, and even less can we hope to hand it on to our descendants. Thus, placed between the graves of our fathers and the cradles of our children, we are stirred by the trumpet sound of our time. It calls us to be the last of a great inheritance in its old form, and at the same time, the first who, with unswerving courage and bound together as brothers in word and deed, shall lay the cornerstone of a new edifice for us and for the generations to come.

FROM THE INTRODUCTION TO THE BERLIN PRAYER BOOK

As we present a revised edition of our prayer book to the members of our Association, we deem it to be our duty to sketch briefly the principal points of view on which this revision is based.

THE CHOSEN PEOPLE

To start with, the way and manner in which the chosenness and priestly vocation of Israel were expressed in our public prayers until now, seemed to require a thorough reform which would be adequate to our religious convictions. The chosenness of Israel as a holy priest-people and as God's own possession appears in our Holy Scriptures as a firmly established historic fact. But on closer examination, this has validity only as a *subjective* fact in the religious consciousness of the Jewish people. To a certain degree, the Jewish people had a full right to consider itself God's chosen people with whom God had entered into an intimate covenant, and whom He had distinguished with a call to priestly service. This was the degree in which it felt itself more enlightened and morally more developed than all pagan nations. It believed itself to be in the exclusive possession of a purified idea of God and of a moral life task to be holy even as God is holy, and thus truly closer to God and more intimately bound to Him than all other pagan peoples. In this sense we still consider it to be true that Israel *was* a chosen people, and that this well-founded conviction of its chosenness worked for the salvation and enlightenment of mankind. But as an *objective* fact, with all its important consequences for our religion, this chosenness has lost its validity. The concept of tribal holiness and of a special vocation arising from this has become entirely foreign to us, as has the idea of an intimate covenant between God and Israel which is to remain significant for all eternity. Human character and dignity, and God's image within us—these alone are for us signs of chosenness. We consider man as chosen and closer to God as he exemplifies these gifts and witnesses to them through virtue and righteousness. In such a sense we may occasionally mention Israel's choice in our prayers, in order to urge ourselves on to noble humanity and true brotherly love, and thus to distinguish ourselves, not as a people, but as human beings and as a congregation who stand together in their devotion to a worthy life.

REVELATION

Closely connected with this concept of Israel's choice and holiness is the idea of revelation, which in our prayers has received a formulation which in every way reflects our religious convictions. Revelation to us is the divine illumination of the spirit of our fathers which does not exceed the natural limits of human ability and which is, therefore, capable of continued development. Consequently, when our sacred texts speak of a revelation which many of our fathers received in the course of supernatural events, we can only consider such texts, in accordance with our religious convictions, as a living expression of *subjective* faith. This feeling, filled with the power of inner truth, invested our fathers with a sense of blessing, but as for us, we must deny its objective factuality. Our ancestors and all of Jewish antiquity were thoroughly convinced that God, of whose holy being and will they had the noblest conception, had illumined their spirit and had revealed to them the highest truths. They felt this so deeply that they could speak of the act of revelation only with a living sense of *immediacy*. To the degree that this conviction had living reality for them, this sense of immediacy was heightened greatly. According to the extensive description in the Holy Scriptures, the Decalogue was revealed at Sinai with the greatest solemnity. This is testimony for us that our forefathers had, as we have, a sense of the infinitely higher importance of these cornerstones of all moral knowledge, when compared to all other laws and ordinances. The Ten Commandments are not more important and holy because they were revealed with greater solemnity; the reverse is true: they were revealed with greater solemnity because they are in themselves more important and holy for the human spirit. The divinely illumined human spirit is and remains the last source of judgment to decide which revelation is of greater or smaller importance.

OUR HERITAGE

The congruence of our feelings and knowledge with that of our most ancient ancestors forms the spiritual bond and historic connection between them and us. This allows us to view and revere the heritage they bequeathed us as *the inheritance of our fathers,* and to call the universal God, the Father of all men, whom our ancestors knew and loved (and whom to know and love they taught us), "God of our Fathers," "Shield of Abraham," "Saviour of Jacob." Hence our prayers quote whole passages from the Bible in which our ancestors' faith in an immediate, apparently supernatural revelation is expressed vividly and with great force. But these citations are given a place only because the warm vital thrust of our fathers' conviction can thus retain its influence on our sense of worshipfulness; there is no yielding in this of any religious conviction on our part. However, such poetry must not sully the purity and clarity of our religious consciousness, lest a grievous contradiction accompany us from the synagogue out into life itself and spoil for our sobered spirit what poetry gained for our warmly aroused sentiment.

OLD AND NEW PRAYERS

What we have said applies to the old prayers as well as to those which have been reshaped to resemble their old examples. Everywhere the national and dogmatically narrow aspects must give way to the living flow of purely human, truly religious thoughts. For a noble, truthful, pious soul, the thought of the Father of all mankind is more stirring than that of a God of Israel. The image of God, imprinted upon every human being as a covenant-sign of divine love, has more poetry than the chosenness of Israel. The general love of neighbor and brother, deeply imbedded in every man, has more attraction than a particular ceremonial law. The universal human bond sanctifies more than does an exclusive pact between Jehovah and his first-born son Israel. All these ideas were deeply rooted in the subjectivity of the Jewish people and had their great historic importance for the development of the human race. For the preacher they provide a treasure of religious thoughts and truths as well as suggestive homilies, but they must not confuse and confound the simple sensibilities of the worshiper. Rather, prayer should be like a clear, transparent mirror of the sea in which the sentiment of the worshiper can reflect itself. Man lives primarily in the present, and its mode of thought and expression are most familiar to him. What is presented to him out of the past should facilitate and not obscure his understanding of the present.

As concerns newly created prayers, they all belong to the religious spirit of the present, to which Judaism owes its reawakening and its revitalization. They belong to the genius of the modern era which has regenerated and rebuilt Judaism from the ground up. Our sense of belonging to this faith is one of pride and joy, for Judaism has passed through the process of purification and has retained its sustaining power despite all the destructive battles which were waged against it from various sides, by the forces of stagnation as well as those of *negation.* This is perhaps a fitting place to say frankly that Judaism hides within its bosom a treasure of ideas and sentiments which has not yet

been unlocked, for it is enclosed in forms and symbols which must be completely abandoned so that those deeply hidden ideas and sentiments may rise
again in their primal force. Some think that it is these symbols and forms
which one must trustingly preserve, so that in practicing them one may acquire
the hidden kernel. It is precisely the position of Reform that one must indeed
value the kernel in its full worth, but can gain access to it only through
shucking the husk. The symbols and forms and the whole history of Judaism
must serve as a lamp so that, by its light eternal, ideas may be distinguished
from ephemeral forms. Only those forms will be granted a relative religious
value which are suitable for the exposition of an idea and for the awakening
of sentiment. The diligent reader of these prayers to whom the reforming
movements of the last decades are familiar, will find that in this fine book the
greatest achievements in this area, the high ideals and sentiments, are brought
together, which, in the purifying struggle on the battlefield of science, have
proved themselves as the ideals and sentiments of the genuine Jewish spirit.
We call special attention to those prayers which contain thoughts of the holiness of God and man, the priestly vocation of Israel, the purified Messianic
idea, and others.

May this prayer book, its contents refined, continue to awaken and maintain
the spirit of true religiosity in our congregation and our whole community of
coreligionists. We remain bound to them in spirit and in love. May it be
witness to the purity of our striving.

Berlin, October, 1848   THE COMMITTEE OF EDITORS
                                      In behalf of the Representatives of the
                                      Association for the Reform of Judaism.

PASSOVER PRAYER

Reader: Our God and God of our fathers! Thou hast chosen Israel from
among all nations, hast graced us with Thy love, hast sanctified us by Thy
Commandments, and hast dedicated us to Thy service and called us to carry
Thy name through the whole earth.

Thou hast given us the Feast of Passover so that, filled with joyous gratitude, we should remember the mercy which Thou didst show to our fathers.
Thou didst take from their shoulders the hard yoke of Egypt's slavery and
didst lead them from servitude to freedom and knowledge. But to us Thou
gavest this festival so that we might increasingly share in this freedom, which
is ours because of our fathers; that we might unswervingly hold fast to the
teachings of eternal truth which Thou didst proclaim for them and for all
coming generations.

Lord, we thank Thee for the freedom which Thou hast given to our fathers
and to us. But with our gratitude, let there also arise to Thee our fervent supplication for the welfare of our distant brethren who are still oppressed by
persecutions, as they were centuries ago; who, abandoned to hatred and
despotism, cry out in their bitter oppression. O Father of Mankind, let the

sun of Thy love illumine and warm the hearts of those who still nourish hatred and contempt against their brothers of different faiths; who believe that they serve Thee, Almighty Father, when they threaten those with ruination who pray to Thee in a manner different from theirs. Make strong the faith and confidence of our persecuted brethren; uphold them in their certainty that Thou canst never be far from those who look to Thee and hold fast to Thy pure law.

But into the heart of the free man plant Thou obedience to Thy will; let him hearken to the teachings of virtue which Thou didst write into his heart and which Thou didst proclaim to us in Thy revelation. Make us firm in our reverence to these teachings, and keep us from the delusion that through license we can honor the right to inner freedom. Help us to be worthy sons of freedom, so that we may use it for Thy glory, for the sake of our Father land, and for our own welfare.

Choir: Praise the Lord, all ye nations,
           Praise Him, all ye peoples,
           For His mercy and truth
           Endure forever.
                  Halleluyah!

8. WORMS, 1848

In one other city did radical Reform find a temporary home. This was in the Rhenish city of Worms, where centuries ago Rashi had taught the traditions of Judaism. The program of the *Reform-Freunde* (Friends of Reform) resembled its Frankfort and Berlin antecedents, but here as elsewhere the abortive revolution of 1848 dealt a death blow to the many high hopes of the liberals.

FROM THE PROGRAM OF THE FRIENDS OF REFORM

We must strive for truth and dignity in our worship service; we must see to it that our beliefs and our life are in agreement. We must uproot empty forms and create new institutions to house the spirit of Judaism. No longer must our lips pray for a return to Palestine, while at the same time the strongest bonds tie our souls to the German Fatherland whose fate is inextricably interwoven with ours—for what is dear and precious to us is embraced by her. We should not mourn for the destruction of the Temple, wearing sackcloth and ashes, for another fatherland has been ours for many years, one that has become most precious to all of us. We may remember the destruction of the Temple from year to year, but why should we pretend a sorrow which no longer touches our hearts; why should we sound lamentations for a historical event in which we see the loving hand of God? We must no longer expose our little ones in religious school to a mass of ordinances which the living spirit of Judaism is casting overboard as dead ballast. We must no longer pray in a dead language when word and sound of our German mother tongue are to us both understandable and attractive. These alone, therefore, are suited to lift us up to our Creator. This contradiction must finally be resolved; this deadly sin of untruth must be banished from our midst. A new Temple for the genuine spirit of our faith must be built on the old foundation, a Temple in which past and future are reconciled and from which once again a burgeoning fresh and free wind blows to animate our ambitious youth.

9. PESTH, 1848

The revolutionary spirit of the year 1848 made itself strongly felt in Hungary also. In this year a group of young men led by Ignatz Einhorn (1825-1875) and Moses Bruck (1812-1849), founded a liberal congregation and directed an appeal to Hungarian Jewry. Einhorn later had to flee the country because of his liberal views and wrote on political, economic and philosophical subjects. Upon his return to his homeland he became a member of Parliament and was a member of the cabinet when he died. Bruck fought as an officer in the fight for Hungarian independence and died during the battle. He was the author of a book on the reform of Judaism. The following is part of the Appeal:

The time long since prophesied has come at last; a beneficent thunderstorm has cleared the political atmosphere; millenium-old systems are destroyed mercilessly and ruthlessly; age no longer sanctifies abuses; whatever mocks the spirit of our time is in its turn now scorned and despised; the eternal truths appear pure and unencumbered on the horizon of our achieved freedom; we have taken the giant leap from pupilage to full and responsible manhood in the course of a few weeks, and shall only the golden content of our religion continue encrusted with moldering medieval ceremonies? Is this possible at a time when everything blossoms and decks itself with the fresh apparel of the new age; is our faith alone to declare itself absolutely incompatible with the new age? No! No! say we.

CHAPTER
III

The Great Controversy
Tiktin vs. Geiger

■■■

IF THE *reforms* which were advocated were brought under the scrutiny and ban of the Orthodox, the *reformers* themselves, and especially their rabbis, had to be exposed in the same manner. The first to feel the full impact of conjoined opposition was Abraham Geiger. He had indicated his belief in the necessity of change, even though he had not as yet proceeded to institute such changes in his congregation. In 1839, he was elected as second rabbi of the Breslau community which desired a more progressive leadership than was afforded them by Solomon A. Tiktin, who had occupied the chief rabbinic post since 1821. Tiktin's opposition to Geiger was absolute; no one who did not subscribe to the inviolable and absolute truth of tradition could serve with him. Tiktin's friends calumniated Geiger before the authorities, and their direct attack on Geiger as unfit for the office of rabbi embroiled all of Western Jewry in its bitterest controversy. At stake was the freedom of a Jew to study, inquire, and search—and to arrive at conclusions different from tradition. Of course, there was only one step from such inquiry to the advocacy and then to the actuality of change, and of this Orthodoxy was desperately afraid. Tiktin gathered the opinions of like-minded colleagues into a volume called *Exposition* (*Darstellung*), and the Breslau community leaders countered with two volumes entitled *Rabbinic Opinions* (*Rabbinische Gutachten*). With representatives of the old and new schools taking part in the debate, a focal point of controversy was created, and thereafter Reform leaders began to move from mere inquiry and general preachment to the advocacy of specific changes.

FOR THE FREEDOM OF INQUIRY (*Bernhard Wechsler*)

Wechsler was District Rabbi in Oldenburg when he wrote his opinion. His name occurs often in the debates of the Reform rabbinic conferences.

Jewish theology is not merely *compatible* with scientific treatment and free investigation, it *demands* them as absolutely necessary. If there is to be light in the chaotic jumble of opinions and viewpoints; if there are to be reasonable limits to arbitrary, subjective interpretation and formulation and to useless recourse to dubious authority, then only a strictly scientific treatment of the whole and its part can correct these abuses. But quite aside from all extraneous circumstances and considerations, one cannot speak of theology if it seals itself hermetically from all inquiry and research, and answers the thinker, not with reason, but with excommunication and persecution. All this leads our religion from the land of the spirit into the wilderness of thôughtless religious formalism, and Moses and the prophets have to call again and again for a spiritual and intellectual understanding of that which is unique to Judaism. Therefore it can only be in the best interest of Judaism when gifted theologians of our day search for free scientific foundations in their discipline, when they sift the mass of available data with sincerity and a love for truth (even if they find in our talmudic tradition many a gap and some aberrations), and when they publish the results of their research and strongly defend them. And what are these results until now? As far as I know, not one single fundamental teaching of Judaism has ever been remotely challenged; not one voice has been raised to quarrel with principles.

For Rabbi Tiktin to detect atheism in the train of such science, is a complete misunderstanding of an opposing system. The representatives of Jewish theological discipline have dabbled neither in speculative philosophy nor in one-sided dogmatism. Instead, they have modestly limited themselves to bringing critical and historical order into what has been tradition, and to drawing from it practical consequences. Here, too, it was not so much the principle of tradition which was investigated and for valid reasons was found to have been corrupted, but rather single points which in the Talmud were put forward as traditional. Anyone who understands anything of history and of the course of human events must admit the possibility of corruption and must thank science for entering the service of religion and for separating the true from the false. If some people think that such results are incorrect—well, they can be investigated, contradicted, and disproved; and indeed, many a point needs further elaboration and a better foundation. But one should not act as if our whole religion were at stake. One should not accuse someone of apostasy and irreligiosity who thinks he can prove—what? That the Talmud is occasionally a muddied spring! I strenuously object to such allegations (unfortunately very frequent in Rabbi Tiktin's pamphlet), and hence I must declare them as profoundly in error, and regret that Mr. S. Tiktin considers Dr. Geiger as unfit for rabbinic duties, because of the latter's scientific achievements, and refuses to treat him as a colleague.

THE PROGRESSIVE NATURE OF JUDAISM (*Abraham Kohn*)

Among the supporters of Reform, Bohemian-born Abraham Kohn (1807-1848) paid the highest price for his opinions, for fanatics poisoned him to bring a promising career to an early and tragic end (see below, p. 258). At the time of the Tiktin-Geiger affair Kohn was rabbi in the Tyrolian mountains.

This rigid immobility, this forced self-isolation of teachers from the influences and demands of the time, while their congregations progress intellectually—this it is which undermines the foundations of a positive Judaism and prevents its wholesome effectiveness. I do not know how many have proceeded by themselves because of this, and have cast off the yoke and even gone as far as deism or atheism. There have been efforts to eliminate the abuses which have crept in during the past centuries and to restore to the worship service its dignity and edifying atmosphere, and wherever possible to bring teaching and life into accord (something that the status-quo people love to decry as "the urge for innovation"). Wherever this has been done under the direction of theologians who proceeded with care and expertness, it has proven itself most salutary and has *nowhere* led to sectarian enterprises. And neither do I know whether and by whom, through word or deed, the elimination of tradition has been attempted, and certainly I do not have the intention to defend such an attempt. Nonetheless, I feel moved to remark (because this seems to be the characteristic spirit of the *Exposition*) that, by their rejection of tradition, the Karaite Jews never came close to deism or even atheism, and that in Russia and Austria they were not only tolerated but even treated better than their rabbinic brethren, and that they had the reputation of exemplary honesty and truthfulness.

To be sure, the ceremonial laws are essential in Judaism, though its creed has never been hardened into binding formulae. Rather, these laws are always of a practical nature, and for this reason there are some who ask for more in this respect than conscientious theologians could agree to. But just because of this, does it not become even more dangerous to oppose stubbornly the justified demands of time and life? The whole history of the Jewish religion proves that certain changes in the customs and ordinances of rabbinic Judaism were not only permissible, but indeed were undertaken at all times.

It must be admitted that post-talmudic teachers rarely dared to assume for themselves the right of change. Generally, they let life itself take the lead, and they followed after with excuses, admissions of exception, and considerations of special circumstances. In this manner, however, some of the most important instances of legal relief were approved (but, of course, even more so was this the case for the minutiae of added commands). It is probable that a history of religious ordinances would show that not a single command has remained unchanged in content and extent since the compilation of the Mishnah, to say nothing of former times. The influences which brought forth such changes never arose as suddenly as in the last sixty years, for they never entered into Jewish life with such force and in such mass. In these latter years barriers have come down. The civil and social position of the Jew has changed. The education of our youth has been improved through good schools, etc. And all of these brought forth new circumstances, needs, and points of view; yet, unfortunately, our Talmud scholars are walled off from the whole world and are, therefore, the least capable of judging and appreciating them.

To be sure, arbitrary changes are never permissible. But is it arbitrariness when we try to sift the chaff from the wheat and attempt to drive out the superstitious observances which, encouraged through the darkness of past centuries, have nested illegally in the halls of the synagogue? Is it arbitrariness if we, in order to restore to religion its dignity and its salutary influence upon life, desire to eliminate from the house of God all that which proves a stumbling block and gives offense to refined taste, and if we want to restore to the forms of religious worship more sanctity and more of the freshness of life? Is it arbitrariness when in our time, as far as is legally possible, we declare as inapplicable those added strictures of former teachers which are not in accord with our present conditions of life and which, because they are always disregarded, only lead to guilt feelings and then to further transgressions? Is it arbitrariness when we approach the Talmud with a scientific attitude in order to separate the results of pure divine teaching (Mosaic tradition) from edicts of a Sanhedrin, from subjective exegesis, and, finally, from the opinion of individuals and even from the conclusions based on false premises (as for instance those which resulted from earlier views of the natural sciences)?

Well, then, truth and peace are dear and sacred to us; and therefore, we must in no wise allow the right of free investigation and of progress along with our times to be abbreviated or stultified. We are truly in accord with the nature of rabbinic Judaism, and because of this, Sadduceeism died and was buried, for it held fast to the dead letter and only looked backwards. In the Talmud, the opinions and interpretations of older teachers were set aside and nullified by their successors; in fact, the Talmud is nothing but a constant development of a clash of opposing opinions. To be sure, in the course of time one notes an increased tendency toward peace and uniformity, so that, after the Talmud was completed, one did not easily dare to contradict it directly (and one must keep in mind that the Talmud was not concluded because of such uniformity of opinion, but only because of the forcible closing of the academy). But even this could not do away with the multitude of changes.

Even less did Judaism ever oppose free exegesis. Our most highly renowned exegetes differ completely from the Talmud in their interpretations of legal commands, even though they set the latter up as guides for life (which in fact was inconsistent and contradictory). Scientific study of the Talmud, with its procedure, with its method of interpretation, its principles—all this is supposed to be a mortal sin and should exclude a man from the rabbinate? The spirit of our time must revolt against such insinuation!

THE PERSONAL ARGUMENT (*Joseph Kahn*)

The bitterness engendered by the affair is reflected in this sharply worded defense of Geiger by the chief Rabbi of Treves (Trier). Kahn (1809-1875) makes reference also to Orthodox objections against the German sermon, an issue which, twenty-five years after Jacobson's and Kley's first preachments, was here debated for the last time.

Before I proceed to the actual refutation of the principles expressed in the *Exposition*, I must first declare myself against the presumption of Tiktin and company, as if they and their friends in spirit were the only people who advance and maintain Judaism, as if they were the only ones who would sacrifice their possessions and shed their blood; as if the Torah and the word of God flow forth only from them to all of Israel. I would have liked very much to be able to remain silent about this because of respect and pious reverence toward the many honored old rabbis who might feel hurt by this, but Tiktin and his henchmen, as well as most of the people of his point of view, have secretly and publicly striven to cast suspicion on the new theologians and called them "New Thinkers" (*Neologen*), deists, and Sadducees, who, as such, would lead the people to unbelief and immorality—they even called them demagogues and revolutionaries. Must not every non-partisan and honorable Israelite be deeply revolted—whether or not he belongs to the old or the new school—when Tiktin says, justifying himself, that he himself did not give *his* lectures in the German tongue and in "homiletically dressed-up" language; that such lectures are inadmissible as synagogue lectures according to government law, as can be documented by rescripts and decrees, etc., etc.? Tiktin then continues much like a Jesuit, saying, "The fact that German lectures are given during services in the synagogue and that they are even given by specially engaged preachers in a number of Jewish congregations in our fatherland (including congregations which have rabbis as their chief spiritual leaders), is not the subject of my inquiry." Tiktin might have brought forth as an excuse that he himself was not familiar with the German language and therefore was not in a position to preach a "homiletically dressed-up" sermon, and that this could not in justice be expected of him as a man of the old school who was educated in the traditional manner and who had occupied himself exclusively with talmudic studies. He might have said that for this reason the Board of Trustees, had they made such a request of him, would thereby have exposed him to chicanery and would have attempted to force him out of office. Or again, if he could not muster enough strength of character to make such a confession, he might have claimed that, according to his inner conviction, such purely German "homiletically dressed-up" lectures could not in any wise have the same effect on the audience as his own, which were given in an improper German and in the Hebrew tongue. Had he spoken thus, then, in the first case, he would have proceeded honorably and straightforwardly and, in the second, would at least have put up an appearance which would have earned him the sympathy of all non-partisans.

But the way things are, we, and with us all decent people, cannot respect his way of proceeding. For what he really had in mind was no less than to call guilty all newer theologians and teachers who committed the crime of having given a lecture in pure German, and to place these people outside the bounds of religion and law, and to describe them to the government as people who, every Sabbath and holiday, diligently transgress the "high rescripts and decrees." In this manner they would be able to get rid of this doubly sinful young brood and be able to kick them out of office and pulpit in one fell swoop. They would also cause the "high rescripts and decrees" to be made stricter, and this would rob our service of one of its noblest portions, namely, the German language which by its use binds us to our noble fatherland, the language in which a child first babbles "father and mother," "God and king," in which the boy and youth, the girl and the young woman, are educated in their schools. The consequence would be that our youth, as well as our adults who have been trained and educated in the pure German language, would either not come to services at all or would not derive any benefit from them. Why should our youth who have been so brought up remain in the house of God when, in the golden age which Tiktin desires, the old talmudic discussions and casuistic arguments and the muddled, half-German, half-Hebrew lectures would once again "adorn" the service? Isn't this really what you had in mind? We, at least, and everyone else who has a little healthy good sense, would be unable to interpret this defense in any other wise. We, therefore, must leave it to Mr. Tiktin himself to justify himself some day before the judgment throne of God. But this much we want to tell him, perhaps for his own peace of mind, just in case this sin, which doubtlessly others already have pointed out to him, should give him pangs of conscience: that however many other similar *Expositions* he will write or cause to be written, they will all remain fruitless and the olden times will not be brought back.

For he should know, if he does not know it already, that even the most uneducated people are too educated to find further pleasure in the former manner of preaching. They flock rather to the pure German "homiletically dressed-up" lectures; they listen to them with pleasure and profit, so that even some of the old honored rabbis in their old age toil to give lectures in the pure German "homiletically dressed-up" language—even if such lectures which are to be read at public ceremonies are often ghost-written for them by a new candidate. Furthermore, our high and illustrious government officials want such lectures and are often present to hear them in the synagogue. Recently a high royal Prussian government in its official journal even recommended a pure German homiletic inaugural sermon which had appeared in print. It had been given by a "new" rabbi at whose installation most of the members of this government had been present. And finally, our wise and merciful king and his counselors fully support this progress, are in favor of it and encourage it, and can only receive with disfavor the false pretenses and insinuations of Tiktin and company.

Now Tiktin and three supporting rabbis put up a great show and unctuously and touchingly proclaim themselves as the true watchmen of the sanctuary. They would be honored as holy martyrs because "in an age like the present, when the religious sense is so frivolous and abuse so easy, these changes can only lead to further degeneration." These gentlemen above would appear to "dam up the raging torrent" under peril of life. Now we truly do not know whether we should cry or laugh over such and similar outpourings. The whole thing has almost a tragicomical aspect for anyone who is acquainted with the doings and activities, or rather with the non-doings and non-activities, of these gentlemen. Our conscience demands that we may and must say to them boldly and loudly: You have done nothing for the maintenance of our faith; indeed, you are to blame for this frivolous spirit which is found here and there amongst Jews in matters of religion; you are to blame! If there is anything that is true in the whole *Exposition*, it is doubtlessly the following sentences so far as they concern themselves with Tiktin:

"But what should I, what could I do, being sadly convinced of the complete overthrow, not only of *traditional*, but also of *Mosaic* Judaism, of the progressive diminution of all religiosity, of the progressive disappearance of many a beautiful custom which had adorned Judaism? The dissolution of the tenderest bonds of society and family is near at hand; there is a progressive increase in the mockery of all that which was sacred to us for centuries and had vouchsafed unity, strength, and permanence in life, and solace and hope in the hour of death. What could I do, faced with all these evils which, alas, were getting the upper hand in Israel? What could I do, myself, to dam the raging torrents, *except to protest?*"

Does he not condemn himself? With all these dangers facing him he could do nothing and also did nothing more than—*protest!* And he did it in the privacy of his own four walls and his own two eyes! If he had really been "sadly convinced" of all that he described so tragically, if he was really serious about damming up the raging torrents—why then does he bargain and quibble with the Board of Trustees about questions which have to do with statutes and the number of sermons that have to be given, etc.? He could have at once proceeded to give lectures on every Sabbath, every new moon, every fast day, every feast day, at every opportunity, in order to admonish the people without circumlocution about their condition, and without tender treatment of the circumstances admonish the people to retain old customs and religiosity. He should never once have rested, and the pulpit should never have been empty on any of the above-mentioned days. Everything, everything, he should have given to one great effort in a time such as this, as he describes it, in order to train the youth in the truths of religion, so that this tender plant would not be infected and poisoned by the bad and rotten spirit of the time! That is what he ought to have done, by God, and should have done. Instead, he folded his hands in his lap and just looked on, regretted, wept, protested, and examined a few poor children in his apartment "without making a solemn and noisy display about it!" Should Tiktin not be ashamed before his own supporters to proclaim himself as the upholder and protector of religion? Is he in the least an imitator of those of our teachers and Talmudists whose defender he claims to be and for whom he wants to fight? Far from it! For these people truly rallied with all their power for their religion and its maintenance and development, as well as for the education and ennoblement of the children entrusted to their care. They were *doers*. They worked and taught honorably and decently without cessation. Everyone must witness to that, even those who do not fully subscribe to their system.

But what did most of the old rabbis do, our immediate predecessors, as well as Chief Rabbi Tiktin and the whole host of his comrades? Nothing. What did they do for morality and the ennoblement of their congregations? Nothing. What for the schools? Nothing. What for the service? Nothing. What for the rooting out of prejudices against people who thought or believed differently, especially against confessors of other religions—prejudices, it cannot be denied, that arose necessarily through the pressure of the times? Nothing, absolutely nothing.

These are not casual accusations, but rather, all congregations, officials, and governments must here be in agreement with us. We newer rabbis do not pride ourselves, like Tiktin and company, and claim to be the sole upholders of Judaism. That be far from us. We are free of such arrogance; we know and recognize that we could still do many things differently and better, that often in our attempts and performances we choose ways which do not always lead to the desired goal. But this we can claim and say of ourselves without conceit: that we *desire* the good and that we rally to its strengthening and progress with all our might; that no trouble is too great for us; that we take a zealous interest in our schools and in our worship services; that we do not neglect any of our official duties; that in fact we do, therefore, more than merely collect our salary. All congregations whose spiritual leaders are new rabbis will testify to this, as will magistrates and governments. But we would accomplish even more, and our efforts would be more greatly blessed, if there were not everywhere, unfortunately, some men like Tiktin and company who constantly disturb us and hinder us in our efforts, who, in the eyes of the people, make us suspect as unbelievers, if there is but the smallest change. They hold fast to a talmudic dictum (which, of course, was meant in a totally different fashion): "Sitting still and doing nothing is the best"; they think that they belong to the thirty-six pillars upon which the earth is founded, and pride themselves that when they die the earth will totter and finally perish.

As we have already indicated, we have not the slightest intent to offend the many rabbis, some of them already gathered to their fathers and others still living as old, honorable gentlemen who were and are sincere in their faith; and neither do we want to offend the congregations entrusted to their care. We have high regard for them and love them with all our hearts, and many of them are our good friends. But we must publicly express our contempt for those who, like Tiktin and company, blindly damn and ban, and in just indignation we must brand them as men who "some day will have to account for their deeds," so that "they should hear and fear and not sin any more."

CHAPTER
IV

Conferences and Synods

---

1. THE FRENCH SANHEDRIN

W<small>HEN</small>, in 1806, Napoleon caused a convention of Jewish notables to be called, excitement ran high among the Jewish masses of France and Western Europe. Recognition, status, equality, autonomy—all these cherished goals seemed suddenly in reach. Unfortunately, the Emperor's plans were less idealistic, and the Assembly of Notables as well as the Grand Sanhedrin which followed it had little visible effect. Yet for the history of Reform they became important as forerunners of future rabbinical and synodal conferences. For the first time in modern days a Jewish body met to contemplate how the demands of the age could be reconciled with the traditions of Judaism. When the 110 Notables had assembled they received these questions:

QUESTIONS ASKED BY NAPOLEON

1. Are Jews allowed to marry several wives?
2. Does the Jewish faith permit divorce? And is an ecclesiastical divorce valid without the sanction of civil court or valid in the face of the French code?
3. May a Jewess marry a Christian, or a Christian woman a Jew? Or does the Jewish law demand alliances between Jews only?
4. Are the French in the eyes of the Jews their brethren or their enemies?
5. In either case, what duties does the law prescribe for the Jews toward the French who are not of their faith?
6. Do those Jews who are born in France and who are treated as French citizens regard France as their native country, and do they feel themselves obligated to defend it, to obey its laws, and to submit to all regulations of the civil code?
7. Who appoints the rabbi?

71

8. What police jurisdiction have the rabbis over the Jews? And what judicial authority do they possess?
9. Does their prestige rest simply upon usage?
10. Are there trades which the law forbids the Jews to practice?
11. Does the Jewish law interdict usury, the practice of usury with their co-religionists; and
12. Does it prohibit or allow usurious practices with Gentiles?

CALL FOR THE SANHEDRIN

Of the twelve questions, the third aroused the most heated controversy. The final answer by the Notables was ambiguous. In a dramatic, if cynical, gesture Napoleon called an enlarged conference, known as the Grand Sanhedrin, to put its stamp of approval on the preliminary debates of the Notables. A proclamation was issued in Hebrew, French, Italian, and German to encourage the various regions in the large French domain to send delegates.

A great event is in the making. That which our fathers did not see in the long progression of centuries, that which we in our days could not hope to see, will reappear before the eyes of an astonished world. The 20th of October is the day which is fixed for the opening of the Grand Sanhedrin in the capital of one of the mightiest Christian empires and under the protection of the immortal prince who rules it. Paris will be the scene for a drama that will play before the world, and this eternally memorable event will open a period of redemption and happiness for the dispersed remnants of Abraham's descendants.

Who would not admire with us the hidden plans of a Providence which we cannot fathom, which changes the forms of human affairs, brings comfort to the oppressed, raises the lowly out of the dust, and makes an end of the trials which divine will has imposed, and which once again restores to the faithful guardians of His law the respect and good will of the nation. Since our dispersion, uncounted changes have proven the instability of human affairs. From time to time nations have expelled each other and at times intermingled with one another. We alone have opposed the stream of centuries and revolution. [There follows an extravagant tribute to Napoleon and the appeal to send delegates to the forthcoming Assembly.]

THE SANHEDRIN RESOLVES RELIGIOUS AND CIVIL LAW

We declare that the divine law, the precious heritage of our ancestors, contains religious as well as civil demands;

That by their nature religious demands are absolute and independent of circumstance and time;

That this is not the same with civil commands, that is to say, with those which touch upon government and which were designed to govern the people of Israel in Palestine when it had its kings, its priests, and its magistrates;

That these civil commands ceased to be applicable when Israel ceased to be a nation;

That in hallowing this distinction, which has already been established by tradition, the Grand Sanhedrin declares it to be an incontestable fact;

That an assembly of men learned in the law, united in a Grand Sanhedrin, can alone determine the consequences of such development; and

That, if the ancient Sanhedrins have not done so it was only because political circumstances did not permit and because, since the entire dispersion of Israel, no Sanhedrin has assembled until now.

Therefore, engaged in this pious enterprise, we invoke divine inspiration from which all good derives, and consider ourselves obligated to advance, as far as it depends on us, the achievement of the moral regeneration of Israel; and

Therefore, in virtue of the right conferred upon us by our customs and our sacred laws, which determine that there resides in an assemblage of the learned men of the time the essential capacity to determine, in accordance with the needs of the case, that which is required by the above-mentioned laws, be they written or oral, we now proceed to declare that obeisance to the law of the state in matters civil and political is religiously required.

Marriage

The Grand Sanhedrin, taking cognizance of the fact that in the French Empire and the Kingdom of Italy no marriage is valid unless is has been preceded by a civil contract before a public official, declares in virtue of the authority granted unto it:

That it is a religious obligation for every Israelite in France, as well as in the Kingdom of Italy, to regard from now on civil marriage as a civil obligation, and

Therefore forbids every rabbi or any other person in the two lands to assist in a religious marriage without it having been established beforehand that marriage has been concluded according to the law before a civil officer.

The Grand Sanhedrin declares further that marriages between Jews and Christians which have been contracted in accordance with the laws of the civil code are civilly legal, and that, although they may not be capable of receiving religious sanction, they should not be subject to religious proscription.

Military Service

The Grand Sanhedrin declares that any Jew who is called to military service is, according to Jewish law, during the entire duration of the service, released from observing all religious obligations which interfere with such service.

2. RABBINIC CONFERENCES

A whole generation passed before Western Jewry was ready for another conference on theological matters. But this time its convener was not the secular power; now the call was the indigenous, inevitable result of the burgeoning Reform spirit which sought clarification and direction. Geiger had repeatedly urged a rabbinic conference, but it was Ludwig Philippson whose organizational talent called it into being. The discussions achieved less than its originators had hoped for, and fewer rabbis attended than had been expected. Withal, the Brunswick conference and those that followed were landmarks of Jewish history. Their slow beginnings, their controversies, their hopes, and their failures all play a part in the drama. Quite naturally, the first conference put in its agenda a reconsideration of the questions which thirty-eight years before had occupied the French Notables and the Sanhedrin. With minor changes they arrived at the same conclusions. This debate occupied the major part of the Brunswick conference, which considered itself primarily preparatory in character.

The excerpts which follow portray the genesis and actual opening of the historic gathering.

PHILIPPSON WRITES TO BRUNSWICK

To the directors of the distinguished Jewish community in Brunswick:

Gentlemen: Your wonderful and blessed activities, your quiet, well thought-out, but consistent and therefore successful, labors for the institutions of your community instil in me the confidence that you would favorably consider the following request.

Some Jewish rabbis and clergymen, some of whom have studied together, have had the idea of meeting together in June of this year, in part to see each other again, in part to come to know each other. To be sure, there is also another purpose, namely, to discuss the religious conditions of their congregations and to pacify those who through literary disputes have grown apart, and thereby to work for a rapprochement in the spirit of peace and common effort, for the sake of the communities entrusted to their care. This thought, which the undersigned has expressed publicly, has found great response, and subsequently the following indicated that they would participate in such a gathering: (Now follow the names of the gentlemen who have so indicated.)

You will notice that your distinguished spiritual leader, District Rabbi Dr. Herzfeld, is among those who have already agreed to come, and therefore the undersigned has asked Dr. Herzfeld whether the locality where this gathering could take place could not be the city of Brunswick. Dr. Herzfeld fully agreed and has told us of the level of education reached by your community, and of the form of its services; he has told us of the pleasant and interesting environment, of the fact that the city is easily reachable through railroad and highways; and he has also indicated the favorable attitude of the Ducal Government, which encourages all good things, subject to legal limits and rightful authority. For these reasons we have come to the conclusion to choose Brunswick as the place of our gathering. Since District Rabbi Herzfeld has declared himself willing to make certain necessary arrangements with some friends, I therefore submit to you, honored directors, the following humble request:

Whether you would not be pleased if we chose Brunswick as the place of our gathering; and

Whether you would be willing to inquire from the respective governmental office whether we would need their permission to meet for the above-mentioned purposes, and if so, to obtain such permission.

I look forward to your kind reply and am,

Respectfully,

RABBI DR. PHILIPPSON

Magdeburg, March 26, 1844

THE TRUSTEES WRITE TO THE CITY COUNCIL

To the honorable City Council of the city of Brunswick. From the directors of the local Jewish congregation concerning a projected rabbinical assembly.

We have the honor to transmit to the honorable city council a letter which has been addressed to us by Rabbi Dr. Philippson of Magdeburg (of March 26). This letter expresses the desire to hold a projected meeting of several rabbis and Jewish clergymen in June of this year and asks us, in case we would be willing, to take the necessary steps and procure the permission of the respective official body. As far as we are concerned, we declare that we are not only agreed that the meeting take place here but at the same time we are very willing indeed to do everything in order to make the visit of these gentlemen here most pleasant, and to justify the flattering confidence they have put in us. We greatly value in every respect the noble and self-sacrificing striving of these honored clergymen, and we hope that much good will come to our coreligionists from such an assembly, especially in respect to the possible resolution of different points of view through friendly discussion. This will also bring about that the reforms of our ritual, which in almost all congregations have either already taken place or are in the process of being introduced, would take a common direction as a result of progressive education.

Our gracious national government, together with our honored city council, has in the past constantly encouraged and protected all that which we have permitted ourselves to suggest for the welfare of our congregation, and has done so with such truly fatherly concern that we confidently expect the granting of today's respectful request, namely:

That the city council be kindly pleased to intercede with the Ducal Ministry of State and obtain for us the permission for an assembly in June, in the city of Brunswick, of the projected assembly of several rabbis and Jewish clergymen.

Since time is very short to make the necessary preparations and to obtain a suitable locale for the assembly, and since a part of the rabbis and clergymen who live far away would each one in his own realm of activity have to make a number of preparations for such a journey, we add the most respectful request for the early disposal of this matter and remain, your obedient servants of the honorable city council,

DIRECTORS OF THE JEWISH CONGREGATION

Brunswick, April 1, 1844

Reply

We transmit to you herewith a copy of the letter of the Ducal Ministry of State of the twelfth of this month, from which you will see that there is no objection to the gathering of various rabbis in our city.

Brunswick, April 16, 1844   CITY COUNCIL

THE FIRST SESSION (*From the Transcript*)

The assembly met in Brunswick on June 12, 1844 at 9:00 A.M. Present were the following gentlemen: Church Counselor Dr. Maier; District Rabbi Holdheim; Rabbi Dr. Klein; Preacher Dr. Salomon; District Rabbi Dr. Hess; Rabbi Dr. Soberheim; Preacher Dr. Jolowicz; County Rabbi Goldmann; Preacher Ben Israel; Rabbi Dr. Philippson; Rabbi Schott; Chief Rabbi Dr. Formstecher; Preacher Dr. Frankfurter; District Rabbi Dr. Herxheimer; County Rabbi Dr. Adler; Preacher Dr. Adler; Rabbi Hoffmann; Preacher Heidenheim; District Rabbi Dr. Herzfeld; District Rabbi Dr. Bodenheimer; District Rabbi Dr. Hirsch; Preacher Edler.

Opening of the Assembly

After the local Rabbi, Dr. Herzfeld, had greeted the assembly with a fitting and appropriate address, and Dr. Philippson had done the same, the election of the chairman was on the agenda. Church Counselor Dr. Maier of Stuttgart was elected with sixteen votes out of twenty-two. He mounts the rostrum and gratefully declares his acceptance of the election which gave him so significant a majority. First of all, he expresses thanks to Rabbi Dr. Philippson for his initiative and his effort to bring about the assembly. He further expresses the deep-felt thanks of the assembly to the committee on arrangements for this first assembly, as well as to the honored Israelitish community of Brunswick for their quite extraordinary hospitality and their fine arrangements. Thereafter, he calls attention to the importance of our task, which he delineates briefly but succinctly, and he asks that the different factions should have confidence in each other, for all are deeply motivated by the sacred cause which we represent. He further asks to keep in mind the tasks of everyday life which make urgent demands upon us. The assembly will be more successful if it keeps strictly to questions of the day. At the same time he asks the support of the whole assembly for his chairmanship of the discussion.

The question whether a vice-president should be elected was decided affirmatively (the members either rose or remained seated), and the choice fell with a six vote majority on Dr. Holdheim.

The assembly then proceeded to the election of a secretary, which office went to Dr. Frankfurter with a seven vote majority. In the same manner, the question whether a second secretary should be elected was decided affirmatively; equally, the question which of the members had received the most votes for second place (in the first voting which had elected Dr. Frankfurter to secretaryship). Dr. Hirsch of Luxembourg was then declared to have been elected second secretary.

Next on the agenda was the question whether the sessions should be public or secret, because Mr. M. of Hanover desires to be present at the sessions even though he is not as yet an officiating minister. A divergence of opinion developed.

Shall the Sessions Be Public?

Relevant questions are debated in a discussion in which Dr. Bodenheimer, Dr. Hess, Dr. Salomon, and Dr. Philippson participate. A side issue is debated concerning the printing of the discussions and similar matters, but finally the main question (whether or not the session should be public) is debated again. The following speak or vote:

Dr. Herzfeld: No.

Dr. Holdheim: Absolutely public, in order to allay suspicions. This is accomplished best by having everyone able to hear and convince himself of the purity of the purpose and convictions of the assembly.

Dr. Formstecher: No, for the discussion would be debating ideas not yet fully mature, which are not suited for the public at large. However, the results of the discussions could be published.

Holdheim tries to disprove this, saying that people of evil intentions are in any case casting suspicions on our assembly.

Dr. Philippson completely agrees with Dr. Holdheim, for our century demands light and publicity, which we do not need to avoid. Whoever has an opinion should state it or should stand up for it, and he who cannot do this should be silent.

Dr. Hess also believes that the consecrated nature of the assembly demands absolute public procedure.

Rabbi Schott believes in the public nature of the sessions, not so much because we are children of our time, but because confidence cannot merely be asked for; we must prove ourselves worthy of it.

Bodenheimer is for the negative, because with public sessions, people will mistake discussions for results.

Dr. Herzfeld is now for public sessions and so is Dr. Klein.

Dr. Hirsch believes that public sessions are absolutely and unconditionally important, both because of our opponents and because of our congregations. What about evil intentions, he asks? An individual, to be sure, may have a difficult time with this, but the assembly will just have to disregard it. The person who comes here is not destructive and neither is he of uncertain motivation; on the contrary, he is enthusiastically devoted to Judaism. Therefore, we have nothing to hide from the public.

Dr. Hess repeatedly seconds Dr. Hirsch and stresses the aspect of freedom in the Jewish religion, which we must respect here also. Shall we not also keep in mind the good-will which shall speak strongly for us, more strongly than what evil intentions can do to us?

Rabbi Goldmann: No—We would miss the purpose of our assembly if misinterpretations would distort our debates.

Dr. Jolowicz: Since we will be publishing the results, we might as well have the sessions public.

Dr. Adler calls attention to the historic element. The old Sanhedrin too was public. Shall we be less advanced in our time?

Secretary Dr. Frankfurter believes that only practical reasons speak for secret sessions, but both theory and practice speak for their public nature; therefore, it must be unconditionally public.

Thereafter the debate is closed and the question is put: Shall the sessions generally be public? Seventeen vote "Yea"—four "Nay."

The request of candidate M. of Hanover to be admitted to the assembly and to listen to the proceedings is therefore granted.

Summary

Joseph Maier (1797-1873), who later won the unique distinction of being ennobled by the King of Württemberg, was the president of this first rabbinic conference. The following is his concluding address:

As we conclude our labors for this year, I deem it necessary to address a few words to the distinguished Assembly. As we look back over the progress of our discussions during this first and certainly most difficult and important Assembly, we have every reason to be satisfied. Even though the results are not of great import, at least so far, still what has taken place is assurance that greater things will happen in the future.

The statute on which we counseled and which we accepted contains, to be sure, only formal regulations which shall govern future assemblies and discussions. However, in so important a matter as that which brings us together each year, even the form is not unimportant. It gives to our association a firm basis and brings order into our business; it facilitates it and advances it. In addition to some less important matters, three highly important subjects were prepared and referred to commissions for further study.

The revision of Jewish marital law will help to do away with essential defects in this portion of Jewish life and in the future will also help to do away with many inconveniences and conflicts.

Even more important is the preparation of a new liturgy and a new prayer book for home and public worship. If the commission, which has been created for this purpose, will undertake and complete its task in the sense and spirit in which this distinguished Assembly has expressed itself, then indeed it will have the most wholesome influence on the religious life of the Jew.

Finally, you gentlemen have recognized and appreciated in its full extent the importance of the matter which we have just discussed, namely, the Sabbath.

To be sure, those who would like to make sweeping reforms will not be satisfied with these results. However, we cannot let these people deter us. One must sow first in order to achieve spiritual harvests. The spiritual tree must first be planted and nurtured before one may have fruit from it. On the other hand, those of rigid and formal belief will accuse us and will throw suspicion upon us, and perhaps the thoughtless will mock us. But even these will not deter us, for, conscious of our good cause, neither suspicion to the right of us nor mockery to the left of us will bother us, and with a zeal which will not cool, with a self-assurance which will not be moved by every whim, we shall pursue our task with that thoughtfulness which takes time and circumstance into consideration. This task is to maintain and develop our religion and to revitalize the religious service. Let us understand the time and let us utilize it, but let us not force from it that which it cannot give us, for "He who forces time, time will force him" (*Kol hadohek et hasha'ah, hasha'ah doheket oto*). Let us take away from here the conviction that the good cause to which we have dedicated our time, our effort, our life, will remain victorious, and finally, that our holy religion, purified of all dross and additions, cleansed of all that is merely local or ephemeral, of all disfigurations which adhere to it, will rise in new glory, to fulfil its mission to mold mankind into one brotherhood.

HIRSCH VS. FRANKEL

There was one man above all whose absence in Brunswick was keenly felt. He was Zacharias Frankel, one of the recognized leaders of German Jewry who was known to favor moderate reforms (see above, p. 24). But not only did he not appear at the conference, he proceeded to criticize it sharply in the press. Samuel Hirsch (1815-1889), then Chief Rabbi of the Grand Duchy of Luxembourg (he later became the spiritual leader of Keneseth Israel in Philadelphia), came to the defense of the Reformers. Hirsch, who acquired his fame through his philosophical writings, well demonstrates the prevailing tone in Jewish polemics. Even the most highly placed personalities were not sacrosanct in the face of the great cause.

I have just come across the eighth issue of Dr. Frankel's *Zeitschrift (Journal for the Religious Interests of Judaism)* in which the editor denounces the Rabbinical Conference (which took place in June in Brunswick), with a bitterness which was painfully noticeable. Dr. Frankel announces to the world, at the end of his essay, that the Conference was a failure, and though he pretends to be greatly pained, one cannot avoid detecting a certain malicious gloating on his part. In a sense we agree with Dr. Frankel: indeed, we admit that the undersigned, and certainly some of his colleagues, had journeyed to Brunswick, aware that this first Assembly would almost have to be a partial failure! Not all those present at Brunswick were in as sound a financial position as Dr. Frankel, and there was hardly one among them who had the hope of ever becoming Chief Rabbi of Berlin.[1] Those living in the more remote areas learned about the date and place of this Conference so late that they hardly had time to make the necessary arrangements. Nevertheless, they made great sacrifices in undertaking the journey; their stay at Brunswick, notwithstanding the magnificent hospitality of its congregation, was rather costly and thus had to be of short duration. Under those circumstances how could anybody have persuaded himself that in such a short time all important questions would be solved and significant results be achieved? That members who met there for the first time could have reached an agreement on important matters? That an Assembly which had hardly come into existence, could already have gained the stature necessary for mutual trust and authority? And yet, despite all difficulties, these men did convene; they came, knowing that they would most likely expose themselves to accusations—though certainly no one had expected such an attack from a man like Dr. Frankel. And why did these men make an appearance? Only because they believed, by the mere fact that this Conference would

[1] (Ed. note) The Berlin community had offered the post to Frankel, but after protracted negotiations he declined the offer.

come into being and reconvene annually, that the illnesses of Judaism might be healed. These men laid themselves open to possible embarrassment, conscious of exposing their good name to criticism. Yet, they did it so that a beginning might be made; they were convinced that, in time, experience would teach them how to avoid further mistakes. For that they deserve appreciation and gratitude; instead, they were subjected to personal attacks by another publication, and to piqued invectives by Dr. Frankel, who in his long article did not find the smallest space to express a desire that this Conference might reconvene in order to achieve better results than the first time.

Dr. Frankel knows he is the least entitled to make such denunciation; however, he thinks he can get by with high-sounding phrases. Why did he not stand by his pledge to appear personally? Certainly it is not difficult to travel from Dresden to Brunswick! Dr. Frankel states he does not have to account to anyone but himseif. Well, we shall not let you get off that easily, Sir! One who can say so much about what the Conference should or should not have done; one who with such hair-splitting precision can point out the demands and claims that should have been made to this Assembly and its individual members; one who is so aware that this Conference and most of its members had convened without the slightest desire or intention of meeting these demands— such a man does not only owe it to himself, indeed he must account to all Israel for his failure to appear. Dr. Frankel should presume that each member had come with the good intention of doing his best; what was lacking was a leader like Dr. Frankel who alone could have told the Conference what it ought to be; alas, he did not come. Whose fault is it then, that, instead of achieving some good, it did the opposite? Thus, is it not a fact that all the accusations against the Conference must of necessity turn back to Dr. Frankel himself? Who is to blame when this Conference found so little support that it might possibly not reconvene, as Dr. Frankel seems to hope? Or is there perhaps no need for such an institution? According to Dr. Frankel's utterances about the people, its sound mind and deep religiosity, it might almost seem as though pure wantonness had brought these men together, as though levity was the order of the day, something not to be forgiven a layman, much less so a group of rabbis. But has Dr. Frankel never been in Leipzig during the Fair? Has he never walked through the streets on a Sabbath or a holiday? Has he never seen a table d'hôte or a similarly appointed place for eating and drinking? And he presumes to brag about the religious sense of the people! I do not exaggerate when I say that seven-eighths of our German-Jewish youth are completely estranged from any and all meaning of Jewish religious feeling; I claim that this cancer advances daily. And Dr. Frankel could not find the smallest word of praise, of love and encouragement, if not for the men of that Assembly, at least for an institution that has taken upon itself the task of finding a solution to this dilemma!!

I shall now proceed to discuss Dr. Frankel's accusations one by one. After dealing with the question of mixed marriages, which I shall not take up at this point, Dr. Frankel deplores the fact that the Conference had made a decision in favor of open meetings. Every argument Dr. Frankel puts forward was taken into consideration and backed by experience. I had, for instance, not spoken as strongly against the Shulhan Arukh as Dr. Frankel makes it appear on page 16. The question involved the obligation to consider the resolutions of the Conference (for those who supported them) as binding and to translate these decisions into everyday practice. It was at this point that I stressed the need for such a resolution. I showed how, against our better judgment, we were bound in our present-day practice in religious matters by some precepts of the Shulhan Arukh which appear obsolete to everyone, including, most likely, Dr. Frankel himself. I suggested that in the future such passages of the Shulhan Arukh should be confronted with the authority of this Rabbinical Conference, leaving it up to the individual which authority to follow. I cannot be blamed, therefore, when one among our respected members became so impressed with the publicity of the proceedings that, roused by a holy zeal, he arrogated to himself the functions of the President and imputed to me the intention of attempting to ridicule the Shulhan Arukh. No one who knows of my scientific endeavors will take this seriously, for I have always sought to evaluate every event in the area of religion in its historical importance; thus the accusation that I want to make anything appear ridiculous defeats itself. I am just a little responsible for the fact that the President himself, infected by the same passionate zeal, censured *me* instead of the person deserving it. This was proved by the fact that Dr. Adler, who followed me, took up my ideas, pursued them along the lines of my own intent, and, when said member got carried away once again by his fervent zeal, the Chairman, now performing his duties with greater fairness, protected the freedom of discussion against any inopportune outbreak of holy passion. Notwithstanding these abuses, the Conference decided in favor of public meetings.

Why? Has Dr. Frankel completely forgotten about the massacre of Damascus and the manner in which German journalism behaved? Would not a conference behind closed doors have offered new weapons to the enemies of the Jewish people? It was better that the Assembly take the risk of an occasional speaker who would be carried away by his vanity and try to shine before the public, or the risk of another who, because of shyness or consideration, would hold back his true feelings—better this than to give rise to renewed, unfair, and slanderous accusations against Judaism. "But the layman could cause annoyance, could become confused in his religious belief by some assertion, the refutation of which he might not be able to follow!" Well, we have an opinion different from Dr. Frankel. We say there are no such laymen among the Jewish people. We feel that the layman, too, must reflect and ponder on matters of his religion. Therefore, he really does not have to be so anxiously sheltered from every little draft. His priest does not have to offer him ready results, purporting to be the dogmas of his church, which he is obligated to adopt under the threat of forfeiting his salvation; but rather, he may and should share the path the rabbi takes in his search for Eternal Truth. And if at times he blunders on his way, it will certainly be more agreeable to God than if he merely swears by what his Chief Rabbi could offer him as ready truth.

Furthermore, Dr. Frankel is most dissatisfied that the Assembly elected a committee for the reform of Jewish marriage law. Is there a way to satisfy Dr. Frankel? In regard to mixed marriages, he felt one committee was quite sufficient. Now, when the assembly shows more prudence and cautiousness, choosing not only a committee, but also demanding that its work be closely examined by distinguished talmudic authorities before reaching the Rabbinical Assembly for discussion, it is still, in Dr. Frankel's opinion, not doing enough. He states: "Present day circumstances do not urgently demand reforms in this area." How is that, Sir? Blinded by your hatred against everything this Conference has done, *how can you dare to put these words on paper?* Suppose someone dies childless. According to Hebrew and talmudic law, the brother is obligated to marry the widow. If he does not comply, he must endure public disgrace. Through the synod of Rabbenu Gershom, that which is obligation according to the Bible, is now forbidden,[2] yet the disgrace is retained as punishment. Suppose this case happens today. The surviving brother is somewhere in America, China, or his whereabouts are simply unknown; the young woman can never remarry, because a ceremony, the significance of which has ceased to exist, cannot be performed. And this obstruction to a person's happiness means so little to you, Dr. Frankel, that you are not even in favor of establishing a committee that would ponder at least the possibility of some remedy? A "Cohen" may not marry certain women; how often does this fact not only mean thwarted happiness, but also a turning away from Judaism! And all this means nothing to you? Indeed, you deem proposals for a reexamination and reevaluation entirely superfluous? Suppose a young man takes it upon himself, in the presence of two witnesses, to give a young girl something of the value of a peruta[3] while using the well-known marriage formula? Does the ensuing anxiety and sorrow, the strife among the families, mean nothing to you? These are by no means invented stories. Indeed, these are cases that have happened in real life. Yet Dr. Frankel states: "Reform is urgently demanded neither by the existing situation nor by many people!!" And what if some day the state's assistance at a religious wedding ceremony would no longer be required—a hopeful wish, justified not merely from the philosophical viewpoint, but also by Jewish talmudical law, whereby in fact the bridegroom and husband, and not the rabbi or his deputy, contracts or dissolves a marriage. Considering the cultural level of today's Jewry, how long do you believe people will continue to submit to a ceremony like that of Halitza, or how long do you think they will acquiesce to rules governing marital unions prohibited to a "Cohen"? If anywhere at all, it is right here where the damage ought to be repaired before it spreads too far. Precisely that which exists in the consciousness of the people *is without foundation in Jewish law,* namely, the necessity for the presence of a clergyman when a marriage is contracted or dissolved. Yet we owe it to this very fact that much evil has been avoided. Could anyone blame the Rabbinical Conference when it wishes to elevate to the status of real law this practice which has been sanctified through custom, but which hitherto was not considered legally essential? Indeed, only Dr. Frankel would be capable of doing that.

The same is to be said about Dr. Frankel's objections to the discussion con-

---

[2] About 1000 c.e., a synod called by Rabbenu Gershom of Mayence, had issued a decree prohibiting polygamy (which the Bible permits) to Jews living in Christian lands. Hence, he prevented the obligatory Levirate marriage in cases where the surviving brother already had a wife. The "disgrace" refers to the public ceremony of Halitza.

[3] A small Palestinian coin, the exchange of which validates the wedding contract.

cerning the oath. The question was simply this: Is an oath binding upon a Jew when taken without any additional ceremony, not excepting that of the *nekitat-hefetz?*[4] For the Rabbinical Conference was not called upon to promulgate a law, nor was it asked to make arrangements for making the oath more solemn. It was merely asked what makes an oath sacred to the Jew? At this point Dr. Frankel, referring to R. Hai Gaon, admits that sacredness has nothing to do with *nekitat-hefetz,* but that an oath is binding even without it.[5]

We learn now for the first time from Dr. Frankel that in France the oath has nothing to do with religion. A non-religious oath is no oath at all. However, it is quite another matter when, as is falsely presumed, the Jewish religion lays down special formulae, the observance of which alone makes an oath valid under Jewish law. And this was precisely what the Conference disputed. Indeed, it would have been detrimental had they not done it and instead had maintained an untruth, as, for instance, that a Jewish oath had to take place with *nekitat-hefetz.* It is possible that such an explanation could have brought about complete annulment of the emancipation of the people in Luxembourg.

Dr. Frankel must have noticed from the minutes that the majority of the Assembly was in favor of retaining at worship services the Hebrew language (but not exclusively, as goes without saying). However, this question was not on the agenda to be passed on as a resolution, therefore the discussion on it was an informal exchange of ideas rather than a real deliberation. It could be that the Conference looked into that particular matter more out of politeness toward the person who brought it up, since at any rate it was only a matter of choosing a committee for laying the ground for (note this!) *preliminary* studies. Therefore, it was more a question of refuting each other's arguments than keeping sight of the question whether or not to pray in Hebrew. Thus it came to pass that someone, even though for the retention of Hebrew prayer, still disagreed with someone else who was for the same thing but for apparently wrong reasons. One may look upon all of this, if you wish, as a *savoir vivre* on the part of the Assembly, or as a blunder that should be avoided in the future, but under no circumstances should any of this offer material for questionable accusations.

This is the first time that I have taken the opportunity to commend or criticize Dr. Frankel publicly. Therefore, it pains me deeply that in this essay I could only criticize and not praise him, but *Bimkom she-yesh hillul hashem, en holkin kavod larav* (When God's name is being defamed one need not respect the diginity of a rabbi). I have no intention whatsoever to win my spurs with Dr. Frankel whose superiority in talmudic knowledge, as well as his general erudition, I gladly acknowledge. But it pains me deeply that Dr. Frankel, whose pledge to appear at the Rabbinical Conference was as much expected as it was hoped for, did not find a kind word for said Assembly and its members and behaves like a crusader against it. Instead of helping this insti-

---

[4] The grasping of a sacred object during the oath. The need of continuing this practice was extensively discussed by the Reformers; see below, p. 233.

[5] Hirsch proceeds to quote from Git. 35a which shows that a woman's oath is valid under circumstances which have no reference to *nekitat-hefetz.*

tution, which could be so beneficial to Judaism, to remain in existence, he chose to nip it in the bud. And thus this article was indeed written *cum ira,* immediately after reading of Dr. Frankel's notions and ideas.

"POSITIVE, HISTORICAL JUDAISM" (*Zacharias Frankel*)

Frankel finally was prevailed upon to come to the second Rabbinical Conference, in Frankfort, 1845. It was hoped that he would lend his great authority to the task of reconciliation and orderly progress. He first spoke from the floor on a committee report which dealt with the question: "Is Prayer in the Hebrew tongue objectively necessary?" Here Frankel made his famous statement on "positive, historical Judaism," which was to have a profound impact on the Reform movement and which provided the basic platform for European and, later, American Conservative Judaism.

The following is taken from a transcript of the discussion.

Zacharias Frankel takes the floor. He finds it necessary to begin the discussion of so important a subject with some general considerations. The Rabbinical Conference consists of guides and teachers of the people. They know the people's needs and sorrows and it is their obligation to do what can best satisfy the former and meliorate the latter, and above all prevent any schism. It is the duty of the Rabbinical Conference to show and attest that it is animated by a sincere and holy motive. Its leaders have to let it be known, first of all, what their spiritual foundation is and by what principles they are guided. It is the pride of Judaism that no individual and no class can arrogate to itself any authority, but that all decisions must flow organically from principles and receive their validity only from them. Of course, everyone is free to vote and express opinions, but without principles this remains only the expression of private opinion. The people at large have a right to ask of us above all the exposition of our guiding principles.

Even those matters which are generally disposed of without difficulty have value only in relative proportion to the reasons which underlie the decision. Take, for instance, the question of eating leguminous food on Passover. Everyone may be in agreement, and yet much depends from what point of view the decision proceeds. Does it recognize the prohibition of all leavened food to its full extent, or does it take the matter only as a question of form which could be satisfied by a simple change of terms? The true process of reforming consists always of building up, but this is not the case when reformations proceed in an unprincipled manner. The absence of principle is the greatest enemy of faith and must be fought in every way and with all possible force.

The speaker now declares his principle: he stands on the ground of *positive, historical Judaism.* In order to understand what it means in the present, one must first look to the past and to the path which Judaism has traveled.

The positive forms of Judaism are organically integrated into its character and form a part of its life and, therefore, may not be coldly and heartlessly disposed of. Where would we be if we would allow our inner life to be torn to shreds and, instead, would let new life spring forth from our minds as Minerva sprang forth from the head of Jupiter? We cannot return to the letter of Scripture. There is too great a gap between it and us. On the other hand, a new exegesis is subject to the changing phases of science and, therefore, also unsuitable for the construction of a firm edifice. Or shall we grant the spirit of the time [*Zeitgeist*] its influence? But the spirit of the time changes with the time. Besides, it is cold. It may appear rational, but it will not satisfy the soul; it will not comfort, calm, or enrapture it. Only Judaism is always truly inspiring and enrapturing.

The reform of Judaism, furthermore, is not a reform of faith but of practices demanded by law. These still live within the people and exercise their power. It is not our task to weaken this influence but rather to strengthen it as much as possible. We need pay no attention to those individual few who do not practice the customs; we are not a party, but ours is the task to care for the needs of the whole people. We must maintain their true sanctuary and prevent any schism in Israel; we must not bring new parties into existence but rather must reconcile those which exist already.

There is yet another principle to which we must hold and that is that of *science,* which must be the foundation for every reform. But science can stand only on a positive foundation, for this alone offers a secure path for progress. There are men in Israel who are not present at this Assembly, who do not belong to the circle of religious officials, yet whose presence is desirable because they possess the equipment for the science of Judaism. If that which will be decided here is to have validity, then those men, too, ought to be asked as was customary with *sh'elot uteshuvot.*[6] The decisions of the Rabbinical Conference will in any case be weighed and examined outside of the Conference and must make their way first by gaining the support of the experts. Only then will they achieve validity. It would be advisable, therefore, if, prior to voting on a subject, the matter would already be published in print.

Finally, says the speaker, he believes the Rabbinical Conference to be a very useful institution. However, he wishes to state that he will be able to approve of its meetings only as long as these will always keep in mind the whole of positive Judaism. He would ask, indeed he would implore the Conference, to express itself above all about its principles. It should particularly avoid those discussions the only purpose of which would be to express private opinions and views.

President Stein replies. He did not interrupt the honored speaker, even though the latter really did not speak to the subject matter. However, he wanted him to express himself fully, and he is happy with what Dr. Frankel in his address did say. For he, the president, would hope that the whole con-

---

[6] Inquiries from Rabbinic authorities and their responses.

ference could agree with it. Mr. Frankel maintains that no reform must leave its historic foundation. Gentlemen, is that not the foundation on which all of us find ourselves? (General approval) Dr. Frankel declares that the letter of the Bible is far removed from us and that we can no longer return to it. Therefore, positive, revealed Judaism is *his* principle—a Judaism which in the course of time has unfolded itself historically and must in this manner be carried forward and developed by science. Gentlemen, is that not also *our* point of view? (General agreement) Dr. Frankel further declares that we should try to reconcile the parties to heal the rift which goes through our congregations, that we should try to come closer together rather than to drift farther apart. Gentlemen, do we not all strive for this? (General agreement)

FRANKEL RESIGNS

On the third day of the Conference, Frankel left and submitted the following letter:

To the honorable officers of the Second Rabbinical Conference in Frankfort:
    The maintenance of Judaism is the basic aim of my life and the goal of all my efforts for which I in my turn am prepared to bring every sacrifice. Hence, I find myself in irreconcilable opposition to contrary tendencies. Already at the second session of the Conference (May 17), I brought up the question of principle, so that we could understand each other and be entirely clear about the spirit of the Conference. However, this point was not treated any further. Yesterday's session had a result of which I can think only with sorrow. Only with deep pain do I recall that in a rabbinical assembly a question could come up for voting and could fail of agreement, concerning a subject which is an absolutely integral part of the religious interest of Judaism, a subject which should have been expected to enjoy the protection of the religious leaders of the people. The question was whether there is a legal—and if not a legal, an objective—necessity for the maintenance of the Hebrew language in prayer, and whether this necessity is founded on religious considerations. When this question was discussed in its practical implications, it was declared that the question at issue was whether rabbis should attempt to safeguard the remaining portion of Hebrew in our prayers. This, mind you, happened after a discussion in which all sides agreed that German prayers, too, ought to be accepted and made a part of the worship service. The alternative question was whether the maintenance of Hebrew was only *advisable,* that is, a concession conditioned by circumstances of the present, but that a real effort should be to make advisability superfluous and to eliminate Hebrew entirely from the worship service. It was in vain to show how the Hebrew language, the antiquity of which has been sanctified by millenia, gives sanctity and exaltation to prayer. It was in vain to point out that the Hebrew language must be safeguarded like a precious gem, for the sacred documents are written in it, and

the understanding of these documents must not be lost as once it was amongst the Hellenistic Jews. In vain it was stressed that, once Hebrew disappears from prayer, it will be lost altogether, for it will then be banished from the schools and thus another religious element will have disappeared from their already sparse curriculum. In vain was religious sentiment appealed to, for this should be significant in prayer, which is heightened by the sacred sound of Hebrew. In vain it was emphasized that Hebrew prayer especially is a characteristic mark of the religious community of the Jew, for through it the Jew, wherever he meets another Jew, would recognize him as his coreligionist, would recognize his temple as his own house of worship, and find his prayer to be his own. In vain was the contention disproved that the youth would study Hebrew only with antagonism. For it can simply be said that if the parents do not nourish this antagonism, and if the school strongly supports Hebrew education, this obstacle will disappear by itself, as can be proven from examples.

In vain it was explained how, even for the female youth, the understanding of Hebrew prayers (of which there would not be a large number in any case) could be facilitated. In vain, finally, were the devotion, the religious force and sanctity of Hebrew prayer and its edifying powers stressed. In vain—the majority of the Rabbinical Conference decided that Hebrew prayer was only *advisable* and that it would be the task of the rabbis to eliminate it gradually altogether.

I disagree with such a decision, not only because I have a different point of view, but also because I disagree with the tendency of the decision. For this spirit leaves unheeded so many important elements and eliminates the histori-cal element which has weight and power in every religion. In my opinion this is not the spirit of preserving but of destroying positive historical Judaism, which I declared distinctly before the Assembly was my point of view. This spirit of the Assembly deprives all its further decisions of any validity in the eyes of those who adhere to the positive historical position. As I explained to the Assembly, not only voting is important, but also motivation. Only those who have already made up their mind and merely want a formal approval for their position can find a superficial satisfaction in general voting procedures.

For these reasons I find myself moved to protest, not only against the above-mentioned decision, but at the same time to declare that my point of view is entirely different from that of the Assembly, and that, therefore, I can neither sit nor vote in its midst. But I must also express my regret that the Assembly has not kept in view its stated high aim, "to obtain general confidence and thereby bring about compromises." Rather, it has again removed any opportunity for such compromise and has repelled the many thousands who will be deeply hurt by its decisions. How much I had the above-mentioned aim before my eyes is emphasized by my presence in the Assembly and by my desire to do my share in bringing about a compromise. I wanted to work jointly with others and make this young institution one of reconciliation, one which would mature into a body which would represent general religious needs. Therefore, I over-looked many misunderstandings which my participation would elicit and many other things which were in opposition to my personal interest. It is this same high and holy consideration which now moves me to separate myself from this Conference. For when God, to whom our whole life belongs, admonishes, and when an inner conviction calls, one must follow without respect to misunderstanding or misinterpretation of motives. The honest man values his conviction above all; he must primarily ask himself, his inner judge. If he is justified before him and finds his judgment validated, then he goes firmly on his way, and all other considerations yield before those of religion and truth. I trust that as soon as possible the honorable officers will inform the distinguished Assembly of the contents of this letter and that it will be made a part of the minutes. I have the honor, etc.,

Frankfort, July 18, 1845   CHIEF RABBI DR. Z. FRANKEL

*Declaration of the Rabbinical Conference regarding the
   letter of Dr. Frankel.*

The Second Rabbinical Assembly has received with great astonishment a letter from Chief Rabbi Dr. Frankel, of July eighteenth, which states that he resigned because of the debates of the seventeenth concerning the objective necessity of Hebrew in our prayers. In the *Allgemeine Zeitung des Judenthums* of last year, No. 26, Dr. Frankel declared that he would appear in this year's Rabbinical Conference if the moderate views were represented by a number of men. He did appear. The result of the vote on the seventeenth was that thirteen members declared themselves for the objective necessity of Hebrew in prayer, three abstained, while fifteen declared themseleves for the non-existence of such a necessity. The vote showed that in this respect Dr. Frankel did not at all stand alone and, therefore, if he wanted to follow his published declaration, he had the obligation to remain further in the Assembly. On the other hand, the Conference vehemently denies that, through the vote of the majority, it has forsaken the view of a positive historical Judaism, which it had made its own on the sixteenth, by acclamation, together with Dr. Frankel. Yet Dr. Frankel in his letter suggests that the Assembly had done the opposite. But the majority did not fail to recognize the high significance of the Hebrew language for the Israelites and the necessity of learning it in the schools; only it did not hold that it was unconditionally necessary for the worship service. On the other hand, the minority which held the latter view, did not in any wise claim that its opponents had left the positive historical point of view. Different points of view were involved here, not different tendencies. The positive historical point of view desires progress out of that which exists. It does not desire haphazard creation without limits and without foundation. Therefore, our prayers shall be built on existing prayers and as much as possible develop in form and content out of tradition. The Assembly cannot admit that the foundation of historic tradition is denied if one prays in a non-Hebraic tongue. Similarly, Dr. Frankel would have to deny that the Talmudists tampered with positive historical Judaism when they prayed the holiest of our prayers in Aramaic, indeed, when they permitted the entire service, with few exceptions, to be held in a non-Hebraic tongue. Even Dr. Frankel admitted this in his vote concerning the non-existence of a *legal* necessity of Hebrew prayer. The Assembly, therefore, believes that Dr. Frankel made this question forcibly into one of tendential import, and when he left the Assembly, he left also his own point of view and its consequences.

3. THE SYNODS

The failure of the 1848 revolutions and the resultant large-scale emigration of Jews from central Europe dealt a severe blow to all liberal movements. Nearly a generation passed before the Reformers succeeded in creating a new, if short-lived, platform for discussion. In 1868, twenty-four rabbis, led by Philippson and Geiger, assembled in Cassel to lay the foundation for what they hoped would be a widely inclusive synodal conference of rabbis, scholars, and communal leaders. They issued this invitation:

INVITATION TO THE SYNODAL ASSEMBLY

TO RABBIS, JEWISH SCHOLARS, AND CONGREGATIONAL BOARDS

At the close of the past century the European Jews began to participate in the general life of the world, in consequence of the gradual removal of the barriers which had excluded them from industrial life, social amenities, general and scientific culture, and public service. Under the influence of these completely changed conditions, a new and fresh religious life awoke in our midst in the province of religion, with the result that different views and many conflicts arose. In spite of the indestructible fealty of the Jews, which is as ready today as at any time in the past to bring all sacrifices in deed and suffering, there arose growing confusion and an almost indescribable diversity among individuals and congregations. Every individual was a law to himself as far as religious practices went, and the same was the case with congregations in their religious institutions. From these conflicts, parties issued which called into being inner divisions, and in many places violent conflicts took place whereby the condition of Judaism became ever more confused and precarious. A religion of a minority, a religion of scattered small groups, can be exposed to no greater danger than to become internally divided, quarreling, hesitating, and agitated by violent party strife. It is readily comprehensible that such a condition could be cured only by organization and united action. Real improvement and betterment of the conditions can be accomplished only by the union of many, and such a union alone can obtain real and sufficient authority. With this in mind, twenty-four rabbis from all parts of Germany and Switzerland met at Cassel on August 11, 12, and 13 of last year. These rabbis recognized that the most effective remedy for the present conditions of Judaism lies in the creation of a union of the best intentioned and ablest elements, but that such a union was not to be found in the assemblage and the resolutions of a smaller or greater number of rabbis, but only by having mature scholars of Judaism and representatives of the congregations themselves join the rabbis. The Conference at Cassel, therefore, resolved unanimously: (1) to convene a synodal assembly of rabbis, Jewish scholars, and representatives of the congregations; (2) to choose committees who are to formulate propositions for the synod.

The object, above all else, is to lay the foundation for a large and more closely knit, but altogether free union, devoid of all outer coercion—yes, for a visible and more effective organization and cooperation.

We, therefore, approach Jewish congregations in general, and the governing boards in particular, with the request to participate through one or more representatives in the synodal assembly that is to be convened during the summer of 1869. We do this with the consciousness that the honorable board is fully able to appreciate the real significance, the beneficial bearing, of the proposed assembly. We do not doubt that you have no wish to dissociate yourselves from the community of Israel, and that you will contribute with pleasure toward ensuring its well-being and providing for its future. We see no other means whereby, in the spirit of our religion, whose loftiest principle is brotherhood, as well as in the spirit of faith and freedom of conscience, we can effectually prevent further ruin. We can think of no cogent reason for refusing to participate in this gathering. Every view, every tendency, will have the right to express itself. Verily, only that peace is upright, only that union real, which results in mutual understanding and agreement, even though these involve much contention and struggle. All these things we submit to you for consideration and beg of you to let any one of the undersigned committee know within four weeks whether or not you will participate in the synod.

May we all, mindful of what we owe to the glorious heritage of our fathers, the religion of four thousand years, soon see the work of union take shape before our eyes under the providence of God!

RESULTS OF THE LEIPZIG SYNOD (*Moritz Lazarus*)

Some eighty-three congregations were represented when the synod opened in Leipzig in 1869. Prof. Moritz Lazarus (1824-1903), the synod's most prominent non-rabbinic leader, was elected president. He had gained his fame in the field of national psychology, was a philosopher of the Kantian school, and later occupied many important positions in Jewish life, including the presidency of the Berlin *Lehranstalt*. His book, *The Ethics of Judaism*, went through many editions.

The following is an excerpt from his concluding address to the synod.

There will be some who stand outside this conference and will ask, "Well, what did they do away with this time, and what do they want to put in its place?" Gentlemen, to be sure we want to eliminate, but especially do we want to eliminate the feeling of indifference. We want to eliminate—yes, eliminate ignorance. (bravo) But that is not all—we do need reform. We honor the old, but we honor it truly by nurturing it, not by letting it fall prey to neglect. A vintner knows that if his planting is to bring forth good and sufficient grapes, he must prune the proliferating shoots so that the strength not be dissipated. But he also knows that when he cuts away all shoots, the stem will wither. (bravo)

Far be it from me and you to criticize here what other religions say or teach. But we can note the simple fact that all religions of our time, all of them in all their denominations, uniformly complain about the lack of religious life, the lack of religious enthusiasm, the lack of religious sentiment. We complain about it for our own sake. Now, then, there is a new task for the synod which until now it has not grasped. It is this: not merely to make denominational studies and to think continuously of one's own lacks and defects, but to place oneself into the front of those who fight for idealism and religiosity and against materialism in general, against the everyday, against all shallowness. (bravo) What is necessary, therefore, is to search for the real reason for the lack of religiosity in our midst, and this is not found simply in our institutions. In this regard let us compare our religion with other religions. They have few ceremonies, they have few rituals, they have nothing of that which, it is claimed, in Judaism constrains the religious sense and drives people out of the synagogue—they have nothing of it and still they complain over the lack of religiosity. (bravo) Therefore, the real reason lies much, much deeper than in the rituals, which we can and will change; it lies in the spirit of the time itself. What is demanded, then, is that we all join hands, that each one in his own place should help. Therefore, it may be specially recommended to this synodal assembly that it should work for the elevation of the mood of idealism, for the renewed encouragement of the religious sentiment. (bravo) In our first declaration we spoke of the unity of mankind as a dogma of Judaism, one which has never been disputed, which has been maintained at all times, and which is found at the very beginning of the oldest source, the book of Genesis. In contradistinction to all other myths which other people have created concerning the origin of humanity, and in which they always speak exclusively of their own primal parents, the Bible speaks of the creation of man in general. We find the thought expressed in various places, not only in Genesis, but frequently elsewhere, that the unity of God is a principle as is the unity of mankind. Therefore, we too must make its spiritual grandeur and purity above all our goal.

We strive to recreate the unity of Judaism in all phases and forms of its development, but not in all its customs and regulations. We can well bear it if one congregation introduces something which we have recommended here and which another congregation refuses to do, as long as both acceptance and refusal proceed from the religious sense. (bravo) We must look to the heart and not merely to the external form.

From of old, Judaism has been the bearer of the one idea of God. And in fact, it has borne this thought at all times and in all forms. Sometimes it was a yoke, sometimes a crown. Therefore, the unity of Judaism is for us not a phrase but an expression of living continuity. First, let us look to this continuity in a horizontal direction, that is, in the present. Let us look to the Jews in all lands, in all parts of the world. Let them form this union, gathered around the banner of the idea of God. But let us observe, maintain, and nurture this continuity of spiritual development in a vertical direction also, that is, in the passage of time and history. This spirit of unity is the spirit which has manifested itself in this assembly also.

There is none amongst us who refused to abrogate simply because it was traditional. There is none here who wanted to conserve at all costs without taking cognizance of all ethical development of our time or without regard to all spiritual currents or to the needs of the present. The principal thought which has been expressed here, with various modifications, has always been to keep to the middle of the road. We do not wish to belong to those who either arrest the hands of the clock or even want to set it back, and in doing so imagine that the clock has stopped. But we also do not want to belong to those who constantly wind the clock. (bravo) For it is well known that while you wind the clock it does not move forward. Therefore, those who constantly wind and re-wind it do not even know what time it is. (bravo) You gentlemen here who are theologians, you know that the service in the holy of holies was sacred but also dangerous. Sacred yet dangerous is the service which we have rendered here, but we must find in our holy of holies that which we have sought, and that is *conciliation*. (bravo)

THE AUGSBURG SYNOD

Once more, in 1871, did the leaders of Reform make an attempt to tackle pressing practical and theological problems through synodal decision. The setting of the Augsburg Synod was similar to that of the Leipzig gathering. It was, however, a more intensive work conference, and dealt not only with important specific questions, but also produced the first general platform of Reform Judaism and outlined the tasks facing the modern Jew.

The Synod declares:

1. Since the earliest period of its history, Judaism has passed through different phases of development. A new, highly important turning point in its history is now at hand. The spirit of true knowledge of God and of pure ethics more and more fills the consciousness of humanity in government, art, and science. Judaism cheerfully recognizes in this the approach of its own ideals which have illuminated its historical march.

2. The essence and mission of Judaism are today the same as they have been in the past. The powerful change, however, which has taken place in the minds of mankind at large and of the adherents of Judaism in particular, and the changed position which the latter occupies in the midst of the nations, has called forth the urgent need to regenerate many of its ceremonies.

3. Judaism, from the very earliest period of its history, has laid special stress upon knowledge, and has demanded at all times the agreement, equally, between thought, feeling, and deed. To do this, it goes to work courageously and fearlessly in order to set that regeneration in motion. While fully appreciating and venerating the past, Judaism strives, in accord with earnest scientific reasearch, to set aside what is obsolete and antiquated, so that it may unfold itself in the spirit of the new age.

4. The Synod desires to be an organ of this unfolding. The convictions and aspirations of modern Judaism shall find it in their firm expression. It intends to labor with clear purpose so that the reform of Judaism for which we have striven for several decades should be secured in the spirit of harmony if possible and, taking into consideration the wants of all our coreligionists, should be successfully consummated. The Synod wishes to preserve the bond which unites all Israelites, and desires to further, to the best of its ability, the higher goals of life in general and of science in particular.

5. The Synod makes no other pretentions and demands for its resolutions than those which the power of truth, of sacred earnestness, and of firm convictions bestow upon it. It is, however, well aware of the fact that this power, the only one which ought to exercise an influence in the realms of religion, is overwhelming, irresistible, and is bound to conquer in the end, in spite of all impediments and difficulties.

6. The Synod, while striving to yield to the requirements of the age, is convinced that in doing so it works for the preservation of Judaism. In this manner it is at one with the spirit of Judaism in its entire historical evolution, at one with all its coreligionists, no matter to which party they may belong. Thus it hopes to labor in the cause of harmony, not for the next moment and not by a denial of its convictions, but by the spirit of truth which, according to the principles of our ancient teachers, is the fundamental condition of peace.

7. The task of the Synod is not concluded by these preceding declarations or principles. Considering the intimate relation between religious life and social and civil circumstances, it appears to be the indispensable duty of the Synod to lend adequate expression to the consciousness of the unity of our coreligionists in all questions pertaining to their civil and social condition.

CHAPTER
V

New Patterns of Thought

JUST as it is impossible to compress the philosophy of Judaism into rigidly defined outlines, so the thinking of Reform cannot be sharply limned. There were—and are—wide divergencies of opinions; there were —and are—bitter controversies on some vital issues. In addition, one would expect a revolutionary movement to give birth to extremes, and these are indeed not absent in the history of Reform. Still, there is a mood which overlies the whole; there are certain threads which even in the heat of battle were never lost.

All Reformers agreed on the urgency and legitimacy of dynamic change, but, with few exceptions, they wanted all changes to be organic, growing out of the historic fabric of Judaism. Some Reformers were "Mosaists" and near-Karaites, but they did not prevail.

Reform redirected Judaism to its prophetic goals and its universal ethic. There were those who would lose the particular distinctiveness of Judaism in this universal sweep, but they too did not prevail.

Reform had its roots in the surging idealism and optimism of the age. It saw the possibility of fulfilling the ancient dreams of human salvation, and it reemphasized the prophets' concept of Israel's mission in the world. It never moved far from the traditional concept of revelation, and even its rationalists stood firmly on this basis.

The Reformers were champions of emancipation, of equality, of social progress. They were also apologists par excellence, and while assimilationists were often found in the ranks of Reform congregations, the leadership was staunch in its defense of Judaism and frank in its critical appraisal of Christian doctrine and practice.

Reform had its greatest problem when it dealt with the nature of *halakhah,* the binding nature of law and tradition. It distinguished between the ethical-religious content of Judaism and its ritual or ceremonial aspects. It could not accept the equal importance of all *mitsvot,* but it could not fully resolve the question of differentiation: which *mitsvot* were divine obligations and which were not? A hundred years later this dilemma has still not been solved, and reflects itself in the controversy over ritual guides and codes.

1. GENERAL CONSIDERATIONS

JUDAISM MUST BE THOROUGHLY JEWISH (*David Einhorn*)

The fiery orator who began his rabbinic career in Birkenfeld, Germany, made his imprint on two continents. Einhorn (1809-1879) was already well-known in Europe when he decided to accept the call to Har Sinai Congregation in Baltimore. In America he became the principal exponent of radical reforms, and especially through his prayer book *Olat Tamid* exerted a permanent influence on the nature of the Reform service. The following is an excerpt from his inaugural American sermon, preached in 1855. It is included here because it is still part of his European experience.

Above all, Judaism must be thoroughly Jewish—based on divine revelation. In our day we cannot lay too much stress on this point. The more mere ceremonialism loses in significance and observance, the more it is necessary for us to seize upon the essential character of the Jewish faith, upon that which, divested even of the whole ceremonial law, would still stand out in sharp contrast to all other faiths. Here we see the real source of our strength, the real cause of our wonderful endurance, the real glory of our historic strength: the belief in the one and only God, eternal, invisible, and incorporeal, who has revealed Himself to man in His marvelous works, but chiefly in man himself; whose Presence pervades the whole universe, the earth as well as the heavens, what is transitory as well as what is everlasting, the body as well as the soul; the belief in the original goodness and purity of all created things, especially of those beings who, fashioned in the image of God, are gifted with reason and, with no native bar to a state of holiness, need no other mediation than their own efforts to obtain divine grace and their eternal salvation; the belief in a humanity of which all members possess one and the same natural and spiritual origin, the same native nobility, the same rights, the same laws, the same claims to blessedness—a blessedness of which they may partake even on earth when all nations shall unite into one people of the Lord, when, according to the prophetic utterances, also non-Jews "will be chosen as Levites and priests," and, acknowledging God alone as the Ruler of all, will put away forever selfishness and falsehood and hatred, together with the purple of human rulership incarnadined with the blood of men. These and similar teachings which had first to appear behind the veil of Judaism in order that the eyes of the world might not be dazzled by their brilliancy, these are yet to this day Israel's heritage. The possession of these teachings is their sole pride; the recognition of them their only hope. Every one of these teachings spells universal salvation. It is our most sacred duty to bring to the light of day these treasures imbedded in our literature, to exhibit them in their full splendor, and to enrich with them heart and soul by making them applicable to the life of our present day.

Thoroughly Jewish, inspired by divine revelation, should our conduct be. Our whole life should breathe a reverence for the Holy One, an ardent zeal for the welfare of our fellow man, compassion and respect even for creatures and plants, seeing that these, too, are divine manifestations—thus, I say, should we attest to our reverence for the Sinaitic Law. Our whole demeanor should become instinct with the idea of God; with a humanity unconfined by difference of creed; with unabatable ardor for enlightenment, for justice, for truth; with indomitable courage in our battle against the forces of darkness, falsehood, and superstition; with growing fervor for the glory of Israel and its mission.

Even the religious symbols, such of them as still have soul in them—some religious idea—shall be holy unto us. Man, creature of the senses as he is, requires, on the one hand, a physical impulse to permit free action to the current of religious life within; and on the other, an external expression by which, in the very flood tide of his work-a-day world, the ideal—that reaching out for the infinite—may assume tangible form. Judaism in positing the relation between God and man can ill afford to dispense with such outward expressions; especially, as every objective representation of the Supreme Being is strictly forbidden. In the one case, the ceremonies are like the wood with which the priests were wont to renew the altar flames. In the other, they serve as a mirror in which the human mind, unable to see the real image of God, would see God's image in itself—like those cherubim, their wings sweeping heavenward and facing each other in human form over the ark of the covenant, as though they sought here on earth Him who is throned in the heights of heaven, beyond the grasp of the mind of man. Clearly we see the futility of religious usages that are dead; for the wood perishes in the very flame it feeds, and the mirror serves the purpose only so long as it remains clear and bright and free from dust. But just as obvious is our constant need of religious forms that are still quick with religious ideas, and the sad error of those who would hold aloof from them. When Moses asked for a pledge of his divine mission, the heavenly voice directed him to the future worship on Mount Sinai. When he further inquired under what name he should proclaim the God of our fathers to the people, the same voice answered—again pointing to the future—I SHALL BE is my name, which means more correctly, according to the Midrash, I shall be with you to glorify Myself in the midst of you. "Say to the children of Israel," the divine voice seems to intimate, "EHYEH sends me to you, He who for the present seems to have forsaken you, but will later have His dwellings among you to reveal Himself for the salvation of all men." And yet Moses proclaims this God of the future also as the God of the past, the God of our forefathers. We, likewise, will answer those who inquire about the name of Judaism: it is the Judaism which will be, the Judaism of your children and yet also that of our fathers, only conceived more deeply as to its source, more truly valued in its historical progress and glorious aims; not kept under lock and key, but placed aloft on the watch-tower of time, prepared to come into its own; not as a widow mourning for Zion and Jerusalem, but as a bride adorned for her nuptials with mankind.

CAN SCHISM BE AVOIDED? (*Isaac Samuel Reggio to Samuel David Luzzatto*)

Reggio, mathematician, biblical scholar, and Rabbi of Gorizia in Italy, where he lived most of his life (1784-1855), translated the Bible into Italian and held very advanced views concerning the accuracy of its text.

Luzzatto (1800-1865), a friend of Zunz, one of the pillars of the new scholarship, taught in Padua, Italy, at the first modern rabbinical seminary in Europe. With his vast learning, Luzzatto combined a critical faculty which at first aligned him with many endeavors of Reform. Later, however, he developed a staunch conservative philosophy. The two scholars carried on a lengthy correspondence in the public journals.

Let us examine whether the obstacles, which, as you say, stand in the way, are so large that they could have led you to decline the noble task of bringing the two opposing parties, which keep the synagogue in dissension, closer to one another; the task of enlightening our brothers in the true spirit of Judaism, thus achieving among ourselves a uniformity of view without which we cannot take a position of dignity among the civilized nations.

You are citing two obstacles: the power of habit and the power of human passions. However, both appear of small significance to me. I do not dispute that habit and passions exercise great power over our mind; daily experience convinces us sufficiently of that. However, I do deny that these influences are supposed to be so utterly unconquerable that man must yield irresistibly to these two tyrants, without ever being able to extricate himself from their power. If this were so, philosophy would strive in vain to enlighten and properly guide the human mind, since habit would incessantly compel us to be a slave to prejudices which we absorbed with our mothers' milk. Equally vain, also, would be any effort which teachers of morality make to guide man's actions in the way of justice and honesty, since passion would always lure us to the path of sensuality and vice. In actuality, however, man is endowed with free will and can, though perhaps not without effort, overcome these obstacles, break the influence of bad habits, conquer his own passions, and rid himself of prejudiced notions. He can follow the directives of his own sound reason; he can take a dispassionate view of himself, of his intellectual and moral abilities; he can obtain clear ideas of his spiritual faculties, his rights and responsibilities—in short, he can meet the demands of a charitable Creator and arrange his life in accordance with his high destiny.

Though I agree with you that it is a difficult undertaking to rise in the struggle for the defense of a Judaism which, once it is purified of all that is superfluous and unseemly, would perhaps satisfy neither one nor the other party, nevertheless, I completely disagree with your statement concerning the impossibility of success. Not all are inclined to lend an ear to reason; yet there is cause for hope in our century that the voice of truth will not fade away completely, and that particularly because of these obstacles the perseverance and courage of the loyal-minded will increase.

THE BREACH IS UNHEALABLE (*Luzzatto to Reggio*)

You are astonished, my dear friend, when I explain the schism which has arisen nowdays among our coreligionists simply as a quarrel between rationalism and supernaturalism. You maintain that true Israelites may not be called supernaturalists, since they do not recognize any authority placed above human reason.

My friend! I am using two terms—supernaturalism and rationalism—to define the belief or unbelief in a revealed religion. In Christianity, where belief is a fundamental principle, unbelief could be termed rationalism, since the principle of following no other norm in our judgment than that dictated by human reason contains a renunciation of belief, and hence apostasy—that is, unbelief. On the other hand, faithful belief could be called supernaturalism, as something based entirely on supernatural illumination.

However, in Judaism, which does not command belief in religious truths but rather the assumption of certain rules of life, the term rationalism does not exactly describe unbelief, since anyone (as is actually the case with you and me) can still be a faithful Israelite, despite the admission that in his judgment he follows only the demands of his reason.

Nevertheless, instead of the hostile expressions, "unbelief, irreligiousness, heresy" (terms dictated by intolerance), I much prefer to make use of the customary term rationalism, by which I understand the teaching that man has never had any other illumination, guide, or law but that of his own reason. Moreover, I call the belief in revealed Judaism supernaturalism, not in the sense of the dogma restraining freedom of thought, but certainly in the sense of the dogma which admits the supernatural meaning of any events that happen contrary to the usual order of nature, like miracles and revelation.

Now that I have defined the words rationalism and supernaturalism, I hold that the conflict that in our day divides the scholarly Israelites of Europe and particularly those of Germany, in regard to the enforcement of ceremonial laws, is only a secondary quarrel which stems from the main argument between rationalism and supernaturalism. I say that anyone who admits to revelation, who recognizes Moses as a true prophet, who attributes a divine, supernatural origin to the laws of the Pentateuch, cannot have any doubt whatever about its binding force for all times and all places, with the exception of only those which are known under the term "pertaining to Palestine." A few other isolated exceptions have also become unavoidably necessary because of present circumstances which are so different from those of Moses' time; and, of course, there is also the well-known exception concerning danger of life. I hold, furthermore, that any Israelite, convinced of the divinity of his ancestral religion, cannot remove himself in the least from Mendelssohn's decision, which says: "We are permitted to ponder over the law, to search into its spirit; nevertheless, our sophistry cannot free us from the strict obedience we owe the law."

Precisely for this reason I consider a rationalist one who, in these times, defends the non-obligatory nature of the ceremonial laws and still accepts the laws of the Sabbath, of unleavened bread, etc. There is very little hope for the conversion of such a man to supernaturalistic Judaism. It is easy for you to say that Judaism contains no dogmas running contrary to reason. The rationalist will answer you that they did not appear so to Bacon of Verulam and Newton; yet the rationalists of our century find them to be absurd, and you will certainly not demand that, on Newton's authority alone and without being convinced in their own minds, they recognize these as true. On the other hand, the great question as to the truth of revelation has been debated for so many centuries by so many capable writers and has been so examined from all sides, that neither you nor I are in a position to produce completely new and hitherto unknown evidence.

Yes, my dearest friend, the conversion of a rationalist is a task that causes despair. Perhaps you have never made the attempt. I, however, have engaged in it for many years and have not as yet succeeded in bringing about even a single one. To be sure, I have succeeded in bringing back one or the other from atheism to deism, but never from deism to the acceptance of revealed religion. I am presenting things as they are, since I do not like to delude myself or others.

HERE ARE THE WEAPONS (*Letter of a Jewish Householder to the Reformers*)

There was danger that concern with minutiae might crowd out the need for dealing with some basic questions. Reform, as this anonymous correspondent points out, must not lose its basic revolutionary thrust. It must boldly expose all superstitions and magical elements in Judaism. That, in fact, Jewish life today is largely clear of these cobwebs is one of Reform's lasting achievements.

It must have irked you gentlemen repeatedly that neither your supporters nor your opponents consider your personal influence on our nation as great as you desire. Especially in the large congregations it is considered as something ephemeral and transitory. Will you, therefore, permit a layman (I take the word in its popular, not in its Catholic meaning, for all Israelites are priests) to explain the reason for this situation.

Frankly speaking, we find your efforts directed too much toward side issues and too little toward the main point.

On what do you expend your strength? On hierarchical questions and those of public prayer. You want both of them to resemble the prevailing religion of the land as much as possible. Is it this that we need most of all?

You are concerned with creating for yourself an independent and honored existence which will be supreme in your line of work. In other words, you aim to gain the position of the Protestant or even Catholic clergy, and you have valid reason for making such attempts because of the prevailing bigotry and indifference of many congregations.

But we Jewish *Yehudim* desire to have a word of our own in these matters and want to speak out in accordance with our best insights. We do not understand what it was that the Christians or even our own ancestors gained when they subordinated themselves so much to their theologians. Certainly the example of our French brothers cannot encourage us to imitate their hierarchical centralization.

For fifty years now, every Jewish householder who was not entirely satisfied with the old forms has managed as well as possible. Now we are to have unity in these matters and we see manly efforts to beautify the public worship service and always only the public worship service, and to do what?—to introduce sermons! But are we already so far removed from the old believing times to have forgotten that visiting the synagogue accounts for only one-hundredth of our Jewish religious obligations? To be sure, Christians are to derive their faith from the sermon, but with us Jews, who still have some theological education as our common possession, this faith must pre-exist. Otherwise, we can appreciate only the negative element of a modern sermon and never the positive.

So much of the too highly touted side issues. Now to the much-neglected main point.

What has happened in this new age since German Jews have become more aware of their spiritual treasures—what has happened in order to disinfect us from the "pagan disease," that is, from all superstition? Was not the whole Jewish religion sent forth into the world in order finally to eradicate from our midst such superstition wherever and however it shows itself?

Has the borderline between faith and superstition been clearly and unmistakably delineated? Have we created a bulwark against the importation of new twaddle? Does Israel's church have fewer superstitions than those religions which do not twice daily proclaim that God is uniquely one? I fear we have easily as many!

In vain did Jeremiah call, warn, and plead that we should not be like the other nations (10:3ff.). But what do we do when we conclude a marriage? Certain days must be chosen. There is a fear of Monday. There is hesitation to get married when the moon wanes, there is the bad reputation of the first week of Av, and many more superstitions which are in general use and which our ecclesiastical officials formally tolerate and recognize. Astrological tomfoolery is brought into play even where the biblical texts themselves have long suffered from the acid of philological criticism. Yet, where is the pious man who doubts the dictum, "He who changes his place also changes his lucky star"? Where is the rabbi who congratulates others except with the words "mazel tov," who denounces the belief in fatefully "happy" and "unhappy" people, places, and houses? And are not the *Simanim,* the omens and dream interpretations, permitted by law? In vain did Moses in his Old Testament (in the chapter *Ha'azinu*) call heaven and earth as witnesses against the people who would turn to the idols; the "new testament" of Rabbi Yehuda He-hasid"[1] is being more meticulously observed than the former. Even today it will interfere with the love of young people if the first name of the man is the same as the first name of the girl's father.

In vain does the Torah prohibit necromancy, but even the book *Sefer Ha-hayim,* which was recently published in an otherwise enlightened congregation, and even the schismatic prayer book of the new Temple addressed the deceased in the second person; and in times of general need people go to the graves of old rabbis and ask for their intercession.

In vain did Scripture and tradition name only repentance, prayer, and charity as means of obtaining mercy. But no, right in the middle of a public worship service, a sick person will have his name changed. There are people who measure a grave and interpret letters. There are children whom parents pretend to sell.[2] Even those people who think that the wearing of phylacteries is nonsense, still put amulets of all kinds on the necks of babies. One begins the week with the sentence, "God is with me, I do not fear"; but next to the deity, a pious Jew fears the evil eye just as much, and perhaps even more.

And look what we do with our ritual objects. We use the *essrog* for pregnant women, the *lulav* against fire, the *afikomen* against water, the *havdalah* wine for good fortune in commerce, etc.

I will not say anything about the superstitious forms that have grown up around *shofar, kappara,* and *duchan,* especially at the time of death.

Have modern Jews freed themselves from this agglomeration? Oh, no! To be sure, they laugh about the sanctions of the Talmudists, but privately they keep it all up because of indolence, and they add to it the offal of Christian superstition, like reading reunion out of the stars, hope out of the singing of angelic choirs (of which we can read in German hymnals with great and touching edification); there is the hesitation to eat when you are thirteen in number; etc.

Where now are the zealous fighters against such paganism? We see so many efforts to help the cantors regain their old position in order that every one of their words be understood clearly; why not also, then, the words of the prophets? You reformers, be convinced that if you do not get a full hearing for

---

[1] (Ed. note) The writer has reference to *Sefer Hasidim,* a book of ethical and mystical teachings which contained many superstitions and which was very popular up to modern times. Yehuda died in 1217, in Germany.

[2] (Ed. note) At the ceremony of *Pidyon ha-ben.*

the prophets, those scrupulous, far-seeing guardians of pure Jewish ideas of God, then your ritual reforms will be effectual only in the synagogue, and that only with the help of the police.

Unless we Jews can stand in the European world as strict, uncompromising fighters, as stiff-necked Puritans representing our genuine faith and Jehovah-monotheism, which does not admit of partners or mediators (as it says expressly in the *Adon Olam*); unless we recognize the deity only in direct relation to, and influence on, the universe and mankind; unless we children of our time protect the kernel even more zealously than did our predecessors, because we look less to the outer husk—unless we do this we are nothing, absolutely noth-ing, and do not have the right to ask of our children that they, completely re-signed, suffering obloquy, disadvantage, and privation, should remain with a religion which is as impure as any other.

Now, then, if you are serious, if you want to keep your children as Jews, then, gentlemen, attack and jump into the breach. For here and only here is the Achilles heel of the opposition, and here are the weapons with which we can overcome an opponent who commands the majority, who wears the harness of far-reaching scholarship and who wields the sword of unremitting persistence, proceeds with the enthusiasm of an army and who, with every step and with every flag and symbol, can call out as Napoleon did to his army, "Forty centuries look down upon you from these monuments."

THE TIME IS NOW! (*Moritz Abraham Stern to Gabriel Riesser*)

Stern (1807-94), a mathematician, wrote this letter in 1843 to Riesser (1806-63), who was then emerging as Germany's foremost Jewish po-litical and liberal leader, an ardent fighter in the struggle for full Jewish rights.

The idea of emancipation has conquered for all times; it can confidently be entrusted to the currents of world history which will lead it into safe harbor. This does not worry me at all; however, I am concerned that Judaism will come to a deplorable end if, as up to now, we remain as spectators, witnessing the decay of its religious conditions. I fear that that segment of our people who are lacking in intelligence and strength to make progress on their own, will again cling desperately to the extinct, antiquated faith, believing the corpse of positive Judaism to be really alive. Our theologians are constantly striving to embellish this corpse through sermons, confirmations, choral singing, all sorts of philosophical interpretations, and whatever else these masquerades may be called. For centuries to come they will thus once again delay those religious developments which are irresistibly sweeping over Christian Europe. I am afraid that the more intelligent group, disgusted with extinct, oppressive rites, will be unable to resist the luring voices of Christianity for long. I feel that it is our duty to counteract this; I consider it our duty to make a breach in the old ruin, a breach as wide and high as possible, a breach through which the salutary air of spiritual freshness can at last enter Judaism, as it has been moving through Christianity in ever wider circles since the days of Spinoza. This is the core of our reformatory efforts. I want to be sure that the most wholesome and noblest part among the members of our race will remain with us; I do not want Christianity to swallow them and use them, when opportunity presents itself, against the remaining miserable and unhappy company which, through our fault, has become numb and dumb.

TO SAVE THE FUTURE (*Gerson-Lévy*)

A sense of desperation speaks from this impassioned address of the French reformer (1784-1864), who was a teacher and administrator of the rabbinical college in Metz and later became an honorary member of the Imperial Academy. He, like many like-thinking friends, was deeply troubled by the catastrophic deterioration of Jewish life. It is well to reiterate that a good deal of ritual reform was advocated, not because of any craving for innovations or a cheap lust for imitation. Quite on the contrary, reformers like Gerson-Lévy wanted to conserve Judaism from its threatened dissolution. It is the same sentiment which speaks from the preceding letter of Moritz Stern.

Dear brothers! The heart of the righteous man is the temple which the Lord loves most, but in order to impress the heart it is necessary to make it receptive, through edification by majestic ceremonies and through sentiments of concord, charity, and brotherly love, which are the center of our duties.

It is necessary that our senses be stimulated by certain symbols which will lead us to spiritual ideals. This is the goal of ritual, the splendor of our temples, the solemnity of our holidays, and of most of our ritual observances.

If our ritual is denuded of all that is basic to taste and art; if it revolts our conception of the beautiful and the grand; if in place of a religious melody you hear only the proverbial babble; if grimaces and contortions replace contrition and absorption; if you are interested more in quantity than in quality; if the eloquence of the lips substitutes for the elevation of the soul; if the heart takes no part in that which the mouth professes—then these ceremonies can only produce that which in effect is contrary to their original institution. They will give rise to disgust, repugnance, and contempt, and will lead our religion into the paths of entire dissolution.

When a building threatens to crumble, one must abandon it or at least shore it up. Only the insane would run the risk of having themselves buried alive under the ruins. Similarly, we say that our religious edifice has for some time shown cracks and dislocations, and it is only a sorry relic of its former self.

Formerly, as an oppressed minority, the Israelites created amongst themselves a community of mores, opinions, and language which were the natural consequence of a community of slavery and misfortune.

Isolated, repulsed by society at large, they found refuge against human injustice only in the consolation of religion. From then on, everything came under the purview of religion. The most unimportant acts of life were dealt with in the code and aimed to contribute to the welfare of the mass whom society had condemned to forced idleness and ignorance. From this there developed an invincible attachment to minutiae which, in turn, led to an obscurement of the grand principles which were to make man good, just, sensible, loving, and truly happy. We became enslaved to ritual practices which for us no longer make any sense. Of the ancient Egyptians it is said that to them everything was god except God Himself. One can say the same of our degenerated cult where everything is religion except religion itself. A half-century has passed since the bell of liberty first sounded for us. If our age has engulfed us with its progressive onrush, so that we confuse the abuse of religion with religion itself, then we have had the misfortune of falling into an indifference a thousand times more alarming than the most outrageous superstition.

Would it not be shameful, indeed, if the freedom of religion which our social order guarantees would have no other results for our families than to have them abandon the ancient religion which our fathers and our contemporaries consecrated with precious blood? Millions of victims gave their lives for it, since the time of Antiochus and Ptolemy-Philopator until the butchery of Damascus and the Isle of Rhodes. And now, that finally wise and liberal governments call upon us to enjoy the rights common to all men, shall we not respect the ashes of our fathers better than by deserting the banner of religion under which they sacrificed themselves? Ah, if they had like us wanted to surrender the wisdom of their principles and give up that model law which they kept alive in the face of all opposition, how many rivers of blood would have never flowed, how many evils would they have escaped, how many innocent victims would have been saved? And the culpable usage that we shall make of this liberty, toward which they yearned for twenty centuries, shall be to renounce their religion, to betray the noble cause to which they sacrificed fortune, life, and all earthly goods? So unreasonable a conduct would surely cause us to lose the respect of every impartial and well-thinking person.

Still, we would be unjust if we were to search for the spread of irreligion merely in the depravities of the heart. Is it not also true that every idea of reform has been repulsed? Have not those among us been called extreme innovators, who demanded a reasonable ritual, regular chanting, the reduction of those pieces of rhymed prose which were introduced in the Middle Ages and were of excessive length; who desired some form of confirmation for both sexes; frequent sermons in the national language on the exalted and sublime verities proclaimed by our religion; order, discipline, respect, and decency in our temples; the introduction of funeral services in honor of those who marked their career with generosity, zeal, and devotion? If thirty years ago our leaders had given way to the demands and had sensed the exigencies of the period and had restored to the divine service that grandeur which is its due, indifference would not have taken the offensive, and we would not have to blush when coming to our temple. Then our public worship, freed from the mass of useless and incomprehensible rubble which repels men of sense and taste, would be judged according to its heavenly origin and could still count as many adherents as disciples.

But instead of this, there was temporizing until the whole body became gangrenous and the illness almost beyond remedy. It is time to erect a dike against this dissolution, to save the future generation from the demoralization with which it is threatened. It is never too late to achieve something worth-while, and if there are some amongst us who cannot themselves join in this labor, let them think of their children. Let them imitate the old man of the Midrash who plans for the welfare of his descendants; let us bring our ritual into harmony with the state of our progress, with our mores, our education; let us follow the numerous examples given to us in Germany, Holland, Belgium, and England. And if we are not as yet sufficient in number to erect a temple for our God who has sustained us in the hardest trials and has saved us from oppression, let us at least open a modest sanctuary where together with our families, brothers, and friends, we might elevate our hearts to God with more fervor and contemplation.

It is farthest from our mind that we cherish the idea of a reform society in order to sow dissension in the family. Every one of our followers is free to follow in his private life the traditional rites which he holds dear and has received from his ancestors. We do not concern ourselves at all with the domestic ritual which, if it is sincerely observed, is full of gentleness and consolation.

But as regards the public worship service, we formally protest the purity of our intentions before God and man. We have as our goal a religious regeneration. We want to rekindle in all hearts the faith that has been extinguished. We want to render our ritual more simple, more edifying, and more fit to touch the soul and to elevate the noble sentiment of man's love for his Creator. In one word, we want to save our religion for religion's sake.

This reform is desired by all those whom our coreligionists count amongst the most prominent in business and enterprise. Amongst them are industrialists and literateurs, doctors, professors, lawyers, workshop overseers, civil and military servants. And reform is demanded above all by that sensible sex whose piety increases its gentleness—the woman—whose destiny it is to be on earth either angel or demon, depending on whether she is pious and devoted. Reform is supported also by our children whom we must prepare for the hazards and calamities of life, a task which religion alone can accomplish.

All of you who still have a Jewish heart, do not confuse practices and hardly-edifying ceremonies with the spirit of our religion, which is the root of the religions of all civilized people. Rally to us, lend us your approval and your assistance. With confidence do we make this appeal to your generous hearts and to your willing charity.

Who amongst you would refuse to contribute of his efforts to the ennoble-ment and grandeur of such importance? Future generations will bless our memory for the treasure which we shall transmit to them.

2. THE "SCIENCE OF JUDAISM"

Reform Judaism is intimately tied to the free search for truth, and the scientific study of Judaism, which contemporaries often called the "science of Judaism," became therefore a principal part of its structure. The term originated with the group of young men around Zunz (see above, p. 16) and was popularized by their journal, from which the following is taken.

ON THE CONCEPT OF A SCIENCE OF JUDAISM (*Immanuel Wolf*)

Judaism, based on its own inner principle and embodied, on the one hand, in a comprehensive literature, and, on the other, in the life of a large number of human beings, both can be and needs to be treated scientifically. Hitherto, however, it has never been described scientifically and comprehensively from a wholly independent standpoint. What Jewish scholars have achieved, especially in earlier times, is mostly theological in character. In particular, they have almost completely neglected the study of history. But Christian scholars, however great their merit in the development of individual aspects of Judaism, have almost always treated Judaism for the sake of a historical understanding of Christian theology, even if it was not their intention to place Judaism itself in a hateful light, or, as they put it, to confute Judaism. Even though some important scholarly works written from a general literary standpoint and interest have emerged, not merely as vehicles or propaedeutics for Christian theology (which is admittedly difficult to separate from Jewish theology), these achievements apply only to individual aspects of the whole. But if Judaism is to become an object of science in its own right and if a science of Judaism is to be formed, then it is obvious that quite a different method of treatment is under discussion. But any object, no matter of what type, that in its essence is of interest to the human spirit, and comprehensive in its diverse formation and development, can become the object of a special science.

The content of this special science is the systematic unfolding and representation of its object in its whole sweep, for its own sake and not for any ulterior purpose. If we apply this to the science of Judaism, then the following characteristics emerge:

1. The science of Judaism comprehends Judaism in its fullest scope;
2. It unfolds Judaism in accordance with its essence and describes it systematically, always relating individual features back to the fundamental principle of the whole;
3. It treats the object of study in and for itself, for its own sake, and not for any special purpose or definite intention. It begins without any preconceived

opinion and is not concerned with the final result. Its aim is neither to put its object in a favorable, nor in an unfavorable light, in relation to prevailing views, but to show it as it is. Science is self-sufficient and is in itself an essential need of the human spirit. It, therefore, needs to serve no other purpose than its own. But it is for that reason no less true that each science not only exercises its most important influence on other sciences but also on life. This can easily be shown to be true of the science of Judaism.

The aim will be to depict Judaism, first from a historical standpoint, as it has gradually developed and taken shape; and then philosophically, according to its inner essence and idea. The textual knowledge of the literature of Judaism must precede both methods of study. Thus we have, first, the textual study of Judaism; second, a history of Judaism; third, a philosophy of Judaism.

This would be, in general outline, the framework of the science of Judaism. A vast field embracing literary researches, compilations, and developments! But if the object, as such, is important to science and the human spirit in general, its progressive development is bound to follow. The truly scientific spirit, therefore, cannot on account of the multifariousness and the vast scope of the field doubt the possibility that such a science might be established. The essence of science is universality, infinity; and therein lies the spur and the attraction which it has for the human spirit whose nobler nature rejects any limitations, any rest, any standing still.

It remains to indicate in a few words that aspect in the light of which the establishment of a science of Judaism seems to be a necessity of our age. This is the inner world of the Jews themselves. This world, too, has in many ways been disturbed and shaken by the unrelenting progress of the spirit and the associated changes in the life of the nations. It is manifest everywhere that the fundamental principle of Judaism is again in a state of inner ferment, striving to assume a shape in harmony with the spirit of the times. But in accordance with the age, this development can only take place through the medium of science. For the scientific attitude is the characteristic of our time. But as the formation of a science of Judaism is an essential need for the Jews themselves, it is clear that, although the field of science is open to all men, it is primarily the Jews who are called upon to devote themselves to it. The Jews must once again show their metal as doughty fellow workers in a common task of mankind. They must raise themselves and their principle to the level of a science, for this is the attitude of the European world. This attitude must banish the relationship of strangeness in which Jews and Judaism have hitherto stood to the outside world. And if one day a bond is to join the whole of humanity, then it is the bond of science, the bond of pure reason, the bond of truth.

NEEDED—A STUDY OF THE WORSHIP SERVICE (*Leopold Zunz*)

Ten years after the *Journal for the Science of Judaism* first appeared, Zunz published his magnum opus, *Die gottesdienstlichen Vorträge der Juden,* literally, "The Sermons of the Jews," but in fact a volume dealing with the whole history of the Midrash as the primary source for the development of the sermon. The book is often described as the most important Jewish work published in the nineteenth century, for in source analysis and method it set the highest standards for scholarly treatment of Jewish subjects. Zunz showed that public instruction had never wholly disappeared from the service, and he pleaded for the reintroduction of the free, courageous, untrammeled sermon which was to be given in the native language of the congregation. Zunz' introductory plea for complete freedom of the pulpit was suppressed by the Prussian authorities. The following is taken from the Preface.

The neglect of Jewish science is connected with the civil disabilities of the Jews, under which they had labored so long. By a more comprehensive mental culture, a more profound knowledge of their own affairs, the Jews would not only have achieved a higher degree of recognition of their rights, but many an ill-advised step of the legislature, and many a prejudice against Jewish antiquity were the immediate consequences of the abandoned condition in which Jewish literature and the science of Judaism have been plunged for the last century.

And although publications against the Talmud and the Jews shot up like mushrooms overnight, there existed no book of any moment whence statesmen might have drawn advice; no professor lectured on Judaism and Jewish literature, no academy offered prizes thereon, and no philanthropist undertook travels for its promotion. Legislators and authors had mendaciously to follow the authorities of the seventeenth century—Eisenmenger, Schudt, Buxtorf, etc. —or were obliged to borrow from the questionable wisdom of modern official reports. Nay, most of them candidly admitted their ignorance in this branch of science, or betrayed it in the first sentence. The real knowledge of Judaism stands now where a century and a half ago Eisenmenger had presumed to place it; and the knowledge of philology has remained immovable for the last two hundred years. Hence it follows that even esteemed authors assume an entirely different, if not a spectral garb, the moment they approach the Jewish question; hence it results that all quotations are copied from the sources of subsidiary works of the sixteenth and seventeenth centuries, long since triumphantly refuted. Many authors ignorantly or malignantly construed from an imaginary Judaism and their own Christianity a kind of conversion system, or demonstrated the necessity of retrogressive laws. And although excellent Christians have already raised their voice for, and directed their activity to, Jewish science, no decided improvement can be noticed yet in this respect. Even the incomparable Oppenheimer library had to emigrate to Oxford, in spite of all the wealthy and pious Jews, and could find no asylum in Germany, which just in that branch is considerably behind the libraries of Parma, Florence, Rome, Leyden, Paris, and Oxford.

Meanwhile the Jews have not remained idle altogether. Since Mendelssohn's period they have wrought and written for civil rights, for public instruction and reform, and finally also for their down-trodden antiquities. In life and in science, in education and in religion, in ideas, wants, and hopes, a new era has manifested its vigor; goodly seed has been sown, and prodigious strength has been developed. Yet we require a protecting organization which will serve as the foundation of progress and science, and as the religious center of the community. The physical and communal life of Jewish congregations is provided for by hospitals and orphan asylums, poor-relief boards, and burial grounds. But religion and science, civil freedom and intellectual progress, require schools, seminaries, and houses of divine worship. They call for the activity of able communal boards, competent teachers of the young, and well-instructed rabbis. If emancipation and science are to be no empty sounds, no vain and delusive articles of fashion, but the life-spring of morality which we recovered after a long wandering in the wilderness, then it must fertilize *institutions,* seminaries of a higher class, general religious instruction, elevated divine worship, and appropriate exhortations from the pulpit. For the requirements of the ecclesiastical collective body formed by the Jews, these organizations are indispensable; but for their foundation we stand in need of religious zeal and intellectual activity, of fervent public interest within and cordial acknowledgment from without. The unrestrained word of instruction has no equal in importance. Whatever treasures the human race possesses, it has acquired by traditional instruction and by education progressing through the ages of the world. At all times the word of instruction has been heard in Israel from mouth to mouth, and every further prosperity of Jewish institutions can only flow from words breathing wisdom and enlightenment. Hence the stirring and ardent desire for verbal instruction, and hence the frequent call for rabbis and teachers who are competent to deliver instructive and edifying discourses to children at school and to adults at the synagogue.

These reflections suggested to us the desirability of a strictly historical investigation into the institution of the sermon in Jewish tradition. Whatever we have been able to ascertain as to its origin, development, and vicissitudes since the epoch of Ezra, till the present time, will be submitted to the public through this volume.

MIRACLES AND THE HISTORIAN (*Isaak Markus Jost*)

The founder of Jewish historiography (1793-1860) wrote the first systematic history of Judaism and the Jewish people. When he wrote about Reform he showed himself of the moderate school, inclined to a conservative approach. The following is taken from the Introduction to his first work on history, which sets forth some of the standards to which the modern historian must adhere.

We come now to a consideration of miracles. These are of a dual nature. To begin with, we are face to face with facts which are to reveal to us a direct intrusion of God into the course of events by unexpected and astonishing natural events. Secondly, they ascribe to great men who guide the fate of the people the power to overcome nature in cases of necessity and, contrary to all ordinary laws, to do what cannot be explained without a direct connection with the omnipotence of God.

How can the historian connect these miracles in a causal fashion with history? Do not such sudden changes in the course of events break through all bonds of history? Is it altogether possible to find events believable which cannot be justified by generally recognized laws? Some have tried to reconcile these difficulties by explaining everything through natural law, that is, to see in the so-called miracles only the everyday which fantasy in relating them exaggerated so that they could no longer be recognized. We consider this impossible. Those great events to which history assigned obvious progress maintain their place in history. They are turning points, even though they did not come about through human preparation nor lie within the realm of human reckoning. In fact, that is the essentially miraculous element: while human beings pursue a great ideal and attempt forcefully to realize it with admirable enthusiasm despite all obstacles, there are unforeseen events which suddenly come to their aid and through higher help make possible that which appeared impossible. Such astonishing natural events appear also in the histories of other people and bring about, through unexpected or unforeseeable ways, a development which without it would probably have taken a different turn. The historian can only describe humbly that which has happened and must recognize that higher guidance which a higher unfathomable Providence has wrought. He must abstain from attempting to search out the intention of the Almighty. In the same fashion, the natural historian is not obligated to prove the higher origin of all things. In consequence, this becomes a historic fact and influences the whole spirit of all participants. It enters into the poetry of the people and then becomes itself a witness to the truth of that which it reports.

3. THE BIBLE AND ITS TEXT

THE NEED FOR BIBLICAL CRITICISM (*Abraham Geiger*)

The Mosaic origin of the Pentateuch and its basic unity had been cornerstones of traditional Jewish belief. The nineteenth century saw the full flowering of radical biblical criticism. Protestant scholars were its chief advocates, but it was natural that Reform Judaism with its historical, evolutionary orientation, should make the critical approach its own. With few exceptions Reform leaders accepted the basic proposition, set forth forcefully by Geiger, that the Torah was a composite document which could reveal the early spiritual history of Judaism.

The treatment of the historical content of the Bible as part of the science of Judaism must be subject to all laws which may be termed the science of history. The authenticity of the sources must be investigated, their genuineness and their reliability must be studied, and it must be seen whether these sources give us the complete rendition of reality or whether they enclose it—in accordance with a certain outlook which we must understand—into a husk, the kernel of which we must liberate. No dogmatic presuppositions must interfere with the methods of such scientific criticism. Judaism need not fear such an un-prejudiced critical approach. Such an investigation is indeed difficult and its complexity may prevent us from reaching undoubted certainty. However, science must not allow itself to be repelled by the difficulty of the task.

It is the wonderful distinction of Jewish history that it reaches from the dim-mest antiquity into our immediate present. We are driven by more than mere curiosity to search out its secret of becoming. Our desire is justified by the very process of growth which discovers that in the growth of the seed the essential development of later centuries is anticipated.

4. THE AUTHORITY OF TRADITION

How far does the binding force of tradition reach? Does *halakhah* partake of the divine quality? What are prerequisites for the admissibility of change? These were fundamental questions with which Reform had to wrestle. In a way, the deeper implications of this problem were given secondary consideration, because Orthodoxy adopted an unyielding "no-change-whatsoever" attitude, which focused the principal attack of Reform on the status quo of Jewish law. The Reformers were not hard put to show that dynamic change in Judaism was not only permissible, but that it was demanded, and that in fact it had always been part of Jewish religious history. Thus Reform invoked tradition to justify its changes, and this principle of organic development was firmly adopted by the main body of Reformers. But there were others, notably Holdheim, who dis-agreed and felt that constant reference to the authority of tradition would in the end be self-defeating; that the past had little or no weight when it came to questions of contemporary relevance. In the following selections, Holdheim's point of view is represented along with the prevailing Reform opinions.

AUTHORITY AND CRITICISM (*Joshua Heschel Schorr*)

Among the proponents of the East European school of enlightenment, the *Maskilim,* none was more radical and few more vocal than Schorr (1814-1895). A scholar of many attainments, he entered the great controversy with contributions to the various new journals and finally founded and edited *Hechalutz.* The following is an excerpt from one of his many articles, which were originally written in Hebrew.

For quite a while the thought has been on my mind to contribute my bit, for the benefit of all, by making public some views concerning all of Israel; to this purpose I am availing myself with pleasure of the *Annals,*[3] hoping that thereby I can be of true service to our brothers in faith. Everything has its time, said one of the wisest of all men; there is a time to tear down and a time to build. Our own time is one when many a thing torn down must be rebuilt.

The holy Torah, as given to us by Moses, lies before us. Who dares criticize it or doubt its veracity? Who would deny its divinity? Who cannot see that it is imbued with the divine spirit? The purity of its language, the clarity and grandeur of its teachings, the portrayals which leave far behind anything other old nations have to show forth in their myths, must convince even the most ordinary mind that God's spirit is revealed therein! Looking at the sources of the so-called oral teachings which are accessible to us and which are meant to constitute a supplement to the Mosaic law, any expert who examines them without prejudice will have to realize at once that their expression and wording is merely the work of earthborn humans, and therefore subject to error. Nevertheless, it stands there as an authority, surrounding the pure Torah like an iron wall to keep away any beam of light. However, instead of serving it as a defense and bulwark, the Torah wastes away inwardly because no criticism has been permitted.

In stating this I presume by no means to rebuke the sages of ancient times, much less reject their teaching or even join the Karaites. Not at all! On the contrary, I am an adherent of tradition, and I honor its representatives. Indeed, I believe that they have developed these conclusions from the Torah with true piety and the purest intention. Also, through their assiduity and faithful care amidst the manifold persecutions and sufferings and among strange religions, they have energetically preserved our holy religion; without it, our religion might perhaps have vanished completely. But I maintain with the deepest conviction that the yoke which, for the prevention of error, they have imposed on our coreligionists, is in our time oppressive and can easily lead to the point where one might rather cast it off completely and withdraw altogether from any positive religion. Thus, what they wanted to prevent might, instead, be furthered by the very means they employed. Hence, in order to ward off in

[3] *The Israelite Annals (Israelitische Annalen),* a short-lived journal (1839-41), was edited by Jost.

time the hovering danger of spreading irreligiousness, all present-day scholars and teachers of the people have the holy duty to fix their eyes sharply on their task and to examine carefully what our wise men thought proper to ordain in their time; and only after having gained this insight will they be able to judge our own times and abolish anything that is not in conformity with it, and instead, take measures corresponding to the new circumstances.

Our brothers in Germany have set a good example for us. There, learned rabbis first called attention to this condition; they endeavored, with true religiosity, to express in newspapers their often sharply differing opinions in order to enlighten one another on important points without consideration for the person and with sincere love of truth. Hail to them! Anyone who is concerned with the truth must be grateful to them for striving so openly to establish true piety.

I was hoping that our [East European] rabbis, too, would at last awaken from their lethargy and state their opinions on such important matters, but nothing could arouse them. They did not hear the voices of the German rabbis, partly because they live too far away, partly because they do not understand their language. Who knows how long they would have remained in this lethargy, laboring under the delusion that all is the same as it was many centuries ago, had not the famed and noble friend of truth, S. D. Luzzatto, presented and evolved new views in his letter last year,[4] in a language they could all understand. His views struck deeply at the entire existing system. They can be expressed in short by the following theses:

1. Mishnah and Talmud were originally not conceived as law-books for all times; rather, they represent late written collections of various decisions.
2. The ancient sages wished by no means to prevent posterity from modifying, adding to, or taking away from their decisions, in accordance with new times and circumstances.
3. They intentionally set down the most differing views, specifically also individual opinions and maxims, so that there might be a choice of assenting to one or the other opinion, according to the circumstances.

We are in debt to the valiant Luzzatto for having aroused the people from their stupor and for having given speech to the dumb. The debate is active and the result can only be a beneficial mutual understanding among all Israel. This being the case, everyone able to speak out must feel an obligation to contribute all he can in furthering the search for truth; he must particularly reject all bitterness and injection of personality, so that the quarrel does not degenerate into enmity and blind passion. Only calm, friendly, and thoughtful discussion can bring about the desired result.

As far as I am concerned, I would like to call attention to an advantage which has not been used by criticism so far, and which may be the only one capable of questioning the authority of the Talmud. Until now, of course, criticism has

---

[4] The letter appeared in *Kerem Hesed* and contained a critique of Geiger's views on the origin of the Mishnah.

always been arguing on the ground of authority itself, to demonstrate that this authority itself offers ways out of its own stipulations. Naturally, this makes it easy for the opponent to crush every objection by parading an endless number of other authorities. What can a single sentence in the Talmud accomplish against the great mass of opposite dicta? For as long as the Talmud is considered an inherently perfect, infallible monument of true divine tradition and is being accepted as such, no reform can take place through it. That being the case, why do we not get ready to expose the inner imperfections and the many irrefutably obvious faults from which the work suffers? This would clearly prove that what we possess here is a work created by humans, distorted by many errors, and that the writing of this volume is not imbued with one wholly integrated spirit. No matter how important its contents or how essential it may be for religion, nevertheless, the work can by no means be considered infallible! Its very nature demonstrates in many passages that the ancient scholars themselves no longer had the correct versions before them and that they frequently quarreled about things which must have sounded quite different in the original text.[5] Therefore, any critique should at first reconnoiter its terrain more closely and prove that authority itself is standing on shaky ground! Only then will we be able to judge with some certainty the importance which ought to be attached to its decisions.

The apprehension that the pillars of religion will be weakened through critical treatment of the Talmud is entirely in bad taste and without basis. Besides, it does not mean that criticism will shatter the entire work, discarding the old only because it is old; for the unbridled rage for innovation produces nothing good in itself. On the contrary, we must examine from every point of view what already exists, improve the structure wherever damages are found, and take the proper measures wherever necessary, so that Judaism may represent a house of God instead of resembling a heap of ruins. This task is great and difficult, it needs many laborers, it encounters many obstacles, and time urgently demands its completion. Therefore, it is the duty of everyone competent to join and collaborate, and the Almighty will give His blessing to it!

WRITTEN AND ORAL LAW (*Abraham Kohn*)

If the institutions of the Jewish religion are anything, they are not unchangeable, for they always kept pace with the civilization and the civil and social circumstances of the Jews. This is especially apparent in our ritual. At first it consisted merely of sacrificial acts; then, when poetry and music flowered in Israel under David, the singing of spiritual songs (psalms) with organ accompaniment were added, and not until Solomon's time was there, in the splendid Temple, a fixed place for ritual. In the period of the Second Temple the synagogue came into being and common prayer was introduced, mediated through a messenger of the congregation (the cantor), who expressed the members'

---

[5] The author supplies us with interesting proofs from the most important passages of the Talmud; unfortunately, because of lack of space, the *Annals* cannot publish them here.

yearnings. In part these prayers became fixed, since general events usually came in cyclical order; but nonetheless, with every change of circumstance the liturgy was increased through new additions which mirrored the religious mode of thought, level, and education, and the ideological currents of the time, and which gave adequate expression to their common sufferings and joys, tribulations and anxieties, desires and hopes.

To be sure, we must always and everywhere observe and carry out those ordinances of the Torah which are not dependent on the circumstances of time and situation, and do so in a manner which is commanded by Mosaic tradition, in so far as it concerns itself with such observances. However, this does not exclude varied changes and modifications in the application of religious statutes and customs.

For the statutes of traditional Judaism, despite their extent and complexity, have never been so strictly interpreted that they disregarded life in its wider scope; rather, the principal rule applied: "Man should live and not die by them." From this we learn, says Maimonides (Hilkhot Shabbat, ch. 3, #3), that the commandments of the Torah are to bring to the world, not revenge (unremitting strictness), but mercy, forbearance, and peace. Now, since our century has brought to European Jewry entirely new circumstances which in former times could not have been imagined and which, therefore, could not have been covered by ordinances, analogies must be found which, providing amelioration for exceptional cases, can be applied today, *not that we might make life more comfortable, but that we might better fulfil our duties toward self and society without breaking with our religion.*

Many so-called rabbinic statutes and customs (declared as holy by the status-quo apostles) are merely adhesions stemming from the habits belonging to centuries vanished long ago and originating under entirely different environmental and climatic conditions. Such statutes have no right to eternal existence, because not only has the reason which brought them forth disappeared long ago, but life itself, to which they owed their origin, has largely displaced them again. While religious institutions and statutes were forcibly kept to the viewpoint of past ages and were not touched by a refreshing godly spirit, life itself drove forward with full abandon. Since the guardians of religion, lacking all education and all knowledge of world and man, dreamed of entirely different times and circumstances, and thus estranged the most vital part of the new generation from themselves and from tradition itself, a most unfortunate schism has developed in Judaism: there is a rigid, contentless, formal religiosity on the one hand, and a shallow, negative, anti-historical pseudo-enlightenment on the other.

However, there are of late widespread manifestations of attempts to rejuvenate religious forms in accordance with the needs of the time and to restore much needed harmony between life and law. Nothing but good may be expected of these, and the development of a new sect need not be feared, because in rabbinic Judaism significant variations always existed side by side both in ritual and religious custom.

To be sure, the Talmud is absolutely necessary for the explanation of the ceremonial law, and in this respect its scriptural exegesis has retained its validity, even though such exegesis has not remained without contradiction. However, since such interpretations were in large part not binding but the result of human research, they have no claim to infallibility and untouchability. Rather, it is in the interest of both science and religion to subject such interpretations to a searching critique. One may only ask of the theologian who comes to a different view on some commandment, that he should not translate his views into practice until he has found support from competent authority, and such caution may indeed be expected of every scrupulous person.

WHICH PORTION OF THE TALMUD REMAINS BINDING? (*Michael Creizenach*)

Creizenach (1789-1842), a teacher at the Frankfort Philanthropin, was the first Reformer to attempt a systematic exposition of his theology. Characteristically, he called his chef d'oeuvre *Shulhan Arukh,* in which he treated the traditional *mitsvot* in their biblical, talmudic, and modern relevance.

The intention of the law was that the Israelite ritual system should never sink into the state of an old, amorphous mass of stone, but rather that it preserve itself with everlasting vitality and that it develop continually according to the needs, circumstances, and educational levels of succeeding generations. This was actually brought about by the prophets, the Sanhedrin, and the Talmudists. Likewise, the Talmudists were far from expecting the slavish obedience we give them in ritual matters. They took all measures which they imagined were necessary for the preservation of religion in their days, leaving it up to later generations to proceed in a similar way. But they were unable to foresee that the precepts regarding the organization of the Synod might later on no longer apply. It is also not true that they used their religious authority mainly to impose burdensome strictures on the people; on the contrary, wherever they deemed it necessary, they introduced such significant relaxations of the rules that our rabbis of today would recoil if they were expected to introduce such measures. These were relaxations concerning not merely some milder interpretation of a passage in Scripture or the suspension of a synodal decision, but indeed, in some instances they discontinued the practice of certain precepts altogether.

It is only due to ignorance and the excessive anxiety of later days that our religion has taken on a mummy-like appearance, that indeed it has become isolated from real life by a deep chasm; that it consists of thousands of precepts which the people do not heed or do not even know. Most parents no longer know how to proceed in order to give their children a religious education which is to last them for life. The decrees of the various synodal assemblies were of necessity brought about by contemporary conditions and, therefore, cannot bear the character of laws which are binding for all times. Had the scribes issued laws for all times, one might well ask: Why were these laws not already introduced by Moses? However, a law decree, which at its very inception was understood to be temporary, cannot become irrevocable through the fact that the authority which created it has ceased to exist. Its validity ceases by itself, with the fall of that power, and particularly so in the case before us, when it is a matter of obeying only the authorities of one's own time.

This, however, does not mean that all measures and decisions of the ancient scribes should be disregarded. To do so would rob us of all those useful means in the observance of the Pentateuch which we owe the Talmud, and would put us into the labyrinth in which the Karaites have found themselves for many centuries, without being able to achieve a satisfactory organization of their religious affairs. On the contrary, we wish to leave untouched many a custom which through universal esteem has attained even in our own time a high degree of venerableness. Take for instance the beautiful, scientifically accomplished calendar computation of which it can be said, indeed, that it is an attestation of our wisdom and insight before the eyes of the other nations. It is only necessary that, in our awe for tradition, we do not exceed the boundaries which our ancient sages themselves would have set for us, had they foreseen our present-day conditions and had they not firmly believed that Israel's dispersion would not last half the time that it has lasted already. These boundaries can be described in a few words and can be narrowed down to these few maxims:

We recognize every interpretation of the scriptural passages, propounded by the regularly constituted synods, either as traditional or as derived by means of the well-known hermeneutic rules—provided such interpretation was reached in unanimity. On the other hand, wherever there was a case of divided opinions, we follow the less strict version so long as it does not contradict our own conviction.

However, we shall maintain institutions and legal safeguards only if they still factually exist in most communities, and if they are of such character that the Israelite can continue existing with them; in other words, if he, as merchant, worker, farmer, and civil servant can practice his profession without grievous restraints. Within these boundaries lies, at the same time, the assertion of the degree of obligation that we concede to the statements of the Talmud; yet it is better that we also discuss this matter clearly. Let us proceed with all the candor and love of truth that befits an Israelite, and let us fear neither the accusation of heresy by the few Jews whose convictions we may offend, nor enmity on the part of certain Christians whom, in any case, we shall never be able to please.

We recognize the Talmud as being, at least for the present, a serviceable means for the interpretation of those ritual commandments which, according to the individual concepts of each man, are binding to this day; and we adhere to these interpretations in observing them within the already established boundaries.

We regard those portions of the Talmud which do not elucidate the Mosaic laws as merely humanly instituted decrees; however, for the furtherance of good morality and pure piety, we gladly avail ourselves of anything that appeals to our reasoning.

We consider those passages in the Talmud which are not consistent with the principle of the universal love of man, as outbursts of passionate hatred of which unfortunately quite often the best men cannot free themselves when they are oppressed in a disgraceful way and when they see that all considerations to which the dignity of human nature gives them undeniable claims are being violated against themselves. Statements of that kind, regardless of where and into what book they might have gained entrance, are not only alien to the spirit of our religion, but indeed, contrary to its letter.

AUTHORITY AND FREEDOM (*David Einhorn*)

The following is part of Einhorn's responsum in the Tiktin-Geiger controversy (see above, p. 63), and addresses itself to the following question:

Question: Does a rabbi forfeit his right to occupy his post when he departs in some respects from biblical interpretations and traditionally valid rules of the Talmud, and if so, under what conditions?

Answer: Departure from the Talmud in respect to the exegesis of biblical passages and the validity of traditional laws results in inability to occupy a rabbinic post if the following three conditions exist together:
   a. The rejected talmudic interpretation and the disputed traditional law must concern a tradition which in the Talmud is described and recognized by everyone as genuine and undoubted (Maimonides, in his introduction to the Mishnah, enumerates such traditional interpretations);
   b. When such departure is not sufficiently motivated by changed conditions of time and place; and
   c. If it is not merely expressed as an opinion, but is meant to be practically applied either by the person advocating such departure or by others.

Ad a. Every adherent of talmudic Judaism is obligated to observe all those ordinances which, even though they lack every biblical basis, are listed by the Talmud as having been handed down by tradition and which as such are disputed by no one. The practice of these laws, which have come down to us from the Men of the Great Synagogue, makes a Jew a "Talmud Jew," and this is the chief distinction between him and the Karaites who recognize the biblical word exclusively and do not want to hear of any tradition, whatever its name. However, this category of laws forms and completes the whole circle within which the faithful Israelite concedes authority to the Talmud. There is no legal foundation whatever for a further extension of this authority to ordinances lying outside this circle, to subjective exegesis, and to those laws the traditional character of which is a matter of dispute between the Talmudists themselves. Therefore, one cannot deny the name Jew nor his fitness for the rabbinic post to one who objects to the kind of authoritarianism which would make Judaism an unreplenished swamp and condemn it to eternal stagnation. We cannot, we must not, ascribe such infallability and apotheosis to the Talmud. We believe in its validity, but at the same time we must reject its deification and say to it: Israel believes *you* but not *in you;* you are the channel of the divine but not divinity itself!

"But," it is said, quoting Maimonides as an authority, "after the codification of the Talmud, Israel sanctioned and accepted all its views, expositions, and ordinances!" Where are the documents of so solemn a vow which was to bind all future descendants? How is it possible that so important an event is never mentioned in the Talmud and is not, as at the conclusion of the Book of Esther, documented as a memorial for all time? But suppose, indeed, that our forefathers had pledged themselves and all their descendants to accept the Talmud with everything it contained, how could such a pledge, the existence of which is seen as the reason for the immutability of the Talmud, result in a binding obligation for us? Quite aside from the fact that such a conclusion would be in contradiction to all the laws of normal reason—and especially so in religious matters—it is, in any case, a fundamental rule of talmudic Judaism that no father can burden his minor child with a vow against the latter's will. And, even if the child has agreed to it during his minority, once he reaches his majority he is no longer under any obligation to fulfil such a vow.[6] (Of course the obligation to fulfil a *divine* command needs no intermediary justification; it follows directly from our relationship to God, and is not dependent on any voluntary agreement. This is stressed so that what was said above should not lead to dangerous conclusions regarding Deut. 29:14.[7])

Maimonides, in his Introduction to the Mishnah, already acknowledges as genuine tradition only that about which there is no difference of opinion in the Talmud.[8]

This is not the place to engage in an extended discussion about the traditional character of the hermeneutic rules (*middot*), the denial of which is the real *corpus delecti* of the *Exposition*.[9] A few words will suffice to enable us to judge the principles which the above-mentioned *Exposition* follows.

The Talmud itself is not definitive on this matter. Often there are differences of opinion concerning the laws which are to be deduced from these rules, not because the rules are claimed to be untraditional, but because a conflict arises when a subject is under discussion and one rabbi applies this hermeneutical rule, and a second rabbi prefers another.[10] This results in the type of uncertainty of which Sab. 132a is a glaring example.[11] Who could deny, therefore, that the laws and rules which flow from the application of these *middot* have

[6] See Maimonides, Hilkhot Nezirot 2:15, and the commentary of Yom Tob Lipmann to Mishnah Sota 3:8.

[7] See also Nedarim 25a.

[8] (Ed. note) Einhorn proceeds to quote from Hilkhot Tumat Ha-met 2:10, 5:4, and other sources, to prove his point.

[9] P. 29. (Ed note) The Talmud knows 32 of these rules in accordance with which the Bible was interpreted and a conclusion drawn for the traditional law. The *Exposition* referred to is Tiktin's collection of rabbinic views denouncing Geiger; see above, p. 63.

[10] Cf. Git. 41 b.

[11] (Ed. note) The talmudic dispute to which Einhorn refers concerns itself with this question: What are the halakhic foundations of the law that a child must be circumcised on the eighth day even if this day falls on a Sabbath?

far less value and foundation than the express ordinances of the Bible and the simple *halakhah?*[12]

Ad b. Unfitness to occupy the rabbinic post cannot be caused by a divergence from ceremonial laws, if such divergence is not just frivolous tampering with the sacred, but rather is founded in the spirit of Judaism and represents a pressing demand of its natural development. Of course, such divergence must have nothing in common with mere fashion or convenience or with forced application of an un-Jewish view to Jewish matters, or reflect merely a subjective attitude or a kind of general antipathy to the status quo. It must be the product of profound, honest, and unprejudiced research in the sacred documents, of pious sincerity, of a glowing enthusiasm for God's work, and, finally, of mature advice from several God-intoxicated men who are experts and whose judgment has carefully weighed the causes and consequences of the matter. Such procedure, far from being objectionable, is highly commendable, and it was often followed in both talmudic and post-talmudic times.[13] The well-known ordinances issued by Rabbenu Gershom amply show that the conclusion of the Talmud could not limit the development of Judaism in accordance with the needs of the times.[14]

But suppose even that the divergence of a rabbi would occur relative to a ceremonial law which until now was recognized as indisputably divine, and for the elimination of which changed conditions could offer no reason; and suppose the divergence is founded solely on the conviction, obtained through scientific research, that the law is not of divine origin. If the rabbi does not transgress the bounds of theory and gives it practical expression in neither his private nor his professional life, how then could he lose the right to occupy his post? As a Jew in general, and as a rabbi specifically, he is indeed obligated and duty-bound to observe and practice strictly all biblical and genuinely traditional laws. But when did Judaism ever ban and damn a mere expression of opinion which runs counter to the status quo? When did it ever declare as unfit for rabbinic office someone who took such a position, and even brand him with the name of *kofer* [a denier of the principles of faith]? Genuine Judaism which, despite Maimonides, knows of no binding dogmas, looks at deeds, not opinions. Now, if in addition, I live fired by love for my sacred religion; if without surcease I search and seek for truth in the books of life, but have the misfortune to gain an opinion which differs from the status quo; if, driven by noble zeal, I at once express this opinion without fear and hesitation for the honorable and pious sake of my faith—if I just *express* this I belong (according to the *Exposition*) to the category of thieves and murderers! Worse, I am said to have no share in that

[12] (Ed. note) Einhorn next shows how Rashi, the revered commentator of Jewish tradition, would have fallen under the ban of the authors of the *Exposition,* because he too disagrees with certain hermeneutical applications. Then follows a discussion of the extremes to which a slavish use of *middot* can lead. This concludes his argument *ad a.*

[13] Cf. Yeb. 90b, 39b; Sota 48a, et al.

[14] See Isserles to Orah Hayim 128:44 and to Eben Ha-ezer 165:1. In this passage the relative who with the best of intentions would carry out the divine Biblical injunction of the Levirate law (Deut. 25:5-10), is prevented from doing so if he would thereby commit bigamy, which is prohibited by post-talmudic ordinance. All this in contradiction to Yeb. 39b! See also Abraham Ibn Daud to Maimonides, Hilkhot Mamrim 2:2. (On Rabbenu Gershom, see above, p. 83.)

divine possession for the sake of which I loathe all falsehood and hypocrisy, and am to forego all community with the house of Jacob, which I at least try to cleanse of dirt and refuse! Is such tyranny the preachment of Torah which makes *knowledge* a duty and which calls itself Israel's wisdom and reason in the eyes of all nations?

But listen to the judgment of the Talmud itself in this matter! In Sanh. 86b and 88b it says: The *zaken mamre* [the heretic teacher] becomes guilty only if he either practices his divergent opinion or by *direct teaching* attempts to lead others to do so, but not if he only holds to a point of view. Furthermore (in Sanh. 88a), Akabya ben Mehalalel could not be held to account for his opinions which differed from those of the sages, "because he did not teach in order that his interpretations might be practiced."[15] From this it is abundantly clear that Maimonides, when he speaks of the teacher who decries the traditional interpretation,[16] refers exclusively to one who not only denies tradition as such (which is the distinction between *epikoros* and *mamre*), but who also gives practical expression to his heretical teaching.[17]

TALMUD AND REFORM *(Samuel Holdheim)*

Holdheim (1806-1860) was the principal exponent of radical reform in Germany. He became the first rabbi of the *Reformgemeinde* in Berlin and the author of its revolutionary prayer book (see above, p. 57). In his work on *The Ceremonial Law in the Messianic Era* (from which the following excerpt is taken), he set forth to prove the time-bound qualities of talmudic law. Note especially the last sentence which became famous, not only for its memorable formulation, but also because of its unlimited exaltation of the *Zeitgeist*. In his subsequent writings Holdheim went to the consequential extremes of his position and advocated the change from Sabbath to Sunday and the abolishment of circumcision (see below, pp. 190 and 209).

Anyone who knows the spirit of the Talmud knows that it is built on the view of the eternity of the ceremonial law and its complete fulfilment at the time of the arrival of the Messiah. Although the Talmud deals so meticulously and in such detail with the past, it is because, in its opinion, the past has an interest only in so far as it will again become present. The Talmud lingers over things which are absolutely and forever gone only to the extent that a better understanding of the Bible is involved. The most exhaustive discussions, however, concern such matters that have practical value for the *future*. Take,

[15] The passage in Men. 18b speaks rather for than against this view which is deeply rooted in Judaism. Cf. the conclusion of *Mebo ha-talmud*.
[16] Hilkhot Mamrim 3:1; Hilkhot Teshubah 3:8.
[17] Hilkhot Abodat Elilim.

for instance, the passage in Yoma 5b where the question is asked how Moses helped to put the priestly gowns on Aaron and his son. This question, simply because it relates exclusively to the past, is then declared idle and empty and is changed to read: How shall these garments be put on in the *future,* that is, in the Messianic era (compare Hul. 17a and Asher ben Yechiel)?

Dr. Herzfeld, with all due recognition to his laudable progressive efforts, cannot be excused of a certain weakness, namely, propounding liberal reform ideas as being founded in the Talmud, a view which he shares with many other honored rabbis.[18] This view must in any case be rejected because it is untrue; but, besides, by proclaiming it, one places weapons into the hands of the enemy, who will raise a hue and cry that reformers are trying to fool people and persuade them that the wholly innocent Talmud encouraged atheistic ideas of progress.

It is an unpardonable weakness. Reform must avoid as much as possible to press the banner of progress into the rigid hands of the Talmud. The time has to come when one feels strong enough vis-à-vis the Talmud to oppose it, in the knowledge of having gone far beyond it. One must not with every forward step drag along the heavy tomes and, without even opening them, wait for some innocent remark, therewith to prove the foundations of progress. Incidentally, the Talmud has found its own nemesis; for exactly what the Talmud once did with the Bible, the rabbis of today now do with it. The Talmud, too, was cautious and anxious because it did not have a real, strongly founded, invigorating, reforming principle. Therefore, constantly, with every single step it glanced back at the Bible and, without having recognized that the Bible only spoke from a theocratic point of view, the Talmud superimposed upon the text of the Bible those reforms which changed circumstances had forcibly brought into existence.

Dr. Herzfeld and many others do exactly the same. They speak from their own present day ideology and yet do not trust it quite completely. They, therefore, imagine erroneously that their ideology is founded in the Talmud. But just as the Bible, if one understands it correctly, earnestly rejects all talmudic re-interpretations, so must a more exact knowledge of the Talmud earnestly and decisively reject these modern ways in which the Reformers treat it. Dr. Herzfeld should not place before us so absolute and general a statement as: "The Talmud is right." Rather, he should say, *"The Talmud speaks with the ideology of its own time, and for that time it was right. I speak from the higher ideology of my time, and for this age I am right."*

Holdheim held that eventually the ceremonial law would pass away entirely, for it exists only to safeguard the holiness of Israel in a pagan world. As paganism gives way to monotheism (be it Christianity, Islam, or Judaism), the ritual laws are less and less needed; and with the arrival of the Messianic era they are absolutely superfluous.

[18] (Ed. note) Dr. Herzfeld, a fellow reformer, had written an article called "Reform Attempts and Emancipation," and Holdheim in this book takes issue with Herzfeld's reform theology.

A large part of the ceremonial law exists because of the sacred nature of the Jewish people. The very essence of our people's holiness is the separation and election of this people from all other peoples in custom and habit, so that it might be a monotheistic nation devoted to the service of God. Hence, holiness expresses itself almost exclusively—with the exception of the eternally and generally valid moral laws—in laws of separation. How often is the Jew told: You must not do this or be that, in the same manner as other peoples, for you are a holy people unto the Eternal, your God. If one searches after the reason for most of the ceremonial laws of the Bible, one will find that they were given only because of the existence of pagan peoples and had as their purpose separation from these people. We must admit, therefore, that these laws would either not have been given at all, or would have been given differently had the Jewish people been the *only* people in the world and had other peoples or human beings *not existed at all*. There is only one reason for Israel's ceremonial law and that is the holiness of the Jewish people in relation to other people, that is, its choice from amongst these other nations. This may be compared with the holiness of the priestly tribe; that is, its election from all the tribes of Israel for a specially sacred service is the reason for the respective priestly laws. If no special tribe had been chosen as the priestly one, then there would have been no priestly law; had the Jewish people not been chosen from amongst all other nations, had all of mankind been called for the purpose to which Israel alone was called, then there would be no special ceremonial law, but rather would there be a law for all mankind, that is, a pure, simple, moral law. Only because so many nations, indeed all men, were so little developed, and because Israel, in accordance with the promise made to our forefathers, had alone been called as a holy people, was a ceremonial law necessary. For it was not sufficient for Israel to be given a moral law consisting of pure faith and true conceptions of the one true God, but it had to receive the ceremonial law in the whole context of other peoples and Israel's relation to them. Should all other nations perish from the face of the earth because of a flood and Israel alone remain; or should the rest of mankind accept the faith of the patriarchs and be converted to pure monotheism—in that very moment the ceremonial law would cease to have binding force for Israel also. For then the condition for this law, namely, Israel's relationship to pagan peoples, would have ceased, and the law would sink into complete insignificance.

CHAPTER
VI

A People and Its Faith

----

1. REVELATION

DESPITE Reform's early affinity for a critical approach to the Bible, its exponents held firmly to the doctrine of revelation. God had shown Himself to Israel in a special way, and in a unique manner they in turn were able to comprehend Him: this was the center of Reform teaching, and in this regard it remains close to Jewish tradition. But the nature of this revelation received widely different interpretations of which the following selections are broadly representative. Geiger speaks for what may be called the "folk" theory (which occasionally had near-racial overtones). Despite his anti-nationalism and pervasive idealism, he considers the Jew endowed with "a native energy" to apprehend God. Steinheim's mysticism and anti-rationalism stand in strange contrast to Francolm's "rational" approach—yet the central acceptance of revelation unites them both.

ISRAEL'S NATIVE ENERGY (*Abraham Geiger*)

We have essayed to draw, in a few short outlines, a comparison between the convictions, presentiments, and assertions, which predominated in antiquity in general, and those presented by Judaism; even this incomplete outline must convince the unprejudiced mind that a *native energy* enlists our attention which has preserved its significance for all times, which has proven to be a creative power.

The Greeks boast of being autochtons, i.e., of having been born upon, and from, their own soil; whether this claim be justified, we will not now examine; but another claim, no doubt expressing the profound meaning of the above, must be admitted; to wit: the autochtonic character of their mind, the aboriginal nature of their national talent. The Greeks had no teachers or patterns in art and science, they were their own teachers and masters—they speedily appeared with such perfect accomplishments, as makes them the teachers of mankind for all times.

It is as though a higher, more vivid taste for the beautiful, the harmonious, the symmetrical, and the pleasing had been innate in the Greek nation. We observe a national genius that enabled it to produce masters in every art and science. Therefore, even later centuries willingly listened to the words of this nation, hastened thither where they could see the works of the plastic arts, where they could enjoy, as it were, a rejuvenating bath in the spiritual fountain that springs thence and carries its waters through the streams of centuries. *Is not the Jewish people, likewise, endowed with such a genius, with a religious genius?* Is it not, likewise, an aboriginal power that illumined its eyes, so that it could penetrate the higher life of the spirit, understand more vividly, and feel more intensely the close relation between the spirit of man and the Supreme Spirit, that would more distinctly and clearly behold the innermost nature of human morality, and then present the result to the world as its native-born knowledge? If this be so, we may speak of a close contact between the individual spirit and the Supreme Spirit, of an illumination of individual spirits by the power that fills everything, so that they could break through their confining limits: it is—let us not hesitate to pronounce the word— revelation, and this, too, as it was manifested in the whole people.

The Greeks were not all artists, were not all Phidias' or Praxiteles', but the Greek nation was alone capable of producing such great masters. The same was the case with Judaism. It is certain that not all Jews were prophets; the ex- clamation, "Would that all the people were prophets!" was a pious wish; the other, "I shall pour My spirit upon all flesh," is a promise which has never been realized. Nevertherless, Israel is the people of revelation, the favored organs of which came from that people; it is as though the rays of light had been dispersed, and were concentrated into a flame by those gifted with higher endowments. A thorn-bush produces no wine; a neglected people produces no prophets, such as the people of Judah gave to the world. It is true, the historical books of the Bible mostly inveigh against the morals, the depravity of the people at the time of the Kings; they intend to prepare us for the devastation that came upon them as a punishment for their sinfulness. Yet, that people must have possessed noble powers in great abundance; it must have had a native endowment, considering that it could produce, that it could rear such men. Judaism was not merely a preacher in the wilderness, and though it did not prevail altogether, it was nevertheless a power which existed, it is true, in many men in a small degree, yet in such a measure that it could produce—being concentrated in individuals—such heroes of the spirit. Nor does Judaism claim to be the work of single individuals, but that of the whole people. It does not speak of the God of Moses, or of the God of the Prophets, but of the God of Abraham, Isaac, and Jacob, of the God of the whole race, of the patriarchs who were equally gifted with that endowment, with that prophetic vision; it is the revelation which lay dormant in the whole people and was concentrated in individuals. The fact that the greatest prophet left his work unfinished contains a profound truth: he must not be regarded as the Atlas who bears the whole world upon his shoulders, who completes a work without the cooperation of others, who gives the impulse thereto and, at the same time, finishes it. It is not known where he is buried, and our ancient teachers remark: "His grave should not serve for a place of pilgrimage whither men go to do honor to *one,* and thus raise him above the level of man." Moses did his share of the work according to his great capacity as one of the whole people.

Yes, Judaism has grown from the people of revelation. And why, then, should we not employ the term where we touch the fundamental source; the illumination which proceeds from the Higher Spirit, which cannot be explained, which is not a composition created by a process of development, but which all at once presents itself as a whole, like every new creation proceeding from the Original Spirit? We will not narrow down the term within certain limits in the manner of dogmatical theory; it may be understood in different ways, but as to its essence, it is ever the same; it indicates the point of contact between human reason with the Fundamental Source of all things. The ancient teachers of Judaism never denied that this sublime phenomenon was, after all, connected with some human quality. "The spirit of God," they say, "rests only upon a wise man, upon a man possessed of moral power, who is independent because he is contented, having conquered all ambition, all desire"; a man who bears his importance within him, who feels the divine in him, is alone capable to receive the Divine; he is not a mere speaking trumpet through which words uttered pass without his being conscious thereof; no, a man in the true meaning of the term, touching upon the Divine and, therefore, susceptible of it. A man of the Middle Ages, alike a profound thinker and true poet, Judah Halevi, emphatically maintains that revelation animated the whole people. "Israel," he says, "is the heart of mankind, which in its unity ever preserved its higher susceptibility, and the several distinguished men were the hearts of that heart." Maimonides speaks of "a lightning-like illumination as which revelation must be regarded; to some, this illumination was granted only for a short time; for others, it was repeated; but with Moses, it was a lasting one; an illumination which lightens the darkness, affording man an insight into all that is hidden, that discloses to him what remains concealed for others." Judaism is such a religion of revelation; it has grown from such visions of the Divine, and has connected into a whole all that it did behold; Judaism is a religion of truth, because the view into the nature of things is infallible, discovering as it does the unchangeable and everlasting: this is its everlasting essence.

THE INCOMPREHENSIBLE IS CENTRAL (*Solomon Ludwig Steinheim*)

This highly original philosopher, who was a physician by profession, lived from 1789 to 1866. He made revelation the center of a complex philosophic system which had few followers in his day, but which has lately been given new attention (chiefly through H. J. Schoeps). "Jewish peoplehood is religion and nothing else," he wrote, and religion was founded on revelation. In some ways Steinheim may be said to resemble his younger contemporary Kierkegaard.

The old maxim of philosophy, "From nothing comes nothing," has always been, and remains to this day, a triviality. This axiom was, and still is, the real cliff against which all higher tenets must dash in pieces. For without freedom on the highest level, namely, in creation, there can be no freedom of conduct for those whom the Almighty has created.

This most formidable barrier to human thinking, however, was removed by an entirely new concept; and with this barrier fallen, access was gained to the whole new era of a well-founded, no longer purely intuitive, set of ethics. It is the dogma of world creation which in our holy canon stands at the head of all others. The first verse blasted a gateway through the old doctrine, breaking through the primeval, rational concept of paganism and a hitherto dogmatic philosophy. We have here the first actual protest which we may call revelation, so as to differentiate it from our own inherent, innermost, and naturally derived concepts, without being concerned at this time about the way it has succeeded more recently in penetrating the world of the human mind. It is enough that we find a written, historical document which contradicts the rational dogma, which stands in contrast to man's primeval way of thinking, demanding that he accept a definitive position, repugnant to him and almost impossible of acceptance. However, as much as this new doctrine offends against the old, natural theory of inherited reason, it follows that it must also be in agreement with that same ancient intuitive freedom of the very same reason, when it shifts from the area of knowledge to that of action, from the realm of a succession of cause and events into the circle of the ethical man whose actions are freely completed and executed.

Once the basic rational dogma, "From nothing comes nothing," was cast aside, the struggle had to spread across the entire endless chain of conclusions and institutions, and each practice based on an old premise was consequently contested and opposed. It is the conflict we have described earlier, which began with Abraham's quarrel and his banishment from the ancestral hut; it is the fight of freedom against necessity, of morality against sensuality, of theology against idolatry, of revelation against paganism, of the new against the old.

Just as to this day moral freedom has, or can have, little place in paganism, so in contrast has the concept of destiny, of iron necessity, little place in the chain of ideas of revelation. This was carried to such a point that in the language in which this strange new document was written, the concepts of necessity and destiny, for which the Greek had such sharp, well-defined terms, are entirely missing.

Not Oriental asceticism, not mortification of the flesh, are meant; those were indeed nothing new, nothing unheard of. What is meant is, rather, the subservience of the mind to a superior reason by way of free resolve, and effectual insight into the truth of the dogma of revelation. Not the body but the soul shall be reborn, altered in its naturalness, transformed from its old way of thinking, recast into a new spirit; "Something from nothing"—that is the solid concept which, like the power of electricity, melts the fireproof metal of primeval pagan mentality, forcing it out of its rigid mold. This dogma, long since accepted by us, is today the center of the decisive struggle between philosophy and revelation.

The idea of revelation has appeared to us as a new concept, standing against our own innate ideas of reason in their original forms and their derived teachings. This is the substance of our struggle and it will remain so as long as the old, ingrown ideas retain even the smallest fraction of their mastery over the human soul. However, the concept of revelation appears—we repeat—in the same sense, as something new, in which we regard each true enrichment of the mind; not only as something unfamiliar and unexpected, not known *a priori* and therefore only to be remembered, but rather as something new to be learned. Knowledge is a twofold thing in our visible world; it originates in part from mathematical ideas, the other part consisting of acquired sense perceptions. The former concerns form and relationship; the latter, the content and substance of knowledge. A similar relationship can be recognized in those incomprehensible things we call divine, which exert no less influence on our spiritual existence than do the others on our external life in our thousandfold relationships with the external world.

Wherever we were in exile, our faith in revelation was influenced by, and tainted with, exotic views and dogmas. This happened in our contact with Parsism, as well as the philosophies of Greece and Germany. Moses Mendelssohn, and more especially his disciples after him, endeavored to do away with the anthropomorphic admixtures which had found their way into our religious system from the Persians and the Greeks during the first and second exiles, having created from it a fantastic hodge-podge of belief and superstition of substance and formalism, of the serious and the ridiculous. Still, they themselves misunderstood the true nature of the revelation dogma. They thought they were rendering it an admirable service when they helped it to acquire the alleged advantages which they found in the systems of the prevailing *a priori* theories of philosophy and scientific dogmatics. It was because of this prejudice that even Mendelssohn, who otherwise was so strong in his belief, completely accepted the prevailing ideas of his time and left to the dogma of revelation only the institution of ritual, denying to revelation the communication of God's so-called eternal truths.[1] Mendelssohn took away from the old definition of religion the first part, namely cognition, as *a modus cognoscendi et colendi Deum*. He left it only the second part, namely, the mode of worship. With this, he cut through its essential vital nerve, thus preparing for the conversion of his immediate successors which he himself had resisted despite all of Lavater's importuning. Mendelssohn had misunderstood, platitudinized, and misinterpreted the holy concept of revelation, thus opening the gate to the shallow rationalism of the day. Not much more was left of Judaism except periwig and beard, and these, too, soon had to make way for the more modern, pomaded, and powdered queue.

[1] See the selection from Mendelssohn's *Jerusalem,* above, p. 5.

Each new discovery fares like the large strawberry in the strawberry-patch. As soon as one of the youths has plucked an unusually large strawberry and shown it to his companions, they all hasten to the area where he found it, in the belief that from now on they will find only big ones. We find that the whole effort of Mendelssohn's successors aimed at unearthing the great philosophical strawberry in the field of religion, their highest goal being to turn religion into philosophy. In order to halt this course of destruction in God's vineyard, I wrote the paper *Revelation According to the Dogma of the Synagogue*. It pained me greatly to learn that it was not an unfounded assumption when one of my friends wrote to me that this doctrine would experience less opposition from the outside than from within the ranks of Judaism. I see that some among our men of progress pride themselves greatly when they succeed in inoculating Judaism with modern philosophical ideas, persuading themselves that they have made forward strides by following the spirit of the times; or perhaps that they even anticipated it, since they merely substitute for our theology the chameleonic, changing, old, primeval concept of a philosophical system. As in its time the Leibnitz-Wolff theorem was introduced, so now Hegel's procedural system is to be introduced into our synagogue. *More mathematico* as well as *de facto,* we would very soon see the external aspects of Judaism blotted out, and its spiritual aspects reduced to an empty skeleton-like concept, leaving nothing but a *tabula rasa,* which would then—just as outside the synagogue—bring about and justify the ardent longing for a new revelation.

The men of progress, as they like to be called, misunderstood and platitudinized the old heathenish externalism of Judaism, particularly its ritual, as well as its basic ideas. On the other hand, the adherents of the status quo with stupid obstinacy hold on to formalism, as if it were Joseph's coat of many colors. They do so even at the expense of Judaism's most ancient concept, the eternally new idea of the revelation of God—and thereby risk the loss of both. It is the task of the present to fight these two parties simultaneously. The latter, calling themselves formalists, have for a century already been confronted by a thousand opponents. Therefore, it is needful and high time that fighters gather to defy the former in a battle for life and death. The latter only committed the sin of having defaced the holy place with trifles and heathenish picture rubbish, exposing it to mockery. The former, however, aim at stealing the gem itself in order to throw it into the depth of the seas.

The struggle is and will remain the same. It is the contest for our minds, the struggle of the new against the old, the primeval concept in it which wants to gain a place within the idea itself—here, as an added contribution to the ritual, there, as its principal object. Now then! The path is opened! Light and air are justly apportioned! No sword, no ban, no stake blunts the speech any longer! May thus the battle against idolatry continue, as it has been carried on, in the same way, for over three millenia. Only its methods have varied with place and time. The masses do not matter here. Gideon shall be our symbol. Before the battle he had his army kneel to drink the water, and he sent home all those who drew the water as if they were idolaters.

A spiritual trait grows and thrives in every Jew. He gets it with his mother's milk, it enters his soul with the very games of his youth and suffuses it with vitality, it penetrates it forever with its strength and stamps it with its mark. It is the same characteristic that is absorbed by the Jewish youth of the cold North as on the sweltering Ganges; it is the same trait that is assimilated by the youngster in Barbary as in the free land of North America, the Asian as as well as the European. Early in life his spirit becomes imbued with a sustenance which heathendom never afforded; it becomes impregnated with ideas and thoughts which paganism could not conquer and indeed barely approached. Thus, when it came to divine things, the most primitive Jewish lad was master over the most educated and thinking Greek. What the latter was not capable of grasping, was the Jew's property, a gift from heaven which he accepted unconsciously, without realizing or appreciating it fully, without recognizing its value and its difference from heathendom. This great and most unique endowment of the mind, this holy treasure was his universal possession, even as it was the people's inner flame. It was this element which formed the nation.

Thus arose the phenomenon of a people who disregarded and defied the destruction of all those factors which ordinarily are necessary to hold a people together. It was the power of God's revelation which was a spiritual seal, which produced a sharp difference of mentality, an indelible disparity of mind in the highest concepts of God, freedom, and creation. It was this power which was able to create and maintain a people for so long. This quite unique character of the mind, which reigns in the same manner and with the same strength even where peoplehood, in its ordinary significance, has been submerged and completely obliterated by another nation, has nothing whatever to do with any earthly business. It is the pure imprint of spiritual power on religious consciousness, and the expression of an ideal citizenry in extra-mundane areas. What is this most unique keynote of Judaism which has its utterly unmistakable basic color shine from the very depth, through the overlaying lacquer of local European custom? It is this: each individual member of this people, as long as he has not solemnly separated himself and voluntarily excluded himself from its community, accepts his share in that great mission of dispersion. Every member, wherever he may be, is, by the very fact of his personal existence, a part of that great, ancient missionary institution, which continues to exist under the immediate direction of that same invisible Master, who had dedicated and founded it in Mesopotamia three thousand years ago and whose first missionary was Israel's revered Patriarch, Abraham, who was its first priest as well as its first victim. One knows not how, but this missionary institution has spread all over the earth, and one can say about it what the great sovereign of Spain used to say of his realm, that the sun does not set in it. Indeed, its envoys do not receive pay, but on the contrary, more suffering; they do not achieve honors, but on the contrary, more scorn. And each individual is, *eo ipso,* a living protest against all heathendom and philosophical dogmatics.

Yet, on the part of a whole nation this entailed a resignation of great significance, which it demonstrated for millennia across the inhabited earth, from the rising of the sun to its setting, an unbelievable renunciation of all things that otherwise make life beautiful and desirable: greatness, power, and honor, indeed life itself. It entailed a voluntary endurance of a thousand and yet another thousand-year-old misery, which could not dull this nation's spirit and which could be explained only by an ever stronger counterweight, meaning and always having meant more to this people than the entire earth with all its splendors and treasures. Only the heavenly gift of a thoroughly God-filled consciousness, only the power of the truth of the one unique and holy kingdom of God could, and still can, bring about this miracle of all miracles, and will retain its power for as long as alluring earthly beauty, the seducing charms of enticing pleasures, evil corruption, and merciless violence will wield the scepter and rule the world—that is, until the arrival of the Messiah.

In conclusion I repeat: the nation-forming and preserving element of Judaism is revelation, the hope and certainty of belief which, humble or exalted, neither fears nor spurns any tribunal. In it, as an indestructible vital force, lies the eternal youth of the people, the indestructible, continued existence of the House of Judah. In this manner each individual member of this people is part of the holy covenant *only as a religious person,* since Jewish peoplehood is religion and nothing else. Thus, Judaism continues to be a great institution for the maintenance and preservation of those documentary revelations, vital, abundantly alive, a perpetually self-rejuvenating vessel. It is the problem that has existed throughout the ages, from generation to generation, the problem of a presentation by word and deed of the only true idea of God and man. It is the ever-living promise of the realization of what is to be God's kingdom on earth. Aside from ourselves, that day is awaited also by those who otherwise differ widely from us in manner and custom and who in many places still hate and torment those who, like loyal messengers, have given them the idea of God and have prepared them for its comprehension. Here, unchanged, stands the perpetually blooming old olive tree of Palestine on which the wild sprig was grafted. Here it still stands with its thousand-year-old branches and roots, spread forth into the light, reaching a thousandfold into the soil of all the kingdoms of the earth. With great patience it still endures the unbearably painful operation in order to nourish and improve with its own vital sap and vigor those wild grafted sprigs of the nations. Israel still waits at the post of honor which a wise Providence has assigned to him, until his time is fulfilled.

REVELATION AND RATIONAL JUDAISM (*Isaac Asher Francolm*)

Francolm (1788-1849) was rabbi in Königsberg and later became principal of a school in Breslau. Among his numerous works the best known was *Rational Judaism,* in which he developed a guide for modern Jews which was most moderate in its reforms. His philosophy attempted to bridge the gap between rational criticism and the traditional acceptance of the Covenant relationship—the gap which Reform Judaism still struggles to bridge adequately.

The word of God has been given unto us to enlighten us and to afford us salvation. It is as exalted as it is simple, as exultant as it is natural. It solves every secret for us; its rays fall across the earth and brighten the sky. We cannot comprehend how it was possible for Moses to behold such magnificence. We can only praise God that for our sake He found him worthy of this grace. It was a deed of divine love which we honor as a miracle. However, no change of eternal natural laws was bound up with such a miracle. The potential which was given to every human being through the original revelation came to its highest realization in Moses. Moses is the flower of mankind. We do, indeed, consider this as an act of mercy on the part of God and as a miracle, but it was an event which took place within the bounds of nature, an event which can be explained as the development of human potential. For this reason, our point of view is called *rational.*

2. THE JEWISH PEOPLE—DISPERSION AND RESTORATION

It was in the nature of Reform as a child of Enlightenment and of nineteenth century idealism, to be strongly universalistic in its religious emphasis. Israel was a people, to be sure, but it was not a "nation" like Germany or England. Jews were eager to eschew all dual loyalties and to profess their respective patriotism. The dispersion—however much tragedy and suffering it had brought in its train—was God-willed, for Israel was destined to spread His law to all men, and this could only be accomplished in the Diaspora. Prayers for the restoration of, or return to, the Land of Israel seemed, therefore, out of place. There was a straight line that led from early anti-nationalism to later anti-Zionism, but there remained within Reform also a keen sense of Jewish peoplehood and Jewish needs. This made possible the identification of other Reformers with Zionism and the eventual reintegration of the concept of restoration in the philosophic structure of the movement.

For additional selections on this subject see below, pp. 200 ff., on the observance of Tisha b 'Av.

THE JEWISH PEOPLE (*Ludwig Philippson*)

In the first number of the new magazine, *Allgemeine Zeitung des Judenthums,* which called itself a "non-partisan organ for all Jewish interests," editor Philippson began a series of articles entitled "What is Judaism?"

The first article, from which the following is excerpted, deals with the political aspects of the question.

Politically speaking, Judaism is, in its historic sweep, the miniature reflection of all mankind. It mirrors man who struggles and strives to rise from a crude and asocial condition toward the highest development of a civil free society. When Moses brought the Israelites from Egypt into the desert, they were nothing but a mass of human beings, atoms of a people and a state. In the first period they adopted all the political forms of antiquity, experienced and then abandoned them. They tried a republic with a military and afterwards a theocratic head (Judges, Eli and Samuel), a hereditary monarchy (Judah), an elective monarchy (Israel). In the second period, the time of the second Temple, they had alternatingly the overlordship of foreign powers (when they were a Persian, then a Syrian, then a Roman province), a theocracy, and finally the union of theocratic and monarchical powers in one person, limited, however, by an independent senate (the Great Assembly and the Sanhedrin).

With the dispersion of the Jews into all parts of the world and with the loss of independence and homeland, our people started anew on a political road. Once more they were thrown back into an asocial condition. They were once again a formless, non-organic, atomistic mass; they had to start once again from the bottom, for unnumbered Jews had once again been sold as slaves. It once again became necessary to rise from this lowest rung of society to the free civil level. But now it was a new world into which they entered. Their task was different. Formerly they had striven to create a nation, an independent state, but now their goal was to join other nations and reach for the highest rung of development in human society. It was the task of a new age to form a general human society which would encompass all peoples organically. In the same way, it was the task of the Jews not to create their own nation and their own state or a separate political entity, but rather to obtain from the other nations full acceptance into their society and thereby attain to participation in the general body social. This pure inner tendency, which is far from being realized in the present, is clearly recognizable. Naturally, external circumstances and conditions played an important role in this respect, because the Jews were not, as in former days, left to themselves and able to control the course of their development, but were in complete dependence on the nation in whose midst they lived. Thus the Jews stood and stand in the cross-fire of two conditions: how the other nations progressed in their political education, and how these nations related to the Jews themselves and their striving for progress.

ONLY GOD CAN END OUR DISPERSION (*Abraham Kohn*)

However much we may differ in our interpretations of the Messianic dogma and the promised redemption of Israel, the real purpose and the culmination of divine promise remains the spreading to the whole world of the knowledge of the One God and the realization of His kingdom, a kingdom of truth and love.[2] In order to hasten the fulfilment of this promise, it is our sole task to practice righteousness and virtue (Isa. 56:1). Is the restoration of Israel in the Promised Land absolutely necessary for this purpose, as was generally believed in former days? Do the so-called Messianic promises of the prophets refer to an earthly state or not? This is not easily decided from a theological point of view and may be left as a moot question to be decided by the good Lord Himself. For we ourselves not only do not *have* to do anything about changing our external condition, we *must not* do anything.[3] Despite this, our fathers never failed to pray for the restoration of a Jewish state. But one must realize that they did not know of any other salvation and had no other expectation for bettering their oppressed condition. For them, temporal and spiritual desires and hopes for each individual and for all men coincided. Is this the case for us also? Or does not he whose religion moves him to expect trustingly a political rebirth of Israel in the days to come, really have entirely different hopes for himself and his dear ones? Is he not much more concerned with the welfare of the German fatherland and the improvement of conditions for his coreligionists? Ought not, therefore, such a natural and pious wish, which we ourselves can and should help to realize, be expressed more frequently in our prayers than an expectation the fulfilment of which we must leave to God alone?

CAN WE STILL PRAY FOR RESTORATION? (*Moses Gutmann*)

One may boldly state that only the very fewest who say this [restoration] prayer really mean it. Compared to the oppressive conditions of former times, the Israelites of today rejoice in all lands in the most favorable treatment, and they hope and desire nothing more fervently than that they might soon be freed from those restrictions which are still imposed upon them, and that they might soon be admitted to full citizenship. Is it not then a great contradiction when, on the one hand, we daily implore our Heavenly Father to lead us back to a far-away land, to found there our own state; and on the other hand, implore our earthly rulers to grant us full citizenship and constantly protest our faithful devotion to, and unlimited love for, our rightful princes and our native land? To be sure, religion has precedence over all temporal concerns. If it were truly an indisputable teaching of our faith that our desires and hopes for the future must be directed exclusively toward Palestine, then indeed—if we wanted to be forthright and honest—we should renounce all expectations and hopes which we harbor concerning full citizenship in the state whose temporal members we are. But this is not so. Judaism always harbored two views about redemption. One concerned a Messiah of flesh and blood; the other was spiritual in nature, and the latter view of this important dogma rests on very

[2] Maimonides, Hilkhot Teshubah, ch. 9; Hilkhot Melakhim, ch. 12.
[3] Ket. 3a.

important pronouncements of our greatest prophets. They did not view the redemption which the Messiah was to bring as dependent on a specific country, nor even as limited to the members of the Jewish people. In the magnitude and fullness of their divine inspiration, they rose above the narrow conceptions of their contemporaries and looked to the appearance of the promised savior as a time of total human redemption, which would lift them from spiritual servitude and its concomitant physical misery to a clear understanding and knowledge of eternal truth, and bring them to a realization of the great ethical ideals on which the happiness of man in this world and his salvation in the next is dependent. For this we should pray day by day, morning and evening, in soulful and deep devotion to the Lord, the all-Holy One, for the redemption of Israel and all mankind, that great and marvelous goal toward which all teachings and all prophecies of God's anointed ones were directed. In so doing will we nourish and strengthen within us the sentiment of brotherly love toward all men who share their fate with us, but not by constant remembrance of Israel's former separateness and the less-than-forthright yearning for the restoration of this separateness, which would incur for us the accusation of pride and lack of love.

A PATRIOTISM AS GLOWING. . . . (David W. Marks)

Because of its location the West London Synagogue was often referred to as the Burton Street Synagogue. Three years after its founding it was still ostracized in the wider Jewish community. The publication of a sermon by its minister, in the new Jewish Chronicle, was considered a significant concession, and the editors felt moved to explain their repeated liberalism as follows:

"It afforded us great satisfaction to print in an early number of the Jewish Chronicle of last year, a sermon of the Rev. D. W. Marks, in which were detailed the views of our brethren of the Burton Street Synagogue with regard to ritual observances. With equal satisfaction do we now open our columns to the following sermon of the Reverend Minister, on the doctrine of the Messiah, and the restoration of Israel to the land of promise. At a time like this, when the most loose and extravagant notions obtain in Jewish Germany with regard to the Messiah and the final restoration, the sentiments of our brethren of Burton Street, in reference to these important doctrines, ought to be made known."

Brethren, from what has been advanced, it must be evident to you that the restoration of Israel is not an event about which mankind can proceed systematically, as if they were engaged in the political settlement of an ordinary state; but that it is to be accompanied by such wondrous occurrences as must totally change the physical and political relations of all the countries of the earth. This is the reply which we, as Israelites, return to all those narrow-minded men who assume that we do not regard England as our home or our country, but that we seek both in our future restoration to Judea. We hesitate not to tell such men that they grossly calumniate the disciples of Moses in charging them with entertaining such sentiments. It is true that we look to our restoration to Judea, but only at that time when the whole tone of society will be changed, and when all nations will be subjected to a system of government totally different from that which now obtains. But until that period arrives—and mark well it is to be attended by such wonders as are to eclipse the miracles of Egypt—we unequivocally declare that we neither seek nor acknowledge subjection to any land except the land of our birth. To this land we attach ourselves with a patriotism as glowing, with a devotion as fervent, and with a love as ardent and sincere as any class of our British non-Jewish fellow citizens. For the honor of this land, for its glory and independence, we all manfully stand up; and for its liberties, its constitutional rights, and its ancient bulwarks, we are prepared to contribute our means, to devote our energies, and, if necessary, to shed our blood, as cheerfully and as readily as the rest of our compatriots. When God shall be pleased, by means of a mighty moral revolution, to bring back the seed of Abraham to Judea, we shall then rejoice in our title of "a kingdom of priests and a holy nation"; and in that title we shall give glory to God in being permitted to become His instruments in bringing all mankind to acknowledge the unity of His name, and in making blessed all the families of the earth. But since this time is in the hands of God, and since we take no account of it in our relations to countries and to mankind; and further, since we act as men amongst men, and as citizens amongst citizens, we boldly claim every right of humanity and every privilege of citizenship, because we are prepared, both as Jews and as Englishmen, to discharge all the duties which these rights confer, with honor and fidelity.

3. THE MISSION OF ISRAEL

Reform's emphasis on the universal character of Judaism brought in its train a re-formation of Israel's destiny. To bring all nations to the house of God, to lead them in their climb to higher moral standards, to bring about peace and brotherhood—these were the goals which Reform leaders saw for their people. Israel was the leaven of mankind, its mentor in religion and ethics. It was a grand mission which was to be accomplished not by conversion but by example, a mission which could be fulfilled only in dispersion.

THIS IS OUR TASK (*Samuel Holdheim*)

It is the destiny of Judaism to pour the light of its thoughts, the fire of its sentiments, the fervor of its feelings upon all souls and hearts on earth. Then all
of these peoples and nations, each according to its soil and historic characteristics, will, by accepting our teachings, kindle their own lights, which will
then shine independently and warm their souls. Judaism shall be the seed-bed
of the nations filled with the blessing and promise, but not a fully grown
matured tree with roots and trunk, crowned with branches and twigs, with
blossoms and fruit—a tree which is merely to be transplanted into a foreign soil.

Already 2,000 years ago Judaism began to face its historic task and in this
manner it must continue to face it. All these unnumbered peoples and nations
which were once governed by paganism were converted to ways of thinking which are based—who can deny it—upon the principles of ancient Judaism,
which gave them their singular color and form. A forced egalitarianism, which
desires that all peoples of the earth should express their innermost thoughts
and feelings with the same words, is neither the task nor the content of
Judaism. From the beginning it expressed its decisive disapproval of the
building of the tower of Babel, that is to say, of the desire to bind men to a
single tongue and a single mode of speech and to extinguish their individuality
and singularity. Judaism wants to purify the languages of the nations, but
leave to each people its own tongue. It wishes for one heart and one soul, but
not for one sound and one tone. It does not desire to destroy the particular
characteristics of the nations. It does not wish to stultify the directions of spirit
and sentiment which their history has brought forth. It does not wish that all
should be absorbed and encompassed by the characteristics of the Jewish people. Least of all does it wish to extinguish the characteristics of the Jewish
people and to eliminate those expressions of the living spirit which were created
through the union and spirit of the Jewish faith.

As a mere philosophical idea, denuded of its historic characteristics and
forms, Judaism can never become the common property of mankind. Our
ancient Jewish sages correctly understood this important question of the relationship of Judaism to mankind and expressed it felicitously, even though
they had a much more limited view concerning that which should be the
norm for the internal aspects of our faith. Regarding the peoples of the earth,
they spoke of the seven Noahidic duties, the fundamental rules of faith and
morals, but reserved the whole Mosaic law for Israel exclusively. We must
spread the Noahidic laws to all nations, but we must safeguard the Torah as
our exclusive possession. To be sure, we do not follow the letter of our sages'
pronouncements slavishly, yet we must not fail to acknowledge their spiritual
meaning and substance. Translating their words into our more purified expression, we would say: "It is the Messianic task of Israel to make the pure
knowledge of God and the pure law of morality of Judaism the common
possession and blessing of all the peoples of the earth. We do not expect of
the nations that, by accepting these teachings, they would give up their historic
characteristics in order to accept those of our people; and, similarly, we shall

not permit the Jewish people to give up its innate holy powers and sentiments so that it might be assimilated amongst the nations."

Thus, my friends, we shall safeguard our position internally and externally. What the ancient sages called the seven Noahidic duties in their universal human application, we now call the Jewish idea of God and the Jewish ethical *Weltanschauung*. When they considered the whole Mosaic ceremonial law as the eternal and exclusive heritage of Israel, we call it the inextinguishable historic characteristic of the Jewish people, the singular spiritual life of Judaism.

This, then, is our task: to maintain Judaism within the Jewish people and at the same time to spread Judaism amongst the nations; to protect the sense of Jewish unity and life and faith without diminishing the sense of unity with all men; to nourish the love for Judaism without diminishing the love of man. We pray that God may give us further strength to search out the way of truth and not to stray from the path of love!

ISRAEL'S DESTINY (*From the Prayer Book of the Berlin Reform Association*)

Holdheim was the Association's first rabbi, and the following prayer was most likely his work.

Unfathomable is Thy wisdom, O God, unsearchable Thy counsels, incomprehensible Thy decrees. Thou guardest all Thy creatures; Thine eye rests upon all Thy children, and from Thine unreachable heights Thou pointest and clearest a path for the sons of earth. In Thy hand rests the fate of peoples and nations, and from the beginning Thou didst know and see the goal toward which at the end of time Thou wilt lead mankind.

Therefore, O God, grant that we may come to know Thy divine task by the way in which Thou didst lead Israel among the peoples of the earth; by the fate which Thou didst decree for those who acknowledged Thy name in the course of the millennia. Make us firm and unswerving in our confidence in Thee and Thy wisdom, so that we may courageously look upon the path which Thou hast stretched out before us and our children for the days which are yet to come.

O God, to one only amongst the thousands who walked in darkness didst Thou give the vision to see the light of Thy knowledge; to the one who strove after virtue and who surrendered to Thy fatherly will with confidence. Our father Abraham was a light in the desert, a light which no eye beheld and which no mortal's foot did follow—and yet this light was never extinguished; for from generation to generation it was transmitted and faithfully guarded, a sacred possession of the people whom Thou didst raise from the loins of that just man.

To be sure, Thy light was darkened; it threatened to go out forever when the descendants of Abraham languished under Egypt's yoke of slavery, but

Thou didst bring them from servitude to freedom; and to the liberated people who saw Thine omnipotence so visibly displayed, Thou didst reveal Thyself anew. Brighter and purer and more radiant did the torch of Thy knowledge shine, borne by the loyal servant Moses before the wandering people into the land of promise.

There it stood, tall and erect, on Mount Zion, the Temple of worship dedicated to Thee, who didst reveal Thyself as the One invisible, and infinite. Into its halls flocked the sons and daughters of Thy people, making supplication to Thee and professing Thy holy name. Tall and erect stood the lamp of Thy knowledge in Jerusalem and in Israel, but a dark, impenetrable night hovered about its borders, and no ray of Thy light reached the nations all around.

But behold! The Temple's mighty edifice crumbles, the columns break asunder which bear its dome, for Thy hand, O God, has dashed them in pieces, Thine arms have shattered them and torn down the walls of Jerusalem. With lamentations the sons of Israel now went forth into distant desolation, and at the rivers of Babylon they sat and wept. And when once more they returned to the place of Thy Temple, to build it anew, Thy right hand again took them up and dispersed them over the whole globe, as far away as the sun casts its rays.

And now? Have we sinned so grievously, O gracious God, that Thou didst banish us without recall? Have we sunk so low, O God of mercy, that Thou wilt leave us forever? For derision has mounted upon our shoulders to mock us in our disgrace; the heel of hatred has pressed upon our backs to relish our woe; and contempt has lain about our feet to drag us into the dust. Oh, how heavy did Thy hand, O God, lie upon our heads! But Thou dost not forsake us; Thou hast never forsaken us. No! Thou hast called us, O Lord, to found the kingdom of truth and love on the whole earth. And for this Thou didst disperse us, so that the sparks of Thy light might fly to all nations, to dispel the darkness of delusion from the farthest corners of the globe. For this Thou didst surrender us to bitter persecution, so that their pride might consume itself before our humility; so that their hatred destroy itself before our confidence in Thee; so that their faithlessness perish before our faith. And lo! Love has flowered where hatred was sown; light has come where darkness dwelt. The sun of knowledge is rising over the earth, and they who carry Thy name among the nations stand erect, and Thy praise resounds more loudly and audibly in the ears of the sons of men.

Marvelous are Thy ways, O God; incomprehensible are the decrees of Thy wisdom. Lead us, O Lord, according to Thy will, for Thou hast again taken hold of us and hast again put the torch of Thy light into our hand. Show us the way that we stray not, make even our path that we stumble not, and grant that the realm of Thy knowledge increase in strength, and the realm of Thy love expand for the blessing of all mankind.

ISRAEL'S POSITION IN PAST, PRESENT, AND FUTURE (*Häster's Reader*)

The following is taken from a widely used nineteenth century textbook for Jewish parochial schools in Germany.

Eighteen centuries have passed since Israel's dispersion, and they could change neither its nature nor its religion. Despite all attempts to annihilate it, it maintained itself with astonishing force before the might of unfeeling tyrants. But now the chain of suffering is broken, and out of the confusion and tumult of former ages the stars of freedom shine once more. The ridiculous prejudice against the Jews has largely been buried. The vicious nonsense of darker days has lost its passing value for all privileged classes, while we still walk before the Lord of our fathers—Abraham, Isaac, and Jacob—and we shall do so as long as the earth will circle around the sun. Therefore, we neither fear nor tremble when the earth is rocked to its foundations and the mountains tremble, for the guardian of Israel sleeps not and neither does He slumber; and heaven and earth may pass away, but the word of the Lord will stand forever.

But woe unto us if in the full use of our liberties our heart turns away from the exalted God in heaven; woe unto us if we pay for our higher and larger knowledge with our hearts. Increase in knowledge and decrease in morality is more decrease than increase. Indeed, woe unto us if a reform of our hearts does not go along with the reform of religious life which people are now seeking. Culture without religiosity, enlightenment without piety and without a sacred enthusiasm for the honor of Israel and for the maintenance of our faith, would debase us into people who do not know who they are and what they ought to be. The Jew of the present, finding himself on the eve of undoubted religious changes, looks wonderingly at the religious horizon and searches it intently to see what a good star and the future hold for him. With calm confidence we may look into this future, as long as we are conscious of the priestly vocation of Israel, which demands that we should lead all mankind to advance in morality, humility, love of man, and true worship of God, so that Israel might be as a lighthouse for all who seek truth, near and far, a refuge for all who are ready to suffer for the sake of virtue. That is Israel's vocation and it is the desire of Providence that we should fulfil this destiny.

When thus Israel will place itself under the banner of God, then today and evermore will it be covered by His pinions. Then will it find the courage to remove completely the many obstacles which still stand in the way. Then it will be able to suffer, to bear, and to raise itself above earth, time, and space. Then all of mankind will sink into its arms to thank Israel for sharing the exaltation of Sinai's light. Then mankind will requite the iniquities of former days and "the whole earth will be full of the knowledge of God as the waters cover the sea."

THE CAPITAL OF THE WORLD (*Ludwig Philippson*)
(Comment on Isaiah ch. 60)

Babylonia had fallen. Cyrus had given permission for the return to the Holy Land. Now the main objective was to make that return as imposing as possible and to assemble an ever greater number of Israelites for that purpose. The prophet effects this by proclaiming the glory of the future Jerusalem. It is at this point that his entire world concept meets with specific temporal goals. To him, the restoration of Jerusalem for its own sake has more than national significance, just as he does not expect future greatness merely for nor from Israel itself. He is much more concerned with the true restoration of the new higher calling of Israel, to serve all mankind as focal point for the knowledge and worship of the one and only God. All nations will recognize Him; they will worship Jerusalem as the site of His revelation and adoration; they will seek it out and will adorn it. Thus he no longer views Israel's purpose as an end in itself, but far beyond that, as involved in all mankind. Likewise, the significance of Jerusalem is broadened from the capital of its nation to the capital of the whole world. This is the basic idea of the sermon in question, which mirrors the whole characteristic uniqueness of this prophet, the combination of noblest ideas and warmest tenderness of expression. Regardless of whether the prophet has seen Jerusalem's splendor and greatness as imminent or in the distant future—for which, however, the intended return of the captive Israelites was the necessary point of departure—his proclamation, notwithstanding the ruins into which Jerusalem has fallen once more and despite the misery in which it still exists, has come true and will increasingly be proven true.

A thousand years after the situation which the prophet discusses one could already see the West wandering to Jerusalem, piously worshipping and hallowing each foot of earth; another five hundred years later, Orient and Occident fought the bloodiest wars for the possession of this tiny patch of earth, for they all regarded Zion as holy, the focal point of religious knowledge. Today, more than ever, the nations' eyes are turned toward that place, and he is short-sighted who would deny that Jerusalem still has a great future. But even aside from the external locale, note this: in the midst of a captive, humiliated Israel, under the impact of horrible battles of powerful Asiatic nations, a prophet arises who proclaims that the religion of Israel will gather the nations to its banner, that it will penetrate and rule the world of man, that its recognition and effect will spread over the entire earth. How astonishing, indeed gigantic, is this phenomenon, yet the millenia have served to demonstrate its truth more and more. Christianity and Islam are the modifications of this religion for Occident and Orient, but as time goes on, these modifications come increasingly nearer to the original teaching of God.

4. THE MESSIAH

At first, the traditional Jewish idea of the personal Messiah continued as an integral element of Reform teaching. In the selections which follow, Gutmann defends the doctrine of the Messiah against the position of the Frankfort radicals (see above, p. 50), while Stein already believes that the idea is no longer relevant to Judaism. In time most Reformers gave up the concept of a personal Messiah. Instead, they believed in a Messianic age which mankind itself would achieve by its forward development. The Messiah might never come, but Israel would soon lead all men into this blessed era.

A THREAD THROUGH ALL OUR SCRIPTURES (*Moses Gutmann*)

As regards the third point in your statement, concerning the expectation of a Messiah and the hope of a return to Palestine, there is good reason to assume that such a belief exists but in the hearts of a very few Israelites, that is, the faith and hope that some day God will send a special person who will lead all Israelites back to Palestine, there to build an independent state of their own. The majority, including you, recognize no other fatherland than the country to which they belong by birth and civil circumstances. But even the manner in which you treat and dismiss this article in your explanation illustrates quite clearly your negative attitude. Thus, your intended reform could not be called anything but an undermining of the honored edifice of the Mosaic religion. To be sure, we, too, neither expect nor do we wish for a Messiah to lead us back to Palestine. However, the promise of a Messiah—a redeemer from bodily suffering and spiritual slavery—this concept runs like a thread through all the books of our Holy Scripture. It carries with it our most glorious and cherished hopes, and we shall not permit any decree to rob us of this sacred belief. It is woven into the inner fabric of our faith, and our religion would lose its supreme ornament if these hopes were to be torn from us. As much as any other belief or teaching, the Messianic promises have their firm foundation in the revealed word of God Himself, and every orthodox[4] Israelite feels obligated to live or die by it.

However, we do not interpret those promises in a narrow, particularistic sense, which would have the Messiah redeem only Israel and grant it the power to rule over the rest of the world; no, indeed; we base our hope mainly on the sayings of the God-chosen prophets, in which the Messiah is assigned an infinitely greater, nobler role, namely, the salvation and redemption of all mankind, the union of all nations into one peaceful realm, to serve their one true God. The first and best means by which the Kingdom of God can be brought about is, in our view, precisely the pure and unadulterated teaching of the Almighty. The more power and influence it gains amongst ourselves, the closer will we approach the fervently awaited moment of salvation. Therefore, we must earnestly reject any attempt which is calculated to lead us away from the pure teaching of God. We feel we must label your intended Reform Association as precisely such an attempt.

THE MESSIAH IN JUDAISM AND CHRISTIANITY (*Leopold Stein*)

Stein (1810-1882) was among the early leaders of the rabbinic conferences and chaired the second assembly, held in Frankfort in 1845. A prolific scholar, poet, and dramatist, he attempted a chef d'oeuvre which he intended as a Guide for Jews (see below, p. 260).

---

[4] (Ed. note) The writer uses the word "rechtgläubig," denoting "traditionally right-thinking" or orthodox in the non-technical, pre-modern usage of the term.

In the intellectual communication of people and nations, few circumstances have produced a greater confusion than the usage of foreign words which one people or one era transmits to another. It is the same sound but it has acquired different meaning. This is particularly true in the religious field, where the foreign word can so easily become the vessel for an entirely new content. What is the original meaning of "Messiah," *mashiah* in Hebrew? Nothing else but "anointed," a word which is used in biblical writings for "king," since he, like priest and prophet, was anointed with holy anointing oil. And what has the term Messiah come to mean later? It became an infinitely flexible word, wherein an entire new religion found shelter. That word, which already among the Jews had an uncertain meaning, passed afterwards through still another language, Greek, whose foreign frame helped to cover the original concept completely. In Greek, the anointed one is called "Christos," and therefore Christianity means—but in an entirely new sense—"Religion of the Messiah," "Teaching of the Messiah-Redeemer." It is based on him; it stands and falls with him.

It is usually assumed that the main difference between Judaism and Christianity is that for Christianity the Messiah has already come, while Judaism teaches that he is still being awaited. The truth, however, is that the contrast is quite different and goes much deeper, distinguishing the two religions in their innermost structures, in their basic approaches to life. Judaism is the teaching of God, Christianity is the teaching of the Messiah. Take away the person of Messiah from the Messianic religion, and religion itself is taken away with it; but take away the person of the Messiah from the religion of God, and religion does not only remain firm but it becomes even firmer; for, since it is not dependent on any prop, it stands revealed in itself, in God. In Christianity, the Redeemer becomes God; in Judaism, God becomes the Redeemer. "Our Redeemer, the Lord of the Universe is His name!"

This is a biblical viewpoint. In the twenty-four books of Scripture there is nowhere any mention of a Messiah-Redeemer. Where, above all, should it be mentioned, if not in Moses' own writings, specifically in the passages where he speaks of the gloomy, and then again of the bright, future of his people? But nowhere is there the slightest indication!

In the other biblical writings, where the term *mashiah* occurs quite frequently, it is always used only in reference to a worldly king, so that even the heathen Cyrus was honored with this designation. However, this term never occurs in the meaning of a future redeemer and restorer. The same is true of the term "Savior" (*go'el*); that term is not used anywhere to describe an envoy, but rather everywhere refers only to God Himself. Thus, we may pronounce with full biblical conviction that the personal Messiah has no foundation in our Holy Scriptures, and whatever mention is made of David's descendant is, as was stated earlier, allegory, figurative speech, as indeed it says: "My servant David shall be king over them," or: "I send you the prophet Elijah," without anyone assuming that David and Elijah will really ever return. The King-Redeemer-Messiah is of very late origin; he does not even appear in the writings which lie between Bible and Talmud and which are designated as Apocrypha. Now, while we show our respect to some later *forms* of worship service, though they may not appear in the Bible, we must categorically deny recognition to later *dogmas,* which are not founded in the Bible; otherwise, there would be no protection against error. In the outward description of religious life, the Talmud represents a historically significant period which we must not deny and to which we must, indeed, grant its temporal justification. However, we must be most careful in regard to the Talmud when it comes to its dogmas. These can claim no obedience whatever, for Aggada has no influence on Halakhah. And the Messiah doctrine is merely the product of the talmudic period; it is exclusively a result of a desire for national restoration gone astray.

This is the same sad situation into which the Christian teaching inevitably had to fall, as was demonstrated on innumerable other occasions. Christianity took up the viewpoint of talmudic times and felt compelled to defend it as its basic religious principle. Thus, religious research has a much wider field in Judaism, since it can confront the talmudic views with equal authority, while the Christian scholar sees himself opposed to the basic constituent parts of his evangelical books. Early Christianity, however, could not avoid following the then fashionable expectations and contemporary idioms. At that time, all hopes among the deeply humbled people were set on a restorer; all salvation for a renewal of the old stately glory was expected from him, the "redeemer," the liberator from tyrannical oppression. He was the last sheet-anchor of the shipwrecked Jewish state. Thus, the new dogma inevitably had to make use of the ancient word to which it gave an entirely different meaning; it used the old frame, investing it with completely new content. In this manner, a word which was misunderstood and was completely estranged from its original meaning had created a religion. And this religion, in turn, precisely because of its absolutely new content, was supposed to shape a totally new world which would help, under God's miraculous guidance, to lead paganism on a millenia-long, circuitous journey toward a future religion of monotheism and unity of nations.

5. JUDAISM AND CHRISTIANITY

Mendelssohn had begun the great debate with Christianity which lasted well into the middle of the nineteenth century. While no startling insights emerged from the discussion, two matters must be kept in mind. One, the element of apology, which was present in earlier days (and in part again later on), was almost totally absent during the main period under consideration in this volume. The Reformers presented a Judaism which was spiritually superior to its rival. Second, the subject matter itself (and especially the figure of Jesus), which had been taboo in Jewish circles, now became familiar and acceptable for discussion.

JESUS AND JUDAISM (*Leopold Stein*)

Did Jesus actually wish to found a new religion? By no means! "Hear, O Israel" is the most important word from his mouth. Had he declared himself a god, he, who so expressly and exclusively proclaimed himself a teacher for Israel, could never have harbored the faintest semblance of hope to find even the least support from his people, who adhered so undividedly to strictest monotheism and who rejected and repudiated so categorically any and all concepts of God's own embodiment and physical manifestation. They would not have persecuted this as heresy, but rather ridiculed it as madness. Indeed, strangely enough, talmudic law declares that whoever invites Israelites to idolatry merits death; but this does not apply to one who pretends to be God. "For they will say: how is he different from us? And his assertion will be met with laughter."[5]

Or did Jesus wish to declare the Mosaic law as abolished or perhaps even, as Paul so categorically stresses, to declare it to be a degrading sign of slavery? Not at all! He himself, as well as his disciples, adhered to it, and Peter would not have had to wait for a sign from heaven in regard to a violation of the dietary laws had his master abolished that law.[6] In fact, Peter claims emphatically at that point that he had formerly never violated the dietary laws —and that was after Jesus' death. No! Jesus states categorically: "Heaven and earth shall perish rather than that the smallest letter or tittle of the law be abolished." In regard to his mission, he says: "You must not think that I have come to abolish the law or the prophets. I have not come to abolish, but on the contrary, I have come to fulfil."

What then did he want? While isolated passages, taken out of context from the speeches ascribed to him, indeed offered hints to the subsequent founders of the dogma of the divinity of Jesus, nevertheless, the general impression we gain from those reports give us the certainty that Jesus grieved over the sad religious conditions of his people and, indignant over the degeneration of the two large religious parties, aspired to nothing else than a purification of religious life among the Jews. That is why to the Sadducees he so emphatically stressed the teaching of eternal life, while to the Pharisees he emphasized the importance of observing the divine moral law. Thus he did not wish to abolish the Mosaic law, but indeed he wanted to fulfil it, that is, restore it in its purity.[7]

Indeed, he even honors the pronouncements of the sages, making manifest use of their magnificent sayings and allegorical speeches in his parables, which can nearly all be traced back to talmudic sources. But he fights against hy-

[5] Sanh. 61b.

[6] Apostles 10:11.

[7] We shall later on examine closely those contrasts to the Mosaic commandments which so sharply stand out in Matthew's sermon on the mount, particularly the one which so unjustly slanders Judaism, saying that the Mosaic law commands: "Thou shalt love thy neighbor and hate thine enemy." All those contradictions rest on false premises, and are certainly not by Jesus. Strangely enough, the sermon related by Luke (6:20 ff.) repeats the main ideas of the sermon on the mount, without mentioning the attacks on the Mosaic law.

pocrisy and Pharisaic arrogance, against the display of the broad phylacteries, the long *tsitsit,* against outward sanctimoniousness along with inner depravity —a zeal already displayed by the prophets, and which men of truth will display at all times. The Talmud itself criticizes this type of Pharisaism most severely.[8]

Paulinic Christianity

After Jesus was rejected and disavowed by his coreligionists both as Messiah and religious reformer, there could remain no doubt that he, as well as his name and his teaching, would soon have vanished completely, had his disciples continued the interpretation which Jesus himself had pronounced in regard to his mission, and had they been satisfied to preach only to the deaf ears in Israel. Paul above all others—and, in the beginning, in contrast to many— grasped this dilemma. He was a rare man, of tremendous spirit and of most resolute will power. He was, indeed, the true founder of Christianity.

It appeared clear and absolutely necessary to Paul that the new teaching had to be brought to the heathens. For that purpose, however, two stirring concepts were needed as tools. Both were the exclusive invention of this ingenious mind, familiar with all the twists and turns of the Talmud. One was negative and the other positive. *The old law had to be suspended; a new law had to be founded and formed.* Both events occurred through the untiring zeal of this extraordinary and energetic man, who went about with deep seriousness, making his view known everywhere in person or in writing—in Rome, in Greece, in Asia Minor, in Judea.

Thus, while Jesus had everywhere shown respect for the Mosaic law, indeed had practiced it himself, it was now dragged through the dust,[9] branded with the disgrace of slavery,[10] and its adherents, stigmatized as "sons of the maid servant," were literally banished from the house of Abraham.[11] Jesus did not wish to be a god, but now he was made into one, and the belief in him was decreed as an essential condition for salvation. To be sure, in Paul there is not yet any mention of trinity, but the divinity of the "son" is being taught unequivocally,[12] and since this "son" had appeared in the form a visible godman, the transition from paganism was thereby facilitated considerably.

For a long time, indeed, the early Christian world opposed the "worship of images," so as not to infringe upon the spirituality of the new teaching. However, almost as a natural consequence, imagery had to triumph at last—with one extraordinarily strange difference from ancient paganism. Instead of using the art of sculpture, which the heathens used almost exclusively for religious purposes, it was the art of painting which prevailed for religious presentation in the Christianity of the Middle Ages. First of all, painting does not throw

[8] Sota 22b.
[9] Phil. 3:8.
[10] Gal. 5:1, and elsewhere.
[11] *Ibid.* 4:30.
[12] Rom. 9:5.

into bold relief any forms,[13] and secondly, its lively colors were doubly suitable, for they served the mediating mission of Christianity by affording physical perception to a teaching which greatly relied on the passion of the power of imagination.

Thus the single curtain was torn which shielded teaching and law; indeed, the tear was completed in two ways: the old law was abolished and, instead, a new God had appeared. Thereby, however—and after a long and necessary interruption we return to our main subject—a division in God's holy, unique being itself was created. The "Father" was stern ruling justice; the "Son" represented tender, conciliatory love. So unfatherly, so stern and harsh does this justice appear that this God demands as atonement not merely the blood of animals, but indeed the blood of a man—a concept which even the pagan Greeks had overcome.[14] In our religion it had at once been abolished forever as soon as monotheism, through Abraham, began its journey from the horrible religious realms of the Orient to the friendlier ones of the Occident. Hence the fine symbolic narrative of "Isaac's sacrifice." Indeed, in Christianity the angry God not only demands the blood of a man, but indeed claims the blood of his own son! Is this not the God of vengeance in His most terrifying appearance? Thus Christianity brought the antiquated and obsolete sacrificial cult once more to the very center of its teachings.

Therefore, the basic principle of Christianity does not represent any progress; but on the contrary, in order to find the way to convert the pagans who were lagging behind Judaism, it had to make a large step backward. It assumed an outdated viewpoint at the very time when, as the Temple collapsed, the synagogue took over a loftier task, smoothing the way for worshiping God without sacrifices, "worshiping Him only in spirit and in truth."

Thus, Judaism has the right and obligation to reject as false the new concepts of the Christian teaching according to which God does not appear as one and the same self-contained Being. It must proclaim a monotheism which, forever immutable, reveals itself so gloriously in the teaching of the two opposites, justice and mercy. This is the only true teaching. For this is the only true "dogma of atonement": the contrast between justice and mercy achieves its blessed harmony in God and through Him, in ourselves.

JUDAISM AND CHRISTIANITY *(Sigismund Stern)*

Our study of Christianity and its development shows us that indeed it has no right to consider itself as that higher development of Judaism through which the latter lost its claim to independent continuity. On the other hand, Christianity is perhaps called to do its work in the name of Judaism. For to be sure, through its activities the external might of paganism has been broken, but pagan elements and forms have found refuge in Christianity and through it have been kept alive. And, while Christianity has succeeded in freeing religion

[13] This differentiation occurs already in talmudic Judaism in regard to pictures which are made not for idolatry, but merely as ornaments. Statues and sculptures are forbidden, paintings are permitted. Maimonides on Idolatry 3:10.

[14] See the story of the rescue of Iphigenia.

from the fetters of national separatism, it has not as yet been able to bring itself to recognize the equality of all men before God. Judaism had to consider Christianity an apostate son until such time when, in the period of the Reformation, the latter turned to a struggle against those pagan elements which in its defeat of paganism Christianity had absorbed into its own system. Judaism will gladly stretch out its hand to the prodigal son and value and recognize the true significance of the work which he has achieved.

The first and most significant step which Judaism must take is the recognition of Christianity as a religion which has its necessary and historically valid existence outside of Judaism. As soon as Judaism recognizes the existence of another religion, outside of itself, as a necessary and valid one, it admits at the same time its own inability to fulfil the religious needs of all people by itself and completely, as long as it occupies its present rung of development. Therefore, it will find itself urged to reach a higher level, where it will be closer to that goal which until now it has been unable to reach. It will have to make an effort to come to know those elements of its sister religion through which the latter has been enabled to do what Judaism was incapable of achieving. It will have to ask whether it is not also called to make these elements its own, so that thereby the circle of its influence be widened. On the other hand, Judaism will also become conscious of that singularity of its own character which, vis-à-vis Christianity, gives it its unique significance and necessitates its own existence. It will, therefore, guard and develop these unique aspects with special care. The recognition of one religion by another should be of salutary significance as long as it can be mutual, for only then an ethical relationship between the two will be possible, just as it exists presently between various states and between individual persons. Then religions, too, will be able to devote their various powers for common purposes.

I hope that Judaism will here take the first step, just as the earliest manifestation of a higher knowledge of God first appeared here. In the same way its relation to Christianity can hew out a new path for a common effectiveness of religion. May Judaism acknowledge its awareness of the fact that in its present form its own perfection has not been reached and thereby exhibit its desire to reach an ever higher rung of perfection, so that the highest may be reached in the end.

This recognition of Christianity by Judaism implies the insight that in its final destiny the latter would be congruent with Christianity, although Judaism must presently pursue a different task. In its appearance Judaism is different, yet in its true character the same. The recognition also implies the admission of a special historic relationship in which Judaism and Christianity stand one to the other. Christianity is not a foreign branch grafted upon Judaism's trunk, but rather a trunk which came from its own or, at most, from common roots. Christianity is not an apostasy from original Judaism, but rather a development, if but a one-sided and preparatory one. The final aim of Christianity is not the destruction but the realization of the knowledge of God with which Judaism first came to mankind.

Thus, Judaism and Christianity must hold out a brotherly hand to each other, for the sake of their common work for mankind. And when that is done, no one will be able to say whose work it was. As long as you can still distinguish one branch from the other, you will know that it is still winter and that you cannot expect any fruit from the precious tree.

Would this recognition of Christianity by Judaism become part of the latter's code; would it be publicly proclaimed in the synagogue? Would anywhere a monument be erected to the newly compacted peace? No. The believers will write it upon the tablets of their hearts. They must love their Christian fellow men, not merely as fellow human beings, but feel related to them in faith and bound to them with special ties. Their deeds of brotherly love will be the messengers which proclaim the new law in both church and synagogue. The monument of peace will be the common works which Jew and Christian do together, and these will be for later generations a sign of the new covenant.

But will Christianity on its part meet us with like recognition? Would our rapprochement lead to unified striving and working together if we do not find a like sentiment on the other side? This question should not move us from our conviction and decision, even if it is to be answered negatively; for neither may an individual make the fulfilment of his ethical obligations dependent on the attitude of others.

THE INFLUENCE OF CHRISTIANITY ON JUDAISM (*Solomon Formstecher*)

Formstecher (1808-1889), a native of Offenbach, served his home town as rabbi for over fifty years. He participated in the Reform rabbinical conferences (1844-46) and was best known for his philosophical work, *Religion des Geistes,* which stressed the universal elements in Judaism.

The internal and external character of Judaism is conditioned by its own world-concept and by that of its environment. Therefore, its distinctiveness has one coloration amidst heathendom, another amidst Islam, and another yet in the midst of Christianity.

The presence of an overwhelming mass of heathens in mankind demands that, in order to accomplish its missionary task, Christianity accept various pagan elements as essential parts of its system, thus setting itself in contrast to Judaism. This mutual relationship takes on a variety of aspects, depending on the course and the aspirations of Christianity. There are two main tendencies by which the various movements of present-day Christian life may be characterized. In the first place, there is the movement from the periphery of Christianity into heathendom; and secondly, the movement within the periphery of Christianity itself, from the pagan to the Jewish element.

The first tendency finds its task in the conquest of actual heathendom; it considers Christianity as perfect and final, recognizing in its amalgamation of the pagan with the Jewish elements its own unique Christian nature, which will always constitute a contrast to Judaism. The second tendency is a rising of the spirit from the pagan into the Jewish sphere within Christianity itself.

It affords Christianity a course of development dependent on varying world concepts and ascribing to it an inner perfectibility. Nevertheless, Christianity quite inconsistently considers this tendency, too, as incompatible with Judaism. Both tendencies appear in the Catholic as well as in the Protestant churches and in all the other sects, with the one or the other predominating. Hence, Christianity should be classified according to these two trends, if the prevailing relationship between it and Judaism is to be appreciated.

The first, primarily a movement to convert the heathens, is in its aspirations even farther from its goal than the second, since it still has to overcome some rudimentary obstacles. The latter merely follows an already hewn-out path. However, even the first tendency does not find the objects of its activity exclusively in far-away India; indeed, in Europe, too, Christianity finds itself often reduced to the necessity of starting its education with fundamentals, thus showing both tendencies next to each other and closely entwined. The predominance of one or the other tendency influences the character of Christianity, which in turn affects Judaism, thus indirectly influencing the shaping of Judaism itself.

Now, where Christianity declares itself as stabilized and regards as permanently essential all those procedures which it required because of its passage through heathendom; where it struggles to maintain its medieval appearance and position in mankind and, despite the objective progress it has made, subjectively resists all change—where this occurs Judaism, too, will follow. It, too, will demand that its followers enfold themselves in separatistic forms, isolate themselves through manner and custom, banish from life anything that has a Christian appearance, thus even turning away from the arts and sciences, showing in their entire way of thinking and in their actions that they consider themselves as outsiders in Christendom.

However, where Christianity admits that it has progressed in its thinking and action under the guidance of and along with progressive ideas; that, in its very inception, it had included local and temporal influences in the mass of its teachings; that, in its passing through heathendom, it had absorbed foreign matter into its organism; and that the more it approaches true selfhood, the more it will have to eliminate all unessential and foreign matter—where and when Christianity will come to this realization and will endeavor to represent it in day-to-day living, then Judaism, too, will adopt a freer form. Then it, too, without endangering its very existence, will step forward from its isolated position and in its way of thinking and acting will accept the present within the limits of its own essential, basic structure. Then it, too, will show by its way of life how it strives for an ever-clearer comprehension of the difference between absolute and relative truths.

Judaism's own world concept, combined with that of its environment—these are the two factors which produce its character in any given region of the earth, at any given time. These are the two elements which are in conflict through the entire history of Judaism: the ancient and the modern, the pagan and the Jewish. Both are mutually interdependent; both gave Judaism its relative character and its temporal position in mankind, and both determine the demands of Judaism in relationship to itself and its environment.

CHAPTER
VII

Worship Reform

∙∙∙

GREAT movements often receive their impetus from relatively insignificant events. Reform was a sweeping ideological revolution against the intellectual and emotional rigidity of tradition; it was a child both of eighteenth century rationalism and nineteenth century idealism, and the industrial and political revolutions of the age were godparents at its birth. But the earliest outward stirrings of Reform were modest indeed—at least, judged by today's standards. They were worship reforms and dealt at first with such subjects as the introduction of a sermon in the language of the land, with the admissibility of the vernacular in the service, with music and confirmation, with the elimination of certain late accretions, like cumbersome, hard-to-understand poetry, and the like. Each of these reforms was bitterly opposed and, since the average Jew was directly affected by these controversies, the battle soon embraced all Western Jewish communities. Worship reform was not the heart of Reform, but it became the index of its growth and served as the visible focus of its adherents.

1. CHANGING THE PRAYER BOOK

THE LITURGY MUST BE CLEANSED (*Aaron Chorin*)

Chorin first published his views during the Hamburg Temple controversy of 1818-19 (see above, p. 32).

Question: Is it permitted to cleanse our liturgy from the additions which have crept in by the bye?

Answer: Prayers are generally divided into two categories:

1. Prayers which are said daily, and these again fall into two subdivisions: obligatory prayers (like the *Shema* or the *Shemone Essre*) and hymns of praise and song (*Pesuḳe dezimra*).

2. The so-called *Yotsrot, Kerobets,* and *Piyutim,* which are to be said on Sabbath and holy days.

As concerns obligatory prayers, there can be no question: these have not "crept in," they originated with the Men of the Great Assembly and should not be changed in either content or language. High antiquity has given them a place of respect; they are surrounded by an aura with which one would not easily dare to tamper. And while our tradition permits the saying of the *Shema* and *Shemone Essre* in any language which one understands, nonetheless, the congregations which have for some time instituted an improved ritual did not try to have these two obligatory prayers said in German. Whatever they felt necessary to change they confined to external form, to the manner in which these prayers were spoken until now. They banned indecent swinging to and fro, swaying from one side to the other, irreverent screeching, senseless facial contortions, all of which were formerly customary during prayers. The cantor alone, in a reverent manner, chants these prayers with prayerful dignity, and the congregation silently and reverently repeats every word.

It is an entirely different matter when it comes to the *Pesuḳe dezimra* (the hymns of thanks and praise). These were assembled from Psalms and other less famous poetry and have grown into a voluminous book, and they deserve the cutting knife of the winegrower who labors in God's vineyard. . . . The heart of the reverent Israelite, however warm in its devotion when he approaches the temple, must become cool as the litany wears on for hours. In the Ethics of the Fathers (ch. 2) it says: "Do not make your prayer a routine." All later rabbis agreed with the maxim: "Better few prayers with devotion, than many without." And it further says: "Prayer without devotion is like a body without a soul." These opinions alone suffice, in my opinion, to abbreviate the all-too-long *Pesuḳe dezimra*. Similarly, the inspired Preacher said (Eccl. 5:1): "Be not rash with thy mouth, and let not thy heart be hasty to utter a word before God; for God is in heaven, and thou upon earth; therefore let thy words be few."

I could cite many other passages which confirm the truth of what has been said; however, I believe that the truth of a proposition is sensed more by the force of our reason than through an accumulation of quotations. Proofs are like prayers; they lose in depth as they gain in length.

Only a few words concerning the second category of prayers (*Yotsrot, Kerobets,* and *Piyutim*). In the whole Talmud there is not one relevant passage concerning the nonsense of these prayers (if they deserve such names at all!). They were generally written much later, at the time of the darkest persecutions. They bear the mark of the extreme suppression of the human spirit.

In the writings of the real scholars of that age, like Maimonides (More Nebukhim 1:59), David Kimchi (Grammar, *sub 'atar*), and especially Ibn Ezra (commentary on Eccl. 5:1), we find bitter attacks, not so much against the authors as against those who repeat these pseudo-prayers. Hence, also, the great divergence of practice in these prayers. The Polish Jew has other *piyutim* than has the German, and vice versa. The Spanish Jew never did admit any of this into his liturgy, hence the advantage which the Sephardim [Spanish Jews] have gained over the Ashkenazim [German-Polish Jews]. There is, consequently, no doubt that the liturgy must be cleansed from additions which have crept in by the bye.

THE NEED FOR A NEW PRAYER BOOK (*Joseph Maier*)

The chairman of the first rabbinical conference in Brunswick (1844) made the following statement in support of a motion to establish a commission for the creation of a new prayer book.

Gentlemen: It is not unknown to you how in recent times the religious sense has unfortunately diminished in many Jewish families and how it has disappeared from others altogether. Perhaps we may blame this in part on an unfavorable attitude to religion in our time. However, the larger share of the blame must be placed on the fact that the presently available books of worship and the present ritual of public worship do not conform to their original purposes. Our ordinary prayer book, *Seder Tefillah*, suffers in formal as well as material respects from so many ailments that it is no longer in a position to satisfy the religious needs of a progressively educated generation. The language in which it is written has for many centuries been unintelligible to half of the congregation, namely the women, and now it has become a secret for nine-tenths of the people, a thick wall of separation between the worshiper and his God, which makes a spiritual attitude and true exaltation of the spirit impossible. Attempts have been made to relieve these defects by adding to the Hebrew text of the prayers a German translation, but this in itself proves the purposelessness of a dead language and its inability to achieve a vital, life-giving spiritualization. When with every word he speaks the worshiper must look to some translation printed below or above in order to understand it, then worship becomes an exercise of the mind rather than an exaltation of the heart.

Another technical defect of our prayer book is the repetition of individual prayers in the very same prayer service. For instance, in the early morning service the *Shema Yisrael* occurs twice, the *Ashre* [Psalm 145] also twice, and the *Kedusha* even three times. This defect is emphasized and made worse in the public service, since here certain prayers are repeated five, six, and even seven and eight times (for instance, *Birkat Shemone Essre* and *Birkat Sheva, Kaddish,* and others). Every repetition is boring, tiresome, negates devotion, and makes the whole service a formal *opus operatum*.

Finally, I consider the lack of the truly poetic element as a technical defect of our prayer book. With the exception of the Psalms which are found in it (and these are only spoken as prayers), there is an almost complete lack of hymns and songs, in fact, of any kind of piece that can be sung.

But our prayer book appears even more defective in its material than in its technical aspect. We find passages from the Talmud which are not even of a didactic nature, to say nothing of having devotional character. Take, for instance, the passages *Rabbi Yishmael, Bamé madlikin, Ayzayhu mekoman.* If it had been the intention to take from the Talmud the most sterile and least attractive pieces and make them part of the prayer book, one could not have made a better choice. The prayer book further contains passages through which breathe animosity against people of different opinions. This can be explained and justified only because of the occurrences and circumstances of the age in which these prayers originated, but it cannot be defended by anyone in our time. These passages cannot be eliminated quickly enough. Finally, the prayer book contains prayers and pieces which are in contradiction to the beliefs of a large part of the congregation, as for instance, the prayers which have reference to a personal Messiah, the return to Palestine, and the sacrificial cult. But even the purer and better prayers suffer from a certain poverty in religious thought and sentiment. Thus, a single religious idea is not infrequently repeated five, six, or more times in the very same prayer—only with different expressions—and this renders these prayers in their present form equally sterile. It we except the Psalms and a few other prayers, we find in the whole prayer book very little which truly speaks to a soul longing for edification and exaltation. In addition, the prayer book collection has no prayers for the special times, situations, and circumstances of life in which the heart yearns for consolation, atonement, and peace. In vain will the father or mother of a family take the prayer book to hand on the occasion of a sad or joyful event, for they will find nothing in it which will speak to their sentiment or is relevant to their needs.

The defects from which the prayer book suffers are not improved by the form and manner in which it is used during public worship. We already noted the frequent repetition of individual prayers which make the service boring, halting, and unedifying. In addition, there are the long and un-understandable disquisitions which of necessity cause boredom, encourage talking and conversation with neighbors, interfere with order and quiet, and contribute nothing to the dignity of the house of God or of the worship service. The calling up to the Torah, the *Teki'at shofar,* and the *Netilat lulav* are customs of which no one would claim that in their present manner of practice they encourage meditation and edification. Finally, the whole manner of conducting the public worship service is not adequate to its purpose. Even though recently many improvements have been made through the adoption of synagogue rituals and choral song, the basic evil has not been eliminated. The song of the synagogue must be accompanied and carried by a fitting instrument if it is to make a contribution for exaltation and edification. Keeping in mind the principle, *day lehakima birmisa,* I will limit myself to mere hints, knowing that you gentlemen here have long recognized the defects of our prayer book and our ritual order and are entirely convinced, even as I am, of the necessity of a new prayer book and a new liturgy. However, the more important such a subject is, the more careful thought must be given it, and, therefore, I do not ask of the commission, which I have suggested be instituted, that it should immediately begin considering the creation of a new prayer book and a new worship agenda. I ask only that it lay the necessary groundwork for it. Such a commission, it would appear to me, would have to keep in mind the following six points, and they should report on these to the next assembly:

1. Whether it is necessary to say one's prayer in Hebrew, and if it is not necessary, to what degree it is advisable to retain Hebrew for the time being, at least in a part of the public worship service.
   Even though this question has been raised several times, it has never been done in such a manner as to render a thorough inquiry superfluous.
2. Is it necessary to mention in our prayers the teaching of the Messiah and all that is connected with it?
   This question, too, has recently been raised in connection with the controversy over the Hamburg Temple, but has found neither a solution nor even a thorough airing.

Connected with this are the further questions:

3. Whether those parts of the *Musaf* which refer solely to the former sacrificial cult of the Temple must be kept in the prayer book, and:
4. Whether the repetition of the *Shemone Essre* and the *Birkat sheva* is necessary.

Finally, the commission will have to express its opinion on:

5. How the reading of the Torah and the calling up for it, as well as the ceremonies of the *Teki'at shofar* and *Netilat lulav* can be arranged so that order and devotion should not be disturbed, and:
6. Whether the use of the organ in the synagogue is permissible.

You will see from these questions that even though I urge the adoption of a new prayer book and a new liturgy, I do not in any wise ask for something which does not find its historical connection with Judaism and the religious life of our congregation. Rather, I ask for both, so that we may hold on to the traditional pattern which has developed from the religious life of our people, and so that, in fact, we keep all that still bears within it the seed of new life. But I do desire, both for private and public service, such means as will be entirely adequate to the religious needs of our time and will represent in a dignified manner the religious consciousness of the congregation, which expresses itself primarily in public worship. It shall be my privilege to present a complete plan for such a prayer book and ritual order to a forthcoming assembly; for the time being I only ask that you should consider my proposal and vote upon it.

SOME SUGGESTED CHANGES (*Abraham Geiger*)

Reform is not a half-measure simply because it does not one-sidedly pay obeisance to some arbitrary principle and eliminate mercilessly everything that opposes it. Rather, our Reform is historical, and all of us serve as organs of history. As we draw from the past, we nourish the future; as we prepare ourselves for higher goals, we yet rejoice in our heritage and heighten its value for the present. I do not underestimate the difficult task which such procedure demands of us. Its conditions are devotion to the religious sentiment, supremacy of the religious idea, and at the same time a truly intimate connection with the history of Judaism. The history of Judaism is so vital, it has so many sprouts and shoots even in contemporary life, that once it is cleansed of weeds, its power of growth will not have diminished. Based on such principles, how would the Jewish worship service be arranged for the present?

The essential difference in the thoughts and feelings as they relate to the religious convictions of the Jews exists in the relationship of Israel to mankind. Now, as always, the true Israelite testifies gladly to Israel's high vocation to carry the faith in the One and Holy God in all its purity to the world. Joyfully he witnesses that Israel was providentially called to this vocation and has remained faithful to it. Joyfully he expresses his gratitude that this holy life-giving thought of Israel is increasingly realized in the world, and with all the fervor of his confidence he looks to the day when this thought will bless all mankind and bind it into one brotherhood. We have prayers in which this thought is expressed with all the majesty of an inspired and deeply believing soul. I only mention several New Year's prayers, to which also the *Alenu* belongs.

But on the other hand, this historically developed faith attracted to itself ideas and sentiments which have become entirely foreign to our time, which in fact are strongly rejected by it. The former relationship of Israel to other nations intimately connected the sense of peoplehood (which had its full justification on its own soil) so closely with its vocation as God's witness that independent peoplehood came to be considered as a condition for the task of witnessing to the true faith. The plaint over lost independence, the petition for and the hope in its restoration, the exaltation of the land in which Israel once rejoiced in its own nationhood, the maintenance of those institutions which were conditioned by ancient days and related to the land at that time—all these desires and hopes, directed to the restoration of these circumstances, pervade a large number of prayers and in some respects form their sole content. Need I remind of the plaint over our dispersion, the petition for the ingathering of the dispersed in Palestine, the restoration of the priestly and sacrificial cult, and the like?

The joy over so beautiful a task as has become the share of Israel must impose upon it the responsibility to prove itself even worthier of it through knowledge and its way of life. Such joy, however, would be indeed irreligious if it would nurture the thought that Israel, without any other reason and without any effort of its own, is something better than other men, and if it would lead Israel to arrogant conceit and smug contemptuousness of others. Let us not overlook the fact that such views existed in the past and found expression in our prayers. We must admit that oppression and contempt from the outside necessitated an overcompensating pressure from within. We even admit that in order to avoid error, one must draw a very strict line between the legitimate pride of being in possession of a worthwhile good, and ignoble snobbishness towards others who have no share in it. However, in our days we have apparently achieved a proper balance. Israel is now far from that self-satisfaction and delusion which are roadblocks to true piety. All the more, therefore, must the residue of outgrown attitudes which still appears in our prayers be eliminated. Today, as always, we can say with conviction, "Thou hast chosen us for Thy holy law," but not, "Thou hast chosen us from among all nations, Thou hast elevated us above all tongues."

It is natural that historical memories, too, in so far as they relate to the history of our people, no longer have the significance which they once had.

The *people* of Israel lives no longer, not even in the hearts and desires of the present. It is resurrected as a congregation of *faith* and only what touches it has an undisputed right to our concern. The exodus from Egypt will not lose its significance as the first cornerstone of the genesis of Israel, but it should no longer be given the exalted position which it has in our prayers, which as a national event outranks even the giving of the law at Sinai. The incessant repetition with which our prayers speak about this theme must go.

Similarly, Amalek and his alleged descendant Haman can no longer rouse in our hearts the revulsion which former days had for them. The sufferings of the Middle Ages, to be sure, will, as historic facts, not disappear from our memories, but they must cease to be the subject of prayer. Besides, many religious concepts have taken on a more spiritual character and, therefore, their expression in prayer must be more spiritual. From now on the hope for an after-life should not be expressed in terms which suggest a future revival, a resurrection of the body; rather, they must stress the immortality of the human soul. We must eliminate the whole physical pictorialization of the divine household, the detailed description of angelic choirs and holy beasts, which is found especially in the morning prayers. We must recognize the force of prayer and the fulfilment of all our obligations toward God more through the blessed effect which they have on our ennoblement, rather than as necessary obeisance to a command imposed from above. We must value our holy days more because of their potential elevation of our sentiment, rather than because of their historic origin, and in this fashion they must be made part of our prayers. The changes which must be made to achieve these purposes will not be very extensive, for in this respect our prayers do possess a treasure of deep thoughts and sentiments, which only need to be cleansed from disfiguring additions. The change of the order of prayers in accordance with these principles will not deprive the service of its sanctity which a long, honorable history has given it—instead, it will significantly strengthen the force of its inwardness.

2. THE SERMON

WORSHIP AS AN EDUCATIONAL FORCE (*Leopold Zunz*)

The education in one's religion is concluded neither in school nor by confirmation. Throughout his life, man should listen to the teaching and the law, and the congregation should be able to strengthen its religious sense through public worship and fill its thirst for the word of God in the synagogue. Therefore, when Judaeo-German language and education made room for their German counterparts, when exclusive occupation with the Talmud, the reading of cabalistic books, and the taste for humdrum interpretations decreased, an increased knowledge of the Bible became observable and with it a rise in the level of scientific culture. This had come to the Jews with their civil emancipation, and through better schools and religious classes we became more receptive to worthwhile things. Then there arose in Israel a longing for a worship service which would bring edification and instruction. Old abuses and the neglect of sermons bespoke all too vividly the decay of former times, especially in view of the new edifice erected by language and civil life, by literature and religious education. Thus, reform was in a way ready-made, but it lacked form, particularly in the synagogue from which, as in the early days, prayer and teaching should shine forth as emanations of the divine spirit and of Judaism's eternal light.

The institution of the synagogue still does battle with the new age. Until this very day, no organic growth can be seen in it—only old and new things in chaotic confusion, progress and regression, efforts attempted and efforts prevented, disintegration and budding seed—all side by side. It was not so much the sermon or its language which was at issue. Sermons during the worship service, understandable lectures, have a long history in Israel. They were intimately interwoven with Jewish institutions and were not only admissible but required. In two thousand years of religious literature they built their own monument. But the manner of these lectures, the right to hold them, and the changes in the service which were connected with or related to them and the whole rabbinate—these elements lent themselves to inner division and external interference. In some places certain congregations came into existence which were independent of rabbis and which entrusted the preaching of sermons, as well as confirmation and other ritual functions, to their own "teachers of religion." They erected "German" synagogues into which they introduced a changed ritual, German prayers, or prayers translated into German, regular sermons, and choral singing with organ accompaniment. In other congregations people were only concerned with the reestablishment of external order and the introduction of more frequent sermons. But in most places the result was generally nil, even though the desire for worship reform had awakened in many, and especially among the female sex.

Of special importance in synagogal reform is the elimination of these shortcomings and abuses[1] and, first and foremost, the reintroduction of regular sermons. Whether the preacher be called preacher or rabbi, teacher or lecturer—as long as he will know to find the word of God in Bible and Aggadah, as

[1] Zunz lists the various defects and abuses which he observed in his time and in each instance shows that these abuses and measures for their rectification have already been mentioned in ancient, medieval, and pre-modern sources: disorder, yelling and shaking at services, lack of devotion and attention, employment of disqualified cantors, use of unfitting melodies, superfluous singing, chanting of the Pentateuchal lesson according to the cantillation, auctioning of Torah functions, presumptuousness of rich people in the synagogue, absence of rabbis from the service, lack of qualified synagogue inspectors, and above all, as the text indicates, the neglect of adequate and regular sermons.

long as he will be able to find genuine gold in our old and new achievements, to show the present its true vocation and speak to hearts in a language we can understand. Then, O daughter of Zion, the divine spirit will return to your temples and will be heard in the living word which enthusiastically will urge us on to deeds, creating institutions for Israel. The spark once kindled will not again be extinguished. Persecutions will only serve to fan it into a bright flame, for the reform and the triumphs of the word which reform will reveal are irresistible, just as is the victory of freedom and civilization and of the civil equality of the Jew and of their scientific culture. Let the sermon of the rabbi, the lectures of the teachers of religion bring blessing and joy along with solace and hope, teaching, and edification—a blessing for Israel and joy for a reconciled Europe.

A WORD ON THE FRENCH SERMON, 1840 (*Samuel Cahen*)

In an earlier edition the editor of the *Archives Israélites de France* had stated categorically that there was no French sermon worthy of the name (see above, page 22). This editorial opinion called forth a good many replies, which in turn moved Cahen to elaborate on his opinion:

We are told that there are sermons preached in Strasbourg—in German, of course, for that is the language of that Province. If indeed we would learn that these sermons are given weekly, as we have a right to expect from the Grand Rabbi of a city such as Strasbourg, and if the preacher would know how to move and edify his audience, then indeed we should admit that preaching exists in the synagogue of Strasbourg.

We are further told that the speaker discontinued preaching because he lacked an audience. Taking into full consideration the indifference of people on the one hand and the desire of others to prevent French preaching alto-gether, nevertheless, we think the speaker ought to have persevered, for it is the speaker who must create his audience.

But sermons which are pedestrian, full of banalities, and recited from a man-uscript like a lesson, without gesture, without movement, without pathos—such sermons are not likely to captivate the spirit of the listeners.

Why did people listen to our old Maggidim and Darshanim? Because the orator was full of his subject; because he spoke words that went straight from heart to heart; because the speaker stood up and faced his congregation and looked them straight in the eye; his presence commanded silence and his small-est word was listened to. Today the people are no less impressionable, but one must learn how to move them.

We founded this journal neither to flatter some nor to irritate others. We wanted to create a platform which would serve the truth and which would advance the well-understood interests of our religion. If our rabbis—who are no busier than Catholic priests or Protestant ministers—will give themselves with zeal to the art of oratory and follow the example of their colleagues in Germany, then perchance there will also be found among them a Salomon or a Mannheimer.[2] Until then we will be right in saying that preaching does not yet exist in the French synagogue.

Apparently the editor received further protests on the subject, and the following year he had this to say:

We have been told that there are sermons in some places, but this really does not contradict our assertion, because we have not learned that there is a truly facile preacher who, knowing that the sermon should be an integral part of the service, preaches frequently and with success.

The honorable Grand Rabbi of Paris did preach a sermon on the Sabbath before Passover. This venerable Grand Rabbi, as everyone knows, does not have the gift to move people, but if he had had the courage to depart from past practice, he could have at least rendered his instructions useful. His last sermon was followed by a brief talmudical explanation on the subject of Passover; then came a recommendation of several virtues which was founded on biblical verses and talmudic passages. In this way his total instruction was actually divided into three parts: the first and longest was rhetorical, the second theological, and the third exegetical. The first produced little effect, the second even less—there were perhaps four or five people in the audience who could profit from it at all—but as regards the third, there was a difference. It was comprehensible to all listeners and we have the pleasure of reporting that the speaker acquitted himself very well of his task. Well then! Why not give to this kind of instruction the time which is reserved to the preceding parts? We know that this would not be a *derasha* as it used to be given formerly, and it would also not be the kind of sermon that might really be preached. But even if this were not the kind of preaching we would desire, it would still be the style of the ancient Maggidim, and it would be an opportunity for public speaking—and orators are made, not born.

As for the city of Metz, there is no preaching there either. The *Courrier de la Moselle* of the tenth of this month reported that it had received an anonymous letter which complained that the honorable Grand Rabbi preached only twice a year and that he does not even preach in French. It would appear to us that the Grand Rabbi would do well to preach more frequently and in French, for the young people understand nothing but this language, and it is the youth who must be instructed. The honorable Grand Rabbi of Metz should at last have the courage to grant the beautiful language of Racine and Voltaire asylum in the synagogue.

---

[2] Salomon was preacher in Hamburg, and Mannheimer in Vienna (see pages 38 and 42).

3. VERNACULAR AND HEBREW IN THE SERVICE

FROM THE DEBATE AT THE SECOND RABBINICAL CONFERENCE,. 1845
(Zacharias Frankel, Abraham Adler, Ludwig Philippson)

The conference had raised the question whether Hebrew was *objectively necessary* in the service, i.e., whether public prayer would *theoretically* require the use of Hebrew to be a proper Jewish service. After discussing the historic foundations of Jewish prayer, the majority answered the question in the negative. This left the amount of Hebrew and of the vernacular up to *subjective* judgment. However, opinion was strongly divided, and in consequence of this debate Frankel left the assembly (see above, p. 87). In the following excerpts the opposing views of Frankel and Adler, and the conciliatory position of Philippson (which prevailed) are represented.

Abraham Adler (1813-56), a fiery Reformer, was not only a scholar of note, but also one of the political leaders in the revolutionary movement of the 1840's. He was imprisoned but was acquitted later on. Elected to the pulpit of Temple Emanu-El in New York, he had to decline because of poor health, and eventually his brother Samuel (see below, p. 189) accepted the post.

Frankel: The debate up to this point is far from bringing forth new ideas. It has only confirmed my previous views. Geiger believes that language is something national and that the continued use of Hebrew would apparently testify to a desire for nationality. However, this point is not at issue in our present question. The problem of emancipation is far removed from religion and no religious aspect must be sacrificed in order to obtain emancipation. We must maintain that which is religious, and if nationality were religious, then without hesitation we should acknowledge it.

Fortunately, experience shows that in the countries of emancipation, as in Holland and in France, Hebrew has not prevented the Jews from being genuinely patriotic and from fulfilling all their duties toward the state. One should be very careful with such statements. Our assemblies are public; therefore, "Ye sages, be cautious with your words."

When Geiger furthermore maintains that German edifies him more than Hebrew, he expresses something entirely subjective. Most of those who know Hebrew will feel differently, for Hebrew expresses the religious element more forcefully. I am sure that the majority of the rabbis present, to whom Hebrew is a second tongue or to whom it is at least very well known, would witness to this.

The Hebrew language is the Bible itself, which encompasses all our religious elements. Religion as an abstract must have an external bond which constantly reminds us of God. Many individual ordinances, as for instance, *Tefillin, Mezuzah,* etc., have this as their purpose. The use of the Hebrew language at prayer fulfils the same purpose, that is, to remind us constantly of the biblical words and at the same time of our covenant with God. These different aids to memory are similar to the bundle of arrows in the well-known fable. As long as the arrows are tied together they are unbreakable, but as we draw out one after the other, the whole bundle will soon be broken. So much that is characteristic in Judaism has already been obliterated. The time has come to call a halt.

There is still another aspect which should be stressed. The Holy Scripture is a pledge which has been entrusted to the Jews and is to be held in safekeeping by them. For many thousands of years already, we are called to carry this word to the world. All of Israel, not merely the priests, have this vocation. But if the original text of Holy Scripture will become merely the property of the rabbis, of a special class, then we would soon once again have priests and laymen—and all of us are strongly against a priestly caste and want to wipe out all memory of it. Our youth must, therefore, be taught Hebrew in order to understand the service and the Bible.

To be sure, it is urgently necessary that a part of the service be held in German. However, I believe that Hebrew must predominate, for it carries with it the sentimental elements of edification and stimulation which otherwise are missing in our service. This edification and stimulation is provided by Hebrew, because we are thereby reminded that it is the language of revelation in which God spoke to Moses. For us, Hebrew in the worship service is necessary and it should perhaps have been so ordered by law. Indeed, this would have been the case had our forefathers been able to imagine that we would ever attempt to forsake Hebrew. The old teachers who did permit another language at prayer only had weaklings in mind, who without such permission would not have found themselves at ease with a non-Hebrew prayer. But they never thought that Hebrew would be eliminated from the house of God.

Adler: We must search for the truth and nothing else, and we must keep ourselves far from all sentimentality. It may be painful to give up certain things; but it must be when necessity demands. The proofs for the necessity of the Hebrew language are all spurious.

It is said:

1. The Hebrew language is sacred. Not at all! That language is sacred which conveys the sacred. If I speak the truth in German, then that German word is sacred. If I lie in Hebrew, then that Hebrew word is unholy. Not the letter, not the sound makes the Bible sacred, but its content.

It is said further:

2. That the Bible would perish. Not at all! Even Philo does not prove the contrary. With all his ignorance of Hebrew, he exhibits a deep knowledge of the Bible through its Greek translation and shows greater fervor and deeper religiosity than are portrayed in many passages of the Talmud. A language is

maintained by the eternal creations of the spirit. The Bible is immortal because of them. It needs no crutches.

3. People fear for the unity of Israel. But language does not create unity; it is rather the other way around. Therefore, the continued use of Hebrew does not fill this purpose.

4. It is said that the worship service needs the mystical element. Yes, there is indeed truth in the truly mystical, which is the direct impact on the soul and its deepest grasp of truth. But just because of this, the mystical is not the same as that which is un-understandable, and lack of understanding does not reveal truth.

5. If one really is afraid of a hierarchy, why then are the last remnants of the priestly caste still allowed to stand, to wit, the *Birkat kohanim* and the other prerogatives of an extinct priesthood? Why does one even pray for its restoration?

On the other hand, there are many reasons for the elimination of the Hebrew language.

1. The Hebrew language encourages hypocrisy and lip service, and this is a cancer on the body of religion which was already excoriated by Isaiah (29:13): "With their mouth and with their lips [they] do honor Me, but have removed their hearts far from Me." Hypocrisy and lip service bring about the decline of religion and genuine religious knowledge.

2. The adulation of the letter has caused many to be indifferent to the sense of the Bible. Hebrew is un-understandable and unknown even to the many pious people who pray frequently in Hebrew. Hebrew prayer has harmed the knowledge of the Bible instead of encouraging it. If one ceases to sanctify the letter, then everyone can get to the content itself.

3. Whatever one may say about it, the Hebrew language is poor in words and expressions. Therefore, it is difficult and unclear. In any case, it is dead because it does not live within the people.

4. Already the ancient teachers recognized this. The Men of the Great Synagogue considered it necessary to render the holiest portions of the service in Aramaic (as, for instance, the Kaddish prayer) so that the people would understand them.

Philippson: All extremes must be avoided for we have already reached some common basis of understanding. For the time being nobody wants to eliminate Hebrew altogether and no one opposes the introduction of German. The question, therefore, is: how much? We do not, however, work merely for the moment and for individual congregations, but rather for the entire future and for the whole household of Israel. Therefore, Hebrew and German elements must be organically integrated.

In this respect we must differentiate between prayer and formal worship service. Prayer is the expression for all special circumstances and feelings, for happiness and unhappiness, for joy and trouble, sorrow, repentance and atonement—here, full understanding is necessary and a foreign language is entirely unusable. But the worship service does not speak to such individual situations. It wants to be a stimulus, it wants to teach, it wants to be an expression of our faith.

Now, Hebrew is indeed a means of stimulation, for through it, *Shema Yisrael,* the unity of God, was first pronounced. Through it, the principle of pure love of neighbor first received its expression, as did the principle of the equality of all men before the law. Through it, Moses reverently spoke to God (Deut. 3:24): "O Lord, God, Thou hast begun to show Thy servant Thy greatness." The use of the original expressions, therefore, is a powerful stimulus for the worship service.

Hebrew also is a means of teaching through reading from the Torah. This must not be eliminated because otherwise the Bible would be entirely removed from the eyes of the people. The sermon further complements the teaching.

The Hebrew language is indispensable as a central point of our religion. The German Jews are German, they think and feel German and want to live and work as patriots. But Judaism is not German; it is universal. The dispersion of the Jews is not the dispersion of Judaism. And, therefore, it must have a unified character. Its content is its creed; its form is represented by each.

In civil matters we strive for unity with all our compatriots. However, in religious matters we may and must hold fast to the distinguishing elements. The minority needs these elements vis-à-vis the overwhelming majority. Hebrew in our service is such a distinguishing element.

The Hebrew language is neither poor nor dead, as has been maintained. Masterpieces have been written in it which will never perish; and, as a language of religion, it has everything and indeed is still full of life.

Hebrew, therefore, must be retained, but it must be integrated organically with German elements.

4. SYNAGOGUE MUSIC

THE USE OF THE ORGAN (*Jacob Hayim Recanati*)

The use of the organ in the synagogue was one of the earliest issues in the reform of the worship service. The Reformers mustered a number of authorities who would permit such use, and who buttressed their views with quotations in the accepted manner.

Amongst the respondents was Recanati (1758-1824), scion of an eminent rabbinical line in Italy and a distinguished scholar. Recanati treats the subject in the traditional form of the rabbinic responsa and considers three aspects: first, whether the playing of an organ is forbidden because it is reminiscent of idolatry; second, whether synagogue music is permitted after the destruction of the Temple; and third, whether organ music interferes with synagogue devotion. His conclusion, taken from his responsum *Ya'ir Netiv,* is as follows:

In sum, it appears that in accordance with evidence, truth, and justice, as adduced above, and also according to the heads of the hosts of Israel, the honored rabbis—may they rest in peace—I see nothing that would prohibit the playing of the organ in the synagogue for the glory of God, to sing songs and praises unto Him in pleasant voices, except on Sabbath and holidays, when an Israelite ought not to play it, even as it is explained in *Orah Hayim,* 338, No. 1. See also *B'er Hetev, ibid.,* 100, No. 3.

REPORT OF THE RABBINICAL COMMISSION
(Rendered to the Frankfort Assembly, 1845 by Leopold Stein)

The question consists of two parts:
  One, whether the playing of the organ itself is permitted in the synagogue;
Two, whether its playing by a Jew may be permitted on the Sabbath.

1. The question whether the playing of the organ in itself is to be permitted in the synagogue falls in two sub-questions:
  a. Whether the organ is admissible at all in a Jewish worship service because it is a musical instrument, and further,
  b. Whether the organ may be admitted to the synagogue because it is used in Christian churches.

The first sub-question, whether the organ as a musical instrument can be used in a Jewish worship service, which for many centuries now has been without instrumental accompaniment, is to be studied with reference to three aspects:
  Whether such playing is admissible at all, whether it is advisable, and whether it is necessary.
  a. The question of the admissibility itself relates to the question whether after the destruction of the Temple a Jew may, in some other house of worship, give himself over to the kind of joyful expression which music excites in every sentient heart. In the old Temple itself, instrumental music was not only permissible, but a prescribed obligation (cf. Maimonides, *Kelé Ha-mikdash,* III, IV; Er. 10a). After the destruction of the Temple, to be sure, a somber view prevailed in Jewish life, as will be seen from various talmudical passages:[3]

In this world man is forbidden to fill his mouth with music;

After the Sanhedrin was abolished, the song too was abolished from the house of drinking;

The ear that hears song will burst;

A song in the house means destruction in the house;

Whence do we know that song is forbidden? (Commentary of Rashi on "The House of Drinking," Git. 7a.)

[3] (Ed. note) The original text gives all quotations in Hebrew only, without translation.

Basing themselves on this tradition, several rabbis declared themselves, in the Hamburg Temple dispute of 1819, against the playing of the organ (*Eleh divre ha-berith,* pp. 10, 61). It is true that because of said circumstances music disappeared from the Jewish house of worship, but a prohibition of such music certainly did not exist, as is erroneously maintained by these rabbis ("But in the house of God it is especially forbidden," *ibid.,* p. 10). Even the above-mentioned talmudical dicta only refer to worldly joys, but music is permissible for a religious purpose (in a matter of *mitzvah*) as, for instance, the rejoicing of bridegroom and bride (cf. *Or Nogah,* p. 17). Thus Maimonides, in commenting upon these talmudical prohibitions of music and song, remarks (*Hilkhot Taan.* 85:14): "At this time all Israel have adopted the custom of singing religious songs when they drink wine." What about the opinion of one of the rabbis (*ibid.* p. 61) that only song and not instrumental music be permitted in the house of God? The reply is simple: In the temple vocal music was the main thing (see Maimonides *Kelé Ha-mikdash, loc.cit.*). If even from the strictest rabbinical point of view such music is permissible outside of the temple, how much the more then instrumental music which was only of secondary importance.

Furthermore, experience shows us that in many Jewish congregations—for instance, in Prague and formerly also in Corfu—worship with organ accompaniment was held (cf. *Nogah Tsedek,* p. 17). Also, Jewish life in modern times has become so pleasant, and music has entered the dwellings of even the most pious Israelite so generally, that to doubt that music is *admissible* in the synagogue would be to put the latter into the crassest contradiction with all else.

Another question, however, is its *advisability.* Here we must answer with a "No," at least as far as our present service goes. For our prayers have been extended so greatly, simply because there was no regular song with adequate instrumental accompaniment, and only in this way was it possible to have the service last the desired length of time. In our present worship service, prayer and cantillation take up too much room, and there is little left for a choir assisted by organ. Also, it must be admitted that its introduction probably would not meet with much sympathy. This would have to be created first through the elimination of many prayers and through an entirely new organization of the service. If we put an organ into our present-day worship service, it will be out of place—a strange element which does not harmonize with the rest.

It is not a paradox if we go on to say that the introduction of the organ in the synagogue, even though it is not advisable, is still *necessary.* For no service needs elevation as much as ours, in which somnolence and nonchalance are predominant. There is no more exalting means of encouraging devotion than the music which issues from that grand instrument. Already our ancients said: "The spirit of God enters only through the joy of doing the commandments" (Pes. 117a). And the biblical verse on which this saying is founded says: "And it came to pass when the minstrel played that the hand of the Lord came upon him" (II Kings 3:15). From this we see that a prophet like Elisha used music in order to exalt his heart. How much more, then, is it our duty not to overlook such a means of creating devotion. The author of *Or Nogah* (p. 17) notes correctly that the Talmud permits the farmer to sing while plowing so that his work be easier. How much more, then, must we utilize this means for exaltation during our worship service so that such service not become a burden, as unfortunately it is these days for so many. For, "he for whom his prayer is a burden, for him prayer is no devotion" (Ber. 28b). Therefore, we ought to bring the *advisability* and the *necessity* of our present matter into agreement. Let us order our worship service in such a manner that the organ has an integral place in it.

b. We have answered with "Yes" the question whether the organ is altogether permissible as a musical instrument in the synagogue. There arises the further question whether it may be admitted to the synagogue because it is used in Christian churches, or whether this imitation of a strange mode of worship should be kept out of the synagogues.

Every worthwhile custom may be imitated by the Israelite wherever he may find it. ("You never accept their best customs, only their worst," Sanh. 39b). The verse, "Neither shall ye walk in their statutes" (Lev. 18:3), only refers to pagan abominations, as may be seen from the subsequent words, "Ye shall not do any of these abominations" (18:26). This is also noted by the commentator *Kesef Mishne* (to Maimonides, *Hilkhot Accum* 11:1), who in regard to clothing says, in the name of Rabbi Joseph Kolon: Even amongst the pagans the Israelite may imitate the pagan in his attire except where such clothing relates to paganism itself; however, if the custom does not have pagan implications, then there is no objection to imitation. Compare also what Rabbi Nissim says (to A.Z. 2b): The Torah prohibits only the actually pagan, senseless, empty customs which contain something that has reference to idolatry; customs, however, which are reasonable are permitted to be imitated. Similarly, Rabbi Moses Isserles says, in the name of the above-mentioned Rabbi Joseph Kolon (*Yore De'a* 178:1): Only immoral customs which contain pagan elements are forbidden, but that which is done with reasonable intent or to honor someone or for some other similar reason, is permitted. Now, if this applies to pagans, how much more does it apply to Christians, of whom already a medieval rabbi remarks (Rabbenu Tam, *Tos'fot Bekh.* 2b; *O.H.* 156, Note) that even though Christianity is not purely monotheistic, still its heart is set upon the Creator of heaven and earth. Therefore, there seems no reason that we could not imitate so beautiful a custom as the elevation of the worship service through instrumental music.

There is even some reason to believe that the organ, the origins of which are lost in antiquity, does, in fact, come to us from the Jewish worship in the Temple. The Talmud speaks of an instrument called *magrefa*, which has many pipes and which brought forth a hundred (according to others, a thousand) sounds and resounded so loudly that, according to legend, it could be heard as far away as Jericho (Tamid 3:8).

We see from this that the *magrefa* was an instrument which, similar to the organ, had a wide range of harmonic sounds and sent forth its devotional music into the far reaches. Therefore, we have, if we actually need it, a historic home-base for the transplantation of the organ into the Jewish worship service.

We now come to a consideration of the second article, namely, whether the organ may be played on the Sabbath by an Israelite.

Present usage has prohibited the playing of instruments on the Sabbath by Israelites ("for fear that one would do some work on the instrument," Er. 104a; Beza 30a, 36b).

However, it has already been remarked by Tos'fot (Beza 30a): "This caution is not necessary for us because we have no skill to make such instruments." From this, the commentator Magen Abraham (*O.H.* 338:8) says that in effect the playing of musical instruments is permitted to Israelites on the Sabbath, especially at dances. How much more then would it be permitted at the worship service! We may add that the organ (as is pointed out by the author of *Berith Emet,* p. 34) is so complex an instrument that improvements or repairs are not quickly made. This is not the business of the organist, but rather the organ-maker. Also, the worship service itself in its public nature makes the feared desecration of the Sabbath impossible. According to the Talmud it is forbidden to read with a light on the Sabbath eve so that one should not be tempted to adjust the light. However, it says, two people may read because one would remind the other in case the prescribed action would be initiated (*O.H.* 275:1). How much more, then, would this be the case in a house of God when there are so many Israelites present, which would prevent any action that would infringe upon the Sabbath.

If, then, the playing of the organ itself is permissible in the synagogue, then it is a *duty* to arrange the beautification of the worship service through a coreligionist. That is the way it was once in the Temple, where Jews took care not only of the singing, but also played the musical instruments. Thus we find an opinion of the former Rabbi of Amsterdam which speaks *against* the playing of an organ on the Sabbath (*Eleh divre ha-berith,* p.62) and says that if such playing were permissible, it would have to be done exclusively by coreligionists. Furthermore, another opposing opinion by the Rabbi of Livorno (*ibid.* p.67) says that the playing of the organ in the synagogue on workdays is permitted, but only if it is done by Israelites. And he adds: "We have permitted this only if it is done by Israelites, through men in whose hearts dwells the fear of heaven, so that we might find favor before our Creator to worship Him in fear and awe, and in the knowledge of God to honor Him as it befits us—and not through someone else." Indeed, the right kind of organist must be thoroughly suffused by the spirit of worship which he attempts to elevate, and we can best expect this from someone who, as a coreligionist, is a participant in the worship service. Now, since already twenty-five years ago a number of well-known rabbis permitted the playing of the organ through a non-Israelite (*Nogah Tsedek,* pp. 3-28), then, in accordance with the above arguments, it is the more permissible to permit the playing to an Israelite. The observance of the Sabbath will in no wise be diminished, but, on the contrary, it can only gain through the added beautification of the worship service, and especially so in rural communities which are unable to maintain a choir. There the organ will render manifold services as a means of elevating the worship service and exalting the soul on festive days.

LET US HAVE CHOIRS (*Anonymous French Correspondent*)

Lesser innovations than the introduction of an organ aroused the ire of the old-line leaders. Even such relatively minor changes as the institution of choral singing were bitterly opposed.

In one of our most important communities it was suggested that choral singing be introduced into the service. The Grand Rabbi forbade any such singing of the stated prayers because, as he said: "It is forbidden to interrupt the prayers." Well then! On the holiest day of the year we have counted eighty-nine musical notes between the verb and the subject in the Kaddish prayer and as many syllables to separate two words, and the same again between the nominative and the genitive. This happened in the year 5601 [1841]. If we do not protest energetically against such scandalous practices, we will still have the same in the year 5701, and I am speaking of a city which has three rabbis, a synagogue consistory, and ten administrators of the synagogue. The heart revolts with repugnance when one thinks of such a state of affairs. Do we need a synod to relieve this kind of extravagance which offends nineteen-twentieths of the community?

FOR HIGHER MUSICAL STANDARDS (*Solomon Sulzer*)

Sulzer (1804-91) did probably more than anyone else to make fine musical standards a part of the Reform program. He was Mannheimer's cantor in Vienna, and his compositions still have an honored place in all synagogues. At the Leipzig Synod (1869) he submitted these proposals:

The Synod in Leipzig should declare that it is desirable:

That our young Jewish people be instructed in liturgical song;

That the main portions of the Hebrew service which form its most typical aspects should be sung to the same melodies in all synagogues;

That the instrumental accompaniment of all worship songs should be introduced everywhere in order to make it easier for the members to participate actively in singing;

That schools for the education of cantors should be established in the interest of better ritual.

WE NEED BETTER CANTORS (*Lazarus Adler*)

At the subsequent synod, in Augsburg, Sulzer's proposal was brought forward again by Lazarus Adler (1810-1886), rabbi in Cassel, who played a leading part in both synods.

A third proposal of general nature was made by Mr. Sulzer at the last Synod. The proposal aims at attaching greater importance to synagogal singing; it suggests that the training of our teachers give closer attention to their development as qualified cantors. I have had occasion to convince myself that their courses give the greatest and almost exclusive care to the subject of education and certainly justifiably so. But on the whole, almost nothing has been done up to now for the development of good cantors. Yet, think of the many to whom religion in its externals is almost entirely confined to attendance at public worship. Consider that in our time which—praised be the Lord—is no longer a time of suffering, the inner impulse to seek the house of God is no longer present for its own sake. We, therefore, have to realize that the place of worship must offer something to attract us, something to arouse our longing, so that we all should look forward with gladness to the return of the Sabbath, to bring us edification and inspiration. For these reasons the divine service must, indeed, have something to induce devotion. I have convinced myself of the important contribution a cantor can make in this respect. I have visited the synagogues in Vienna. They are very well attended, and many among the visitors have confessed to me that they were present because of the beautiful service and the inspiring singing. It is the chanting of these cantors, who are well educated and qualified, which accounts for a beneficial, edifying service. I wish, therefore, to support Mr. Sulzer's proposal that the Synod pass a motion that the next assembly decide on ways and means best suited for the training and development of qualified cantors, and that the subject, therefore, be referred to a committee, with the purpose of making practical proposals to the next Synod.

5. BAR MITZVAH AND CONFIRMATION

Historically speaking, the reform of the Bar Mitzvah rite belongs to the earliest milestones of the progressive movement. In time, the ceremony gave way to what was called "Confirmation," for girls as well as for boys (and in some congregations for adults also). Confirmation became a new rite, and its eventual adoption by most branches of Western Jewry marks it as one of Reform's significant contributions to the ceremonial practices of Judaism.

FOR A REFORM OF BAR MITZVAH (*Maimon Fränkel*)

Fränkel was a teacher at the Jewish free school in Dessau. He wrote this article in 1810, the very year when Israel Jacobson introduced the first modern Confirmation ceremony.

In the Jewish religion we presently find amongst many honored ceremonies some which can hardly pass the test of common sense. These not only often miss their purpose but are frequently harmful to it. Among these latter we count the meaningless ceremonial at confirmation time.[4] It is customary amongst practically all peoples to introduce a young man through special celebrations to his religious majority and to his participation in religious rites.[5] Amongst the Jews this takes place at the time of the thirteenth birthday.[5] Solemnity undoubtedly makes a strong impression upon a person, and especially in the moment when the young citizen moves from the lower sphere of childhood into the higher realm of youth and is introduced to life's seriousness. At such a time a clear conception of the future and the intimate touch of pure goodness will impress their stamp upon his moral character. But what kind of result can an indifferent ceremony have which leaves the heart cold and the spirit uninvolved? I do not know what wholesome effect one may expect from such a luminous moment when the boy has been adequately prepared. But most certainly a harmful impression must result when such a theatrical act happens to an entirely unprepared youth, and the more so if in either case the whole community follows this *religious* act with indifference.

Our ancestors, for whom home life itself had a religious aspect, generally reached the goals of morality more securely than is the case in our enlightened time. From the earliest youth on, a child was taught reverence and love of God and unlimited respect for religion. All his actions were conceived to be in the service of God and, thus prepared, the growing youth came into the circle of the honored assembly shyly but suffused by a holy enthusiasm. At confirmation time he read several paragraphs from the Pentateuch and delivered a rabbinic sermon (of which, to be sure, he did not understand much) and then observed punctually and conscientiously his newly accepted obligations. But now, with the change of form, many have lost also the spirit. In our frivolous times we do not infrequently note a certain indifference to, or even disdain for, the religion of our fathers. Many have the illusion that the intellect can be enriched only at the cost of religion, and show their lack of conscience by abandoning all religious practice. That moral religious training of our forefathers of which we spoke has disappeared along with respect for religion.

---

[4] (Ed. note) The author introduces the term "Confirmation" when speaking of Bar Mitzvah. His intent is to propose a reform of Bar Mitzvah, not its abolishment or replacement by a new ceremony.

[5] To be sure, there is no special treatise in the Talmud about confirmation, but there are some hints here and there. See especially Hulin, Kiddushin and Nedarim.

That which is Mosaic, like that which is rabbinic, is often disparaged because adequate understanding is lacking. Many are even ashamed of worship itself, and thus the celebration of confirmation is either neglected altogether or is observed without enthusiasm. Thus the young man often enters the arena of life without any intellectual or moral education. He is left to himself and yet one expects from such a person that he should be useful to country and mankind. What logic!

But this creeping evil, which threatens to destroy the sacred remains of former glory and to dissolve our religious unity, could well be stemmed. All that is necessary is to infuse our whole life with the true spirit of Judaism, which is nothing else but the spirit of justice and humanity, and though we cannot restore the olden times, yet can we restore the old appreciation for what is good. One should train the child, as soon as spiritual life awakens within him, to a love of and kindly regard for men, to reverence and holy awe before the highest Being, whose name he must never speak without feeling deeply moved. All frivolity and expressed lack of virtue must be carefully eliminated by negative or positive means. Spiritual and moral perfection can develop only if they are the boy's highest ideal. We should pursue this ideal ceaselessly, and with added years his interest in the *truly good* must increase. May he always call virtue his sister and wisdom his companion. Every worship act must be important and solemn for him, and thus it must be with the day of his confirmation when he reaches religious independence. On this day, especially, he should be carefully instructed about his new duties as a human being, as a Jew, and as a citizen. The importance of his new vocation should be vividly explained to him and this should elicit from him the free confirmation of the basic truths of his religion and the solemn vow to live in accordance with the religion of his fathers and the laws of the state. And finally, in order to increase the impression of the moment, the boy himself should speak emphatically on a fitting theme, chosen either from the field of religion or morality. Thus the youth, trained from childhood to like only that which is true, good, and noble, will become a man who will be able to stand up courageously against all storms of fate, and under the protection of reason and virtue will walk unswerving upon his way toward the grand goal of perfection. Then and only then, my dear coreligionists, may we look with justified hope to a happy future in which Israel will shine again in its pristine purity, when the kind genius of enlightenment will lovingly enfold all of mankind in its benevolent arms. Then our descendants will bless our ashes because we taught them not only to think right but also to act right.

SIMPLICITY, NOT POMP (*Isaac Asher Francolm*)

Francolm was probably the first to introduce the confirmation of girls.

According to the rabbinic view a boy, as soon as he has passed his thirteenth year, is obligated to fulfil all ceremonial laws which, in part, he could transgress before that day and, in part, was not even allowed to fulfil, since he did not count as a person for the purpose of religious acts. For instance, a younger boy was allowed to eat on a fast day. However, he was not allowed to put on phylacteries and his presence did not count in the required quorum at a worship service or at the spoken grace after meals. Therefore, the day on which he finishes his thirteenth year is a significant landmark in his life. From this day on, religion claims the boy and he must observe all its commands and is put on an equal footing with all adults in regard to his availability for religious ceremony. The entrance into this age, which obligates him to fulfil the laws, is observed at a festivity in the home on the Sabbath following his birthday. The synagogue takes notice of this in so far as it admits the boy to those customs which are reserved for adults.

There is no definite age at which girls begin their obligation to obey the laws. Hence, no festivity of this kind is held for them. Once again, the female sex is here treated as less capable, as in Oriental custom. In my code there is no ceremonial law which is forbidden to a child, the only exception being the functions of the priests and Levites. The only limits in the synagogue might consist of not calling the child to lift up and dress the Torah. One cannot agree that there is in rabbinic tradition a specific age for taking on the obligations of the law.

But there is a significant landmark in the life of both boys and girls which consists of the knowledge of religion they have achieved, that is, when they have finished their education. For this there is no definite age, for the maturity of knowledge alone is decisive. It is seemly, therefore, that education should climax with a solemn act in a sacred place, and that the soul of the youth be moved and strengthened through a vow to safeguard loyally the knowledge which he has attained and to live in accordance with it.

Such an act, which is not to be confused with the celebration at the end of the thirteenth year, was not customary in rabbinic tradition. It is something new, but it is in the spirit of Judaism. We find the following arrangement as most suited for this purpose.

As soon as the child's education is finished, the preacher arranges for a public examination of the confirmants in a place of his choice.

The next day, or some days later, the confirmants assemble at the synagogue at a certain hour, during which no service is being held. One of them, speaking for all the rest, then pronounces a simple confession of faith, whereupon the preacher admonishes the confirmants to follow the traditional teachings and asks of them a pledge to live religiously. This pledge is then given by all with the words, "Yes, we pledge it before God." The preacher says, "So help you God," and all present call out, "Amen." Then the preacher gives a prayer and speaks the words of the benediction. The observance can be opened and closed with a psalm, which might be spoken alternatingly by cantor and choir, or the choir alone might sing it.

Boys and girls should be confirmed separately. Where there is neither a synagogue arranged in accordance with the new principles nor a teacher, the children should be comfirmed in their homes. The parents may invite friends, but they must take care that the religious act should not become a social function. At the home, the act begins with the examination, then follows the confession of faith and everything else as in the synagogue, and the teacher replaces the preacher. In no case should the boy or girl confirmant hold an address on this occasion, so that a solemn observance which is meant to make a deep impression upon the young soul should not be desecrated through pomp and the satisfaction of idle vanity.

IS CONFIRMATION A "JEWISH" CEREMONY? (*Salomon Herxheimer*)

Herxheimer (1801-1884), a pupil of Creizenach, was a prolific scholar and outspoken reformer. He wrote a popular commentary on Torah and Prophets, and his *Yesode Ha-torah* went through twenty-nine editions.

We finally have to deal with the question whether, how, and when, at the end of the process of education, there should be a confirmation. This inquiry is the more important because the subject matter demands clarification and unification in many congregations, even though, already forty years ago in Brunswick, the strictly Orthodox late District Rabbi Eger introduced a confirmation service. Also, the Israelite consistory decreed confirmation for boys and girls in 1813, and a pious Jew includes a formal "confirmation" in his daily morning prayer when he says the Thirteen Articles of Faith by Maimonides.

In the Protestant church, confirmation is an integral part of the process of baptism, which is necessary for acceptance into the church community. Confirmation completes the covenant of baptism by having the baptized person, who meanwhile has been instructed in religion, affirm and confirm freely that which at his baptism was acknowledged on his behalf by his godparents.

It is obvious that a confirmation of this type and import is not applicable to Judaism. The Jewish child does not need a kind of baptism to be accepted into the covenant of his faith. According to Orthodox principles, he belongs to it already by virtue of his birth and descent. The covenant which obligates him is that of Sinai (Exodus 24:7), which is eternally binding for Israel (Deut. 29:10), just as the Torah which Moses commanded is an inheritance of the congregation of Jacob (Deut. 33:4).

The Bar Mitzvah celebration of a thirteen-year-old boy is not contrary to this principle of the synagogue, for it is not considered an acceptance into Judaism and is entirely different in origin, meaning, and character from the sacramental affirmation of the Catholic church and the later confirmation of other Christian sects. Bar Mitzvah is merely an acknowledgment that the boy has, because of his age, become mature and is, therefore, obligated to observe the commandments (*ben shalosh-essre lamitzvot*).

That at such a time the father has to express his own release from being responsible for his child, proves that the responsibility for carrying out the law existed simply because of the boy's Jewish descent. Consequently, those boys for whom such acknowledgment was not made, as well as all girls, are in any case considered Jews and Jewesses.

The question at hand can, therefore, only be this: Could a confirmation be inadmissible even if it is not an acceptance and affirmation of the covenant, but only a confirmation of it through a confession of faith and a pledge, for the reason that such an act would come too close to Christian purpose and meaning? Would such an observance make the obligation and membership of Jews in their religion appear conditioned on its observance, and make it appear as if all Jews who were not confirmed were not Jews?

Now we believe that, because of the delicate aspects of this subject matter, it might well be that confirmation should not be generally obligatory, and that in any case the confirmant should be given to understand that he is already, as a born Jew, inextricably bound to the faith of his fathers and that he will remain so bound. It is impossible, however, to consider the free pledge of a Jew to remain faithful to his faith as unnecessary or even impermissible, simply because the Jew is already bound to Judaism because of his birth and his Sinaitic obligation.

Moses himself repeats the Sinaitic covenant with Israel toward the end of his life. Joshua and Elijah ask of Israel a voluntary acknowledgment of their faith. Nehemiah renews the Mosaic covenant. The Psalmist says expressly: "I swear it and will fulfil it, to observe Thy just command." And the Talmud (Ned. 8), relying on this very passage from Psalms, allows sacred vows concerning the Torah, despite the existing Sinaitic obligation, for the purpose of "self-encouragement," and similarly the Mishnah (Ethics ch. 4) generally recommends such vows as a "bridle for abstinence." The later rabbis consider such vows expressly as praiseworthy and obligatory (Yore De'a 203:6).

It is obvious, therefore, that according to Bible and tradition, a vow of loyalty concerning individual laws as well as the total content of our religion, is not inadmissible and is neither superfluous nor blameworthy, but rather, may be considered required in the interest of religion, in the same manner as all covenants in the Bible were re-formed and confirmed in order to prevent apostasy.

In order that confirmation may, indeed, produce the intended strengthening and elevation of Judaism, it must of needs receive a form and arrangement which is adequate to its purpose. First of all, it would be necessary that an examination in religion be connected with it. Such examination should immediately precede the confirmation and perhaps would best take place during the worship service right after the reading of the Torah. There seems to be a direct connection between examination and confirmation, and the purpose of the Torah reading, "So that they might hear and learn and fear God" (Deut. 31:22-23). These acts, in their total sacred and worshipful character, belong into a sacred place in the midst of public worship service and the religious assembly which renders them more solemn for all participants. They do not belong, therefore, into some school hall or even into the family circle where they might become a sort of "breakfast confirmation."

So that the worship service should not become too lengthy, the examination should only last about fifteen minutes, but it should not be restricted merely to the Ten Commandments, for people might believe that the rest of the Torah is being ignored or eliminated. The examination should concern itself only with the most important teachings of religion and the relevant sources. Incidentally, the student should not be specially rehearsed and prepared for this examination.

To be sure, such public examinations were formerly neither customary nor necessary at Bar Mitzvah celebrations, because at that time the home life represented one continuous education in religion and an intimate relationship with Judaism. But such a procedure will have two advantages: the congregation will be able to form a judgment concerning the achievements of the religious school and the extent of the religious knowledge of its junior members and, in addition, many in the audience will receive beneficial instruction in religious matters. For every adult, even though he has finished his education, is needful of and aided by a rehearsal of teachings and obligations, or a proverb, or a word of solace.

But chiefly, the examination is of greatest benefit to the confirmants themselves, for by giving public proof of their religious knowledge before parents and congregation in the house of God, they will receive a deeper respect for religion and Judaism. The serious and zealous preparation for this examination, which may last half a year or a full year, will implant the subject matter indelibly into their memory. Their religious sentiments will be more deeply aroused and excited, and thus in a sense they will already be confirmed in advance.

Therefore, we should not limit ourselves merely to a religious examination. The pious sense which is encouraged by it will be still more elevated and increased when, at the end of the instruction period, there is a confirmation ceremony—not a public spectacle, to be sure, but one of high significance, sanctity, and solemnity. It should include all boys and girls who have reached the thirteenth year and have demonstrated their readiness by sufficient knowledge and preparation.

CONFIRMATION IN PARIS, 1852 (*Anonymous Correspondent*)

The ceremony of confirmation which is called *initiation religieuse,* takes place in the synagogue every year after the Shavuot Festival. Even though confirmation has been in existence for only a few years, it has already made a place for itself in the life of the French Jews and has brought them many blessings. Between sixty and eighty children appear at the ceremony. Whether they are poor or rich, they are nicely dressed, and in the holy place confirm their entrance into the synagogue at the end of a meticulous examination.

In this manner children of both sexes from families of the most diverse backgrounds obtain a thorough knowledge and love of their faith. By rearranging and reordering an old form, a need has been satisfied which our times demanded. Such reform is beneficial and after some time it will be firmly rooted in the congregation and amongst our people.

6. COVERING THE HEAD

HISTORICAL FACTS (*Leopold Löw*)

One of Hungary's most profound halakhic and historical scholars, Löw (1811-75) was the first rabbi to preach in the language of that country. A liberal in every way, he was imprisoned during the revolutionary days of the 1840's.

In a long appreciation of Chorin, Löw treats of the Arad Rabbi's reforms, his permission to use the railroad on Sabbaths and holidays, as well as his suggestion to pray without head covering, a suggestion which, in Europe, was followed only by the Berlin Reform Society. It was in America that bareheadedness became an identifying mark of Reform worship. Perhaps no other innovation of Reform aroused greater opposition than this; no other change stirred so many sentiments. Yet the attachment to the custom of covering the head was of relatively late origin, as Löw shows in his detailed historical study. He traces the custom from the earliest biblical days to his own time, and shows that it entered Jewish life very slowly and was originally an oriental habit denoting respect. The article is fully annotated. A few excerpts follow:

Talmudic literature has a good deal of information about the subject of our inquiry. You will find it noteworthy that in the whole talmudic literature there are, outside of the biblical word *koba*,[6] only two other words for head covering, that is, words of Semitic origin.[7] All other words for head covering which occur in the Talmud come from the Greek or Latin, and it is from these people that the custom of using these head coverings came to the Jews. They probably were not generally used because they were foreign products. In any case it is certain that the old biblical custom of bareheadedness was preponderant with men even in talmudic times, but that in Persia already since the fourth century a small beginning was made to supersede this custom, and to introduce instead the continuous use of head coverings.

The Babylonian Talmud lists a whole series of blessings which are pronounced daily before one puts the *sudarium* upon one's head. That is, they were spoken with uncovered heads![8] Of Rab Assi, a famous teacher of the fourth century, it is told that he covered his head with a *sudarium* before he

---

[6] Pea 5:8; Kelim 27:6; Sabb. 120a.

[7] *Ma'aferet*, Kelim 29:1; Sabb. 120a; *Ma'afron*, Targum 2, I Kings 20; 38, and Kimchi *ad loc.*

[8] Ber. 60b.

said grace after meals,[9] which implies that others must have said this prayer with heads uncovered! The night prayer, from which, incidentally, the sages used to excuse themselves,[10] must also have been spoken with uncovered heads, because the whole talmudic literature has no expression for a night-cap or any other nightly head covering, which it certainly would have possessed if in its time such a nightly covering would have been known.

In the twelfth century, one of the most famous French sages, Rabbi Isaac ben Aba Mari from Marseilles, witnesses to the fact that even the pious ones went about during the mornings with heads uncovered until such time as they put the *tallit* over their heads, and that otherwise during the day they sometimes covered the head and sometimes they uncovered it.

Rabbi Joseph Caro, to be sure, attempts to give the words of Rabbi Isaac a different interpretation because he was an oriental rabbi and felt offended at bareheadedness, as was the feeling of his time. However, Rabbi Moses Isserles says quite openly that Rabbi Isaac's words would have to be understood in their natural sense, since no anxiety was necessary concerning the head covering because this was only a pious custom.[11]

At the beginning of the thirteenth century, Rabbi Abraham ben Nathan Ha-Yarchi of Lunel, who had traveled through all Jewish congregations of France and Spain, tells us that it was a *minhag,* or custom, to pray with covered heads. And the Rabbi adds that it is generally right to cover the head in the manner of the Spaniards who ought to be praised for this custom: *yeyasher kohom* [may their strength increase].[12]

This praise for the Spaniards apparently did not move the French Jews. About a generation later, in the middle of the thirteenth century, it still happened in the French synagogue that the Torah reading took place with uncovered head. Even amongst the much more scrupulous German Jews this custom seems to have been permitted to children who were called to the Torah, but Rabbi Isaac ben Moses of Vienna criticizes this very strongly.[13]

Toward the end of the thirteenth century, two famous rabbis, one German and one French, express themselves concerning bareheadedness. Rabbi Meir ben Baruch of Rothenburg, who was the leading German authority of the Middle Ages when it came to customs, says straightforwardly that it was not forbidden to walk about with uncovered heads and to digress from the pious manner of individual sages of the talmudic era. Rabbi Meir's contemporary, Rabbi Perez ben Elijah in Corbeilles, who was the leading scholar of the French Jews in regard to customs, recommends that one should not permit entrance into the synagogue with uncovered heads.[14] The French Jews, there-

[9] Ber. 51a.

[10] Ber. 5a.

[11] R. Jonah in Shéte Yadot, *Derek Hayim* 39b. *Tur Orah Hayim* 8. Bet Yosef and Darke Moshe *ad loc.* Cf. *Sefer Hasidim* (Warsaw 1866), 8c.

[12] *Ha-manhig* (ed. Berlin, 1855), p. 15, no. 45.

[13] Darke Moshe, *Tur Orah Hayim* 282:3. See *Or Zarua* II 20, no. 4g; Löw, *Lebensalter*, p. 410, note 70.

[14] *Kol Bo,* no.11 f 8b Ven; Bet Yosef, *Orah Hayim* 91.

fore, apparently entered the synagogue as late as at the end of the thirteenth century with uncovered heads. Outside of the synagogue even Rabbi Perez does not want to oppose the prevailing custom. At the end of the fourteenth or the beginning of the fifteenth century, Rabbi Jacob Ha-Levi Mölln teaches that mourners should not go about with uncovered heads.[15] There is, in other words, no trace of any general command to cover the head which would be religiously motivated. And this Rabbi Jacob, a contemporary of Johann Huss, far excelled his predecessors in scrupulousness and strictness, and until this very day he is the first authority of our piyutists and pietists in liturgical matters. Rabbi Jacob's more learned and more famous contemporary, Rabbi Isserlein, Rabbi in Marburg and Wiener-Neustadt, received an inquiry from Breslau whether the oath should be sworn with uncovered head. The question noted that Jews in Breslau were being forced to swear in this manner. Rabbi Isserlein answered that he could not find anywhere any prohibition covering this matter. And this considering the fact that during the swearing of the oath the name *Adonai* had to be pronounced![16]

It is often stated that the prevailing custom of covering the head is "a millenium old usage" and that the Jews who uncovered their heads deny their oriental descent. All these errors stem from the fact that the study of biblical antiquities is hardly pursued and that of the talmudic age not at all. Arrogant condemnation is, of course, much easier and more comfortable than thorough study of specialities. But the unprejudiced sense of truth will not be satisfied by the notions of idle romanticism and self-sufficiency, but only by the results of research which does not tire to go to the sources and to be taught by them.

7. TORAH READING AND OTHER PRACTICES

THE TORAH CYCLE
(Discussion at the Leipzig Synod, 1871)

Reformers had long wrestled with the problem of restoring the Torah reading to its central place in the service. The practice of chanting the long weekly portion at high speed robbed this important educational and inspirational act of both its educative and inspirational value. Various remedies were proposed: introduction of a triennial instead of the annual cycle; shortening the readings and maintaining the annual cycle; partial or full translation of the portion; meaningful reading instead of chanting; omitting the procession of persons called up to the reading; abandonment

[15] *Sefer Minhagim* (ed. Sabioneta), 109b.
[16] *Pésakim u-ḳétabim*, no. 203.

of the practice of saying a special personal blessing (*mi-she-berakh*) in behalf of those called up, etc. The two discussants here quoted are Manuel Joel (1826-1890) and Gustav Gottheil (1827-1903). Joel was Rabbi in Breslau and was noted for his research in Jewish religious philosophy. Gottheil, a native of Germany, was serving the community of Manchester at the time of the synod. Two years later he was called to assist Samuel Adler at Temple Emanu-El in New York and later succeeded him. He was among the few early Reformers who actively supported and led the Zionist movement.

Joel: We must all agree if we want to maintain a common worship service. Gentlemen, especially in the discussion of ritual, this is the time to show your colors. It may seem strange to you that I, of all people, make such a statement. With those who know me I have the reputation (which I pray God will allow me to keep) that I am rather inclined to retain than to destroy. But everywhere radicalism assumes the right to show its colors. Gentlemen, in religion radicalism can least afford to show colors because it would read itself out of religion altogether. What I mean here with showing colors is this: We will have to state whether the worship service that we desire shall have only the most distant and tenuous relationship with former worship services, or whether it should grow out of the natural soil of our history and destiny. This is what we will have to manifest above all.

Now, I am convinced that some of you would like to go further than is recommended in these motions. But, gentlemen, we intend to create a prayer book which can be accepted by all reasonably enlightened congregations. The form of Jewish prayer is largely characterized by the fact that it is not so much the individual as all of Israel who are at prayer. It is a sort of majestic chorale which pervades our prayer book. In the revision of our prayer book we should generally be guided by this principle. Our age has many great things which distinguish it from the past. But our honored president has already called to your attention the fact that the past, too, has many advantages over us. Antiquity was great because the totality of the state set limits to the individual; in other words, the individual had no rights vis-à-vis the community. Our time is great because the opposite is the case. Today we emphasize individual more than communal tendencies; but true greatness comes from the community, and this as far as possible we ought to use as a guide for our attitudes. On the one hand, we must express the freedom of the individual, but on the other, especially as far as ritual is concerned, the individual must give expression, not merely to that which moves him, but also to that which affects Israel and the total community. We proceeded from the thought that a shortening of the Torah reading was necessary, but not because such readings were too long for us. Gentlemen, a rabbi has the patience even to listen to a fourth of the whole Torah at one time. As far as I am concerned, I am never bored by any reading from the Bible. But an abbreviation seems necessary to us in the interest of the total community. Therefore, we are concerned with the degree of abbreviation. The commission has proposed a three-year cycle to you. I personally support the suggestion by Wiener[17], namely, that the one-year cycle should be kept, but be divided into readings on Sabbath morning, Monday, and Thursday. However, in the commission proper, I did not insist on my request because the suggestion of a three-year cycle also has in mind a similar abbreviation. But I still lean more to the one-year than to the three-year cycle because, while the former achieves not only the main purpose, namely, the abbreviation of each individual reading from the Torah, it also has the side effect of retaining the names of the Sabbath days and of the Jewish calendar.

Gottheil: Much has been said here of that pious reverence with which, indeed, we ought to listen to the word of God. Now, gentlemen, it would be an act of piety to do that which will increase the confidence in, and the influence of, this word in our congregation. If you want to overcome the objection of the complete reading of the Torah portion by stipulating that it should only be read in part, then, in my opinion—you will excuse this expression—it will be an act which might be interpreted as a lack of confidence. For would we strengthen in our listeners the confidence in the word of God by covering and hushing up some passages? I am against the three-year cycle already for the reason that the bond of unity will thereby be broken. I did not get the full impression of this until some weeks ago I listened to the Torah reading in Hamburg. I thought, "There is a breach in Israel." (bravo) Gentlemen, the idea that the Torah should be read through in one year rests on the talmudic view that the law must in any case be read from beginning to end. This view I cannot share. But you will excuse me, gentlemen, if I say openly—and say this even though I am a young man—that I have long left this opinion of such necessity behind me. I do not recognize it and rely on the spirit of the Bible. Furthermore, if we want to reform formalism, then let us not reform ourselves into a new formalism. For then we will miss our purpose. We must reform ourselves into a new living spirit. (bravo) It is no spiritual accomplishment to stretch out a one-year cycle into a three-year cycle, to broaden it, so to speak, on the anvil. You all know the beautiful and oft-quoted saying of our sages, "The law was not given for angels, but for men."

Therefore, let us treat the whole matter in a human fashion. I understand thereby that we should constantly keep in mind the true and real needs of people and not any false piety vis-à-vis the ancient days. Someone has made the motion that one should either omit or shorten the calling up to the Torah, because this impinges upon the dignity of the Torah reading itself. But what is really important is that what is being read is also understood by everyone. With beautiful words Dr. Joel has called our attention to the characteristics of our worship service and to its common feature. Now, gentlemen, is it a common feature when your women and your youth sit there and at the same time we do not desire that they understand what is being read? (bravo) We learn that it was because of the merit of a woman that Israel went out of

17 Dr. A. Wiener of Oppeln.

Egypt. It was a woman, too, who inspired me to free myself from all mechanical formulae, and I have freed myself from them. In my synagogue there is the custom that every woman, indeed that every child, appears with an English Bible and follows the reading in the Hebrew or the English language. And you ask, how long? For already six years. And the result is that—as you will witness if you come into my synagogue during the reading of the Torah— even though there is no calling to the Torah, the whole congregation, including the children, are involved in a unique religious act. There is a spirit of piety for the declaration of the word of God, a spirit which pervades the whole congregation. (bravo) Because of these experiences and reasons which I commend to you most urgently, I ask you either to accept the proposal of Mr. Leeser[18] immediately or to refer it to a commission, which could then report to us at this or at the next synodal assembly.

After prolonged debate the assembly voted to retain the one-year cycle. Liberal congregations almost universally followed this recommendation, but they often shortened the weekly reading.

PIYUTIM (*Gustav Gottheil*)

Certain religious poems which in the course of centuries were added to the prayer book are called *Piyutim*. Often these poems were complex and their allusions obscure, and only scholars could understand and interpret some of them. In general, Reformers sought to omit most of this poetry, but even amongst them there were dissenters like Gottheil.

Gentlemen: I would like to say a few words to you, not because I really hope that you will favor or even accept what I have to say (since I will attempt to modify your apparently unanimous judgment), but because, according to talmudic principle, a unanimous judgment is always a doubtful one. This, I hope, may help me to find at least good listeners amongst you. I want to say a word in favor of *piyutim*. I am deeply convinced that our festival service would lack its festive character if our *piyutim* were eliminated. The service would then be very similar to the week-day service. But when on holidays we come into the house of God in a very special mood, happy in the thought that we are celebrating a great religious festival of Judaism like, for instance, Rosh Hashanah, when we thus come into the house of God should we find merely the repetition of the everyday and every-Sabbath liturgy? Such a service would not respond to our festive ardor. In fact, it would doubtlessly cool and suppress it. But the *piyutim* will elevate our mood. Furthermore, it is wrong to dispose of all *piyutim* in this manner. Why should we not include in our prayer book

[18] H. Leeser was a teacher in Luebbecke, Germany.

at least a few of them which are unobjectionable, as for instance, some lovely Spanish songs? Besides, the work of learned men has widened the field of the *piyutim* considerably and, leaving the narrow boundaries of custom, there is no objection to accepting some of these. You have tried to make a concession to the festive mood by adding a German prayer. Gentlemen, I fully recognize the rights of the present to change the prayer, but I believe that the religious consciousness of other times also has the right to find expression in our prayers. I do not believe that our time, with its cold rational direction, is especially suitable to create warm, heart-stirring prayers. And for these I would rather go back to the warmer religious sentiment of antiquity and let it supply us with such prayers. Therefore, I must speak out against the generally condemnatory judgment against *piyutim*.

CHAPTER
VIII

Sabbath and Holiday Observance

Reform judaism was essentially the response of a living people to the urgent demands of the time.

There were few areas in which practice and principle posed greater dilemmas than in the area of Sabbath and holiday observance. The whole question of the authority of tradition came here into sharpest focus. It need hardly be pointed out that many of the problems raised here still are matters at issue today, for by definition a dynamic Reform cannot give fixed permanent answers in matters of practice.

1. THE SABBATH

"Even as Israel has guarded the Sabbath, so the Sabbath has guarded Israel," goes a saying. Tradition considered the Sabbath central to Jewish life and the Reform movement was heir to this conviction. But economic pressures had made serious inroads into the old observance, the strictness of which had given the day an aspect of abstinence rather than joy, of prohibition rather than sanctification. How could the essential qualities of the Sabbath be saved in the modern environment? This was the question to which Reform addressed itself, a question which was extensively discussed at the third conference in Breslau in 1846. The answers ranged from proposals for moderate change to a revaluation of the essential nature of the Sabbath. More than a hundred years later the full answers are still lacking.   :

WHAT WORK IS PERMITTED? (*Bernhard Wechsler*)

At issue is the command not to work [on the Sabbath], the stoppage of all commercial activity. To what extent must an Israelite observe this? To the extent that he may not engage in any profession or activity which might at some future time force him to disregard the command? Does it extend so far that the observance of the Sabbath command supersedes all other obligations in case he has chosen such a profession or is subject to a collision of obligations under circumstances over which he has no control? Does the Sabbath command yield to other obligations in such cases? What happens when someone is engaged in commercial activities which are incompatible with work stoppage on the Sabbath, because such activity must be carried on even on that day lest his entire temporal existence be threatened and he be subject to the most severe losses and consequences? Is work stoppage commanded under such conditions and is it an absolute obligation, or may an Israelite make some sort of arrangement for the carrying on of his business by eliminating at least his own personal direct participation in such activity? And finally the last question: What happens in some cases in which work stoppage would lead to the bitterest and harshest losses; where the whole temporal happiness, either one's own or someone else's, is in question? May an Israelite make remedial arrangements; may he let non-Jews make such arrangements if possible; and where not possible, may he himself make them?

Gentlemen, these are some of the questions and circumstances which we must consider and which we cannot avoid answering. These are no idle or casuistic questions. They are taken from present-day life. I need hardly tell you that our people expect from us definitive declarations and well-founded opinions on this point. These conflicts lurk everywhere and urge us on to make a decision. In my opinion we should not, therefore, be frightened by the fact that in making such a decision we may have to make an independent judgment. For the traditional concept, even the biblical point of view, gives us only sparse analogies and hints for the purpose of such a decision. We must be guided by our conscience and our conviction.

We turn first to the question of occupation. Here above all we must make a distinction. There is the occupation which we carry out as a consequence of our general obligations in life, one that we do not choose ourselves, but which comes to us because we are part of state, society, and community. The other is the kind of occupation which an Israelite chooses for himself, such as teacher, lawyer, and so forth. In the case of the former, where it was our obligation to accept an occupation which is incompatible with work stoppage on the Sabbath (as a soldier, as a government official, etc.), it is not necessary to amplify the matter greatly. Everyone must carry out his obligations and must do what his office demands; even though the Bible and tradition are silent regarding such a collision of duties (they only speak clearly about *pikuah nefesh,* the saving of life), history, the development of man, and the ethical consciousness of the present speak of this the more loudly.

More difficult is the decision which concerns an occupation which is incompatible with the Sabbath, but is one that we have chosen ourselves, where we voluntarily took upon ourselves obligations which collide with the celebration of the Sabbath. Who forces anyone to become a doctor, lawyer, teacher, and so forth? But even here, I believe, we must overcome all scruples. Even here we must be satisfied with the answer: Life, conditions, our position in society in general, are forcing our hand. Should the Israelite today avoid all those higher

professional activities which are not compatible with the observance of the
ceremonial law, and especially the celebration of the Sabbath? Would his religion want this of him? Must he resolve to renounce all opportunities of
education? Even if he would make such a resolution, it would not help, for
times cannot be altered through resolution or authoritarian dicta. Incidentally,
while we lack pronouncements on this subject, we do not lack analogies and
historical hints which teach us that in Judaism there never was such an absolute and all-pervasive observance of the Sabbath. Rabbis were doctors, government officials, and so forth, especially in the Moorish period, to cite just one
example. However, we must draw a distinct line between that activity which is
a consequence of obligations which have been assumed, and that which can be
postponed without endangering the fulfilment of such obligations. Therefore,
we must indeed ask of the doctor, even the soldier and official, that he should
observe the Sabbath and stay away from occupational activity as far as his
duties will allow. To be sure, we must leave it to his religious conscience to
draw this line of distinction.

I shall now turn to the question of occupation. According to the *Shulhan
Arukh,* the Jewish customs collector may employ a non-Jew to take in taxes
and customs, or to write receipts, or even to mint coins, with only the condition
that he himself should not draw any gain from this activity, which does, however, not quite fit minting activities (*Orah Hayim* 244). The principle here is
that the strictness of the Sabbath is meliorated because without such concession Israelites could not be tax or customs collectors. It is too bad that in the
ancient days there were not other similar occupations, for had there been we
would not have to search for meliorating excuses in today's occupational
circumstances. Had this been the case, the manufacturer, the artisan, the
merchant, would not be face to face with the sad alternative either to leave his
trade or act contrary to his religious duties. But why should we not be satisfied with these examples which make it possible to declare as permitted that
which has become necessity? We can, therefore, declare with all certainty that
the Israelite is obligated to withdraw on the Sabbath day from business and
trade and, wherever possible, to let these come to a complete stand-still. But in
all cases where such cessation completely interferes with his temporal existence,
he would not be transgressing a religious obligation if he would make arrangements to have non-Jews carry out that which is necessary. From the rabbinic point of view, such an explanation falls under the category of *amirah
lenakhri shevut* (making arrangements through a non-Jew is a further safeguard of the command to rest). Therefore, it does not need any justification if
we suspend such a *shevut* in the face of overriding needs in order to prevent
further transgression. We do not find any command or prohibition in the
Bible which could be applied to our circumstances, because the Bible does not
know of any such collision of obligations. Therefore, we must turn to the
spirit and the reasonable purpose of the Sabbath celebration. The day is
meant to elevate, to strengthen, to encourage, to afford rest and recreation.
How can this be when worry about one's livelihood lurks like a ghost and dis-
turbs the equanimity of the celebration; when on every Sabbath the worry over
one's livelihood battles with higher spiritual ideas?

But, it is said, there is great danger when an Israelite allows a non-Jew to carry on business and trade on the Sabbath, for he would be exposed to the temptation that he himself would take part in such activities, that he would supervise them, pay attention to them, and thus be drawn away from the celebration of the Sabbath. Gentlemen, there is danger here as well as there. The question is, which is the least evil? The question is, how can we bring the present circumstances into possible accord with the needs of religion? To be sure, there is temptation, but that is not introduced through our declaration. It already exists, and it beckons already more than a little. It is our task to inquire what, in the spirit of our religion, is admissible and what is not.

Who would doubt today that in the spirit of our religion it is permissible to violate the Sabbath when one's total possessions are in question, when the house is burning, when the elements are raging and demand quick rescue of one's property? Who would doubt that it would be permitted to act in such cases, even on the Sabbath, rather than look on with outward calm and inner despair and disquiet while misfortune crashes about us and perdition threatens our whole future? For here the principle applies: *Mutav sh'yehalel shabbat ehad v'al yehalel shabbatot harbe* (It is better to desecrate one Sabbath so that one should not be forced to desecrate many Sabbaths). What kind of resignation would be asked of us to observe the commandment in all its strictness? Must we not here remember the wise saying, *Lo nitna Torah lemalakhe hasharet* (The Torah was not given to the ministering angels)? Who can help but publicly contradict rabbinic rigidity in such a case?

In conclusion, I would summarize my suggestions as follows, and would formulate the proposal of the committee in this manner:

The assembly should declare that the Israelite may follow the duties of his occupation in all cases where higher obligations (service of the state as a soldier, doctor, and so forth) come in collision with the celebration of the Sabbath and where they cannot be postponed. He is, however, obligated to observe the Sabbath as far as his professional obligations permit, and must let his business and profession come to complete rest.

The general duty to avert danger to life, be it one's own or someone else's, supersedes the duty to celebrate the Sabbath, and one is not only permitted but even obligated to do everything necessary in this regard and to withdraw from Sabbath celebration to this end.

The assembly should declare that, to be sure, it is the obligation of the Israelite not to seek a livelihood on the Sabbath, to abstain from any gain, and not to worry about his temporal existence, but, instead, to dedicate the day to God. There are occupations which do not admit of rest on the Sabbath because they must be carried on even on this day, and this is the case especially with artisans, manufacturers, and merchants, and some other types of business. Where this is the case, it is permitted to have non-Jews do what is necessary for the carrying on of the business, if personal direct participation by the Jew can thereby be avoided. Where it is a question of one's total material welfare, where one's total possessions, or the means for one's future existence are in question and are threatened, a Jew would not transgress a religious duty if he takes remedial measures and, where others cannot assist him, attends to them himself.

THE SABBATH MUST BE PROTECTED (*Samuel Adler*)

Adler (1809-91) was Rabbi in Alzey at the time of the conference in Breslau, where he made the following statement. After a distinguished career in Germany he was called to Temple Emanu-El in New York and continued his leadership of liberal causes in the New World.

Consider the difference between festival days and Sabbaths in regard to the prohibition of work. With the former, what is forbidden is always called *melekhet avodah* (servile work), and in regard to the Sabbath, *kol melakhah* (every work) is forbidden. What is the difference between *kol melakhah* and *melekhet avodah?* In what respect is one a larger prohibition than the other, and what thought underlies this differentiation? Tradition gives us the key to the answer. To be sure, festival days, too, have as their purpose and goal sanctification and religious edification. But rest is only a subordinate means to this end, and, therefore, what is forbidden is only *melekhet avodah,* an activity which is in opposition to the task and idea of the festival, because its commercial nature and necessary expenditure of energy will divert the mind of the worker. But if such sanctification is not impeded by *melekhet avodah,* it is then permitted.

How then are we to understand the larger prohibition of *kol melakhah* for the Sabbath? Only in regard to the preparation of food? Why only that? The Sabbath is to represent creation completed, and rest is to point to it symbolically. Therefore, *kol melakhah* represents every activity which creates and produces something even if it is not of a commercial or effort-demanding nature. Hence, we have to differentiate between an activity on the Sabbath which deserves the name *melekhet avodah,* and one which, being neither commercial nor effort-demanding, goes beyond it and is expressed simply by the term *kol melakhah.* Just as the Sabbath is not completely expressed through the concept of rest but is also a day of sanctification and festivity and aims at consecration and sanctification of the senses, in the same manner it shares with the festival days the prohibition of *melekhet avodah.* This means that all commercial and effort-demanding labor is prohibited because it interferes with Sabbath sanctification, and this applies under all conditions, whether such labor is productive or not. Thus the Mishnah considers the act of tearing as forbidden labor even where no production is intended. On the other hand, all that which goes beyond *melekhet avodah* and is prohibited, not because it interferes with sanctification, but only because it is a productive labor and therefore prohibited because of its symbolic implications—all this can apply only if there is actually some production or where production is intended.

I believe that this truly expresses the Sabbath idea of Mosaism and the consistent concept of its work prohibition according to tradition. Does this sound strict? Yes, Mosaism is strict. If the task is difficult, we do not, therefore, have a right to misread the task and interpret it differently. That is Mosaism; that is tradition! If they come into severe conflict with the irresistible demands of our time—which, alas, cannot be denied—then we must honestly ask: given such circumstances, must we not sacrifice a part of the strict demands of the Sabbath in order to save the Sabbath itself? Indeed, I would have no hesitation to answer this question with a "Yes." I would agree with the report of the commission and sacrifice all prohibition of productive activity to the pressing demands of our time, *if* such activity is not of a commercial and effort-demanding nature and has only symbolic and ceremonial significance. I say I would do this if in that way we would heal the wounds and satisfy the demands of our age. But our age will not be served with such concessions, which it would consider ridiculous. It wants the entire Sabbath open to all manner of business—and that we cannot, that we must never admit!

A NEW CONCEPT OF THE SABBATH (*Samuel Holdheim*)

The most original contribution to the discussion was made by Holdheim. He distinguished between Sabbath *rest* and *sanctification,* and argued that the true object of the Sabbath was to achieve the latter. Rest was only a symbolic means to the end of ethical sanctification, not an end in itself. And since Holdheim's rationalism expresses itself in a thorough-going anti-symbolism, he finds little to say in favor of any aspect of Sabbath rest which is purely symbolic. The following are a few excerpts from his long and closely reasoned address.

I agree with S. Adler in his opposition to the biblical concept of the Sabbath as it appears in the report of the commission. However, my reasons are different and I, therefore, draw different conclusions. We must rediscover the original Sabbath idea of Mosaism in order to define more closely the biblical point of view and its significance for the present.

In the Bible, that is, in Mosaism proper, the concept of *shavat* means simply rest from daily business, the cessation of ordinary labor. The actual celebration is not the main point. To be sure, this is only one side of the concept of *shavat;* it is negative and does not fully describe it. Cessation from work is in itself of no religious moment, and if *shavat* were to be understood in this way, demanding the cessation of all work so that everyone would have ample time for worship, then we would disregard and hide the really positive aspect of the observance. In that way, we would emphasize what is really merely a premise and condition of the celebration, which should be self-understood, for in no place does the Torah demand such an observance with the exception of the double sacrifice. The Torah is precise and definite when it describes the entire nature of the observance as *shavat*. Therefore, this concept must have a positive as well as a negative aspect, and in fact the positive must be the important and preponderant part.

That God rested after He had completed His creation is for us a symbolic expression of His absolute eternity and exaltedness. All He had created was dependent upon His will and was, therefore, transitory and fleeting. Man's rest on this day is a symbolic exposition and active confirmation of this idea. Rest, therefore, contains not only the negative side of the Sabbath idea—the elimination of every element which would interfere with sanctification—but also its positive realization, namely, the celebration. Any symbolic worship of God is characterized by the necessity to have ideal and spiritual truths expressed and confirmed through the externalities of the senses, and such confirmation must, therefore, in its formal validity be connected to these externalities. This is especially the case in regard to the Sabbath. Absolute rest, although apparently something negative, is, however, the only valid symbolic expression of the Sabbath idea. Rest is, therefore, in the biblical view, symbol and ceremony, and the exposition of the Sabbath idea is closely tied to the other symbolism of Mosaic law.

The sanctification and holiness of the Sabbath by God and man, which in the Bible was only to be understood symbolically, was in later days taken in its purely ethical and moral sense. The strange thing is that the newer opinion was maintained without abandoning the consequences of the older one. We thus see that the historic development of Judaism went, in a very important point, above the attitude of Mosaism, without, however, breaking with it completely, thus avoiding all the far-reaching consequences which such a breach would have had. The sanctification of the Sabbath in its ethical significance leaned upon the Mosaic and symbolic Sabbath rest. It did not thereby replace it, but it reduced it to its true stature as condition and means to a higher positive significance. There was no replacement of the old idea by the new. Rather, we see the two contradictory viewpoints peaceably united because their inner contradiction was not recognized.

But we must finally be done with this contradiction. In fact, we *are* done with it. Let us ask ourselves whether we, who stand in the present and its educational environment, can still identify ourselves in our religious thinking and feeling with the views of antiquity, in accordance with which Sabbath rest was in itself an active profession, and non-rest, an active denial of the most important religious truths. For aside from the ethical sanctification, which Sabbath rest serves as a negative condition, can we find in the Sabbath idea of antiquity an inner connection with the absolute eternity and sanctification of God which would demand such observance? If we want to be truthful we must certainly answer with a "No." It would be a mockery of all experience if one would claim that today's Israelite who desecrates the Sabbath thereby denies the truth of religion, though it be founded deeply in his heart; or if one would claim that the person who celebrates the Sabbath thereby recognizes this truth and thereby had made it his own.

We must admit—and this admission we owe to God and truth—we are no longer at home in the sphere of symbolic religion. The high achievements of the spirit, our newly acquired modern education, have made it possible for us to leave this sphere forever, and there is no power which would bring us back into it, unless history would reverse its course and would lead us who have become mature men back into immature childhood. For us, a religious truth is what it is in nature and degree, not because we bring it to our consciousness and confirm it by some act which has no inner connection with it. For us, it is a truth because we can grasp it through our mental activity and because it is rooted in our hearts. We would recognize the Sabbath idea as a true idea had it become our property in some other manner. But we must declare Sabbath rest as *external and symbolic* by the way in which it appears in biblical antiquity as well as in the later history of Judaism. For us, who are far from symbolic religious forms, this no longer expresses or activates an idea, and, therefore, seen by itself, it has sunk to a mere empty externality. We must claim that he who passes the Sabbath in idle rest does not testify to the truths of any religious idea, nor does he do anything for his ethical edification, even though it cannot be denied that in accordance with biblical and later ideas of the Sabbath he has observed it, even though not completely. We must admit that for us rest in itself contains nothing positive at all and is only a negative condition and means for the Sabbath celebration which is to be observed by spiritual edification. To be sure, we have hereby expressed a contrast between our religious consciousness and that of the Bible. However, the Sabbath is in this respect no isolated incident but is closely connected with the great and general contrast which exists generally between our modern religious consciousness and Mosaic symbolism, and especially with regard to sacrifice.

Now, if one should ask which kinds of labor are forbidden on the Sabbath, then the answer is easy. Just as in the biblical point of view, where rest is the main thing, everything is forbidden which interferes with Sabbath *rest,* so from our point of view, where sanctification is the important thing, rest is only a condition and everything is forbidden that interferes with *sanctification.* In so far as rest is a condition for the sanctification, it is commanded. But where the conditioning element is inoperative, rest ceases to be commanded. The report of the commission establishes two categories: commercial activity and effort-demanding labor, because they interfere with the sanctification of the Sabbath and are therefore prohibited; but all other activity which has as its subject and goal worshipful, religious purposes or recreation, cannot be forbidden because it does not stand in the way of Sabbath sanctification.

Therefore, we must, above all, declare that *the Israelite who does not sanctify the Sabbath does indeed commit a sin against God and himself,* because he discards a means of religious exaltation which his religion affords him. However, he cannot be considered as having become disloyal to Judaism if in other respects he makes it truths his own and the foundation of his life. We must leave it to his conscience how far he will by himself try to reach the purpose of religious exaltation on the Sabbath, even though he does not celebrate it as a general day of rest, and we must avoid judging him in this respect.

SABBATH AND SUNDAY (*Samuel Holdheim*)

Holdheim here presents "the ultimate conclusion" of his view: the institution of Sunday services and the complete shift of the day of rest away from the traditional Sabbath. He was correct in his assessment of the sentiment of the majority who rejected his ideas "with indignation" (as indeed they rejected his extreme rationalism). However, Sunday services (which were at the time of the Breslau debate, in 1846, held solely in Holdheim's Berlin Reform Association) spread eventually to America where they became popular around the turn of the century, only to lose their attraction again a generation later. But the principal issue which Holdheim raised was still unresolved 125 years after he discussed it before his colleagues.

I am not afraid of coming forward with the ultimate conclusion of my view. I will certainly not present it in the form of a motion before this Assembly, since I am convinced that it will be rejected with indignation by the majority of our people, and, therefore, it cannot be expected to be accepted by their representatives and teachers. However, truth and conviction shall not and must not be denied the honor and freedom of expression in our Assembly.

All our efforts for the restoration of a dignified Sabbath observance are in vain, and unfortunately there is no radical means to settle the conflict between Sabbath celebration and the demands of civic life, other than changing the former to some other, occupationally unencumbered day. I protest against any concession which seems thereby to have been made to Christian principles. I have in mind only the possibility of a dignified Sabbath celebration. The wounds from which our religious life suffers cut deeply into all our hearts; and helplessness will be the mark of all our endeavors until the time comes when the only possible cure for the disease will have been prescribed.

The difficulty of changing the historically transmitted day of rest to some other day does not lie merely in the purely religious significance of the Sabbath, but rather in the symbolic biblical statement that God had rested on the seventh day, having completed all creation, hallowing and blessing the day of rest. This was tied later to the commandment to rest, which assured that this commandment referred precisely to that certain seventh day, the *Shabbat bereshit,* and that day alone has, indeed, been celebrated in Israel all along. Thus, the observance of a definite seventh day in creation is connected closely with its symbolic significance. The celebration of that day in ages past allegorically described its basically differing Jewish religious concepts vis-à-vis paganism. However, apart from the ideas which we gained elsewhere and made our own, the Sabbath can no longer have any significance for its own sake. From the narrative which tells that God had rested on the seventh day, we can, if we wish to avoid anthropomorphisms, gather only that God, after creating the universe, manifested himself as the Creator in His absolute distinction from the world. We take for granted that these and all other manifest religious truths which we have accepted are no longer symbolized by man as before, namely, by resting. It says in the Bible: Man shall hallow the Sabbath, which really means that on the Sabbath *man shall consecrate himself.* In other words, he shall celebrate the Sabbath not merely by resting but rather by actively consecrating and dedicating his existence. In this way every reason for observing that particular day ceases to exist by itself, and the purely religious meaning of the Sabbath can no longer contain any religious impediment for its modification, provided such change is governed by other religious motives.

Since the Sabbath is of crucial importance for the preservation of religion, the reasons for changing it to another day must be sought and found exclusively in the needs of preserving our religion. The Sabbath finds itself in conflict with civic life; experience shows that, in this contest, it loses ground daily and there is no hope that we will see it emerge victoriously. The Rabbinical Conference has made it its worthy task to achieve a peaceful compromise in this contest. Should it succeed in solving this problem it would not dream of lessening the importance of the Sabbath. However, if there is no other means of settling the dispute peacefully, our religion will be threatened by the greatest danger, and for the sake of its self-preservation it will and must demand imperatively the changing of the Sabbath to another day, this being the only expedient. Thus, the religious reasons for implementing a change are none other than to rescue our religion from certain perdition.

I consider the reasons resulting from the needs for the preservation and progress of Judaism as a religion of inwardness and moral conduct, as the only valid and qualified ones which can have a say in this vital question. Alongside these, I reject any mention of other reasons, since they must necessarily either be in harmony with it, or else they will not be heard at all. However, these reasons are, as it were, of a completely subjective and individual nature, and must, therefore, be considered only from those viewpoints. If those members of the Jewish community who observe the Sabbath protest against a change, they are within their rights; for they do not see their religion in danger, since for them the Sabbath has remained victorious in its contest with life. However, this faction is in error if it thinks that with its protest it can dispute the need of a change for that considerable portion of Jews who factually no longer celebrate the Sabbath, for whom the Sabbath has been defeated in its contest with life, for here we actually face war and danger, and energetic measures must be taken for the sake of maintaining our religion. So far, the latter faction has nothing to offer but the negative aspect of a change, namely, the non-observance of the historical Sabbath. It must now be granted a positive opportunity if it is not to be completely alienated from religion, if it is not to be lost for religion, and if religion is not to be lost from it.

If the change of the Sabbath can be considered from such a viewpoint, it appears not only religiously justified, but can also be supported with examples from the oldest history of Judaism. No less significant than the Sabbath is the highest and most important national festival, the celebration of the Passover sacrifice, and lack of its observance was punishable with extirpation from God's community. Because of its purely symbolic significance this celebration is firmly bound to a definite day, the eve of the fourteenth of the month of Abib, which is the date of the Exodus from Egypt. Scripture even stresses quite frequently, and with sharp emphasis, the expression *b'etsem ha-yom ha-zeh*. And even so (according to Numbers ch. 9) this particular festival was changed to the next month for those who, because of impurity or absence, could not observe its celebration at the proper time (vss. 10, 11), while those who were ritually clean and present must, under punishment of extirpation, observe it at the appointed time. The fact that the obstacle in the celebration of Passover consists in the ritual impurity or physical absence from the congregation, and that as regards the Sabbath, it consists of an uncompromising conflict with civic conditions, makes no difference either in principle or in spirit. The religious purpose of the Passover festival could be realized through a postponed celebration by those who were prevented from observing it at the given time, just as the religious purpose of the Sabbath can also be realized on some other day. It is a delusion if we think or fear that the preservation of Judaism is conditioned by ceremonial externals. Sabbath year and jubilee, which, as is well known, are intimately and closely related to the symbolic Sabbath concept, representing, indeed, the most widespread expansion and noblest flower of this idea, have not been celebrated for nearly two millenia, and yet the spirit and core of Judaism have not experienced the slightest damage because of this deficiency. We wish to save the Sabbath for Judaism, and to save Judaism through the Sabbath, even if we have to give up its symbolic framework.

SYNODAL DECISIONS (*Augsburg, 1871*)

If the distance from the residence to the house of worship, or age and delicate health prevent attendance at divine service, it is permissible to remove this obstacle by riding to the place of communal worship on Sabbath and holidays, either on the railroad or in a vehicle.

This permission extends also to the practice of charitable acts in such cases where delay would be dangerous.

The same permission holds where the purpose is educational or recreative.

An Israelite is permitted to play the organ in the house of worship on the Sabbath.

2. THE HOLIDAYS

A variety of issues are gathered in this section. There are others not represented here (such as the observance of minor fast days, of the New Moon, etc.), which received the careful attention of the Reformers.

THE SECOND DAY OF THE FESTIVALS (*Salomon Herxheimer*)

The question whether the second day of the holidays should be abolished is to be considered from three points:

1. Is the Bible opposed to this abolition?
2. Is the Talmud?
3. Are the demands of practical religious living opposed to it?

1. If we consider the matter from the biblical point of view we find that the entire Torah does not contain a single word which demands the second day of the festival. Quite on the contrary, the law of Moses commands that on Passover the first and seventh days be observed; that Shavuot be observed for one day; Rosh Hashanah for one day; Yom Kippur for one day; and Succot on the first and eighth days. The Pentateuch, therefore, limits the annual festivals (excepting the Sabbath) to seven, and this number seven plays a role also in the other sacred periods: the seventh day during Passover and Succot, the year of release, and the Jubilee year (see *More Nebukhim* 3:43).

Further, neither the Prophets nor the other books of the Bible have any trace of a second festival. A reduction of the present thirteen festival days to the original seven would, therefore, be entirely in accord with Scripture.

2. Now let us look at the matter from the talmudical point of view. The doubling of all biblical festivals occurred at the time of the beginning of the Talmud. Only the Day of Atonement was excepted, because it was observed by fasting. The supreme court in Palestine determined the beginning of each month in accordance with the declaration of witnesses who had seen the new moon, and the court informed the Jews inside and outside of Palestine of the beginning of the month by fire signals on the mountains. But since the New Year's day is celebrated precisely on the day of the new moon and since the witnesses could testify only on the thirtieth day of Elul, and sometimes only on the next day, that the new moon had been seen, the court arranged to have both the thirtieth day and the day following observed as the New Year's day. This was to avoid all doubt, and this double celebration remained in existence even when the witnesses appeared after the afternoon prayer on the thirtieth.

The double celebration of the New Year is, therefore, as old as the time of the Mishnah, and the Palestinian court introduced it even for Jerusalem itself. Later, at the time of the Gemara, the Jews outside of Palestine observed not only the New Year's day twice, but did the same for all other festivals because their distance from the seat of the supreme court in Palestine often delayed the news of the beginning of the new month, and since it did not come in time for the festivals there was doubt as to the correct day. They wanted to be sure that it would be celebrated at the same time that the day was sanctified in Jerusalem.

The double festivals were called by the Gemara "the second holidays of the Diaspora" because they were celebrated only by those who lived in the Diaspora far away from Jerusalem. Those, however, who lived in and near Jerusalem observed only the New Year's day twice, and so it is today: in Palestine only Rosh Hashanah is doubly observed.

In the latter days of the Talmud the beginning of the month was no longer determined through witnesses who had seen the new moon, but through reliable calculations of the phases of the moon. According to these calculations all doubt which originally caused the double celebration fell away. All double celebrations should, therefore, cease since the original reason is no longer in existence, the more so since according to the Talmud the present calculation is accounted as reliable as the former determination by witness and has the same legal validity. In fact, the Talmud itself asks: Since we now know the beginning of each month by calculation, why do we still continue to observe the double festival? And the answer is: Because the sages in Palestine said, "Observe the customs of your forefathers, for the government might forbid the study of Torah and then the science of astronomical calculation might be forgotten and the correct time of the festival might then be easily missed if only one day would be observed." However, this is surely not enough reason in our time for maintaining this custom of our fathers, for surely our present government will never more be moved, as were the old pagans, to forbid the Israelites the study of their religious books. Besides, the calculation of the calendar no longer depends on theology or Jewish science. It is no longer a secret but is generally known, and is so vital to Gentile nations as well that it is impossible that it might be relegated to oblivion.

But even if that were thinkable, why then do our coreligionists in and about Jerusalem not celebrate double festivals since they use the same calendar as do we as the authority for fixing the festival days? Since they did not have the double celebration in ancient days, why did they not introduce it out of anxiety over the above stated possibility?

(Here follows a talmudic discussion on the legal status of this type of custom. Herxheimer concludes that talmudic law cannot be quoted to prevent the abolition of the second days, except in the case of Rosh Hashanah, which he feels must be maintained.)

3. Now let us consider the question from the practical point of view. We are told that the elimination of the second festival days would not be favored by the general consensus of our congregations. But where is the reform which would elicit such general consensus? Was there a general agreement when we introduced the celebration of confirmation, of choral singing, or of German prayers at the service? If we were to wait with our reforms until we were sure of general agreement, then we should not attempt to reform anything—in fact, there would be nothing left to be reformed, for people would proceed to abandon everything and nothing positive would be left. It is precisely the strictness in the celebration of our important festivals which makes them economically oppressive to the business man, the merchant, and the artisan, for competition is pressing and demands made upon them seem to be growing steadily. The observant Jew feels this pressure strongly and is so disavantaged that only the most unusual person will have the strength to make such a religious sacrifice. Others, considering their need to make a living for wife and child, open their store a little and keep it closed a little, and let their helpers and apprentices work behind closed doors. They begin by riding the railroads, then they get into their carriages, so that by and by they publicly begin to disregard the whole celebration and even the service—not only on the second day but also on the first—and finally they fall prey to religious indifferentism. This is what economic need will do if Jewish law will not deal with it in some

measure. There must be a reasonable consideration for the interest of religion itself and this should move us to reduce the number of the festivals to the original seven of the Bible. The Talmud itself says that in order to maintain our religion in the face of pressing circumstances even the most lenient modifications are an actual duty, and our present situation fits the dictum of Maimonides: "If necessary it is better to violate one Sabbath so that one may observe many Sabbaths thereafter" (Mamrim 2:4).

But there is another consideration aside from our material existence. There is good reason to shorten the number of festival days in order to increase religious sentiment and its effectiveness in this celebration of the holiday. Even those who begin the celebration of the festivals with pious enthusiasm find the excessive length of the festivals bothersome and blunting. There are the complications of the Passover festival, the inability to do work for many days, the inability to travel, the rabbinic prohibition against social amusements, which make of the holidays days of loafing and painful boredom. Only the two days of Rosh Hashanah are an exception. They are still observed with deep devotion and have a blessed influence on our religious life because of their heightened sanctification and consecration. Therefore, we suggest to maintain these as before, but to shorten the other festivals of the year, thereby to make them once again into true days of joy unto the Lord.

ABOLISH THE SECOND DAYS *(Bernhard Wechsler)*

Wechsler reported to the Breslau Conference (1846) in behalf of a special committee whose views were generally adopted by the Reformers.

As a result of what has already been discussed on this point, and what several members of the Committee, as well as other members of the Assembly have published, the prevailing basic idea must have become clear and accepted by everyone, namely, that in our religious records a proper reason for the second days of festivals, which would be applicable in our time, is missing.

On the other hand, however, the Committee does not find any inner contradiction in the continuance of the second days of the festivals, and, therefore, it does not find the abolition of these second festival days everywhere absolutely *necessary.* The reasons which may originally have effected their introduction are no longer applicable to us. Even the rabbis left this original viewpoint, since the main reason for introducing the two-day festival, namely, the doubt as to the precise day on which the festival falls, had been eliminated, thus enabling them to fix the calendar and advise their contemporaries accordingly. Even though the original doubt can no longer have any validity for us, nevertheless, one must not fail to appreciate that the two-day celebration has taken deep roots among the people; that even after the concept of the orginal meaning had disappeared from its consciousness, the people had, nevertheless, kept those days holy and hallowed, attaching to them religious importance.

Therefore, as long and as much as this religious significance, relating to the celebration of all or single second-day festivals, inspires them and has become dear to them, there can be no real objection to their continuance. However, if and when they have become a burden or hindrance in life either because of the many festival days, or when they deprive the celebration of the first day of warm and close participation, as it indeed appears at times, their complete abolition should be insisted upon. How far this is already the case and in regard to what festivals, is a matter on which the members of the Committee have not been able to agree. Likewise, it will depend on the religious conditions and needs of the various congregations and their commercial and other circumstances. Therefore, the Committee does not deem it advisable at all to make proposals to the Assembly in regard to the individual festivals, since the application of such proposals, even if made, would nevertheless have to differ according to the differing viewpoints of the congregations.

On the other hand, all members of the Committee have agreed upon the following universal pronouncements, recommending their acceptance by the esteemed Assembly:

Motion No. 1. The Assembly shall declare that second-day festivals and the eighth day of the Pessach festival, respectively, as well as the ninth day of the Feast of Tabernacles, have no more validity for our time.

Motion No. 2. The Assembly shall declare, therefore, that if their total or partial abrogation is being demanded and resolved in certain communities, these communities do not offend against any religious rule, but are in fact within their rights to do so.

Motion No. 3. The Assembly shall further declare that in the communities in which total abrogation would give offense to the conviction of even a small fraction of its membership, the festival character of the divine service shall be maintained; however, the prohibition of work for the individual shall not be obligatory.

Motion No. 4. Finally, the Assembly shall declare that, accordingly, the prohibition of leavened bread on the last day of the Passover festival shall not be obligatory for the individual.

FASTING ON YOM KIPPUR (*Ludwig Philippson*)
(Commentary on Isaiah 57-58)

Man's whole salvation rests on his sincere repentance. But how very difficult it is for man to attain it! Many are the means our soul possesses to keep us obstinate. How hard it is for us to recognize our own sinfulness; how many excuses and justifications we keep in readiness; how seldom and briefly do feelings of repentance agitate our hearts! Therefore, religion must find ways upon which to lead the sons of men toward knowledge and repentance; it must set up concrete procedures through which their spirit becomes moved and shaken; it must find ways to lead them to atonement. To this end, the religion of Israel has established Yom Kippur, the Day of Atonement. In the calendar of days it has the mission of confronting the faithful with an urgent reminder, with a most vigorous challenge; and all the rites pertaining to it are meant to detach men from their worldly surroundings and occupations and lead them toward the supreme goal. From its very inception and up to the present day, Israel's religion has elevated this day to be the most hallowed, the holiest of the year, and with a deep sense of piety has made it into the highest festival, "the Sabbath of the Sabbaths." We cannot here discuss the observance of this day according to the Mosaic law, nor its significance. However, its basic principle is the fast from sunset to sunset. And indeed, though penance is not in itself the aim of our religion, nevertheless, fasting still remains unavoidably necessary for the meaning of that day. Nothing can better awaken and arouse the sense of reliance on God, the consciousness of man's weakness and frailty, and therefore his humility and contrition. How could this day have its profoundly moving effect if it were interrupted by feasts and banquets? The synagogue further added to this observance by instituting an uninterrupted service from sunrise to sunset, so as to remove the worshiper completely from his worldly concerns for one day, committing him uninterruptedly to meditation, devotion, and consecration. Thus, this day has become a central point of Jewish religious life, the great pulse beat of the Jewish religious organism. This is what it signifies to Judaism in general; this is what it means to each individual Israelite in his loftiest relations to God.

It is precisely for this reason that this most effective means which religion has set up to achieve the noblest purpose, could have appeared to the individual as an end in itself; that, without changing his inner self and without reforming his conduct, he could attach the spirit of atonement to the day itself; that he could regard fasting and praying themselves, regardless of their effect on the nature of his soul, as sufficient means for the redemption of all his sins and for the deliverance from any and all punishment. As it often happens in human affairs, here, too, the end was stifled by the means, and the mere sanctification of form suppressed the true consecration. The word of the prophet, which is being read in this *Haftarah* (Isaiah 57-58), is addressed against this error, and our sages, having prescribed these words for the Day of Atonement, manifested thereby how serious they were when they said that without repentance and reform even the Day of Atonement will not expiate one's sins.

TISHA B'AV AND THE MODERN JEW *(David Einhorn)*

In this sermon, which is based on Gen. 50:51-53, Einhorn proposes to maintain the day as a significant landmark in the Jewish calendar, but with a radical change of its message. The reform of this traditional day of mourning is in effect, he maintains, a reform which God Himself has introduced.

Is the present day in its solemn nature meaningful to us also? Do we, indeed, have reason to commemorate the destruction of Jerusalem devoutly? Does the religion of Judaism, from our point of view, still take an interest in the incineration of the holy Temple, in the death of Jewish peoplehood, in the historic event of universal import which, like a hurricane tearing through the autumn leaves, drove Israel away from its motherly soil, scattering its people in all directions—a few here, a few there, forever hunted anew, driven and drawn into the spinning whirlpool, so that they invented the fairy tale of the wandering Jew, on whom God has inflicted the horrible punishment of dragging along his tormented life in eternity, phantomlike plodding along through the millenia, his shoulder used as a roadway for all the world to step upon, hoping in vain for the *coup de grâce* from even his most wrathful foe? "No!" say those who are unable to value either the root or the goal of our endeavors; for in their opinion today's commemoration can have no other characteristic than that of mourning Zion and Jerusalem and, where such mourning does not take place, there is, according to them, no room for anything else.

Actually, however, today's commemoration has, particularly for us, no lesser importance than the revelation of Mount Sinai; for—hear and remember this word, my friends!—the reform of Judaism recognizes in the destruction of the Temple and its consequences a deed in which God Himself, in the most solemn and decisive manner, reformed the law He had revealed to Moses. Reform recognizes in the decline of the sacrificial cult, of the priesthood, and of the state of Israel, a wise divine revelation to all of Israel, which, though seemingly appearing in conflict with the first one on Mount Horeb, actually is in close harmony with it. Reform recognizes in the flaming Temple mount not a curtailment but rather a continuation of the divine work of salvation, which had begun on flaming Mount Sinai, marking the real beginning of the priestly mission, the conveyance of the divinity to all the children of this earth, for which Israel had been ordained at the Sinaitic choice.

Oh, how many preachers in Israel today strive in vain to find the words which have the magic power to make the long dried-out source of tears flow once again; who use the radiant glow of phantasy to breathe new meaning into a long since died-out suffering. Mine is a more beautiful and easier task, namely, that of showing forth the pleasing stately flower that has arisen from the decay, the healing change our religious life has undergone threefold through the dispersion of Israel, in that it has gained more freedom, more spiritual depth, and wider dissemination.

The Sinaitic doctrine could never be content with purely external works, but, on the contrary, is everywhere most insistent on the sanctification of the soul, on the removal of any sinful temptation, on the love of God with all of one's heart, soul, and might. Therefore, an attempt to keep its adherents forever under the rule of religious restraint would mean a contradiction of its very spirit. Indeed, Judaism regards free self-determination as the very life-breath of piety; it relies on levers of obedience entirely different from the knout. Therefore, the more the word of God was strengthened in the hearts of Israel, the more in the course of centuries God's people followed the call of the prophets and a destiny full of the most miraculous divine guidance, the more they were cleansed from all pagan customs. The more they opened their hearts to God, the more did the state-aspect of their religious life, and with it Jewish national life as a whole, begin to decay. And when, at last, the love of God had gained full mastery, the holy Temple, and with it the shackles of religious coercion, melted away in its flames, to let freedom emerge from the ashes as the triumphant queen and master. God's people went down into dust, and in their stead arose the religious congregation whose members were to endure scourging and death, not because of their *faithlessness,* as had been the case until then, but, on the contrary, because of their *faithfulness* to God. From now on, it was no longer the threatening sword of judgment but rather the heart which was to determine the relationship between God and man, and the divine maxim: "Ye shall be holy, for I, the Lord your God, am holy," was to be truly realized.

From the ashes of that one Temple thousands of places of worship came forth; from the grave of animal sacrifice and separate priesthood rose the magnificent phenomenon of a congregation of priests scattered over the entire world, who offered themselves as sacrifices in the holy service of God. From the ruins of a pompous cult that flattered our hearts by its appeal to sensuality, we received a divine service of the noblest and simplest forms, borne by the strength of world-conquering truth, shaded by the cherubs' wings of prayer and Torah, far from the art of flattery and deception, but powerful in edification, stimulation, and exaltation. And should we not be able to find in this rich inner development an adequate replacement for that external pageantry? To be sure, there are some who, in complete denial of our history, consider the ceremonial law as the core of Judaism and who deplore the immense unbridgeable gap that has separated us from it through the dispersion of Israel. We, however, rejoice over it, for through this gap a ray of light has penetrated the heart of Israel which in dispersion bore fruit a thousandfold. In this respect, Israel, like Joseph of old, lost a coat of many colors and like him wandered into exile, to grow up into the prince of God and to become fruitful in the land of his oppression!

Israel was chosen by the Lord to be the receptacle for the balm of the Sinaitic doctrine; indeed, it was predestined to cause all parts of the earth to become suffused with the exquisite fragrance of this balm. Before the destruction of Jerusalem, Israel was hidden in a corner and concealed by the heavy mantle of the ceremonial law and its distinct national characteristics, and, therefore, could not fulfil its destiny. Now, in obedience to the Lord it had to come forth from its isolation, to be forced from place to place, from land to land, and see its old insulating hulk punctured in every place, in order to permit the pleasing aroma of its precious balm to penetrate everywhere.

And just as Joseph bore two children in exile and was made fruitful by the Lord in a land that he had entered as a slave, so, near that stream, born from his loins, two mighty torrential currents rose, Christianity and Islam, two gigantic sons, eternally nourished by a never-aging mother. It is their mission to prepare the nations in the outer court for their admission into the mother's sanctuary. Yes, my beloved! If our heart wants to bleed in memory of the countless martyrs who were sacrificed for the holy cause of God and the nameless sufferings which our tribe had to endure for almost two thousand years, ever since the day we had to leave our homeland, then let us think of the glorious goal of these sufferings and sacrifices, the many millions who do not belong to our house, but who, nevertheless, owe us their noblest and best. We should think of the countless, proud churches reaching far into the skies, in which other non-Israelitish congregations raise their souls to the heavens in prayer, reciting *our* Psalms. There shall be in our hearts not only comfort—nay, a joyful pride and heavenly jubilation shall thrill our being, because of the magnificent, glorious thing God has done for His people, and because of the even greater and nobler future which awaits us. No! We must not weep over the ruins of Jerusalem; for *beyom she-neherav bet ha-mikdash nolad ha-moshiah*—the Messiah was born in those very ruins! Israel lost a structure of wood and stone so that it might win more souls for God. It lost its homeland so that it might conquer a world. To be sure, its sons despaired when they saw the Temple go down in flames; but God sees farther than man. He recognized in the fallen Temple merely the foundation and cornerstone for the house of prayer for all people. Before His eyes, He could then already view an altogether different scene of distant millenia, unfolding from the dismal devastation; the miraculous sight of a sea of light flowing forth from the flaming fire, and Israel no longer wailing and weeping, but on the contrary, radiant in its Messianic glory, shouting with exultation: "God hath made me forget all my toil and all my father's house. . . . God hath made me fruitful in the land of my affliction. He hath made my seed as the stars of the heavens and as the sand which is upon the seashore."

WE MUST MOURN ON TISHA B'AV (*Ludwig Philippson*)

Philippson's moderation is apparent on all issues. He takes note of the point of view of Einhorn, but he finds reason to maintain the traditional observance.

On the ninth of Ab, 660 years apart, the first and second Temples fell under the sword and incendiary torch of the Chaldeans and Romans. While the first fall was followed by the captivity of Babylon and the subsequent return to Palestine, the destruction of the second Temple was followed by the complete dispersion of the people across the entire earth, resulting in what is now an already eighteen-centuries-old period of humiliation, exclusion, and persecution which afforded only rarely the hope of tranquility and exaltation, and which only in the last century has seemed to point toward new developments and toward a freer civic position for the Jew. Some take the viewpoint of modern times, that there was a higher reason which removed the Jewish nation from Palestine, so as to be witness to and bearer of the revealed religion of the One and Only amidst all mankind, thus stretching the narrow boundaries of a humble country to encompass the whole world. This viewpoint reflects the teaching that divine providence combines a higher, universal goal with all the events and destinies of men. But even if one accepts this view, the ninth of Ab is and must remain a dismal day of mourning, since it embodies the memory of such formidable ruin, such frightful events, the cessation of worship in the Temple, the loss of independence and that of a visible central point, and the innumerable horrors which from then on bore down upon Judah's dispersed little band. Neither civic emancipation nor the most magnificent successes of intellectual development can minimize the sad character of that day. You may institute a holiday for having attained civic liberties, yet what the ninth of Ab contains in utterly sad and touching memories cannot be blotted out by any blessed turn of our destiny. For it is, after all, only a minute fraction of the Jewish race over whom the sun of freedom has risen. Even the European countries, in which the greatest number of our coreligionists live, have at present merely discontinued the practice of persecution and oppression, but not that of exclusion and restrictions of all sorts. Therefore, the synagogue has justifiably appointed this day, which mourns the destruction of the Temple and that of Jerusalem, as the most meaningful day of fasting and mourning in the year.

FOR A REVIVAL OF HANUKAH (*Simon Szantó, Michael Silberstein*)

The Augsburg debate on Hanukah (1871) shows the neglect with which this festival was treated and the influence which Christmas exerted on its revival.

Simon Szantó (1819-1892) was a journalist and teacher, and the supervisor of the Jewish Religious Schools in Vienna.

Michael Silberstein (1834-1910) was then a rabbi in Württemberg. He later served in Wiesbaden and became the author of several noted historical studies.

Szantó: Gentlemen: As the adoptive father of this proposal, I must naturally assume the duty of the mover, and I hereby submit to the honorable Synod certain suggestions for the enhancement of the Hanukah festival. I have taken up this proposal and adopted it because this celebration, though it is a rabbinical observance, belonging to the seven rabbinical commandments, has been neglected in a most irresponsible manner in most communities, in the *shuls* of earlier times as well as in the synagogues of our day, naturally with the exception of the more progressive congregations. There are instances where school children do not even know the significance of the Maccabean festival. It has come to my attention that in the Austrian monarchy the teachers in several schools, which shall remain unnamed, had been requested by the rabbis to relate to the children the meaning of the Hanukah festival. One of the teachers thought he was discharging his obligation by reading to them the story from the Book of Judith, which he, for some unexplained reason, considered to be a canonical book.

Gentlemen, the situation is much the same in the synagogue. Comes the eve of Hanukah, we light one candle, which burns pitifully, since the decision in the argument between the schools of Shammai and Hillel was made long ago in favor of the latter, and we begin by lighting one candle and end with eight. To be sure, the *Al ha-nissim* prayer is said, the complete *Hallel* psalms are recited, but since the festival has not been proclaimed with the pomp it deserves, the whole Hanukah period passes almost unnoticed. Now, my learned friends, I do not have to tell you of the victories of the Maccabees. Permit me to pass over the details. The observance of this festival deserves to be made more significant.

Now, what happens in some of the more progressive communities? Naturally, I am referring to the congregation to which I have the honor of belonging, the congregation in Vienna, where we have definite, precise procedures. This is what happens: First of all, on the eve of the Sabbath, the preacher of the congregation announces to the assembled congregation the advent of the festival. On the eve of the day of Hanukah, when only one candle is being lit, he ascends the pulpit and gives a sermon in keeping with the celebration. Then the *Hallel* prayers, etc., are recited, naturally with great solemnity. In Vienna this is accompanied by the choir, in Prague, by an organ. The holy day is being observed as a biblical holy day. These are the proposals that I would like to submit.

Silberstein: It is a known fact that unfortunately a misuse has arisen in Jewish families, namely, the observance of the Christmas holy day as a day of Jewish sanctity. As has been mentioned before, this stands in the most extreme and gross contrast to all Jewish sentiment and self-consciousness. Therefore, we must attach greater solemnity to the festival of Hanukah, not only in the Synagogue, but particularly also in the schools, and must point out to the parents that the festival of Hanukah should be turned into a family celebration. This, by the way, would not be something new, since it existed in earlier times and has merely been forgotten. We must show them that children and everyone at home will take pleasure in the Hanukah celebration. Then we could, indeed, reach the point when this loss of self-respect would disappear from our families and no longer would a celebration be observed in Jewish circles which, as stated, is in direct opposition to Jewish consciousness.

CHAPTER
IX

The Personal Life

▬▬▬

W HILE the first public manifestations of Reform centered in the synagogue and its worship, the movement was, of course, not confined to such expressions. For Judaism centers in the total person, in his private as well as in his group life, and it was in the privacy of their homes and in their own personal behavior that Reformers made their first changes.

Here, no less than in the synagogue, did the principles of Reform find their practical test and application; and in this area, no less than in that of synagogue worship, did the debates rage. Did the omission of circumcision make a person a non-Jew? Were dietary laws still necessary? Could there be a double-ring wedding ceremony? What about civic and religious divorce? Did the old mourning practices need revision? These were some of the questions which were raised and which scholars attempted to answer at conferences and synods, in books and journals.

Of course, even the most personal of customs had public import, and often the debated practice belonged to private life as well as under the heading of worship reform. The issues gathered in this chapter, however, focus upon the individual and on the way he makes Judaism relevant in his day-to-day existence.

1. CIRCUMCISION

The question "Who is a Jew?" agitated the age of early Reform no less than it does our own time. Is one's membership in the eternal people determined merely by descent, or do factors of faith and ritual enter into it?

In 1843, these questions became acute when the Frankfort Reform Association encouraged its members to abandon the rite of circumcision.

Solomon Abraham Trier, the orthodox Chief Rabbi of the city, tried every means to dissuade the members of the Association from taking this revolutionary step; he even invoked the help of the city senate. But the city declined intervention and Trier caused a volume of rabbinic opinions to be gathered. He approached both traditional and Reform rabbis, and the latter generally joined in declaring circumcision to be an essential mark of Jewish identification.

THE FRANKFORT CASE *(Solomon Abraham Trier)*

A Jewish citizen in this community [Frankfort], failed to have his newly born, healthy child circumcised. As soon as I knew of this, I tried every persuasive means to keep the father from this open breach with Judaism. But the goddess of fashion had done its work in the name of "enlightenment" and "higher spiritual direction," and its supporters were determined to fight the battle under her proud banner. Neither fatherly admonitions nor clear, simple reason availed against these so-called convictions. Now the long suspected secret intent of the so-called Reform Association, which had flourished in the dark, has come into the open through this public manifestation against membership in our faith. The tendency of this Association is now exposed all too obviously before everyone's eyes, for it desires to eliminate an undisputed Mosaic law, claiming that it is antiquated in the edifice of modern religion.

Consequently, on August 4, 1843, I did my duty and informed the illustrious Senate of the fact that a local member of the Jewish congregation, despite my insistent admonitions, would not agree to have his newly born child submitted to the religious act of circumcision, and I added that this was equivalent to a formal separation from the religious bond of our religious group. I said in my document: "If it is a generally known principle in our German fatherland that every subject must confess to one of the generally recognized religions in Germany and must do so in a visible ecclesiastical form, then the illustrious Senate cannot be indifferent in this matter. It cannot allow that a Jewish subject is free to separate himself de facto from the Jewish religion, which is recognized by the state, without joining at the same time another recognized religious association. Otherwise, every person could arbitrarily form some religious system which would be in opposition to the Holy Bible and to all the teachings, laws, and customs which in the past we have recognized and followed." I closed with the request "that the illustrious Senate, in accordance with the law and present legal circumstances, would issue the correct decree, namely, that no child of Jewish parents may be admitted into the local Jewish association as a Jewish coreligionist and Israelite citizen if he has not been circumcised."And I said that I looked forward with confidence to the illustrious Senate's decision.

THE EXTERNAL CONDITION OF ACCEPTANCE (*Nathan Marcus Adler*)

Adler (1803-90) was then Rabbi in Hanover; soon after rendering his responsum he was elected Chief Rabbi of Great Britain.

Many and different are the opinions concerning the reason and purpose of circumcision. Some see in it an aspect of higher priestly consecration, others a symbol of purification from sin, others a social means to aid the birth rate; still others consider it ethical in nature, designed to decrease the sexual urge; others consider it medical because a painful growth of the skin is removed; others believe it to be hygienic because it encourages cleanliness. But however different the facets of this question are—like in a diamond which infracts the light from various sides—most of the commentators agree that circumcision signifies that the Jew is a Jew. This is what Maimonides says (*More* III, 39), that it is the distinguishing sign which unites the adherents of one faith into one nationality group and which, therefore, is the external condition of one's acceptance into the congregation of Israel.

HOW TO TREAT THE UNCIRCUMCISED JEW (*Samuel David Luzzatto*)

Trier's volume of responsa contains some extremely harsh suggestions on how to treat the Frankfort recalcitrants. The violent nature of the answers reflects the deep emotions which the question of circumcision unleashed. Luzzatto's responsum may be classed as fairly moderate.

It is my opinion that he who rejects the mark of the covenant is to be considered as one who rejects the whole Mosaic law and who has ceased thereby to belong to the Jewish religious community, and especially so when the reason for this transgression is not frivolous but principled.

It is, therefore, our duty to avoid contact with such a person so that our children should not learn so dangerous a principle. If he has an administrative post in the congregation, he must be relieved of it, and most certainly may he not have any kind of religious office. He may not contribute to the communal or synagogue tax (compare *Orah Hayim* par. 154); even the poor shall reject his alms. Even if the congregation is in real need of his tax, it would be preferable to sell holy objects than to accept a tax from him as long as he has not had his son circumcised. "It is permitted to receive gifts from the adherents of other religions but not from a heretic" (*Yore De'a* 254).

If he is poor and in need of help, one must have mercy upon him and support him; for if circumcision is the mark on our body, leniency and mercy are the marks of our soul.

If such a man enters the synagogue he should be honored and should be given his seat, just as one honors a stranger, but he may not be counted in the required quorum of worshippers and no religious honor may be given him, with the exception that on the anniversary of his parents' death one may for their sake accept a contribution from him. If he becomes ill and he repents of his sins, then all his former transgressions are counted as naught and he is to be buried like everyone else; but if he does not repent, then he must be buried separately, as is the case with those who have been executed by the authorities (Sanh.VI).

A BARBARIC RITE (*Abraham Geiger*)

A few Reformers shared the Frankfort Association's attitude toward circumcision. Among these were Holdheim, who supported their extreme stand publicly, and Geiger, who did so privately only, because he did not wish to be identified with the over-all program of the Association. In a letter to Zunz, Geiger wrote:

I was not in sympathy with the Frankfort Reform Society; it had no clear idea of what it was striving for, neither was it honest enough in its utterances; instead of proceeding calmly and sanely, it aroused the greatest antagonism by attacking at once the rite of circumcision, which was considered a veritable foundation of Judaism. . . . As for myself, I must confess that I cannot comprehend the necessity of working up a spirit of enthusiasm for the ceremony merely on the ground that it is held in general esteem. It remains a barbarous, bloody act. The sacrificial idea which in former days invested the act with sanctity has no significance for us. However tenaciously religious sentiment may have clung to it formerly, at present its only supports are habit and fear, to which we certainly do not wish to erect any shrines.

THE VIENNA CASE (*Maximilian Engel*)

Engel was a Vienna physician, a member of the Board of the Jewish community, and an editor of the *Wiener Zeit* (*Vienna Times*). His recital of a famous case was made at the Leipzig Synod (1869), which debated the whole issue of circumcision.

The Synod should refer the following questions to a committee for detailed discussion and decision:

    a. Is a boy, born of a Jewish mother but uncircumcised for some reason, to be considered as a Jew according to the existing norms of Judaism which are generally recognized as binding?

     b. In case the first question is answered in the affirmative, how is such a
     person to be treated on ritual occasions later on (again following above-
     mentioned norms), both subjectively and objectively?

Permit me to tell you briefly of the reason for my motion. Until recently we
had in Austria, as in many other countries, the principle of a "must" religion,
that is, every newborn child, through his father, had to belong to some definite religion, and the father, therefore, had to go through the necessary arrangements, such as baptism, circumcision, etc. Now in Austria, thank God, the
new religious laws, which all of you know, have done away with this "must"
religion, but at the same time this has caused a certain schism which threatens
to spread more and more. Since we have religious freedom several people have
declared: We would like to have our children continue to belong to Judaism
but we shall not have them circumcised. Now in Austria the government has
an official register in which the children of all religions are entered, and this
duty has been placed into the hands of the respective clergymen. This appeared
to mean that the government wanted a religious register kept. Now when the
clergyman concerned had to enter into the register a child who had not been
circumcised, he refused such registry because he was afraid that if too great license would be permitted in such cases, the refusal of circumcision would spread
more and more. Now what happened? A certain father brought suit before the
Vienna Magistrates. The Magistrates did not know exactly what to do. On the
one hand they did not want to offend the Jewish religion, and on the other hand
they did not want to act against the new laws. The officials were caught, as is
Austria as a whole, in a problem of dualism and could not decide whether the
register was merely civil or whether it had religious character also. Now what
did the officials do? One Magistrate ordered the rabbi to enter the child into
the registry and supported his opinion with a certain passage in the new laws in
a manner which does not seem convincing. A similar circumstance happened
in Prague. There, a higher Magistrate, the imperial representative, decided that
the child had to be registered. However, he meliorated the decision by stipulating that the clergyman could keep a special private registry for himself in which
he could note whether or not the child had been circumcised.

    Now what did the trustees of the Jewish community in Vienna do? These
trustees had always guarded their autonomy zealously and decisively, and they,
therefore, now informed the Vienna Magistrate that they would file the official
decision but would not follow it. Now it is unlikely that policemen will be
sent into the houses in order to circumcise the children of obstreperous Jews.
But on the other hand, the officials will also not put up with an obvious transgression of the law. The trustees wanted the officials to express themselves
clearly and unequivocally what character they believed the registry to have.
Secondly, they wanted the natural leaders and guides of the people, namely, the
clergymen, to instruct them what religious status these uncircumcised children
had. The Vienna trustees, therefore, asked their rabbis to meet with them and
to discuss this second question. The rabbis came, with the exception of one
single gentleman, who, however, afterwards promised a written opinion. They
debated at great length, which was very sad; but finally they agreed that in any

case such a child would have to be considered a Jew. Since this question had been answered affirmatively, we wanted to know, further, what would happen with such a boy in the future; for the trustees wanted a practical, not merely a theoretical result. Now I must sadly admit that the written answers were so technical in nature—or perhaps we are too limited in our knowledge—that we have not understood them fully and still do not know whether such a child is to be considered a Jew, whether he can be called to the Torah, whether he can be married in a Jewish ceremony, etc. Only one of these gentlemen was very clear in his decision, but he stated it orally and not in writing. He said: "I make a difference between subjective and objective treatment. Subjectively, I consider the child a Jew, for instance at a marriage. However, he can never become a cantor or rabbi."

Now I have been sent here because our people expect that this illustrious assembly will proceed entirely differently in arriving at its judgment, and will base its judgment on generally recognized norms. Therefore, I ask you to refer the matter to a committee. Let me be honest. We in Austria, and especially in Vienna, have a very mixed public. There were two hundred families in the year 1748 and now we have grown to 40,000 souls. We have a lot of indifferent people, but they are interested in this question because it has social consequences. Then we have very orthodox, pious people, and we have also those who use orthodoxy as their sounding-board. Now I admit that this synod, with all the respect that it commands, has a little bit of a progressive, liberal reputation. I do not accuse you of this, and as a matter of fact, I do not even agree with this pre-judgment. However, if you would decide this question at once, then the orthodox gentlemen would not fail to say, "Yes, the majority of the members of the synod were ultra-liberal and we cannot accept their decisions as binding. They acted too hastily." But the matter is different if you will first refer this question to a committee. There is no hurry because it is only a question of one year's delay. Whether such a child will be circumcised in 1869 or 1870 is really unimportant. But it is important what character your decision will have. Therefore, I move that this question be referred to a committee in order to pacify both those who are anxious and those who are entirely opposed, and, therefore, I have also added to my motion the words "based on the existing norms."

(There were bravos from the audience. After some further discussion, Dr. Engel's motion carried.)

RESOLUTION OF THE AUGSBURG SYNOD (1871)

Although the synod premises without any reservation the supreme importance of circumcision in Judaism, it yet declares, in answer to the question propounded, that a boy born of a Jewish mother who has not been circumcised, for whatsoever reason this may have been, must be considered a Jew, and be treated as such in all ritual matters, in accordance with the existing rules regarded binding for Israelites (Yeb. 70b, *Yore De'a* 264:I).

2. DIETARY LAWS

While there was already at an early time in the history of the Reform movement a private neglect of the dietary laws, the question of *Kashrut* was hardly discussed. Geiger wrote a series of articles on the subject, and Creizenach treated of it briefly. There were two reasons for this general silence on so important a subject: one. that observance and non-observance were chiefly personal matters—and early Reform concentrated its efforts of clarification on the realm of public concerns; and second, that many liberals had already begun to disregard certain aspects of dietary observance. Creizenach suggested that the laws of the Torah regarding forbidden foods and the laws regarding the separation of meat and milk be strictly observed, but that the rules relating to the slaughter and preparation of meat by non-Jews be abandoned.

FOR A MODIFICATION OF KASHRUT (*Michael Creizenach*)

Talmudic law states that the Israelite is not allowed to eat the meat of a mammal or bird unless it is ritually slaughtered.

There is probably no command where the talmudic interpretation differs so radically from the natural sense as here. In Deut.14:21 the Pentateuch prohibits eating the flesh of an animal that "dieth of itself" (*nevelah*). The Talmud wants us to understand this as including every mammal and bird which did not die in accordance with the rules of ritual slaughter. It declares such animals as unclean as a carcass, even though birds brought for sacrifice in the Temple were not slaughtered in accordance with ritual. Hence, what the Talmud calls *nevelah* was brought to the very altar from which everything that was unclean was kept with most anxious care.

However, since we do not wish to depart from the talmudic interpretation of the Mosaic law, we too will declare as *nevelah* every animal that was not slaughtered in accordance with ritual, but we interpret the word not in the usual sense, applying it only to a dead animal which should have been ritually slaughtered but was killed in some other fashion.

A sacrificial bird whose head was severed was, therefore, not a *nevelah* because Scripture did not ask that it was to be slaughtered ritually. Similarly, an animal slaughtered by a Christian (and therefore not in accordance with Jewish ritual) is also not a *nevelah,* because as a Christian he does not have the obligations of an Israelite to slaughter his mammals and birds in a ritual fashion.

Of course, we would have to be stricter with regard to pagans, whose meat we may not eat even when they slaughter the animal in accordance with ritual, because we must be afraid that in the process of slaughtering they may have sacrificed the animal to some idol.

The authors of Mishnah and Talmud had this anxiety constantly before them, because it was a time when the ceremonies of paganism flourished. Therefore, the Rabbis made the eating of all non-Jewishly prepared foods so difficult that the Israelite, once he leaves his domicile, is in fact placed in a position of helplessness.

If we wanted to leave the talmudic interpretations, we could easily assume that the Pentateuch itself does not mean this prohibition strictly and intends it only to be a means for the maintenance of ritual purity and not really as a prohibition of food. To begin with, the Bible says expressly, "Thou mayest give it unto the stranger that is within thy gates that he may eat it; or thou mayest sell it unto a foreigner"; secondly, in Lev. 7:24 it says, "And the fat of that which dieth of itself and the fat which is torn of beasts may be used for any other service; but ye shall in no wise eat of it." From this it may be concluded that it is not prohibited to eat other parts of the animal (other than the fat). Finally, it says in Ez. 44:31: "The priest shall not eat of anything that dieth of itself, or is torn, whether it be fowl or beast." This would lead to the conclusion that only priests are subject to the prohibition.

However, let us not look for relaxations of the traditional viewpoint and let us observe all talmudic regulations when animals are slaughtered which belong to Israelites. But, in order to lessen rather than to increase the number of Israelites who neglect all dietary laws in their homes, we would allow the more lenient interpretations indicated here, which make it possible for an Israelite to live in accordance with his religion, which intends to enhance, and not to restrict oppressively, his earthly welfare.

KASHRUT—OFFENSE AND PENALTY
(The Central Consistory of the French Israelites)

The following excerpt from a consistorial session transcript is of interest, not only for the story it tells, but also because of the implication that in 1840 the observance of *Kashrut* was already widely disregarded and that the rabbinate felt moved to take extreme measures to stem the tide of non-observance.

May a Grand Rabbi inflict a religious or other penalty and impose his judgment or decision? Answer: No.

May he officially intervene in order to mete out religious punishment to a religious offender?
May He prescribe that the offender make honorable amends in the synagogue? Answer: No.

Does he have the right to suspend the license of the shochet who violated the

sanctity of the Sabbath, or withdraw from the butcher the license of shochet?
Answer: Yes.

Here are the circumstances which lay before the Central Consistory.

On the Sabbath preceding Rosh Hashanah, 1839, Monsieur Dreyfous, Rabbi
of Mulhouse, found himself in the community of Zittsheim in order to officiate
there. He noted that the three butchers were selling meat on that day. He spoke
to them about the violation of the sanctity of the Sabbath and then brought the
matter to the attention of the Grand Rabbi of Colmar. The latter issued an order
which was read in the synagogue and which declared that the three butchers
were in a state of public violation of the Sabbath, that consequently they were
deprived of every confidence in religious matters, and that they could no longer
sell kosher meat without a supervisor.

The Grand Rabbi added to this order other portions which were not read
publicly in the synagogue and these dealt with the conditions under which the
butchers could recover the confidence of their fellow Jews. Both their penitence
and their further conduct would be determining factors. The son of the one
was to fast two hundred and forty days (six times forty days), and the other two
were to fast two times forty days.[1] Furthermore, they were to make a formal
vow in public before the open Ark that they would not commit similar sins in
the future. Each day of fasting would also have to be supplemented by a gift
of forty-five centimes and also by a lump sum to be decided upon by the
rabbi. Furthermore, the shochet was no longer permitted to work for the
butchers.

Two of the butchers complained to the Ministry of Religion, which in turn
submitted the case to the Central Consistory. The third one submitted to the
rabbinic decree. After considerable discussion, and listening also to the opinions
of the Grand Rabbi, the Consistory arrived at the following decision.

As a general rule the rabbis cannot inflict any religious punishment or impose
other forms of judgment or decision. Their mission is limited to indicating to
the violator of a religious principle the means of expiation which the talmudic
law prescribes. Under the conditions of religious liberty which exist in France,
the rabbis cannot officially issue religious punishment, whether for the violation
of the Sabbath or any other kind of religious obligation, and they cannot demand
that public amends be made in the synagogue.

However, Israelite butchers who sell their coreligionists kosher meat are, of
course, under the necessary supervision of the Grand Rabbi. If one of them
violates the sanctity of the Sabbath, the rabbis may justifiably suppose that such
a man will not have any scruples to substitute *trefa* meat for *kosher,* and under
such circumstances the rabbis may forbid the shochet to slaughter for this
butcher or, if the butcher himself is a shochet, to propose to the Consistory to
withdraw his license. The rabbis have also the right, in fact the duty, to let the
faithful know that the butcher has lost their confidence and that he violates
the Jewish law. They may urge them not to patronize the butcher until further

[1] (Ed. note) By fasting is meant here abstinence from food during the daylight hours, eating
at night not being forbidden.

notice. When the butcher then comes to the rabbi in order to be reinstated, the rabbi has the right to impose upon him such religious punishment as he believes to be indispensable in order to have the man prove his repentance, provided, however, that such punishment does not violate the laws of the state and, as was already stated, that it is not done officially, either for the violation of the Sabbath or any other infringement of religious law.

Therefore, the Consistory states as follows:

1. The Grand Rabbi could not, on the mere accusation of the Rabbi of Mulhouse, use his office to inflict on the offenders a religious punishment redeemable through a gift, and he could not ask them to declare in the synagogue that they would not commit the sin of violating the Sabbath again. The Consistory has, therefore, nullified this part of the decision.

2. The Grand Rabbi did have the right, and even the duty, to declare in the synagogue that the petitioners who had profaned the sanctity of the Sabbath had lost his confidence and that the Israelites of the community should abstain until further notice from buying meat from these places, and he further had the right to withdraw from them the services of the shochet. The Consistory completely approves this part of the Grand Rabbi's position.

3. MARRIAGE

One of the earliest reforms to take effect was that of marriage procedures. Israel Jacobson used his brief span of consistorial power under the Napoleonic regime to promulgate regulations for the wedding ceremony as well as a free rendering of the contractual *Ketubah*. Some of Jacobson's reforms were in time adopted even by staunch opponents of the movement, and the marriage contract has found its way into the traditional ceremony of present-day America, as an addition to the Aramaic original.

THE CEREMONY
   (*Edict of the Royal Westphalian Consistory, 1810*)

So that fitting order and needed uniformity, adequate to the dignity of the occasion, should from now on be the rule during religious weddings of Israelites in the Kingdom of Westphalia, we feel moved to decree the following:

1. Weddings shall take place only in the synagogue, before the Holy Ark, under a canopy (*huppah*) which shall be supported by four poles and shall be held by proper persons. The curtain of the Ark (*parokhet*) may be used for the canopy.

2. The wearing of a cover (*tallit*), which is still customary in many places at such ceremonies, is prohibited both to the rabbi and to the bridal couple.

3. During the marriage ceremony several (or at least one) candelabra shall be kindled near the Holy Ark.

4. The ceremony shall be opened with a brief German address, by which the bridal couple shall be duly impressed with their new obligations.

5. The marriage shall take place in the following manner: After the end of the German address, the officiant (without having his own name called out by anybody) shall speak the first blessing slowly and with dignity. He then asks the bridegroom to present his bride with the marriage ring while pronouncing the customary formula; thereupon he reads, word for word, not the customary Aramaic wedding contract, but the German one which is herewith appended (*ketubah*). And none, save the bridegroom, may pronounce the seven blessings (*sheva berakhot*).

6. Thereafter, no further ceremony, whatever its name, shall take place. We mention here the custom of breaking glass, the singing and blessing by the cantor (customary in many congregations), the procession of the bride around the bridegroom, the improper use of a bottle instead of two wine glasses, the question posed by the bride whether this wedding ring was the property of the bridegroom and whether it really had the necessary value of a *peruta* (questions which could well be asked prior to the ceremony), etc.

7. We further prohibit the custom practiced in many Israelite communities of the kingdom of Westphalia, namely, to conduct a pre-marital processional (*Mahnfuehren*), on which occasion people throw wheat over the heads of the couple.

8. Only extraordinary obstacles, which must be adequately demonstrated, can be adduced as reason for excuse from the rule that the marriage should be held in the synagogue before the holy Ark. In such a case it must take place in an adequate room. However, everything else in this decree is to be meticulously observed.

9. The secretaries of the communities will publish this edict in all synagogues of their district and have it posted, and, together with the rabbis and directors, will carefully see to it that it is meticulously observed.

Marriage Contract

On this day, the fourth in the week, the third day of the month (Elul) in the year (5570) after the creation of the world, this couple, namely the bridegroom, N. N., son of Mr. N. N. from N. N., and the bride, the virgin (woman), N. N., daughter of Mr. N. N. from N. N., have been joined in marriage in accordance with the rites of the Israelite religion, here in N. N. On this occasion, the above-mentioned bridegroom made the following declaration to his bride: Be thou my wife according to the laws of Moses and Israel. I will love thee and honor thee as a husband. I will nourish and care for thee, clothe thee and protect thee, and will fulfil all duties of a religious husband. I will also, in consideration of a dowry of 800 francs (400 francs in the case of a widow) and its increase and everything else to which I have obligated myself in the marriage contracts, faithfully fulfil my obligation.

She, the bride, N. N., on her part, has agreed to take her bridegroom, N. N., and has promised to become his wife, to love and honor him, and to fulfil conscientiously all the duties of a religious wife and also faithfully to fulfil all that which she has taken upon herself as an obligation through these marriage contracts. In testimony of this solemn act, this is being publicly read and is to be signed by two witnesses and is attested by me, the officiant at this marriage.

ONE OR TWO WEDDING RINGS? (*Joseph Aub*)

Aub (1805-1880), Rabbi in Berlin, delivered the following address at the Augsburg Synod. Its argumentation shows how, as late as 1871, even minor reforms faced determined opposition.

I have made the following motion: We should approve the wish frequently expressed by the bride, that during the marriage ceremony she, too, should be permitted to present her betrothed with a ring and place it on his finger while saying the words: *Ani ledodi, vedodi li,* "I am my beloved's, and my beloved is mine."

Gentlemen! The question might be raised: Why this modification? I shall answer simply: Was the presentation of *one* ring in itself not also a change which came about at a certain time? As far as I know, from my studies of the rabbinical writings, there is no mention of the wedding ring in the Talmud.

Going back to the earliest rabbinical manuscripts, I was unable to find a single mention of the wedding ring. From that we must conclude that the wedding ring was introduced at a much later time. We are glad to welcome this innovation, for in the ring we see a beautiful symbol, the band of marriage, embracing, so to speak, the bridal pair for an everlasting union. On the other hand, we find the wedding ring mentioned in the Christian church at a much earlier time; we read about the wedding band in the writings of the Church Fathers, almost as far back as the third century.

Thus, it is evident that our elders did not object to the introduction of a procedure which was so well recommended, regardless of whether it had arisen within another religion or in our own midst. At present, the Christian religions in Germany generally use two rings at the marriage ceremony. On the other hand, to this day the official English church continues the custom of using one ring only, which the bridegroom presents to his bride, saying almost the identical words that we use in our synagogue.

Incidentally, my proposal is not directed at having the Synod pass a decision favoring the usage of two wedding bands, but rather at having the Synod declare that no religious law prevents a bride from presenting a ring to her betrothed if she so wishes. No new code shall be drawn up; no new precept shall be introduced; I only want the mind to range freely at all times. The actual question is therefore: Can we make allowances for the demands made upon us regarding the two wedding bands? Does the marriage law permit us to comply with the wishes of those betrothed couples who express the desire of having two rings at the performance of their marriage ceremony?

Several people in the Committee, which originally consisted of five members, declared themselves against it; they did not wish to permit the bride to present her betrothed with a ring. The Honorable Chief Rabbi, Dr. Landau of Dresden, even attempted to prove in a truly sophistical manner—and I cannot express myself any more charitably—that the presentation of a ring on the part of the bride actually would mean an annulment of the marriage; that, as a consequence, the vows which the bridegroom had made during the ceremony, as well as his presentation of the ring to the bride, would be annulled thereby! In other words, the whole marriage act would become void. Where and how he had come by this proof, since he does not quote from any writing, I, for one, cannot ascertain. It is evidently his own peculiar viewpoint, which hopefully will not be shared by many people here; it is forced and its purpose clearly is to maintain an antiquated custom somehow, and under no circumstance to permit the slightest deviation from it.

Further, the alleged sentiments of women were brought forth as a reason for rejecting this proposal. I shall be careful not to provoke a psychological discussion on a bride's emotional frame of mind at the marriage altar; however, I have been approached in some of my earlier positions, and particularly in Berlin, by many young brides who asked permission to present a wedding ring to their bridegrooms.

These young brides belonged to the most cultured families, and certainly no one could deny their profound spiritual sentiment. These ladies stated that they did not wish to be completely passive at the marriage altar, as if they were objects and as though the marriage ceremony could be performed without their equal participation.

Since in our present time we have achieved complete recognition of marital equality between man and woman, it is only fair that the bride should enjoy this privilege at the marriage ceremony. In Berlin it has come to the point where most betrothed couples desire to have two wedding rings. Neither my esteemed colleague nor I worry as to whether there should be one or two rings used at the marriage altar. Usually, when we step forward to perform a marriage ceremony in the name of the bridal pair or to say the benedictions, we find two rings lying before us. It is evident, therefore, that the usage of two rings is not as repugnant to female sentiment as some would like us to believe.

I have always found the formula which I have chosen—"I am my beloved's, and my beloved is mine"—to make a profound impression on the feminine soul. As you can see, my proposal only endeavors to substantiate the fact (and my colleague and friend, Dr. Geiger, is in agreement with me) that there is no existing law in Judaism which forbids the usage of two rings. We do not wish to introduce them; but freedom of conscience should prevail everywhere. For the validity of the marriage ceremony it makes no difference whether one or two rings are chosen; however, permission should at least be given and no objection should be raised against the usage of two rings. At first, however, the marriage ceremony shall be performed entirely according to the hitherto existing procedures, so that indeed, even according to the viewpoint of the oldest rabbis, there would be no objection for the woman to present a ring to the man. In Mr. Landau's opinion it would follow that, if a new bride who had been married an hour ago came home and presented her betrothed with a ring, their marriage would automatically become void; in other words, the act of marriage be annulled! For certainly nobody would dispute the fact that it could not make any difference, whether the bride places a ring on the finger of her betrothed an hour earlier or later, if thereby the very act of marriage could be annulled.

I move the honorable chairman to proceed at once with the discussion on this first proposal, and hereby conclude my report on the same.

MODERN MARRIAGE
(*Resolutions of the Augsburg Synod, 1871*)

1. It is permissible that during the marriage ceremony, after the bridegroom has presented the ring to his bride with the words, *hare at mekudeshet li,* the bride in her turn also give the bridegroom a ring with a few appropriate words.

2. The Synod recommends that in those countries where the civil marriage ceremony is entrusted to the rabbinical office, the bridal pair should be asked during the religious ceremony whether they consent to the marriage contract. The procedures now in use in Württemberg might be followed.

3. No one can be declared unfit as a witness at marriages or divorces on account of his non-observance of a ritual law.

4. The Synod states that the prohibition of the marriage ceremony on certain so-called unlucky days, namely, the period between Pesach and Shavuot and the so-called three weeks, is without any foundation, serves to advance superstition and does not foster any pious feeling. Therefore, it considers this restriction as annulled, with the exception of the week immediately preceding the ninth of Ab.[2]

5. A widow who has a child by her deceased husband does not have to wait more than one year before contracting a new marriage. Where special circumstances of the widow or the child suggest that the marriage not be delayed for that length of time, the wedding ceremony may be performed earlier.

6. According to Judaism the civil ceremony is completely valid and sanctioned, provided that the Jewish laws of prohibited degrees are not violated. However, the religious ceremony is required as the proper consecration for so significant an act.

7. A valid judgment of the courts concerning the identity of a deceased person and a valid presumption of death have sanction also in respect to ritual.

8. The rule of the Torah in regard to *Halitza* has lost its significance, since the circumstances which brought about levirate marriages and *Halitza* no longer

---

[2] (Ed. note) The Synod makes a distinction between "unlucky days" and days of mourning which are founded on historic events.

exist and since the basic thought underlying this precept has become foreign to our religious and social consciousness.

The omission of *Halitza* is no impediment to a widow's remarriage. However, for the sake of the freedom of conscience, no rabbi will refuse to perform a *Halitza* in appropriate form if the participants so desire.

9. In view of the fact that the statutes of the Christian churches, as well as the laws of the modern countries, apply the prohibition of various degrees of affinity with almost greater rigor than does the Jewish marriage law; and whereas they regard matrimony as an ethical partnership for life and, therefore, forbid at a wedding everything that violates morality, the Israelitish Synod in Augsburg declares: That the talmudic marriage law in regard to proselytes of pagan origin cannot be applied to persons who have turned to Judaism from one of the Christian churches.

10. The Synod resolves to establish a committee for the purpose of submitting to the next Synod definite proposals on the jurisdiction of divorce cases, particularly on the relation of the rabbi to this procedure, and also on the still valid causes for divorce. The committee shall insure the equal treatment of the two sexes, if at all possible.

MIXED MARRIAGE
(From the Debate at the Brunswick Conference, 1844)

The first rabbinic conference had on its agenda a discussion of the questions to and answers of the French Sanhedrin, called by Napoleon at the beginning of the century (see above, p. 71). Napoleon had asked about the validity of mixed marriage, and the Sanhedrin had tried its best to preserve the Jewish traditional viewpoint on this matter without giving grave offense to the Emperor. It phrased its answers negatively, stating that mixed marriage was "not forbidden"; but it did not state that it was allowed. This ambiguity came into play when the issue was reopened in Brunswick. The following is from the conference transcript.

The debate was on the third question asked of the French Sanhedrin:
May a Jewish woman marry a Christian, or a Christian woman a Jew, or is it the intent of Jewish law that Jews should marry only each other?
Answer of this Sanhedrin: Marriage with Christians is not forbidden.
Motion of the commission:[3] Marriage between Jews and Christians, in fact, marriages between monotheists in general, are not forbidden.

Hess:[4] I agree, but with the following addition: "Such marriages are not forbidden and the rabbi is permitted to officiate."

[3] (Ed. note) The commission had been appointed to evaluate the procedures of the Sanhedrin and to make proposals to the Assembly.
[4] Mendel Hess (1807-1871), chief rabbi in the Duchy of Weimar, belonged to the most radical wing of Reform and was probably the first to officiate at mixed marriages.

Schott:[5]   The integrity of the Sanhedrin is proven in the way it formulated its answer. It said: "Marriage between Jews and Christians is not forbidden"; it did not say: "It is permitted." There is a difference. Such a marriage may be permitted, yet there would be practical difficulties, as for instance, in the marriage service or the ritual of engagement or divorce proceedings. Since these questions touch so widely on practical issues, I am for postponing this whole matter for the time being.

Maier: The Sanhedrin was cautious, but it remained entirely in accord with the Talmud. Where there is a *civil* marriage, there is no objection to it from a rabbinic point of view. *Ba'alot ba'al yesh lahen;* but there is no religious marriage: *huppah vekiddushin en lahen.* The President objects to making a difference between "not forbidden" and "permitted."

Holdheim agrees with Church Counselor Maier. However, according to present Jewish religious marriage law, religious or synagogal forms are not necessary for the marriage ceremony. These have been introduced because of a well-recognized need to give marriage a church sanction also. All of us feel urged to consider as legally necessary that which has manifested itself as a need (like the religious form) at the time of the marriage ceremony. However, this is not yet law! First, we must satisfy our conscience and the laws of the Sanhedrin: "The marriage of a Jew with a monotheist is not forbidden."

In a practical sense, however, we can do no other than to advise against mixed marriages if they are to be concluded without assuring the freedom of religious education.

Philippson agrees with Holdheim, but refers to the formulation of his own proposal, namely, that in a mixed marriage the possibility should not be precluded that children might be brought up in the Jewish religion.

Frankfurter:[6]   We would not have raised the question, for we understand its difficulty. We know too well that mixed marriages are neither desirable from a practical nor a theoretical religious point of view, even when it accords with the sense and the words of the Sanhedrin, which closed the matter as far as the law of the state is concerned.

But since the question has come before us, we must answer it forthrightly. A reservation in the answer is not permissible. I am also of the opinion that mixed marriages should be admissible only if there is freedom of religious education for children born in such wedlock. In order to achieve this, an *addition* should be made which should be separate from the answer itself.

Maier: This question is simple: Are such mixed marriages permitted? There can be no reservation in this regard.

Herzfeld: In principle I am satisfied with the answer of the Sanhedrin. However, thinking of practical matters, I would very much like to pass this paragraph by, for we are desirous that our resolution should be accepted by the *people*—and by dealing with this question at all we would act in contrast to this very wish. Furthermore, as one may judge from the teaching which goes on in Christian schools, Christian love toward Jews has not progressed far enough to make a marriage between Jews and Christians desirable.

[5] Leopold Schott, Rabbi of Randegg.

[6] **Naphtali Frankfurter (1810-1866), preacher at the Hamburg Temple, a member of the radical Reform wing.**

(There are many objections in the Assembly against this last expression.)

Hess: What is our objective in this discussion and what are our resolutions on this point? Everything is in vain if we do not add, as I have already proposed: "The religious marriage of such a union may be performed by Jewish clergymen."

S. Adler is against the acceptance of this whole matter because he does not believe that it belongs to the task of the rabbinic assembly. For what does the permission of mixed marriages do to the revitalization of the religious spirit? If one has to say something about it, then for the time being, contrary to Holdheim's remarks, it must be considered as undecided whether the education of the children in the Jewish religion may indeed be a condition for such marriage. (He proceeds to explain his point of view.)

Schott (against Holdheim): Even though the ceremonies could be omitted at a Jewish marriage, the *hare at mekudeshet* must not be missing, for in it the sacredness of marriage is already expressed.

The President asks: Shall the proposal of the commission be accepted in the following formulation: Marriages between Jews and Christians, in fact, marriages with monotheists in general, are not forbidden.

The vote is taken. The majority votes "No."

Philippson rephrases the motion in the following manner: Members of monotheistic religions in general are not forbidden to marry if the parents are permitted by the laws of the state to bring up children from such wedlock in the Jewish religion.

The majority agrees to the motion.

Jolowicz[7] objects to the formulation and wishes his objection to be recorded, because the resolution goes against the expression of the Paris Sanhedrin as well as against the rules of the Talmud at this point. The latter has not been abrogated.

Ben Israel agrees. Dr. Klein, Dr. Herxheimer, Dr. Herzfeld, Dr. A. Adler abstain from voting.

DIVORCE

(Resolution of the Philadelphia Conference, 1869)

The following statement is included here because it reflects most succinctly the prevailing Reform opinion of the time, an opinion which became universally accepted by the Reform movement. Even though the conference was held in America its members were all European born and trained, and they conducted their meeting in the German language.

---

[7] Heymann Jolowicz (1816-1875), rabbi in Köslin, a radical Reformer who was widely known for his prolific scholarship.

A judgment of divorce pronounced by a civil court has full validity also in the eyes of Judaism, if the court documents reveal that both parties to the marriage agreed to the divorce. If, however, the civil court decreed a forcible divorce against one or the other party in the marriage, then Judaism recognizes the validity of this divorce only after the divorce grounds have been studied and have been found sufficient according to the spirit of the Jewish religion. It is recommended that the rabbi should seek the advice of experts for such a decision.

4. MOURNING PRACTICES

RABBINIC DEBATE
(From the discussion of the Breslau Conference, 1846)

Motion: The Assembly declares that the following mourning practices, which have developed from former popular custom, have lost significance and religious value for our time, and, in fact, run contrary to our religious sentiment and are, therefore, to be eliminated:

The tearing of clothes, allowing the beard to grow, sitting on the ground, elimination of leather footwear; and also those which custom has almost entirely eliminated, namely, the prohibitions of washing, bathing, and greeting.

The Assembly believes it advisable that the mourner should stay at home during the first three days (and not seven as previously), beginning with the day of interment, provided that higher duties and considerations of health permit it.

The Assembly further deems it advisable that the mourner, if at all possible, should refrain from all business on the day of interment and withdraw from it during the next two days, but that during these days the carrying on of his business through other parties be permitted.

Güldenstein:[8] I am for the motion because:

1. We are here entirely in the field of talmudic law and custom which leaves us the widest margin for decision. The Bible does not know of a *command* to mourn; it only speaks, in story form, of incidents of mourning which took place. The practices which it notes in these stories are not commands but customs of purely oriental character. The laws concerning mourning are, therefore, an invention of tradition which translated living popular custom into commands and thereby greatly burdened the Israelite. I believe I would not overstate my case if I said that this is recognized from all sides. Even the most orthodox Jews who follow rabbinic tradition admit that mourning practices are excessively harsh. Why not then listen to the popular voice?

2. Mourning practices have the purpose to express properly the sentiments and feelings of the mourner. The mourning practices which have been in vogue

[8] L. Güldenstein was rabbi in Buchau.

until now are, however, no longer the expression of our sentiments but almost elicit the opposite result. They are offensive and do not give solace.

3. Indeed, it is self-contradictory to *prescribe* mourning practices. I remind you that often there are cases of death which wound the heart deeply and produce a sorrow which borders on despair. Why in such cases add customs which will deepen the sorrow and be void of all comfort? Here religion should approach man not as a taskmaster, but as a messenger from on high. It should lift him up rather than bend him low. There are also cases of death which, in fact, are a blessing both for the departed and for the survivors. I remind you of long debilitating illnesses, when death does not bring mourning and when the customary mourning practices are little less than ironic.

Einhorn: In the Holy Scriptures certain mourning practices are never commanded, but only mentioned as prevailing custom. If, however, one would consider such practices as commands, then sackcloth and ashes would also be necessary for the mourner. On the contrary, the Bible forbids the High Priest to tear his clothes and let his beard grow, and forbids it also to the other priests when they are engaged in sacrifice. This apparently belongs to the purely religious laws which are designed to spread slowly to all Israel, since excessive mourning which disfigures the body is, as a pagan custom, forbidden to all Israelites.

Granted, however, that the biblical mourning ceremonies are to be considered as commands (something which even the rabbinic authorities deny); granted also that letting the beard grow, tearing the clothes, etc., is not considered excessive mourning by the emotional Oriental; we say that for us the *Keri'a* [tearing of the garment] is productive of wild, unbounded sorrow which cannot be reconciled with religion and with the teaching of immortality (vaguely projected in the Bible). Further, the drawing off of shoes has no connection with present-day customs and is a thoroughly useless mourning practice. We also should not forget that the ancients deeply believed *en mitah belo het* [there is no death unless there is sin]; hence, each death was a new victory and triumph of sin and Satan which could not be mourned deeply enough. Some believe that because of this the next of kin of the departed were also considered to be touched by sin and were therefore unclean. Hence, the seven-day period of deep mourning, which is the same period assigned to purification from ritual uncleanliness, and hence the prohibition for the mourner—as for a woman in menstruation—to visit the house of God. According to our ideas, death has nothing whatsoever to do with sin. Rather, we enter into a higher stage of life which renders all manner of uncontrolled, wild sorrow entirely impermissible, and which makes it desirable that we give expression to only that natural sorrow which occurs when our dear ones pass on. Judaism never wants to suppress the purely human and, therefore, approves of weeping at the time of mourning: *v'ahekhem kol beth yisrael yivku et ha-serefah* [your brethren, the whole house of Israel, shall weep over the loss].

Stein: We are warned not to engage in a new kind of casuistry, and I, too, am against the institution of a new Shulhan Arukh. However, we should be aware that we are about to eliminate a significant portion of the old code, the *Hilkhot Avelut* [laws of mourning]. Therefore, we are obligated to set forth brief outlines which contain the quintessence of our thinking in accordance with the religious point of view of our own time. Let us not merely negate present custom. We must be positive lest our resolutions will lack all effectiveness.

The motion prevailed after extensive debate.

5. HOME OBSERVANCE

By the mid-thirties of the nineteenth century the neglect of personal home observance was already widespread. Nothing emphasizes more strongly the mood of urgency which animated the Reform movement than does the following despairing outcry by Creizenach. It was precisely because the attitudes he describes were so real that the Reformers pressed forward with a truly divine enthusiasm.

ONLY A MIRACLE CAN HELP US *(Michael Creizenach)*

Neither the school nor the synagogue can instil true piety into the soul if the religious element is lacking in the household; if no devout prayer to God begins and ends each day; if God's gifts are accepted and enjoyed without gratitude, as if they were coming to us; if Sabbath and holidays are distinguished from the workdays through nothing except a somewhat more luxurious life. Unfortunately, very many quite pious Jewish householders see these evils in the circle of their own families, without being able to do anything about it. Should they force the Jewish prayer book into their children's hands, commanding them to recite this or that piece? If the children have managed to learn their spelling, they will reluctantly obey. During the recitation their thoughts will wander at will, and they will put the book aside like someone freed of a burden, without having elicited a single spark of true religiosity from it. Their father will not be able to get more from them, even if he could improvise all the tirades of Horeb from his own soul. Of course, the prayer book could be used in a German translation, or new prayer books could be published.

These things are being done; however, since in that way the devotion at home loses its analogy with the public worship, it takes on the character of an institution created of its own authority, a separatistic exercise in devotion in which, if formality prevails in the least, one appears ridiculous in one's own eyes. If we are not exposed to an approved liturgy we will not for long hold on to the accepted ritual. We will improve, make changes, become indifferent, and finally drop it altogether. This is not something merely to be apprehensive about; it has already happened in many families, and certainly not always because of an indolent love of comfort, which in this instance could not be a very powerful motive. Similarly, the passion (to which quite a few are addicted) to strip off completely all Jewish characteristics from our outward appearance, has not helped either. The thing that deters even men of earnest, stern character from observing Jewish rituals in their family circle is that these rituals have a truly grotesque appearance for European, cultivated people; therefore, as long as they will not be altered in a suitable way, they must of necessity be ineffectual. But youth, especially, will be moved to mockery and derision unless the head of the family embodies all these endowments which can affect the spirit and the heart. Whoever has at any time lived the life of a pious Jewish family of the old kind, who particularly in his parental home has come to know the magic charm of our festive ceremonies, will not shun them as a troublesome compulsory service, even in the face of the most drastic changes in his views. They offer only pleasure to one who is familiar with them, and any small abstinence they may impose is outweighed by an abundance of moral and spiritual joy. A great many who have stopped the practice recall with deep melancholy the spiritual consecration that formerly filled them at the sound of pious songs at the parental table, and they realize painfully that the commonplace, prosaic tone in their homes is never interrupted by a more genial, festive life. Precisely in such moments of reminiscence they realize with regret that they stand alone with their feelings and favorite ideas, that they are not understood by the younger generation even in their own families, and that with their ancient custom of observing the domestic ceremonies, they weaken the devout sentiments of their surroundings, instead of strengthening them.

If we are not dismayed by this observation and nevertheless preserve the old ancestral customs, we can see from year to year with greater clarity how these customs appear more pale, more profane, even downright comical, degraded as empty observances. No angry zeal will help against such evil. There is something here which may be called the spirit of the times or anything else for that matter, against which it is impossible to fight, simply because it is an unequal fight. The younger generation is by no means impetuously insistent that we accept their ideas and sentiments; for, because through our obstinacy, they have for the most part become indifferent in matters of religion. But they will survive us, and the time will come when they, without encountering resistance, will be able to remove arbitrarily our customs which have become meaningless to them, as indeed they have been removed long ago in many a home. They are disappearing, and most people do not even realize that this is something to be regretted. Our immediate successors have seen the religious domestic rituals practiced with such dull thoughtlessness, that they have never been able to penetrate the inner core spiritually, the beautiful ideas which are the basis for many of them. They do not know, for instance, that the *Kiddush* is a beautiful devout greeting, with which one welcomes the holy days, thanking God for the favor of having granted days for the restoration of body and soul. They know actually nothing more than that a Hebrew formula is being recited mechanically in a recitation delivered in bad taste, with a goblet full of wine; they listen to it with disgust, if they are forced to do so at all. Experience shows that to instruct them on this point leads to no good result, for at least in modern times there has been no lack in education of this kind. To instil new life into withered bones can be accomplished only through a miracle. The casting itself should not be thrown away to make the radiant core shine through once again; instead, it must be embellished and cleansed, and for this our rabbis who are aware of the needs of Judaism today must provide the necessary leadership.

CHAPTER
X

The Community

▬▬▬▬▬▬▬▬▬▬▬▬▬▬▬▬▬▬▬▬▬▬▬▬▬▬▬▬▬▬▬▬▬▬▬▬

Rᴇꜰᴏʀᴍ began primarily as a movement responsive to total community needs. Its early preoccupation with worship reform was one facet of its communal orientation. Many of the leaders were active in efforts to alleviate the depressed status of the Jews; Reform rabbis and laymen could always be found fighting for an egalitarian cause, and not a few of them suffered persecution and imprisonment.

The topics assembled in this chapter have some bearing on community concerns. Many of these ceased to be live issues after the battle was over, but others continue to face the Jewish community.

1. THE RABBINIC OFFICE

Tʜᴇ Dɪɢɴɪᴛʏ ᴏꜰ ᴛʜᴇ ʀᴀʙʙɪɴᴀᴛᴇ (*Samuel Holdheim*)

Holdheim had published a lecture on the rabbinic office in which he attacked the existing restrictive laws of Prussia. The censor had passed the lecture, which was called "exceedingly strange" by the *Annals*. The journal, in reprinting these excerpts, noted that the censor's leniency was proof that "noble frankness" was given a hearing by the officials even when it displayed great zeal against the laws of the state.

Only religion and its outward representative, the spiritual head of a religious community, namely, the rabbi, have not yet been freed of that medieval disgrace [of second-class citizenship]; he alone still stands stigmatized by the law. The supplements to the general Civil Code read as follows: "Jewish rabbis and other servants of the synagogue cannot be counted in the category of those ecclesiastical functionaries whose qualifications are judged by the supreme religious authorities of the state. The rabbis, in particular, are nothing but individuals versed in law and biblical knowledge, from whom the Jews can obtain instruction in the interpretation of ceremonial laws as well as the performance of marriage ceremonies and other religious acts. However, Jews do not incur any obligation whatever to make use of these rabbinic services. Hence, the confirmation and inspection of such Jewish synagogue servants on the part of the state authorities can only have the purpose of preventing the election of men declared unfit by the state police, as for instance, those unable to read and write, or subjects with questionable morals." The law says further: "Jew rabbis are not teachers of the young and cannot be regarded and treated as teachers of religion in the sense of Christian clergymen, since they do not have a clerical character in this sense."

What? Is this all to which the clerical activity of a rabbi is restricted or should be restricted? It is being assumed that this activity applies solely to functions indifferent to the moral interests of society and, therefore, unworthy of its confirmation and inspection, thus denying the rabbi any clerical status. How can any creditable rabbi, who knows better and is deeply sensitive to the dignity of his ecclesiastic position, not solemnly protest such disgraceful imputation? Should not a rabbi who is suffused with the sanctity of his calling and aims to further the moral and religious ennoblement of the congregation entrusted to his care, categorically reject such a dishonorable reproach? Indeed, he would deserve disgrace and reproach if he would not strive with all his might for the propagation of a better demonstration and a more correct appreciation of his holy vocation! No, my beloved friends! Instructions in the ceremonial law, marriage ceremonies, etc., do not begin to fill the sphere of a rabbi's spiritual calling!

It is true the laws take care not to revile Israel's religion because of its awe-inspiring name and age; yet they do not hesitate to derogate its representatives. The profession of the rabbi, of the Jewish clergyman, is as inwardly holy and outwardly respectable as that of any other faith. For next to instruction in the ceremonial law and other religious acts, his profession consists mainly in the endeavor to propagate within his own community, through teaching and example, both religion and morality to the widest and most beneficial extent. It is his sacred, dedicated calling to create and strengthen religious belief in all directions, and, wherever his influence extends, to advise the ignorant through public instruction and exalted interpretation of the divine word; to convince the sceptical; to return the erring to the path of goodness and righteousness; to strengthen the weak; to comfort the disheartened; to uphold the falling; to uplift the humbled; to give stability to the wavering; to calm those agitated by passion; to conciliate the ill-willed; and to bestow upon all the blessings and comforts of religion. The rabbi strives to awaken and to restore, to create and to further, to establish and to preserve in all hearts a sense of justice and responsibility, religion and morality, love for God and man, love for one's king and country, inviolable loyalty to the laws and its executors, and to make virtue and religion rule everywhere. His sacred calling is to make the youth, on whose moral-religious ennoblement Israel's future destiny depends, the chosen object of his religious attention and spiritual care, and, through instruction or supervision of religious education, to help raise a future generation who at last shall experience uncurtailed justice and to whom their fathers' hardships may be forever unknown. His sacred calling is to preside over the worship service, that divine institution for the propagation and restoration of moral and religious sentiment; to supervise the religious affairs of the community; to live and work for the noble and divine in every sphere of his influence. Is all this no more than interpretation of ceremonial laws, which naturally must not be excluded from the circle of his responsibilities? Does such activity and work in God's vineyard not bestow an ecclesiastic-spiritual character upon its guardian?

"DOCTOR" OR RABBI? (*Peter Beer*)

The penchant to obtain the secular doctor's hat was neatly scored by a layman. He might equally have scored the congregations who usually wanted a "Dr." to lead them. It should however be noted that the splendid general education of Reform rabbis has continued to be a mark of distinction and has been of inestimable value to the total Jewish community.

The more prominent an object is, or the more value it claims, or the more effectively it influences life in general, or the more frequently it is used—the more abundantly it is subject to misuse. This ancient principle derived from experience has likewise proven to be entirely true in regard to the rabbinical and preaching candidates of recent times. I am referring to nearly all our younger rabbinical candidates who make great haste to obtain their doctor's hat, not only to parade before the world as philosophers, but, indeed, as doctors of philosophy. In regard to this, one might quote the prophet Jeremiah: "Ask ye now among the nations, who hath heard such things. . . ." For among a thousand Catholic preachers we will not find a single one who sought the doctor's title; likewise, among the Protestants we shall hardly find one who aspired to it, since the doctorate is just as little required for the administration of their office as it is for the office of a rabbi or any other Jewish preacher. Only in our nation has this more recently become fashionable, and a rabbinical candidate is as embarrassed to appear without the doctor's hat as without shoes and stockings.

It seems that for the Jewish rabbinical cadidates the doctor's title will be subject to the same misfortune that befell the otherwise so common titles *morenu* and *haver*. These were so common and so easily available from any rabbi for two to four gulden, they became so debased that any educated man was ashamed of them, and, indeed, in the better established synagogues they were no longer used, even for the calling up to the Torah. We have had no Doctor Aristobulus, no Doctor Philo, no Doctor Maimonides, Albo, Candia, Spinoza, Mendelssohn, Salomon Maimon, and many other radiant stars of greatness who shone on the Jewish philosophical horizon in antiquity, the Middle Ages, and the recent past. These great men were no doctors, but—scholars.

Indeed! During the period between the completion of his university studies and the assumption of his office, the candidate for the rabbi's or preacher's office has to occupy himself with much more important and more urgent activities than to prepare himself for the rigorous examinations of the doctorate. As a theologian he must above all acquaint himself accurately with the Bible *in extenso* and with its Jewish commentaries; likewise, as a preacher he must accurately acquaint himself with homiletics and its disciplines. In the first place, however, as a Jewish theologian (which means as counselor on *terefa* and *kasher*) he must endeavor to familiarize himself thoroughly, if not with the complete Talmud, at least with several of its tractates, especially those controversies which are usually submitted to the rabbi for a decision, as for instance Pesahim, Hullin, Nidda, and partly also Yebamot and Gittin. He could not have acquired this knowledge before entering school, being too young at the time, nor could he have had the opportunity and leisure to absorb it during his years of study.

Then, if a candidate has completely satisfied these demands, for which purpose he will require several years, no one will hold it against him if in his spare time he continues to search further in the depths of philosophical disciplines, and, to satisfy himself that he has perfected his knowledge in that area, submits to rigorous examinations, thus earning his doctor's diploma.

IT IS HARD TO BE A RABBI (*Abraham Geiger*)

The rabbi, like everyone else who deals with the practical issues of life, has a most difficult position. If he has made up his mind that much of what is tradition has inescapable disadvantages, then he will find it difficult to safeguard this tradition. Furthermore, there are things which are really bad, and here he must feel the urge to do something about it. Yet there will be elements in his congregation who will oppose even these improvements. Then he has others in his congregation whom he sees turning away from religious life altogether, and whom he may not hope to bring back to Judaism under present circumstances. Yet he would be deluding himself if he would not take note of these very people. He cannot hide from himself the obstacles which many traditional forms place in the way of social and commercial life and also of humane and truly religious attitudes. To eliminate these forms is his obligation. There is most certainly something magnificent in his self-limitation and in the taming of his powers which always threaten to break the bounds of narrow circumstances. We must honor the rabbi's mastery over his dearest desires. It is a small thing to deny oneself pleasures and to live poorly, but it is something great to deny oneself the highest pleasure, namely, to follow one's ideas with boldness and, instead, to accommodate oneself with ever-new attempts to gain some small place for these ideas. It is a great thing to give up the rewarding hope of recognition in wider circles and of prosperity in order to be the more surely effective in the narrower sphere of one's influence.

Who would tell him what to do and how to do it, considering the chaos of our present circumstances, with all the contradictory demands made upon him? Happy is he if he sees his position clearly; happy if he does not delude himself in any wise; happy if he does not become entirely dishonest, if he does not misjudge the potential which even under present circumstances does exist; happy if he does not forget his aims and does not lose firm ground under his feet.

NEEDED—A RABBINIC COLLEGE (*Ludwig Philippson*)

The organizational genius of Philippson manifested itself early in his career. He foresaw the need for a variety of communal institutions and lived to see many of his dreams fulfilled (see above, p. 74). In 1837, he took up Geiger's suggestion and issued his first appeal for the formation of a modern rabbinic seminary. However, it took almost twenty years until the seminary in Breslau opened its doors.

APPEAL TO ALL GERMAN ISRAELITES TO SUBSCRIBE FUNDS TO A JEWISH FACULTY AND JEWISH SEMINARY FOR GERMANY

Israel is in the midst of a significant, decisive crisis regarding its religion, education, and civic position!

Israel stands at the turning point of its internal and external existence!

The four-thousand-year-old history of Israel has presently reached a midpoint from which Providence will lead Israel forward to its high and sacred goal.

We are called upon to prove that four thousand years of experience have not been lost on Israel.

We are called upon not to leave the course of events and of life to itself.

We are called upon to participate actively and to determine our own future through our own deeds and to bring this better future nearer.

We stand before all of Europe, before all of mankind.

We stand before the future and all coming generations.

We must prove to Europe, to the future, and to all coming generations what our will is, what our striving is.

We look back at a long past, at generations long perished. They say to us: We brought you to this point, we came through struggle, death and oppression. Now the battle has turned to peace, death to life, oppression to tolerance. Will you now progress from peace to salvation, from life to knowledge, from toleration to freedom?

Then prove it to all through a deed—a splendid deed, showing that you care not merely for the external material advantages of the new time, that you do not desire merely to get civil equality and to enjoy its fruits, but also that you care for the inner spiritual issues of life. Everything which has happened until now happened individually, for individuals and through individuals. Therefore, it is all piecemeal. Our religion is without university chairs, teachers, our youth and children are without education.

We need a rallying point for all. We need an institution where our religion will be taught, developed, and defended; where our teachers will be trained together. We need a hearth for all our interests.

Only then will our religion be protected from all scorn, will our holy writings be secured from ignorance and perdition, and will we ourselves be saved from degeneration and schism.

We need a faculty for the development and the maintenance of our religion for all the centuries, for the education of our spiritual leaders. We need a seminary to educate our teachers.

(Philippson proceeds to outline the ways and means by which a fund of one hundred thousand thaler may be collected.)

We appeal to all the Israelites of Germany, and to anyone else who wants to help this great work, to bring their gifts.

Forward, then, you Israelites who have acquired the new education. Give us your hand and prove that when you acquired new education and new forms, you did not lose your enthusiasm for the Israelitish faith and salvation.

Come forward, then, you older Israelites, come without suspicion, without fear; for the new institution shall unite everything, shall be the touchstone of peace for all the parties and thoughts of Israel. Already rabbinic scholarship is at a low ebb and the time for its complete disappearance is at hand. For there is no place to teach. Prove, then, that your faith is not mere pretext nor your piety mere façade.

Come forward, you rich people, for though you cannot obtain eternal reward and undying fame through pomp and ostentation, you *can* obtain it here.

Forward, you who are poor, for your gift is not measured according to its amount, but only in accordance with your will. To do nothing is nothing, and is no excuse. You are in the majority; therefore, your gifts count the more.

And you clergy and teachers in Israel, help this great common work along in your congregations and do it without envy, but rather through love of that faith which you teach.

2. THE PUBLIC OATH

The second-class citizenship of the Jew was nowhere more obvious than in the discriminatory manner in which a Jew's oath was administered. In medieval days he had to stand on a pigskin; but while this offensive requirement no longer obtained, there were other regulations which were meant to underline that a Jew's word was not as good as his Christian neighbor's. Special formulae were used, and often the Jewish witness was required to don *tallit* and *tefillin,* and render the oath in the presence of the rabbi.

It was natural that a discussion of the matter should arise at the first rabbinic conference, in 1844. The discussion revealed the scrupulous effort of the Reformers to proceed from the basis of talmudic Judaism.

It is interesting to note that the discussion also touched on the text of the *Kol Nidre.* This text had long served as a pretext used by state authorities to declare Jewish oaths as worthless. Since the formula had lost most of its old meaning, the delegates voted to eliminate it. But such is the nature of Reform Judaism that it was possible, one hundred years later, to reintroduce it, with a positive English paraphrase, into a new edition of the *Union Prayerbook.* For by now the question of vows and oaths was no longer at issue in Jewish-Christian relations, and the old text and melody were again accorded the place which popular sentiment had reserved for them.

Excerpts from the transcript follow:

Bodenheimer:[1]   It is our duty to elevate Judaism internally and to justify it externally. In regard to the latter, he calls the oath *more iudiaco* a serious defect, the abrogation of which we must help to achieve to the best of our ability. None has a more exalted appreciation of the sanctity of the oath than has the Jew. And yet there is many a state in Germany which still believes that the oath of a Jew is sacred only if it is sworn to the accompaniment of picayune ceremonies and if it is done in the synagogue. The saddest situation of all exists in this respect in the kingdom of Hanover. There, the Jew who swears an oath must put on phylacteries and tallit; he must take the Torah scroll in his arm; he must assert that he will not have a Jewish court relieve him from the consequences of this oath, nor that the oath would be nullified through the Kol Nidre prayer, nor that he looks at Christians as idolaters, etc., etc. The speaker shudders every time he has to administer such an oath, for the very formula is contrary to the Jewish religion; it is as derogatory for the clergyman as it is for the one who swears the oath, and is revolting to every decent sentiment. He (the speaker) has already repeatedly undertaken many steps in this regard. He has petitioned both Houses as well as the ministry itself. The Houses have, indeed, recognized the justification of his request; but the honorable ministry has done nothing to do away with these abuses. He now hopes that the Rabbinical Assembly would undertake measures to relieve the sad situation which he has described. Such measures should consist in a solemn declaration by the honored Assembly, to the effect: That the oath of an Israelite, as he calls upon the divine name, has full legal and binding power.

Indeed, continues the speaker, originally the person swearing an oath had to say only "Amen" after the judge had recited the oath first. According to

[1] Levi Bodenheimer (1807-67), orientalist, author, rabbi in Hildesheim.

Jewish law this was entirely sufficient for the complete validation of the oath. The speaker proposed that any resolution by the Assembly should be affixed to a renewed request to the honorable ministry in Hanover, which might lead us to hope for a final, more favorable reply.

Holdheim: The motion of Rabbi Bodenheimer justifies itself. Indeed, it must be said that according to Jewish religious principles the simple expression, "I swear," gives the oath its thoroughly binding force. However, the speaker would like to add a few considerations. The suspicion of the magistrates against the oath of a Jew, according to which the Jew has to swear that Jewish courts would not nullify this oath, is doubtlessly founded in the fact that for all too many years only *Jewish* courts were the legal adjudicators in matters between Jew and Jew. The civil magistrates are doubtful whether non-Jewish courts, which do not adjudicate according to Jewish law, would be recognized by us as entirely *legal* courts. Of course, we know how unjustified such doubt is, since we do not have any other magistrates nor any other laws than those of the state. But we have not done anything in order to bring this fact to the attention of others, namely, that the Jew has ceased to view only the Jewish judge as his proper adjudicator in all legal matters. We must make such a public declaration and thereby oppose the erroneous impression which still exists in many places.

In addition, Bodenheimer mentions that in the above-cited formula of the oath which the Jew has to use, he must say that as a Jew he does not consider Christians as idolaters. This is another matter in which, by a very determined declaration, we must do our share to dispel this delusion. Finally, we recognize the accusations which have been made against us relative to the Kol Nidre. To be sure, they are unjust; but we must not fail to correct this impression with a relevant declaration.

The Hon. President (Maier): Even though the formula, "I swear," gives binding force to the oath, nonetheless we must make it clear to the government that according to rabbinic law we do swear while touching a sacred object such as the Bible. For the oath is not a legal, but a religious matter. The man who swears must swear according to his religious conviction. According to these, the above-mentioned grasping of a holy object (*nekitat hefetz*) is necessary. As far as the evils concerning the Kol Nidre are concerned, the best way out would be to do away with this prayer altogether.

Bodenheimer: I am entirely in accord with the Hon. President with regard to *nekitat hefetz,* and I would indeed like my motion to be understood to include the amendment: "By putting a hand on the Bible."

Hirsch: (He is glad that this matter is now up for discussion. Against Holdheim he says the following:) The reason that non-Jews place less confidence in the Jewish oath does not lie in the fact that Jews are not believed to consider non-Jewish magistrates as their legal magistrates, but rather in the intolerance which darkened former ages. This is what caused the Jews to be burdened by degradations and indignities in this sacred act. The amendment suggested by the Hon. President concerning the *nekitat hefetz* is inadmissible. In this respect the Bible is a symbol of God, but the Jew knows no symbol for God. The oath is "Yes, Yes," "No, No." (The speaker makes reference to a talmudic passage.) The Assembly should make a simple declaration that this is all that is necessary.

Herzfeld calls the attention of his listeners to the fact that our declaration might have better success with the various governments if we would add a history of Jewish oath-formulae. For instance, the sainted Rabbi Eger of the local community, whom Herzfeld once asked for an expert opinion about the oath, came to the conclusion that the use of Torah scrolls by Jews at the time of swearing an oath originated in a time when *printed* Bibles were not available. However, so that the Torah scrolls might not have to be removed from their proper place in the synagogue, the person rendering the oath had to go to the synagogue in order to swear. The witnesses, who incidentally had to be present at the swearing of the oath, had to testify only that the oath had been rendered in the synagogue. However, since printed Bibles are now available everywhere, they substitute adequately for the hand-written scrolls at the time of rendering the oath, and, therefore, the swearing in the synagogue proper is rendered superfluous. The speaker mentions this only as an example, but because of it he is of the opinion that a historical development of court cases involving Jews should be added to our declaration. This would doubtlessly do the most to bring governments to the correct point of view.

Holdheim speaks against the viewpoint of the Hon. President regarding the necessity of *nekitat hefetz,* a custom against which he (the speaker) protests. Such an act was only a demand of Jewish *law* and, as such, no longer has validity for us. It is only Jewish *law* and not the Jewish religion which demands guarantees against mental reservations. As to the significance of the oath for Jews, one need only go for an answer to the Bible itself.

The President: I understand why Holdheim would be against *nekitat hefetz.* This derives from his system, for he wants to make a strict distinction between law and religion, and he believes that what he desires is already a fact. But as long as we are Jews with a talmudic rabbinic orientation, we must swear while grasping a sacred object.

Philippson: Let us not forget the practical point of view. The governments probably will not trust our declaration if we leave the basis of the Talmud. First of all, the oath of a Jew should be rendered in the personal presence of a Jewish clergyman; and second, the oath should have a *religious* formulation. Perhaps this was not so necessary with the Jews of old, who were more scrupulous and had a greater sense of religious reverence than have the Jews of our day. (The speaker is interrupted from all sides with the exclamation that this was an ill-thought out and unfounded remark.)

The President objects in the name of the Assembly against the last remark of Philippson. The President's rabbinic practice of fourteen years' standing, and doubtlessly also that of the majority of the Assembly, has convinced him that Jews who have been subject to the process of modern education have the highest sense of scrupulousness. (General assent)

Herxheimer agrees with Dr. Salomon that the Kol Nidre should be abandoned, and also that we should not allow anything to be required for the Jewish oath which does not apply to the confessors of other religions.

Formstecher: I am against the continuation of the *neḳitat hefetz* because by maintaining it we grant the Talmud the kind of authority which perhaps many Jews would refuse it. (As far as the motion to abrogate the Kol Nidre is concerned, he would agree.)

Herzfeld: If one is to talk at all about *neḳitat hefetz,* one would have to add that there are instances in which even according to Jewish law it is not necessary. (He too agrees to the abrogation of the Kol Nidre.)

Frankfurter: Bodenheimer made his original motion that the oath of a Jew has binding power without any further ceremony. Later on he added in explanation the words, "by placing one's hand on the Bible." The Assembly seemed to be opposed to this addition because the simple "I swear" is sufficient. To be sure, this is true. But even if the government deems the grasping of the Bible unnecessary, we should not abandon it. We should not consider this a bothersome obligation, but rather the recognition, during an important act, of the sacred word God. We should not derogate the maintenance of *neḳitat hefetz* but, indeed, insist on it. On the other hand, contrary to Kahn and Philippson, I believe that the assistance of a Jewish clergyman during the act of rendering the oath is entirely unnecessary. It is altogether sufficient that the person about to render an oath is cautioned as to its signifiance, which can be done in the house of a clergyman.

As far as the Kol Nidre is concerned, I agree with the many previous speakers. This so-called prayer has brought us so much unjustified defamation and so much misfortune that even its beautiful melody cannot compensate for it.

Heidenheim[2] recites a passage from Zunz concerning the origin of the Kol Nidre which shows how it came into use.

Jolowicz: The considerations concerning the oath of a Jew may already be found in Campz' *Annals of Prussian Law* (1772, No. 116). There the use of the psalm verse *Shiviti Adonai lenegdi tamid* has been mentioned as a simple substitute for *neḳitat hefetz.*

Hirsch once again objects to *neḳitat hefetz.* One should abandon it if for no other reason than for the sake of Jews in such countries where they have already been emancipated.

Holdheim agrees. He cannot be moved from his opinion against *neḳitat hefetz,* which is theoretically wrong and practically inadvisable. He cannot agree with Frankfurter. The only important thing is the *significance* of the oath; the *solemnity* which has been mentioned is not really the important thing. One may feel that there are still some people for whom certain formalities are desirable. But on the other hand, we should not force those who have reached the level of our age, as we have, to do something which is superfluous.

Thereupon, the debate is declared closed and the motion is put:

1. Shall the Assembly declare that the Jewish oath which mentions only the name of God has binding force without any other ceremony?
Unanimously agreed to.

---

[2] Philip Heidenheim, rabbi in Sondershausen.

2. Will the Assembly declare that the Kol Nidre is unnecessary and would the members of the Assembly do their part so that in their sphere of activity the prayer might already be abandoned come next Yom Kippur?

The Assembly agrees.

3. APOSTATES

It is often said, and justly so, that Reform Judaism closed the floodgates of apostasy. The number of Jews who in the nineteenth century converted to Christianity was frighteningly large. Reform's unremitting zeal saved thousands of others from taking this step. Geiger's exchange of letters, dated 1858, illustrates this vexing problem.

LETTERS ON LEAVING JUDAISM (*Abraham Geiger*)

Dear Sir:

Please do not think ill of me if a certain rumor causes me to ask you a question. The answer, of course, depends on you. I trust that in my question you will see merely a lively interest in a highly important matter and at the same time recognize my high esteem for you. There is a rumor that you are resolved to forsake your loyalty to Judaism and turn to Christianity. Now, if many a person in our day and in days past took this step, the motives were usually open and easily recognizable. Such a step was explicable, even though I could not sanction it. Some were motivated by the desire to enter into a career closed to Jews; others were driven by vanity, by the desire to climb the social ladder and achieve titles, and to have the kind of social intercourse which from afar appeared in a splendid light. I know that none of these motivates you. Your status in society is such that changing your religion would bring you no status change, for you do not need it. Besides, you are too estimable a person and enjoy too much genuine respect to be moved in your decision by petty vanity.

For a man like you there can only be one reason—and this one, to be sure, is entirely sufficient—namely, your conviction of the truth of Christianity. If you are convinced of the divine origin of this teaching, if you genuinely believe the dogmas of Christianity, the divinity of Jesus, the Trinity, original sin which can be lifted only through faith in the redeeming power of Jesus' death on the cross; if you believe in the ever-renewed covenant with the "savior of the world" through the consumption of His body and blood in the act of communion—then, indeed, it is your duty to convert to this faith. I would not oppose a conviction so honestly obtained, even though I am far from sharing it. I would honor you for a step to which your inner conscience urges you, even though I could not cease to regret it. And yet precisely here I have my doubts, for in so far as I know your way of thinking, I do not deem it probable that you have adopted this religious attitude, and I have such a complete confidence in your frankness and truthfulness that I will receive from you—if you answer me at all—an unambiguous declaration on this matter.

If you declare that you are a believing Christian, then my questioning is at an end. You will remain in my eyes an estimable person who only follows his conscience and disregards all other considerations—even though his conscience and mine differ fundamentally. If, however, this is not the case, as I suspect, then what shall be the justification of this external conversion, what would be its cause? You are too sincere to play with religion, too honest to desire that your conversion cause injury to a group with whose totality as well as its individual estimable members you have stood in manifold relationships. What, then, is your reason and motivation? I ask you most insistently; please speak openly with me, and believe me that you will give me true tranquility if you will share your motivations frankly with me. I must and shall overcome my sadness over losing you, but I would suffer more greatly from the mysterious nagging feeling that a dark power is somewhere at play.

I repeat, the only reason for my letter is my esteem for you. Judaism, you must be convinced, even if you will really turn your back on it, will not perish, even though more than one adherent, however influential through personal fortune or otherwise, will withdraw from it. Even the community is in itself not really hard-hit by such a loss, but it is natural as well as noble to be pain-fully affected when a dear friend leaves the faith. Therefore, you will not feel hurt by my question and will not consider it as importuning. To be sure, I would have to disregard even such misunderstanding, because I am convinced that I would be fulfilling a duty. However, I would be very happy if you would save me such conflict and would be even happier if I would learn from you that the rumor was wrong.

Sincerely,

ABRAHAM GEIGER

Answer

Dearest Sir:

You have honored me greatly by your interest in me, by your frankness, and by the love of truth which you ascribe to me. Therefore, I do not wish to prove myself unworthy of your confidence and will give you an equally frank answer.

The rumor is not wrong. I am in the process of converting to Christianity and my reasons are as follows:

I am no Jew. I have probably never been one. Judaism means nothing to me except that martyrdom which is the share of all Jews. I do not feel the urge to be a martyr. And why should I transmit this martyrdom to my children with-out offering them anything in return? On the other hand, it would be a half-measure to educate my children as Christians and to remain myself within Judaism. Of this you would doubtlessly disapprove even more strongly. Better, therefore, that I take the step externally as well, which internally has already for a long time been taken. The creed to which I would confess at the time of my conversion I can profess with a clear conscience, for it contains nothing which is contrary to my religious convictions. I do not consider the change of religion lightly. I do not take off my faith like a garment which has become ill fitting, for I have carried the whole thought with me for many years and do not do like others who, as soon as they think of it, quickly carry it out. The last thing I would wish to do is hurt the Jews by my conversion. If it were so taken, I would be sad and I hope that this will not be the case. I have only a small acquaintance and the few people with whom I have associated will, I hope, continue to do so. If you would know me more closely you would certainly believe me that I have no other motive for this step.

Sincerely,

• • •

Counter-Answer

Dearest Sir:

First of all, will you please accept my sincerest thanks for the complete openness with which you answered me. This is worthy of a man, and I expected it from you. However, I proceed to the matter itself. For if you did not mind my question, you will not feel offended if I examine your reason. Indeed, you will probably have guessed that my inquiry was only a preparation for such an examination.

You begin your motivation by saying that you are no Jew and have hardly ever been one. You consider this as an admitted fact and treat it in your further discussion of the matter as an axiom. But is this indeed such an indubitable truth? *You are a Jew* when you believe in the one, holy, living God. This belief was always the principal faith of Judaism for which its adherents fought and suffered and in which they found solace and comfort. Even at a time when the ceremonial laws were much more highly esteemed and considered much more binding, the ancient sages said that in fact a Jew was everyone who rejected idolatry and who did not place another power next to the one God. But Judaism developed greatly later on, and especially so during the last century. In the historic process it has reached a level of knowledge which lays less stress on external acts and more on those fundamental convictions of the unity of God. The essence of Judaism is not described by what one or the other Jew considers as binding for himself. Rather, it is the spiritual bond which today encompasses all its adherents, that thought which amongst German Jews is being recognized more and more. It is this which is Judaism's essence, it is this which makes a Jew. And this bond consists precisely of the pure conception of God and the realization of this faith throughout a rich and honorable history. In this sense, then, you are a Jew. You owe to Judaism much in your education and character which has become part of your inner nature, even though you may not be conscious of the fact that these are a beautiful gift you received from Judaism. You pretend that you are no longer a Jew because you have separated yourself from the ceremonial law? Judaism today, on its present progressive level, has given up much of this law. A discussion on other matters is also in progress, and history will finally reserve its judgment on still further issues. And again, much will prove to be vital which touches the depth of the soul and lifts the heart. But these are side issues. What is fundamental is the faith, and this you share with us—this faith which was the possession of your and my ancestors, this faith which educates and elevates mankind. And you will say so quickly that you are no Jew?

You are a Jew; you are not a Christian and will never become one. I find your good letter strangely reserved on this very point which I permitted myself to emphasize especially in my inquiry. This strengthens me greatly in my supposition that you do not subscribe to the faith of the church. For Christianity does firmly demand a belief which is hard to accept for a born Jew. Let us not overlook the fact that however often people have tried to water down the fundamental dogmas of Christianity, they have assumed a more decisive and central position. This proves that Christianity would cease and lose its true character if it would weaken or even give up these credal points, especially the divinity of Jesus and everything that is connected with it.

Perhaps you will counter and say that there are many Christians who share your religious views. I cannot examine that too closely. I rather believe that the born Christian believes in little more than the universal, historic significance of Christianity, which even I share without hesitation. But he experiences other sentiments in connection with names and customs—be it because of his education, be it because of his association or general habits—and these are different from those of a Jew who in his mature age converts to Christianity. But quite aside from that, you will not overlook the difference between the born member of a society and the convert. The former lives within it and does not need to make any explanation. He has the right to express his own views, however divergent they may be (as long as he remains within the faith), and he may hope that his convictions would gain ascendancy even though for the present they may be firmly rejected and have very little hope for recognition. But it is entirely different with the convert. You will have to conform with the prevailing principles of society if you want its doors open to you, and if you have mental reservations you would enter this portal with a lie which could never be justified. You have no right to join a congregation with the intent to weaken its principles, which is precisely what you would have to do as a conscientious person. You do not have the least reason to hope that your divergent opinion would ever prevail, and you, an honorable person, will take so important a religious step which is bound up in such a complete contradiction? Shall this be the dedication with which you will declare yourself as a believer? If I were a Christian, I would say to you, "Remain a conscientious unbeliever rather than one who has lost his conscience."

Still, you have one answer ready for all my arguments and this I read from your letter. I am a practical man, you say; I leave the metaphysics to the philosophers, dogmatics to the theologians; I only want the satisfaction of my spiritual and religious needs; and so you say, "Judaism offers me nothing." But, dearest sir, whose fault is it, yours or Judaism's? Can the latter press itself upon you if you bolt the doors of your house and your heart? Can it offer you the tools of religion if you systematically avoid its house of God? Why don't you visit the synagogue on Sabbaths or holidays if you really have a religious yearning? Why don't you ask yourself whether the synagogue would not bring you full satisfaction? There is a wonderful, vital development afoot in Judaism today, and the generation of the present as well as our youth, who are the generation of the future, find themselves attracted to and truly edified by our worship service, however far they may be removed from tradition and memory. I could give you many examples which are truly pleasurable for me, but you should be convinced by looking at life as it goes on in your immediate vicinity. And yet, despite such vitality and useful thrusts which join hands with honorable high antiquity, you will fully withdraw and needlessly have the sad courage—excuse the hard expression—to issue accusations and say that Judaism offers you nothing?

Judaism with its festive holiness, Judaism with its magnificent history, Judaism with its devoutness in family life, Judaism with its merciful heart, Judaism with its pure faith in God, Judaism with its powerful capacity to suffer—all this offers you nothing?

In fact, it is this last capacity which seems to repel you. "Judaism," you say, "offers me nothing except perhaps martyrdom which is the share of all Jews to bear, and I do not feel within myself the vocation to be a martyr." For the time being I will not deal with the question whether it would not be better and nobler to suffer injustice than to commit injustice. But I must ask you this: What is presently your Jewish martyrdom? When the Jews in the Middle Ages spoke of it, it was indeed bloody martyrdom. It was a testimony which they rendered willingly and steadfastly. When a poor young man has finished his studies and at the very beginning of his career is prevented from pursuing it, then I feel his pain deeply. But I also ask of such a disciple of the spirit to have the spiritual energy not to surrender to timidity. But you, in your independent position, what is your martyrdom? Perhaps that not every narrow-minded person gives you a friendly smile, or distorts his mouth into a friendly smile without bearing friendship in his heart? Is this your heavy martyrdom? As far as I can see, you are honored everywhere in society, and where there is a public honorary office or participation in some activity which touches upon the common weal, you are asked to participate. I do not know whether it is because of or despite the fact that you are a Jew. But where is your martyrdom? Perhaps there is one or another social group which stubbornly keeps you out. It requires a Christian profession—of course, only an external one—as the first condition for membership and otherwise makes itself inaccessible like a fortress. It opens its doors only then, when a Christian profession is given, whether it be true or false. And such a circumstance you deem of such high value that you break forth in a complaint over heavy martyrdom? Are you craving social intercourse with people who exclude you —you, an honorable person—only because and as long as you cannot decide to make a declaration which you really cannot make from your point of view without digressing from the truth? And these are the people who will then gladly greet you as one of their own as soon as you—lie? I must admit that I would find either the honor or the intelligence of such people very doubtful, or association with you very painful.

I am sure you deem character and integrity which enable one to make sacrifices for truth more important than the desire not to have to make any sacrifices at all. This is the lot of humankind, that one must sacrifice from time to time. It is well with him who does it readily and devotedly and with a good conscience that he was not to blame but was subject to the fate of all mortals. It is a lovely heritage to instil such a conviction within our children and to transmit it to them as the way of their fathers. Only weakness will protect children from everything, and in the end it will corrupt them. It is a unique and worthy privilege of truly noble birth to be able to consider that which determines the general nobility of mankind as the possession of one's family and people, namely, worthy deeds, strength of character, honorableness of life. We are strengthened and exalted to receive such an unalienable heritage from fathers whom our ancestors considered their examples. But what if the father denies his fathers because they were oppressed? What if he denies them the cradle of his children and rationalizes himself into a conviction that he is making it a little more comfortable for his children? I ask you, will this instil character and honor in these children?

But I must break off. Perhaps in our discussion I have illuminated one side of the subject which may be new to you, and perhaps I have hurt you with some of my words. The latter, of course, was not my intention, but the former should not be unpleasant to you. One must hear both sides before such an important step, and one must wish to hear them and, in fact, demand their expression. It is not your duty to follow my words, but rather to examine my views thoroughly. You yourself say that you do not treat the matter easily and that for many years you have already contemplated this step without bringing it to realization. Will you not now take the time in which it will be possible for you to evaluate my objections freely? The sharp contradiction which I have offered you is perhaps a thorn which goads and hurts. I know that I do not understand the diplomatic art of persuading softly and of suggesting to the person whom one wishes to convince those thoughts which are really one's own. But I am honest and I know that I face an honest, conscientious man who will not be misled by a temporary ill mood, and who will instead wait until such mood has passed so that he may think with a tranquil mind. I would not know a higher joy and a richer reward for myself than if you would say to me, "Well, then, I have examined. Let us walk together." May God guide you in your thinking and in your decision.

Sincerely,

ABRAHAM GEIGER

4. JEWISH EDUCATION

Reform leaders very early recognized that without effective Jewish education of the youth all their other efforts would be futile. Many of the questions then raised still command our attention: Should parochial schools be encouraged? How can a teacher in a community school deal honestly with questions of Reform—seeing that his teachings may run contrary to some cherished views of his pupils? How much Hebrew can be taught in religious school classes?

GOALS OF JEWISH EDUCATION (*David Einhorn*)

The religious training of our children should be thoroughly Jewish and instinct with the spirit of the Sinaitic teaching. This is a task of supreme importance, a task to which we should bend every effort. Here no obstacle should block our path. The most indifferent and thoughtless must see that here we have to do with a vital Jewish question. We will point out to our children the world-redeeming power, the ever-widening significance of the Sinaitic teaching which is ever-enduring; the changeable character of its outward forms; the glorious triumphs it has achieved outside of the house of Jacob; the unparalleled sacrifices its preservation has cost; the wonderful vitality with which it has marched on, unscathed, amid the crash of worlds. We will also point out the universal union of the nations in God, the end for which Israel was set apart from the rest of mankind; and, finally, the mission of our scattered people to carry the Law of God to all peoples and all climes. When synagogue, school, home, and our life in general are imbued with such a spirit, we can rest assured that we shall have given our heritage an abiding place in the hearts of our offspring and secured for it a glorious future in this blessed land. We shall recognize in this happy outcome of our labors, in this service of God on the height of freedom after our going forth from the land of bondage, a sign of our divine mission.

PRIVATE INSTRUCTION OR RELIGIOUS SCHOOL? (*Abraham Geiger*)

Geiger here attacks the old custom of engaging a private teacher, or *Melamed,* for one's child.

Religion is something essentially human, independent of class and rank, independent even of the degree of one's education. To be sure, it is different with each person. And yet each one experiences the chasm between himself as a finite being and the infinite toward which he yearns. Religion is modified according to historic tradition and conditions, and this history is the common property of the larger community and usually takes on the same aspects amongst its subjects. Now since common instruction is to be preferred for every topic, it is an especially necessary condition for the growth of religious instruction. The child must at an early time gain the conviction that the truths which are here transmitted to him are generally valid, that he thereby belongs to a great community.

The child must progress from the small circle in which he is rooted to a sense of belonging to the larger community of those who feel as he does. As in the house of worship, so in the religious school class, he must see next to him a large number of youthful coreligionists who may be in many respects different from him, but to whom he is closely tied through the same faith. In addition, there are the many advantages which common instruction affords, especially in the field of religion. Religion is not merely a branch of knowledge. Its instruction must aim at the awakening of his deepest sentiments, the stimulation of his inwardness. It is, as it were, a sermon for our youth. Only within the larger circle can the wholesome warmth show forth in both teacher and pupil. Then the word comes forth more vital, more insistent on the lips of the teacher, and the soul of the pupil is more deeply touched by sincerity and devotion. This high advantage can hardly be replaced by any other means. It would, therefore, be a sad sign if there would be a decrease in the inclination of parents in certain circles to let their children attend the religious school, and if they would prefer to give them private instruction. Whatever the reason, it would be regrettable, and it should happen least of all in our own time. Our time demands equality and it also demands equal submission to that which is sacred. Could it be that religion, which in periods of many schisms maintained almost singly the principle of equality, be excluded when finally this principle is recognized?

Therefore, I urge our parents earnestly to regard the real interest of their children and truly to further their moral and religious education. Entrust your children to that institution which belongs to all of us for religious education. Send them early so that gaps in their preparation do not make their work more difficult and diminish their desire. Do not discontinue them prematurely from this instruction before it has reached its rounded conclusion! True understanding comes later, and early instruction receives its true illumination only at the end. If it is interrupted in mid-course it will remain piece-meal and little fruit may be expected from it. The act of confirmation, even though it does not have sacramental character, as well as preparation for confirmation, create a devotional atmosphere which will not remain lost in life. Let us use, then, the not-too-frequent moments in life which are suited to produce an elevation of the soul. Let us not deprive the receptive heart of our children of this act as they enter into a more mature age! One illumi-nated thought often illuminates the path of one's whole life.

THE TEACHER'S DILEMMA (*Michael Creizenach*)

We shall not argue the question at this point whether or not it is a good thing that there be special schools for Jewish children which serve also for the instruc-tion in worldly subjects, since this depends entirely on the local conditions of the communities. May it be noted here, however, that the need for well-appointed schools in religious instruction was never greater than it is right now, since in so many families domestic worship is no longer practiced and the observance of the established ceremonies has been discontinued. Now, if the school does not frequently and with the most earnest urgency remind the children of such families that they are Jews; if at school they do not become acquainted with the holy mission, the high dignity of the devout Jew, and the great world-historical significance of Judaism; if the schools do not instil in them awe and respect in the beliefs and morals of our ancestors, then it is to be strongly feared that they will be filled with the most damaging and unjust prejudices against their own religion, thus making a favorite wish of some people come true. If, by accident, some libelous pamphlet or a book like *Choreb*[3] fell into the hands of such youth, they would be lost to Judaism. All the more, therefore, can the school be an essential aid to parents who hold their children to the strict observance of all established practices and precepts but often do so with lack of understanding, with unfeeling sternness, without any reference to the Holy Books, and without any instruction in the basic concepts of religion. In this way the children consider the observances to which they are being subjected as hateful, needless, compulsory services, rather than acts of divine worship. If the children of such parents are not instructed with great warmth that each festival, each rule of conduct, has a blessed strength if it is informed by humility before the presence of divine, infinite wisdom; if they are not earnestly told to let themselves be willingly guided by their parents in religious matters; if they are not shown that the Holy Books are a venerable source of all the responsibilities of the Israelites; if they are not being imbued with the devout spirit that must hallow all religious forms—then they will submit to the rules of their parents only by constraint and with inner reluctance. This will soon reflect itself in their attitude toward religion itself and make them impatient for the day when they will be able to follow their own arbitrary choice.

[3] (Ed. note) By Samson Raphael Hirsch, founder of Neo-Orthodoxy.

Public religious instruction can accomplish all this whenever it is entrusted to men of proper insight and practical knowledge; however, it should afford one additional thing which is impossible within the present structure of our communities. It should familiarize all children in an equal manner, in no uncertain terms, with everything concerning their conduct as humans, as citizens, and as Israelites. The teacher should exclude from his exhortations nothing which the parental home directs the child to obey as his duty. If he finds himself forced by circumstances to bypass some part of his religious instruction in silence, his teaching would suffer from a disadvantageous incompleteness; for thereby he would be deprived of the means of correcting the faulty, far-fetched ideas which are imparted to many children by parents, servants, and other persons with whom they come into contact. How very important it is that every Jew should know which rites have their origin in the Pentateuch, which are merely an institution of the old scribes, and which were introduced at later times by scrupulous rabbis or by zealous cabalists. How useful it would be if the teacher in his instruction would also have an opportunity to express himself against certain customs which are pure inventions of superstition and which are actually distorting our religion!

The teacher is forced to remain silent on all these things, just like the authors of all hitherto published books of religion, and rightly so. For as long as our ritual code is not reformed, as long as brighter and truer views on the Mosaic law are not sanctioned by broad acceptance on the part of many Jewish communities, the teacher of religion cannot propagate Jewish customs in any detail without acquiring the reputation of a black zealot with some, and at the same time being called an arbitrary innovator by others. What can he do when a pupil asks him one of the numerous detailed questions which present themselves in such great numbers in the ritual code? If he is being asked, for instance, whether this or that routine, which according to talmudic theory is referred to as work, is permitted on the Sabbath day? Shall he forbid it, thus stigmatizing the parents of the majority of his pupils as Sabbath-breakers? Or shall he allow it, and in this way appear in the eyes of other pupils, and indirectly in those of their parents, as a scoffer at religion? "He shall act according to his conviction!" appears to be the most natural answer here. Yet, it only appears to be so, for the teacher has no right to elevate his individual opinion to a universal law, whether he unconditionally subscribes to the decisions of the Shulhan Arukh or not. He may not do this, particularly if he has mental reservations about the rabbinic views, which very likely is the case with most, and perhaps even with all. All that is left to him is either to reply coldly: "Such and such is the decision of the Shulhan Arukh," without supporting the decision any further with his own authority, or not to answer the question at all, referring it to the forum of the family. However, neither makeshift is good and can easily lead to indifference to all duty itself. Therefore, the teacher must state once and for all that he does not wish to engage in questions about the ritual code which are not touched upon in his textbook, and confine himself to impressing on his students that in matters of religious custom they should conform entirely to their parents' views. Thus, our instruction in religious knowledge must necessarily remain quite incomplete, until our religious observances have obtained the necessary regulation through a carefully thought-out reformation.

TEACHING CEREMONIES, BIBLE, AND HEBREW (*Abraham Geiger*)

What place shall ceremonial laws have in Jewish education? If instruction is to aim at a pious life as the result of one's highest convictions—convictions which the students themselves have gained—then ceremonies, too, must be more than un-understood actions which cannot be subjected to inquiry. Either they must be strong stimuli for the worship of God, or they must contribute to our own ennoblement and to the sharpening of our sense of duty toward our fellow men. Only the former are really ceremonies in the strict sense, while the others belong to the category of duty. Therefore, it would be wrong to consider as ceremonies certain biblical laws, as for instance, kindness to animals (not to slaughter the cattle and its young on the same day, not to take the young birds with their mother, not to boil the kid in the milk of its mother, and so forth). These are necessary expressions of loving-kindness, which also expresses itself vis-à-vis the world of animals. Thus the dietary laws of the Bible, in so far as they warn of abominable, harmful foods, are also a result of the respect for human dignity which aims at maintaining the body as the means for spiritual activity and which must prevent that animal lust abuse it for promiscuous satisfaction or sensual needs.

On the other hand, there are a great number of statutes which are merely means for remembrance; customs which make us think of God; symbols which are to express a deep thought. These are ceremonies proper. A question which ought to be considered very seriously is how the teacher ought to proceed in his instruction of these ceremonies, since nowadays they are understood and observed so differently. It is my conviction that he would do best not to go into great detail in his instruction of these ceremonies. He would be treating extensively of worship and festivals which are a means for the stimulation of the worship of God. He would indicate that there are many other means which aim at not letting our soul forget the thoughts of God, but that these must be practiced with the right spirit and conviction. He could give individual examples without trying to be exhaustive. Even less would he be called upon to make choices or to battle against the non-essential customs which have long lost their force. The school is the last place for a theological battleground; and only if some custom contradicts a pure teaching directly, would he proceed to explain the latter without reference to the former. He would teach submission to God's will in suffering and in trial; he would warn not to express wild rebellion against God's judgment on painful occasions such as death, not to indulge in some passionate acts such as the tearing of clothes, and so forth. Eternal truth must be secured amongst the youth of the present, the more so since, upon entering life, youth will soon enough discover the inner contradictions from which Judaism suffers today. The growing generation must receive a foundation which remains holy, even though life and a progressive science will yet eliminate other now existing customs. One would be committing a sin toward our youth if one would make them at so early an age a party to this rift and cause them to doubt what at home they have learned to consider holy, or to be indoctrinated with something which life later on will make uncertain. It would be better to avoid these points, for, either way, the treatment will not be satisfactory.

The instruction must stress especially how Judaism in its whole history represented these higher truths among mankind and has aided in their spread. The respect for its ennobling influence must be nurtured through proof from history. Therefore, religious instruction must be supplemented by *instruction in Jewish history,* which follows this particular purpose and also aims to acquaint the pupil, not merely with the external history of the Jews, but also to instil within him the conviction that Judaism is not a finished product. Rather, it is a truth which is to make holy, which in the progress of time has found different expressions and has a history of eternal vitality. This is to give the growing generation a means of comprehending the present tension and of understanding that highest esteem for Judaism does not preclude great differences in individual points. Naturally, the history of Judaism must have its broad foundation in exact acquaintance with the Bible. This is the indestructible kernel from which all the different fruits grow and which will continue its production inexhaustibly. Therefore, *not merely biblical history but the reading of the Bible* is a necessary subject of instruction, so that knowledge of its content may give a distinct direction to the pupil's whole religious attitude.

We have already talked earlier about the *instruction in the Hebrew language.* This instruction has achieved what, under the circumstances, has been possible. But parents do not sufficiently supervise the student's application to his homework, and our whole environment no longer affords memories of Hebrew, which formerly allowed the pupil—through practical application in life, and however unmethodically and superficially—to learn more than through today's best guided instruction. We may, therefore, agree that as mere language instruction, which has to face so many external obstacles, nothing inspiring and revitalizing will be achieved, nothing which may be considered religious or which will give food for thought and will for inner strength. However, as long as the house of God gives a special place to the Hebrew language, our youth must still be prepared for participation in the public worship service, and religious instruction must, therefore, give it some attention. For the young Jewish man who wants to acquire a higher [Jewish] education, the Hebrew language is in any case a necessity. To a person who wants to mature to greater knowledge, this language gives the means of fully understanding the sources of his faith. And should not a man of scientific education feel the need to make his own independent judgment about the most important matters and subject them to proof?

NEEDED: A REVIVAL OF HEBREW (*Levi Herzfeld*)

Herzfeld (1810-84) served the community of Brunswick throughout his rabbinic career. A prolific scholar, he was host to the first rabbinic conference in 1844.

The Hebrew language has always had definitions for anything it had to define; but the fact that it could create definitions does not hide the difficulty it had in creating them. There were heroes who could force the language to apply to their thoughts; but how many heroes of thought are there who do not happen to be language tamers! Is not one of the chief weaknesses of our Piyutim that precisely in the contest between thought or image on the one hand, and language on the other, the latter failed completely? For every new thought a new word must be coined, put in circulation, become accepted, pass for a time from mouth to mouth, as it were, before its character can claim universal acceptance, and only then can it be permitted to be used even by the less qualified.

However, if I spoke here of ages past, the same applies also to the present, only to a much higher degree. In our days a completely new phase is opening up for the religious language of the Jew. It has established its spiritual creativity gloriously; now it is up to science (of which theology is a part) to incorporate the best from all areas which have recently come into the purview of its research. In this process it must single out those idioms which best satisfy the religious needs of the present. For we do wish to continue the practice of deliberating about our religious matters in Hebrew, do we not? In the first place, having arisen from Hebrew soil, these matters must appear as alien, exotic plants if they are transplanted into any other language; and secondly, Hebrew has become the universal language of our religion. We are beginning to take an interest in the weal and woe of our dispersed, even though antipodal, brothers; we are beginning to regard ourselves as a religious unit and know that, even though Europe and in particular our own Germany promise to become the cradle of our regeneration, the latter especially has taken in only a minute number of our coreligionists. Therefore, we must embrace all of Israel spiritually if we are to prevent two equally deplorable events from happening, namely, that the handsome flower of German-Jewish science would become detached from the tree that bears and nourishes it, the tree which represents Judaism in the east and south; and secondly, that with the disappearance of its blossom, which had barely begun to unfold, this tree would relapse into dull petrification.

We must write for these, our Jewish brothers; we must seek to win them over to reform them, for they are capable and worthy of it. Our young literature shall be the missionary institution, and our new Hebrew language, the medium of our communication. This, then, must be created, and in order to accomplish this feat it is necessary above all to translate the entire cycle of our new ideas into Hebrew, even though they might not as yet be used directly for the benefit of theology. Once these ideas are in circulation, the Jews, who have never lacked genius, shall be able to mold their coreligionists into real Jews, in terms of theological values. Thus it may indeed appear baroque to translate Schiller's *Handschuh* into Hebrew. I gladly admit that on its own merits such a version has not the slightest value. Those who relish Schiller's *Handschuh* understand German, and those who understand German know the difference between Schiller's sweet-as-honey language, his pleasing structure of verses, and the crude scraps as well as the gothic embellishments of a Hebraized ballad. However, once in a while some capable Hebraizers succeed in saving one or the other tender turn of speech of our beloved German minstrel, translating it into their version; this always pleases me, and I would be happy if I knew that it had been brought safely to the altar of our holy Temple of Speech. Even Luzzatto's dramas—though deserving of the criticism voiced recently against the awful inversions and contortions appearing in them which mar any possible pleasure in reading them, and no matter how far-fetched it is to compare his personifications with those of Aeschylus—even these dramas by Luzzatto compensate for the sacrifice their reading may cost, because many a kernel of gold can be garnered from them for the treasury of a new Hebrew terminology. Once we gain an idiom for our new expanded theology with the aid of such and similar pioneers, we can claim that the time is ripe for a national language foundation, and then it will be possible to bring the suggestions of individuals before a collective forum, adding whatever it recognizes as valid to the true facts of our national mission.

A PROGRAM FOR JEWISH EDUCATION
(Resolution of the Leipzig Synod, 1869)

1. The assembly recommends must urgently to the congregations the establishment and support of good religious schools for the youth of both sexes.
2. The assembly recognizes it to be the task of the congregations—yes, of all the Jews of each and every state—to put forth every effort to have Judaism obtain its rights in the higher institutions of learning, which are intended for all confessions, by having it made possible for Jewish students to receive higher religious instruction.
3. The assembly hails with joy the tendency of our age which strives for the general establishment of non-sectarian schools; it recognizes in this tendency no danger for Judaism, but considers it all the more important that, in addition to these non-sectarian schools, there should be institutions which inculcate in the rising generation the knowledge and love of their inherited faith.
4. The assembly recognizes as inalienable portions of religious education not only the usual instruction in biblical history and the compilation of deeply ingrained religious principles, but also the firm grounding in the content of all the biblical books, the cultivation of the Hebrew language as the language in which these books are written, in which the religious idea finds its uniquely deep and intense expression, the language which has been, and should remain, the fresh spiritual source of all succeeding centuries and likewise the firm spiritual bond between all parts of Jewry. Especial stress should be laid upon acquainting the

young with the whole of Jewish history, including the post-biblical, as the richest source for confirmation in the faith and fortification of the religious sentiment.

5. The assembly declares that religious instruction in the school must avoid the critical method; the idealistic outlook of the young should not be blurred by the suggestion of doubts. For this very reason, however, the assembly expects our teachers to be wisely discreet in not ignoring the results of science, but to anticipate and prevent a conflict, which may arise later in the soul of our growing youth, between religion and the commonly accepted scientific point of view.

6. The assembly recognizes the need of special training schools for Jewish teachers, notably religious teachers. It appreciates the existing institutions of this character and desires eagerly their increase. But it does not fail to recognize the great difficulties in the way of establishing a sufficient number of such seminaries. Therefore, the assembly considers it an urgent duty to strive towards having capable Jews, who understand how to train Jewish religious instructors in their future profession and in its specific sectarian character appointed at the general public seminaries.

7. Finally, the assembly regards the establishment of one or more higher institutions of learning for the science of Judaism (theological faculty) as the highest task in the interest of the scientific knowledge of Judaism, and considers it to be one of its essential objects to arouse general interest in this matter. The assembly declares that the significance of such institutions consists primarily in their becoming the nurseries of free scientific knowledge, and that their mission is to strengthen Judaism spiritually and to secure for it its justified influence upon general spiritual development. The assembly, therefore, names a committee which is to unite with all efforts already put forth for the establishment of such higher institutions of learning.

5. THE STATUS OF WOMEN

Traditional Judaism granted to womanhood honor and respect, but certainly neither religious nor legal equality. An enlightened society could not for long tolerate the ancient inequities. Here, as in many other areas, Reform Judaism was ahead of its time. Its leaders soon urged total equality for women, a status which they enjoyed in none but a few other denominations.

THE SERVICE IS FOR WOMEN ALSO (*Aaron Chorin*)

Gone are the barbaric ages when the stronger half of mankind thought to elevate itself above the nobler half, when it was thought sinful to put women on the same level with men. The writer is of the opinion that we owe to our women the larger portion in the moral training of our youth, as well as our mores, our esthetic sense, and all that which is good, beautiful, and true. Therefore, women must not be excluded from the soul-satisfying experiences which come to us through a solemn worship service. But in which language shall such service be held? Certainly not exclusively in Hebrew, of which women do not have the slightest notion and which does not speak in any wise to their emotion! Here I agree heartily with the reformed ritual which has been instituted by so many enlightened and goodly men in Hamburg, Berlin, Kassel, Karlsruhe (and other congregations presently unknown to me). I wish nothing more fervently than that such ritual reforms soon be imitated everywhere.

NO SPIRITUAL MINORITY (*Abraham Geiger*)

Let there be from now on no distinction between duties for men and women, unless flowing from the natural laws governing the sexes; no assumption of the spiritual minority of woman, as though she were incapable of grasping the deep things in religion; no institution of the public service, either in form or content, which shuts the doors of the temple in the face of women; no degradation of woman in the form of the marriage service, and no application of fetters which may destroy woman's happiness. Then will the Jewish girl and the Jewish woman, conscious of the significance of our faith, become fervently attached to it, and our whole religious life will profit from the beneficial influence which feminine hearts will bestow upon it.

FOR TOTAL EQUALITY
(*Report to the Breslau Conference, 1846*)

The halakhic position of women must undergo a change, and it is hoped that all the members will be unanimous on that subject. We may think of one reason or another for the position which Bible and Talmud assigned to woman; and specifically in the province of the Talmud, we may designate either the moving spirit of the Aggada or the rigid attitude of the Halakha as the prevailing one. So much is certain: the religious needs of the present cannot be satisfied with mere motive power, but only with what this power generates.

From the religious viewpoint, it is the same with the dignity of women. A mere theoretical recognition, devoid of all legality, gives them as little satisfaction as, for instance, the Israelites are given in civic matters. They have received assurances of their capabilities for emancipation, without, however, being indeed permitted to become emancipated. It is useless to argue why the religious situation of women has become impaired, since one can neither deny its deterioration, nor can one find it compatible with present religious consciousness. To be sure, according to their viewpoint, the rabbis were absolutely right in systematically excluding the female sex from a significant part of religious duties and rights, and the poor woman could not complain about being denied exalted spiritual blessings, for it was believed that God Himself had pronounced the damning verdict over her. In the face of so many offending slights in civic life, she could not even complain about the fact that the house of God was as good as closed to her, that she had to beg the rabbi's permission for the daily expression of her Israelitish faith, as one begs for alms. She was permitted a share neither in religious instruction nor in certain sacred parental duties. The execution of sacred acts was now permitted, now forbidden to her; and finally, through the man's daily benediction for the good fortune of not having become a woman, she had to experience the most bitter offense in the very house of God. And yet, all this appears most mild when compared to the conferences of a Christian Council in the Middle Ages, debating whether a woman had a soul at all!

For our religious consciousness, which grants all humans an equal degree of natural holiness, and for which the pertaining differentiations in the Holy Scripture have only relative and momentary validity, it is a sacred duty to express most emphatically the complete religious equality of the female sex. Life, which is stronger than all theory, has indeed achieved quite a bit in this regard; however, a great deal is still lacking for the achievement of absolute equality, and even the little that has occurred already is still devoid of all halakhic strength. It is thus our task to pronounce the equality of religious privileges and obligations of women in so far as this is possible. We have exactly the same right to do this as the synod under R. Gershom, 800 years ago, which also introduced new religious decrees in favor of the female sex. When in regard to the Mezuzah commandment the Talmud says: *gavre bo'e hayye, nashe lo bo'e hayye*[4], we want to apply this principle in a far higher sense to all of religious life, thus supplying our religious community with a strength of which it has been deprived for all too long.

On the other hand, there shall no longer occur that religious preference on the part of woman which the Talmud grants the female sex (Nidda 45b, against the view of Rabbi Simon). Regarding the beginning of religious maturity, it is assumed that women mature earlier intellectually. For us, the religious coming of age shall begin for boys and girls alike, with the completion of the thirteenth year.

Esteemed gentlemen, the Committee herewith submits the following proposals for your examination:

The Rabbinical Conference shall declare the female sex as religiously equal with the male, in its obligations and rights, and pronounce accordingly as halakhic:

1. That women must observe all *mitzvot*, even though they pertain to a certain time, in so far as these *mitzvot* have any strength and vigor at all for our religious consciousness;
2. That the female sex has to fulfil all obligations towards children in the same manner as the male;

---

[4] (Ed. note) Men need to live, but women don't? Kid. 34a.

3. That neither the husband nor the father has the right to absolve a religiously mature daughter or wife from her vow;
4. That from now on, the benediction *shelo assani ishah,* which was the basis for the religious prejudice against woman, shall be abolished;[5]
5. That the female sex shall, from earliest youth, be obligated to participate in religious instruction and public worship, and in the latter respect also be counted in a *minyan;* and finally,
6. That the religious coming of age for both sexes begin with the age of thirteen.

6. FOR THE SAKE OF HEAVEN

Reform had its victories and its defeats, its moments of pessimism and its surges of exaltation. It had bitter opponents and staunch defenders, and, in Abraham Kohn of Lemberg, it even had its martyr. Often the bitterness of the struggle made its participants forget that they were all children of Israel; but in the end, history wrote its own verdict. It had been an age of searching and growth. Reform had battled for the sake of heaven, and made a lasting and continuing imprint on Jewish fate.

DISCOURAGEMENT *(Orly Terquem)*

A mathematician of distinction, Terquem (1782-1862) had stirred his French coreligionists briefly by issuing nine pamphlets advocating radical reforms. But these *Lettres Tsarphatiques* (1831-37) elicited little response, and after a decade of literary activity Terquem announced his withdrawal from the field of religious controversy.

I may be forgiven if I express for the last time my principles which are so little known and so much misunderstood. I advocated them because I believed and still believe them to be good and advantageous for our faith, a faith which I prefer to all others and whose continued existence I desire. Honorable and judicious people have thought otherwise; therefore, I herewith renounce all further participation in any polemic which might be termed Reform and shall only occupy myself with purely literary or scientific matters. For the rest, I shall resign myself to the role of reader and spectator.

---

[5] (Ed. note) The Orthodox prayer book contains this benediction: "Blessed art Thou, O God, King of the Universe, that Thou hast not made me a woman."

A REFORMER RECANTS (*Aaron Chorin*)

In 1818, Chorin had published his *Kin'at Ha-emet* which appeared in defense of the Hamburg reformers. Subsequently, pressure from Orthodox colleagues in Hungary caused Chorin to reconsider his position, and he was moved to pen the following recantation. Despite this declaration, the very next year Chorin issued a new tract in which he disregarded the sense of this revocation and further encouraged the reformers.

Since I have learned that the founders of the new ritual have also abbreviated the blessings and prayers and no longer petition for the restoration of Israel (the realization of which we expect in accordance with the principles of our holy religion), and since they change other prayer formulas as well, I apply to myself the scriptural verse, "Let this ruin be under thy hand" (Isaiah 3:6)! Therefore, I declare publicly: All my words in the letter *Kin'at Ha-emet* are annulled and invalid. Besides, I am not worthy to judge and decide this subject matter. Only the sages of Israel and their leaders (Geonim) of the time are justified in doing so. In comparison with their opinions, mine is null and void.

THE ETHICAL WILL OF AN ORTHODOX LEADER (*Moses Sofer*)

Moses Sofer, the greatest Talmudist of his time (1763-1839), was the acknowledged leader of Orthodoxy in its battle with Reform. Sofer lived in Pressburg, where he founded a famous academy.

With God's help, the 15th of Kislev 5597 (November 24, 1836).

Since man does not know how long he is destined to labor for the Almighty, treasure your knowledge of God's teaching ever more, so as to elevate the house of our Lord, and so that you, my sons, daughters, sons-in-law, and grandchildren, and their children, may truly live!

May your mind not turn to evil and never engage in corruptible partnership with those fond of innovations, who, as a penalty for our many sins, have strayed from the Almighty and His law! Do not touch the books of Rabbi Moses [Mendelssohn] from Dessau, and your foot will never slip! Study and teach your children the entire Holy Scripture with Rashi's explanations, the Torah with Ramban's [Nachmanides] exegesis, for this is the main source of religion. Should hunger and misery lead you into temptation, then the Almighty will protect you; resist temptation and do not turn to the idols or to some god of your own making! The daughters may read German books, but only those which have been written in our own way, according to the interpretations of our teachers (may they rest in peace), and absolutely no others! By all means, stay far from the theater. That I absolutely forbid you!

Be warned not to change your Jewish names, speech, and clothing—God forbid—and your motto shall be: "And Jacob came in peace to the city of Shechem" (Gen. 33:18).

Do not be concerned that I have left you no fortune or wealth; for the Father of the orphans compassionately protects all those without father or mother; He will not forsake you either! Do not use God's teaching to make a crown for yourselves or even a bread-winning tool! And even less—God forbid—shall you use it to wander around preaching for money or soliciting a job. Never say: "Times have changed!" We have an old Father—praised be His name— who has never changed and never will change. . . . The order of prayer and synagogue shall remain forever as it has been up to now, and no one may presume to change anything of its structure. . . .

REFORM IS UNNECESSARY (*Israel Deutsch*)

Deutsch (1800-53) was an Orthodox rabbi in Beuthen, Germany. The following is taken from letters to a friend.

. . . I have read only one of the Geiger publications, but I know enough. With the torch of enlightenment they want to burn the graying, venerable structure of religion and build on its ruins a modern Judaism which would essentially be nothing but a poorly corrected Christianity, without Christ and apostles.

Judaism is either direct, divine revelation, or nothing. Almost all religions have the basic moral good in common. . . . However, if Judaism is revelation, then it is above all the ceremonial aspect which prevails everywhere in the law; the dogmatic and moral aspect—though it may be the more important part— does not appear to be the main goal of revelation. Now, if the ceremonial is divine revelation, then there is no need for any arguments founded on reason; and instead of all arguments, it should be enough for us to know that it is the will of the Almighty. Therefore, Judaism without ceremonial is an absurdity, a tattered vestment which neither protects nor adorns.

Now, the more the Jew is mentally attracted to the non-Jew and the more he enjoys the latter's respect, goodwill, and equality as a citizen, all the more is he in danger of denying his nationality and of disappearing into the melting pot of nations, without leaving a trace. It is precisely at this very point that the ceremonial, as an external mark of distinction and as a means of attraction, has its significance. It is precisely here that it can demonstrate its basic strength.

When we see the storming and blustering of the Jewish Reform-Jacobins, we are led to believe (in the words of the Apostles) that "the Heavenly Kingdom is close at hand." They seem to think that as soon as organ and choral singing will resound, and sermon and prayer arise, virtue and purity will mount the throne and all vices will cease and vanish. Would to God that they spoke the truth! I gladly admit that all this can have its advantage, but when we do not adhere to tradition, even prayer cannot be regarded as a positive law and basically founded in Judaism; how, then, shall and can prayer render all expressly stipulated positive and negative commands dispensable?

And if, indeed, we have reached the point where we succeed in hallowing the service through organ, choir, etc., then we shall have achieved only what every Christian village community has had for many centuries. . . .

But were the Jews at any given time—even though without regulated service —ever less moral, or less religiously minded than their Christian brothers? Whoever claims that, slanders them. With some justification they are being reproached in the area of their business dealings, which is a consequence of their civic position in society. But they certainly have practiced more temperance, chastity, and charity in former days than at present, and more so than all Reform heroes of recent times. . . .

YET WILL I SPEAK (*Abraham Kohn*)

The following is taken from the Lemberg reformer's last sermon. Fatefully, it dealt with the commandment, "Thou shalt not murder." The following week Kohn was poisoned by fanatical opponents.

Our ancients who took the promise at Sinai, "We shall do and we shall listen," to mean literally, we will do (what God has commanded) and we will hear it, found in this promise both haste and incomparable zeal to accept and follow the law. I see nothing strange in this, nothing that does not repeat itself with us today. To heed a divine command is indeed something which one delays as long as possible. Instead, one is inclined to say, "We will do it; we already know what is right and what is wrong." And in saying this, one still maintains one's freedom to act in accordance with one's own decision, to follow one's own interest, and still at the same time one appears meritorious and worthy of recognition. But it is another matter to listen to the divine word in order to follow it *after* one has heard it, *because* one has heard it, and *in the way* one has heard it. To do this goes against our sense of independence, and with this the religious sense has its trouble. Thus, I have been importuned from various sides that I should not proceed with the explanation of the divine commands and not give religious lectures and not bring the word of God into the pulpit; but rather, I should speak about political questions of the day or intramural quarrels, because these alone, it is said, command attention and interest. But can I heed such desires? Can I make this place a battleground of unholy struggles? Can I diminish the right of God's word and suppress it when it needs to be proclaimed? May it find fewer listeners then; but he who wants to hear will hear, and he who wants to turn away, let him turn away.

Thus, then, will I turn to the sixth commandment, "Thou shalt not murder."

I WRITE FOR TOMORROW (*Solomon Ludwig Steinheim*)

I do not rely on the fortunate nor the contented nor the wealthy; my eye is set on the youth with their pain and their longing, their susceptibility to light and justice, youth who are not yet weakened by humiliating circumstances, not yet paralyzed by the indolence of comfort, not yet ruined by earthly gain. Here, the word shall pass from heart to heart and do its work where the noblest blossoms of the mind grow toward their full bloom and are ready to burst forth from the bud. I offer my hand as a friend and companion on a path that I endeavored to open for myself and others. I hope that, through a succession of continued studies carried on in earnestness and devotion, I have removed many a thorn and many a stone.

In the last decades the amount of true education has increased tenfold among our people, and a fund of the noblest kind has accumulated. Was it the fault of our youth that, together with the spread of scientific methods, a glossy philosophic system took hold of them? It was mostly their fathers who had made a burdensome ritual into a repugnant burden, for which even they had already lost the ancient reverence. They failed to reveal to them the lofty, open secret, which was hidden like a diamond within the coal. As the saying goes, the child was thrown out with the bath. It is a wonder that even a few maintained their loyalty to the old way; it would be inexplicable were their number greater than it is.

My book is now beyond the realm of my power! As the arrow darts from the string, so does man's word once it is spoken; for he is no longer its master. But was I its master before? Who knows the elasticity of a thought, the power of which breaks through the narrow boundaries of each poor creature, overwhelming him with divine power—who knows it, who can weigh it? And so, I shall eagerly follow these words on their way into the distance. Will they stir up new waves? Will they calm the large ones? Will they vanish without leaving a trace? Who can prophesy it? The author is like many others, as were fools and wise men before him. He has, as a presentiment, the notion of a marked effect and the conviction of a beneficial outcome of his endeavor. If he fails, he can seek consolation in a more glowing future and comfort himself that his voice was not suited to a hateful present, which lacked the right sense of hearing. As the reader will notice, he has already learned from experience and is holding his consolation in readiness.

WE MUST REFORM OURSELVES (*Leopold Zunz*)

I am not responsible for the misfortune of our "status-quo Judaism" and I would be happy indeed if others who attack traditional Judaism—even that which was precious to me—would achieve something worthwhile for the sake of mankind and Jewry. I despise a rabbinical hierarchy, but I also have contempt for a Reform movement that produces namby-pamby programs; and as for those who will attack a defenseless Judaism from an anti-religious point of view, I let them be, if they have pleasure in doing so. The norm for the religious spirit can only be the religious spirit itself and that which we hold dear in a common and living tradition. Our best souls (as in the past, men like Maimonides, ibn Ezra, Mendelssohn) can then build on such a foundation. We must reform ourselves, not our religion. Of course, we must attack existing abuses, both within and without the community, but in doing so we must maintain our sacred heritage.

7. A GUIDE FOR REFORM JUDAISM

How could the teachings and practice of Reform be distilled so that the average Jew would know how to order his religious life? Leopold Stein was not the first to attempt the creation of a guide. Others, like Creizenach and Francolm, had preceded him, and a hundred years later there were new Reform thinkers who prepared such guides. Such catalogues of duties were a normal part of Jewish history, and as such they were indigenous also to Reform. The movement shrank only from creating an official code, but did not discourage scholars from creating their individual guides. Stein's effort found a ready audience and demanded wide attention. His guide was called *Torat Hayim* (The Torah of Life), and came at the end of his two-volume work on the theology of Judaism, *Die Schrift des Lebens* (The Book of Life).

TORAT HAYIM (*Leopold Stein*)
 (*A catalogue of religious ordinances for present-day Israelites*)

1. Judaism is the religion of law, and every Israelite is obligated to sanctify and order his life in accordance with divine ordinance.
2. The single divine source of the religious laws of our life is the Holy Scriptures, as it is written, "Moses commanded us a law, an inheritance of the congregation of Jacob."
3. The Mosaic teaching and law of life is above all *moral law,* which summarizes the *duties toward one's fellow men* with the words, "Thou shalt love thy neighbor as thyself"; which summarizes the *duties toward God* with the words, "Thou shalt love the Lord thy God with all thy heart, with all thy soul, and with all thy might"; and the *duties toward ourselves* with the words, "Ye shall be holy, for I, the Lord your God, am holy."
4. These laws are founded in our very nature and are, therefore, by themselves apparent to reason. However, the Mosaic law contains also *ordinances*

which do not have their source in our inner nature, but which nature and reason welcome because of their wisdom and utility.

5. The Mosaic laws, whose apparent utility was made known to us in the words, "For this is your wisdom and your understanding in the eyes of the peoples," (Deut. 4:6) are clear and understandable in themselves. This is also true of the ordinances in so far as they still apply to us. We cannot and may not suppose that Moses himself, by means of the Oral Law, stripped these ordinances of their simple meaning and enlarged them through countless additions.

6. Under Oral Law in its historically significant meaning, we understand the living word of the religious teachers and leaders of *all* kinds, who have the right and obligation to formulate religious ordinances in accordance with the needs of the time, the needs of reason, and the needs of nature, so that the people may both hear and practice them.

7. The Talmud tells us how, by way of frequent change throughout two millenia of our religious history, the Oral Law discharged its function for the continued development of religious life. However, the Talmud is not for us in any respect a credal book or a basic source of divine communication.

8. God has made Israel a "kingdom of priests," which means: *all* shall know, *all* shall be in a position to learn what their religious duties are. This can only be accomplished by the Holy Bible itself because it is easily grasped and available to all, but not through the Talmud, the precincts of which are open only to the rabbis, but which remains incomprehensible to the people.

9. The post-biblical times brought about many splendid new institutions like the creation of the synagogue (a house of prayer outside of the Temple), which occurred at the time of Ezra and his successors; the creation of the Hanukah festival at the time of the Hasmoneans; the order of the worship service and the prayers which come to us from the time of Mishnah and Talmud. These, as well as other rabbinical institutions, which are in themselves in accordance with reason and nature and which reflect the religious needs of the present, we, too, consider to be sacred obligations to us in the ordering of our religious life and law.

10. All rabbinical ordinances, however, which excessively weigh down and impede life, which interfere with the dignity of religion, which impinge upon the clear divine laws of the Bible and which muddy or even distort them—these, we feel, we not only *may,* but *must,* abrogate and must not give them room in our religious life and law.

11. We mention only these as examples: the prohibitions (as explained by the rabbis) to sew a woolen garment with a linen thread; or to shave the beard with a razor; the punishment of a surviving brother through *halitza,* because he cannot, and may not, enter into a levirate marriage. In these and similar customs there is neither wisdom nor reason, and certainly of these it will not be said, "Surely this great nation is a wise and understanding people" (Deut. 4:6).

12. We have especial reference to the dietary laws of the rabbis, which exceed all measure of reason. The rabbinic dietary laws have as their purpose our

separation from non-Jewish society; precisely because of this, their abrogation is demanded by our time, which encourages association and which places the Israelite into continuous contact with the non-Israelite world.

13. As regards abstinence from the consumption of those animals prohibited by the Torah (Leviticus, chapter 11; Deuteronomy, chapter 14), and also the prohibition of the eating of blood (Lev. 17:12, Deut. 12:23), we consider these as ethical means to achieve temperance, sanctification, and the safeguarding of our nature against harm and indignity—but not as means of separation. Therefore, it says in connection with these biblical laws, "Ye shall be holy unto Me . . . and I set you apart"—and not: "I set you apart from the people."

14. Amongst the rabbinical ritual ordinances we count the following:

a) All prohibitions of *trefa*, with the exception of the clear and simple biblical prohibition of that which was torn in the field;

b) The prohibition of the mixing of meat and milk;

c) The prohibition of the thigh-vein;

d) The prohibition of the eating of meat which comes from an animal *not* slaughtered in accordance with rabbinical ordinances (*shehita*);

e) The prohibition of wine which a non-Israelite has harvested or touched;

f) The milk of a biblically permitted animal which has not been obtained in the presence of an Israelite.

15. For all these prohibitions there is no foundation in Mosaic legislation according to its unambiguous formulation and clear reasonable understanding. Therefore, he who does not observe these encumbering ordinances has not only not transgressed against the holy law, but has contributed in a conscientious and salutary manner to the restoration of the law in its purity, as well as to the possibility of living it in the present.

16. The two fundamental forms of the Mosaic law, sanctified as signs of the covenant between God and Israel, are circumcision and Sabbath. The former is not a condition of entrance into the covenant, for a Jew is born into the covenant. It should be noted that a mark of the covenant on our body is not as exalted as the Sabbath, which is glorified in Scripture in countless places as a mark of the covenant of the *spirit*.

17. Without a celebration of the Sabbath, Judaism cannot be long maintained in family and congregation. Its observance demands sacrifices, to be sure; but our fathers brought great sacrifices of life and possession a thousand times in order to preserve their highest good. And the teaching of the one and only God, which promises the unification of mankind, deserves the most joyful devotion, quite aside from the fact that the sanctification of the heart and of family life, which the Sabbath celebration brings in its train, will more than amply replace the loss of any earthly gain which it might cause.

18. Therefore, all of you dearest comrades in faith, brothers and sisters of the house of Israel, who are so fortunate still to possess this holy day—maintain it, save it; and thereby you will assist, more than by anything else, to erect anew and to strengthen new religious life and law in Israel, on a biblical foundation.

19. Numerous unnecessary rabbinic additions interfere with a rational celebra-

tion of the Sabbath. We have both the right and obligation to set them aside. Jewish real estate men, artisans, and business people may take advantage of such permissible means of gaining their livelihood which would not interfere with their personal observance of the Sabbath. We must consider as forbidden labor all such enterprises through which the sacredness of the day is diminished and through which it is debased into a workday.

20. Besides the Sabbath, there are another seven days of the year, to be observed during five different festivals which have been recommended to us as divinely sanctified times and have been established by the Mosaic code with their respective ordinances. In addition to these, Hanukah and Purim come to us from post-Mosaic times. However, the second days of the festivals added by the rabbis (six in number) have no justification for our time and all should, therefore, be set aside as being actually opposed to biblical law and divine will. *This is a sacred religious duty.*

21. Like the Sabbath, the crown of the week, a day of sanctification and elevation above our earthly labors, so is the Day of Atonement the day of the spirit and elevation above our sensual nature. It is the crown of the year. However, every other day of fasting during the year only interferes with the eminence of that unique day and is, therefore, in contrast to the spirit of the Holy Scriptures. The four fast days, reminding us of misfortunes during the first destruction of Jerusalem, have been expressly abrogated by the prophet Zechariah (8:19).

22. It is through public worship that Sabbath and festivals convey to us their great importance for our religious awareness. Public worship sanctifies that most splendid place where religious life must reveal itself in accordance with our convictions and the demands of the time. For prayer is the expression of gratitude, of our desires and hopes, which we lay before our Heavenly Father. It has its origin in our innermost religious thinking and feeling and must, therefore, be the truest mirror of all that we experience, strive for, and need.

23. Therefore, our prayer above all must be truth before the God of Truth. How can it be considered respect before an old tradition when we still cry and lament before God (as is done in many prayers of the old service) over conditions of persecution which, in His fatherly grace and mercy, He has long done away with? These prayers must be uprooted in all synagogues. They are untruth, lack of understanding, and sinful ingratitude.

24. Similarly, the supplications for the restoration of the bloody sacrificial cult must be completely abrogated. The prophets, in the name of God, often spoke in flaming words; the psalmist clearly and plainly proclaimed the lack of value of these practices; Maimonides, just like Moses, the father of all prophets (Lev. 17:7), has proved beyond a doubt that the sacrifices were originally admitted only as a defense against idolatry, but that they stood below the level of prayer. How, then, can we pray for the restoration of sacrifices in a Messianic era in which idolatry will have ceased? How can one pray for such a regression of the religious spirit? How can we ask this of a God who is the source of all reason, who has promised to lead Israel and all mankind in mercy to an ever-higher spiritual perfection?

25. The same is true of the petition for the restoration of a Jewish realm and

kingdom. Moses set as the highest goal that not a single human being, but God alone, would reign through His law. How dare we direct our hopes for the Messianic future to a lower goal than Moses did for us in the beginning?

26. The Messianic era in which "God will be king over all the earth," when "He will be one and His name will be one," in which all peoples will turn to the Lord and "become His people," in which mankind will unite itself under one God into one brotherhood, in which the earth through "justice, truth, and peace" will become a garden of God and a promised land—these prophetic prayers and hopes, together with the most fervent gratitude to God for the salvation which He already granted unto us, shall find their true expression in the synagogue through new prayers in the vernacular which would warm the heart and lift the spirit.

27. In order to maintain the unity of the synagogue over the whole earth, one certain part of our prayers shall always be in the Hebrew language, but the larger part in the native language which is dear to all from childhood on and which is thereby naturally accessible.

28. In order to maintain reverence and dignity, and in order to give adequate room to the most important part of the worship service—namely, the proclamation of the divine word—the over-abundance of prayers should be limited, and every avoidable repetition, as for instance of the Kaddish, should be omitted; especially, the reading from the Torah which takes place every Sabbath shall be done in shorter sections, but through sermon and biblical exegesis these shall be brought ever closer to the understanding of the people. The reading from the Torah shall take place in Hebrew, the reading from the other two parts of the Bible in the language of the country.

29. The recognition of rabbinic ordinances as being God-ordained is to be removed from the prayers. Thus, for instance, the lighting of the Hanukah lights or the reading of the *Hallel* are of rabbinic and not of biblical origin. When, therefore, in our prayers we call these divine commandments, we are adding to the Torah, which has been repeatedly forbidden by Moses.[6] This will in no wise diminish our respect for the utilitarian institutions of the rabbis; only these institutions must not be designated as divine.

30. The number of ten religiously mature male participants, necessary for the conduct of a divine service, is not founded on biblical law. A common uplifting worship should be permitted also to a smaller number of people, and is to be recommended. This improvement will be especially helpful to small congregations.[7]

31. The biblical ceremony of the festive bouquet on the first day of Tabernacles (*lulav*) and the blowing of the horn on New Year's day (*shofar*) should take place even when the festival falls on the Sabbath.

[6] Instead of "Who has commanded us" (*v'tzivanu*), it should be, "For the sake of whose great name we read *or* light the candles, etc." (*asher l'zikhron sh'mo ha-gadol . . . anu korim,* or *anu madlikin*).

[7] In a talmudic book on religious law, it says about the conduct of worship service with *kaddish* and *bor'chu,* "Our occidental teachers (in Palestine) say that it is permitted to pray with seven persons; others say even with six" (Sofrim 10:7).

32. The religious ordinances of the blowing are fully satisfied with the four sounds, and this institution is highly recommended in order to safeguard the reverence and dignity of every worship procedure.

33. Outside of the public worship service, the very important and highly significant home worship service should be most carefully built up. It is through service that we really come in the most intimate contact with God. At a public service it is as if we were sojourning with God, but in a service at home God comes to us in order to sanctify us and our home. The meditation at home consists of morning prayer, prayer at mealtime, and evening prayer, and should be held, if at all possible, in the midst of one's family and should be connected with readings from Holy Scriptures as well as from other non-biblical edifying writings. On the Sabbath there should be added joyous songs for the uplifting of our sacred Friday evening; on the eve of Passover there is the soul-moving family celebration of the Seder; at the Festival of Joy (Succot), the decoration of the festive tabernacle through the hands of children; and at Hanukah time, the lighting of the lights. The regular observance of home services will awaken joy and a happiness of spirit within old and young—for Judaism is a religion of *joy*.

34. When God's sacred judgment imposes bitter losses upon our home, our customs of mourning should not become symbols of excess and extreme sorrow. This is against the express will of our exalted teacher, Moses, who warns us of this when he calls to us, "You are children unto the Lord your God" (Num. 14:1). Therefore, to let the beard grow wild and to tear one's garments, are customs which are contrary to Mosaic law and to humane sentiment and should be eliminated.

35. The following should be maintained: the kindling of the memorial light —for "the spirit of man is the lamp of the Lord"; abstinence from worldly pleasures, as well as the saying of the Kaddish prayer (the prayer of sanctification). The latter is to be encouraged, not because its recital would ensure the happiness of the souls of our departed (this is a point of view which is un-Jewish and should be abandoned), but so that children be constantly reminded of their high duty to sanctify the name of God among men in their parents' stead, and to help bring about His heavenly kingdom on earth.

36. The synagogue itself must, in our time, cease to be in mourning; for this is a time, as the fate of Israel especially proclaims, when the morning of an era of freedom and justice among men is dawning, for with great mercy God has turned toward Israel, His congregation. Uplifting song and the joy-evoking effects of the musical arts shall glorify our house of worship, which, binding the great past of Judaism to the greater future of Israel and of the human race, shall more and more prove itself worthy to be called "a house of prayer for all people."

Bibliographical Notes

CHAPTER I

TRAIL BLAZERS

1. The First Generation

WHY A NEW TRANSLATION? Moses Mendelssohn. Introduction to the Pentateuch (*Netivot ha-shalom,* Berlin, from 1780). Translated in *HR* n.s., vol. I (1859), No. 34, pp. 584 ff. Even though Mendelssohn considered himself responsible for the whole work, the Introduction from which our excerpt is taken was primarily the work of Hartwig Wessely (see p. 8). The Introduction and translation were printed in Hebrew characters.

Elijah Habachur (1468-1549), more generally known as Elijah Levita, was a grammarian of significance. Isaac (Jekuthiel) Blitz published a translation mostly for the use of Polish Jews who had fled to Amsterdam from the eastern pogroms. The work contained many Dutch expressions. There had been a few other attempts by Jews to translate the Bible into German, but none of them exerted any influence.

THE THREE PARTS OF JUDAISM. Moses Mendelssohn, *Jerusalem,* ch. 2; in *Gesammelte Schriften,* vol. III (Leipzig, 1843), pp. 311 ff.

THE RIGHT TO BE DIFFERENT. *Ibid.,* pp. 358 ff.

STATE OF EDUCATION. Hartwig Wessely. From the translation in *HR,* n.s. vol. I (1859), pp. 51 ff.

APOSTASY IS NOT THE WAY. David Friedländer, *Sendschreiben an . . . Probst Teller* (Berlin, 1799), p. 61.

THE NEED FOR PRAYER REFORM. *Ibid.,* p. 41.

2. The Journals

Ha-Me'assef, publ. in Königsberg, from 1784. First supplement (Jan. 1784), pp. 19-20.

Sulamith publ. in Leipzig, from 1806.

CONTENT, PURPOSE, AND TITLE. Vol. I, p. 9.

RELIGION AND CEREMONY. Vol. I, pp. 332 ff.

The Biblical Orient. German original title: *Der Bibel'sche Orient* (Munich, 1821), vol. I, pp. 22 ff.

Journal for the Science of Judaism. German original title: *Zeitschrift für die Wissenschaft des Judenthums,* ed. L. Zunz (Berlin, from 1822).

FROM THE PREFACE. Vol. I, p. III.

THE SOCIETY. . . . TO M. M. NOAH. From Franz Kobler, *Jüdische Geschichte in Briefen aus Ost and West* (Vienna, 1938), p. 186.

The Scientific Journal for Jewish Theology. German original title: *Wissenschaftliche Zeitschrift für jüdische Theologie,* ed. A. Geiger (Frankfort, from 1835). Vol. I, pp. 1 ff.

The General Journal of Judaism. German original title: *Die Allgemeine Zeitung*

des Judenthums, ed. L. Philippson (Leipzig, from 1837), vol. I, no. 41 (July 27, 1837), pp. 161 ff.
Archives Israélites de France, ed. Samuel Cahen (Paris, from 1840), vol. I, pp. 66 f., 113, 234.
Journal for the Religious Interests of Judaism. German original title: *Zeitschrift für die religiösen Interessen des Judenthums* (Berlin, from 1844), ed. Z. Frankel.
FROM THE PROSPECTUS. *Prospectus,* published by M. Simion (Berlin, 1843), p. 5 f.
MODERATE REFORM. *Journal,* vol. I, pp. 26 f.
The Monthly Magazine. German original title: *Monatsschrift für Geschichte und Wissenschaft des Judenthums* (Berlin, from 1852), ed. Z. Frankel.
HISTORY AND SCIENCE. Z. Frankel, vol. I, pp. 2 ff.

CHAPTER II

NEW TEMPLES, NEW PRAYER BOOKS

1. Seesen, 1810

DEDICATION OF THE TEMPLE OF JACOB. *Sulamith,* 3rd year (1810), vol. I, pp. 298 ff.
DEDICATION ADDRESS. Israel Jacobson, *ibid.*

2. Hamburg, 1817

FROM THE CONSTITUTION. *Theologische Gutachten über das Gebetbuch nach dem Gebrauche des neuen Israelitischen Tempelvereins in Hamburg* (Hamburg, 1842), pp. 4-5.
FROM THE HAMBURG PRAYER BOOK. *Ordnung der öffentlichen Andacht für die Sabbath-und-Festtage,* ed. Frankel and Bresselau (Hamburg, 1819), Introduction.
IN DEFENSE. Aaron Chorin, *Ein Wort zu seiner Zeit (Davar be'ito,* Vienna, 1820), pp. 27 ff.
ORTHODOXY ATTACKS. *Eleh divre ha-berith,* ed. by the Hamburg Beth Din (Altona, 1819), *passim.*
A REFORM REJOINDER. M. I. Bresselau, *Herev nokemet nekam berith* (Dessau, 1819), pp. 12, 13, 16.
DISCOURAGEMENT. Gotthold Salomon, in Kobler, *op. cit.,* p. 75.
THE SECOND ROUND. A. Chorin, in *Theol. Gut.,* pp. 51 ff. (excerpts).
THE TEMPLE AND JEWISH TRADITION. M. Fränkel, in *Theol. Gut.,* pp. 27 ff.

3. Vienna, 1826

FROM FAILURE TO SUCCESS. I. N. Mannheimer, in Kobler, *op. cit.,* p. 72 f.

4. Metz, 1841

A PUBLIC APPEAL. 31 Jewish Householders, *Archives Israélites,* vol. II (1841), pp. 469 f.
PROPOSAL FOR REORGANIZATION. Gerson-Lévy, *ibid.,* pp. 533-535.

5. London, 1842

DEDICATION SERMON. David W. Marks, Discourse delivered at the consecration of the West London Synagogue of British Jews, reprinted in *The Synagogue Review*, vol. XVI, no. 6. (Feb. 1942), pp. 133 ff. (excerpts)

FROM THE LONDON PRAYER BOOK. *Forms of Prayer for Jewish Worship*, vol. I. (6th. ed., Oxford, 1931), pp. IX ff.

6. Frankfort, 1842

A DECLARATION OF PRINCIPLE. From the translation by David Philipson, *The Reform Movement in Judaism* (2nd ed., New York, 1931) p. 121.

THE FRANKFORT PLATFORM. *Ibid.*, p. 122.

THEY ARE SECTARIANS! S. J. L. Rapoport, in Salomon A. Trier, ed., *Rabbinische Gutachten über die Beschneidung* (Frankfort, 1844).

THEY DENY REVELATION! M. Gutmann, in *Literaturblatt des Orients*, no. I (Jan. 2, 1844), pp. 3 ff.

7. Berlin, 1844

I AM NO REFORMER. Sigismund Stern, *Die Aufgabe des Judenthums und des Juden in der Gegenwart* (2nd ed., Berlin, 1853), p. VIII f.

PROCLAMATION OF THE ASSOCIATION. Kobler, *op. cit.*, p. 79.

FROM THE BERLIN PRAYER BOOK. *Gebetbuch der Genossenschaft für Reform im Judenthum*, 2 vols. (Berlin, 1848) vol. I, pp. I ff; vol. II, pp. 177 ff.

8. Worms, 1848

FROM THE PROGRAM. Kobler, *op. cit.*, p. 7a f.

9. Pesth, 1848

APPEAL. From the translation in D. Philipson, *op. cit.*, p. 275.

CHAPTER III

THE GREAT CONTROVERSY—GEIGER vs. TIKTIN

FOR THE FREEDOM OF INQUIRY. Bernhard Wechsler, in *Rabbinische Gutachten über die Verträglichkeit der freien Forschung mit dem Rabbineramte*, 2 vols. (Breslau, 1842-3), vol. I, p. 92 f.

THE PROGRESSIVE NATURE OF JUDAISM. Abraham Kohn, *ibid.*, vol. I, pp. 102 ff.

THE PERSONAL ARGUMENT. Joseph Kahn, *ibid.*, vol. II, pp. 13 ff.

CHAPTER IV

CONFERENCES AND SYNODS

1. The French Sanhedrin

QUESTIONS ASKED. From the translation in *Yearbook of the Central Conference of American Rabbis*, vol. I (1890-91), p. 80 f. Used by permission.

CALL FOR THE SANHEDRIN. From Heinrich Graetz, *Geschichte der Juden,* vol. XI (2nd ed., Leipzig, 1900), p. 266.

THE SANHEDRIN RESOLVES. *Décisions doctrinales du Grand Sanhedrin* (Paris, 1812), pp. 6, 24.

2. *The Rabbinic Conferences*

PHILIPPSON WRITES TO BRUNSWICK. *Protokolle der ersten Rabbiner-Versammlung zu Braunschweig vom 12. bis zum 19. Juni 1844* (Braunschweig, 1844), p. VIII.

THE TRUSTEES WRITE. *Ibid.,* p. IX.

THE FIRST SESSION. *Ibid.,* p. 1.

SUMMARY. *Ibid.,* pp. 128 ff.

HIRSCH vs. FRANKEL. Samuel Hirsch, *Der Orient* (publ. by J. Fürst; Leipzig from 1840), vol. V (1844), no. 49, pp. 378 ff.

POSITIVE, HISTORICAL JUDAISM. Zacharias Frankel. *Protokolle und Akten-stücke der zweiten Rabbiner-Versammlung* (July 15-28, 1845; Frankfort, 1845), pp. 18 ff.

FRANKEL RESIGNS. *Ibid.,* pp. 86 ff.

3. *The Synods*

INVITATION FROM CASSEL. From the translation by David Philipson, *op. cit.,* p. 289 f.

RESULTS AT LEIPZIG. Moritz Lazarus, *Verhandlungen der ersten israelitischen Synode zu Leipzig vom 29. Juni bis 4. Juli 1869* (Berlin, 1869), pp. 212 ff.

THE AUGSBURG SYNOD. From the translation in *CCAR Yearbook,* vol. I (1890-91), pp. 115-17. Used by permission.

CHAPTER V

NEW PATTERNS OF THOUGHT

1. *General Considerations*

JUDAISM MUST BE THOROUGHLY JEWISH. David Einhorn, *Inaugural Sermon,* Sept. 29, 1855 (published in English translation, Baltimore, 1905).

CAN SCHISM BE AVOIDED? I. S. Reggio, in *Israelitische Annalen,* ed. J. M. Jost, vol. I (1839), p. 147.

THE BREACH IS UNHEALABLE. S. D. Luzzatto, *ibid.,* p. 156.

HERE ARE THE WEAPONS. Anon., *AZJ,* vol. I (1837), no. 75, p. 297.

THE TIME IS NOW! M. A. Stern, in Kobler, *op. cit.,* p. 61.

TO SAVE THE FUTURE. Gerson-Lévy. *Revue Orientale* (Brussels, 1841), vol. I, pp. 460 ff. Excerpts of this address were also printed in *Archives Israélites,* vol. II, pp. 531 ff.

2. *The Science of Judaism*

ON THE CONCEPT OF A SCIENCE OF JUDAISM. Immanuel Wolff, in *ZWJ,* vol. I (1822), no. 1, pp. 1 ff.; translated by Lionel E. Kochan, in *Yearbook of the Leo Baeck Institute,* vol. II (1957), pp. 201 ff. Used by permission.

NEEDED: A STUDY OF THE WORSHIP SERVICE. L. Zunz, *Die gottes-*

dienstlichen Vorträge der Juden (first published 1832; 2nd. ed., Frankfort, 1892). Preface; translated in *HR*, n.s., vol. I (1859), no. 1, pp. 3 ff.
MIRACLES AND THE HISTORIAN. I. M. Jost, *Allgemeine Geschichte des israelitischen Volkes* (Leipzig, 1850), vol. I, p. 20.

3. *The Bible and Its Text*

THE NEED FOR BIBLICAL CRITICISM. A. Geiger, *Nachgelassene Schriften*, ed. Ludwig Geiger, 3 vols. (Berlin, 1885), Vol. II, p. 62 f.

4. *The Authority of Tradition*

AUTHORITY AND CRITICISM. J. S. Schorr, *IA*, vol. I (1839), pp. 169 ff., 282 f.
WRITTEN AND ORAL LAW. Abr. Kohn, *Rabb. Gut.*, pp. 113 ff.
WHICH PORTION OF THE TALMUD REMAINS BINDING? M. Creizenach, *Schulchan Aruch*, 4 vols. (Frankfort, 1833-39), vol. II, pp. 69 ff.
AUTHORITY AND FREEDOM. D. Einhorn, *Rabb. Gut.*, pp. 125 ff.
TALMUD AND REFORM. Samuel Holdheim, *Das Ceremonialgesetz im Messiasreich* (Berlin and Schwerin, 1845), pp. 48 ff., p. 28 f.

CHAPTER VI

A PEOPLE AND ITS FAITH

1. *Revelation*

ISRAEL'S NATIVE ENERGY. Abr. Geiger, *Judaism and Its History*, translated by Maurice Mayer (New York—London, 1866), pp. 46 ff. *passim.*
THE INCOMPREHENSIBLE IS CENTRAL. S. L. Steinheim, *Vom Bleibenden und Vergänglichen* (Berlin, 1935), pp. 22 ff. *passim.*
REVELATION AND RATIONAL JUDAISM. I. A. Francolm, *Das Rationale Judenthum* (Breslau, 1840), p. 17.

2. *The Jewish People—Dispersion and Restoration*

THE JEWISH PEOPLE. Ludwig Philippson, *AZJ*, vol. I (1837), no. 1, p. 2 f.
ONLY GOD CAN END OUR DISPERSION. Abr. Kohn, *Theol. Gut.*, pp. 79 ff.
CAN WE STILL PRAY FOR RESTORATION? M. Gutmann, *ibid.*, p. 70 f.
A PATRIOTISM AS GLOWING . . . D. W. Marks, *JC*, vol. II (1845), no. 1, pp. 27 f.

3. *The Mission of Israel*

THIS IS OUR TASK. S. Holdheim, *Neue Sammlung jüdischer Predigten*, 3 vols. (Berlin, 1852-55), vol. I, p. 156 ff.
ISRAEL'S DESTINY. *Gebetbuch etc., op. cit.* (Berlin, 1848), vol. I, pp. 190 ff.
ISRAEL'S POSITION IN PAST, PRESENT, AND FUTURE. *Haester's Lehr- und Lesebuch*, ed. for Jewish Schools by Dr. Emanuel Hecht (Essen, 1863), pp. 606 f.
THE CAPITAL OF THE WORLD. L. Philippson, *Das Buch der Haphtoroth* (Leipzig, 1859), p. 173.

4. The Messiah

A THREAD THROUGH ALL OUR SCRIPTURES. M. Gutmann, *Lit. Or.*, no. 2 (Jan. 9, 1844), p. 22 f.
THE MESSIAH IN JUDAISM AND CHRISTIANITY. L. Stein, *Die Schrift des Lebens,* 2 vols. (Strasbourg, 1872-77), vol. I, pp. 266 ff.

5. Judaism and Christianity

JESUS AND JUDAISM. L. Stein, *op. cit.,* vol. I, pp. 93 ff.
JUDAISM AND CHRISTIANITY. Sig. Stern, *op. cit.,* p. 119, pp. 197 ff.
THE INFLUENCE OF JUDAISM ON CHRISTIANITY. S. Formstecher, *Religion des Geistes* (Frankfort, 1841), pp. 419 ff.

CHAPTER VII

WORSHIP REFORM

1. Changing the Prayer Book

THE LITURGY MUST BE CLEANSED. A. Chorin, *Ein Wort etc., op. cit.* pp. 33 ff.
THE NEED FOR A NEW PRAYER BOOK. Joseph Maier, *Protokolle etc., op. cit.* (Brunswick, 1844), pp. 99 ff.
SOME SUGGESTED CHANGES. Abr. Geiger, *Nachgelassene Schriften, op. cit.* vol. I, pp. 203 ff.

2. The Sermon

WORSHIP AS AN EDUCATIONAL FORCE. L. Zunz, *Gottesdienstliche Vorträge, op. cit.,* pp. 472 ff.
A WORD ON THE FRENCH SERMON. S. Cahen, *Archives Israélites,* vol. I, p. 234; vol. II, p. 197 f.

3. Vernacular and Hebrew in the Service

FROM THE DEBATE. Z. Frankel, Abr. Adler, L. Philippson, *Protokolle etc.* (Frankfort, 1845), pp. 34 ff. *passim.*

4. Synagogue Music

THE USE OF THE ORGAN. J. H. Recanati, *Nogah Hatsedek,* (Dessau, 1818) p. 9.
REPORT OF THE RABBINICAL COMMISSION. *Protokolle etc.* (Frankfort, 1845), pp. 326 ff.
LET US HAVE CHOIRS. Anonymous, *Archives Israélites,* vol. I (1840), p. 647.
FOR HIGHER MUSICAL STANDARDS. S. Sulzer, *Verhandlungen der ersten isr. Synode etc., op. cit.,* p. 250.
WE NEED BETTER CANTORS. L. Adler, *Verhandlungen der zweiten israelitischen Synode zu Augsburg, vom 11. bis 17. Juli1871* (Berlin, 1873), pp. 214 ff. *passim.*

5. Bar Mitzvah and Confirmation

FOR A REFORM OF BAR MITZVAH. Maimon Fränkel, *Sulamith,* 3rd year (1810), vol. I, pp. III ff.

SIMPLICITY, NOT POMP. I. A. Francolm, *op. cit.*, pp. 292 ff.
IS CONFIRMATION A "JEWISH" CEREMONY? S. Herxheimer, *Verhandlungen der ersten isr. Synode etc., op. cit.*, pp. 233 ff.
CONFIRMATION IN PARIS, 1852. Anonymous correspondent, *Monatsschrift*, vol. I (1852), p. 359 f.

6. Covering the Head

HISTORICAL FACTS. Leopold Löw, *Gesammelte Schriften*, ed. Immanual Löw, vol. II (Szegedin, 1890), pp. 311 ff. *passim.*

7. Torah Reading and Piyutim

THE TORAH CYCLE. M. Joel, G. Gottheil. Debate at the Leipzig Synod, *Verhandlungen, etc.*, pp. 128 ff.
PIYUTIM. G. Gottheil, *ibid.*, p. 177 f.

CHAPTER VIII

SABBATH AND HOLIDAY OBSERVANCE

1. The Sabbath

WHAT WORK IS PERMITTED? B. Wechsler, *Protokolle der dritten Versammlung deutscher Rabbiner, vom 13. bis 24. Juli 1846* (Breslau, 1847), pp. 43 ff.
THE SABBATH MUST BE PROTECTED. S. Adler, *ibid.*, pp. 53 ff.
A NEW CONCEPT OF THE SABBATH. S. Holdheim, *ibid.*, pp. 59 ff.
SABBATH AND SUNDAY. S. Holdheim, *ibid.*, pp. 70 ff.
SYNODAL DECISIONS. Translation from David Philipson, *op. cit.*, p. 319.

2. The Holidays

THE SECOND DAY OF THE FESTIVALS. S. Herxheimer, *Protokolle etc.* (Breslau, 1847), pp. 209 ff.
ABOLISH THE SECOND DAYS. B. Wechsler, *ibid.*, pp. 209 ff.
FASTING ON YOM KIPPUR. L. Philippson, *Haphtoroth*, p. 221.
TISHA B'AV AND THE MODERN JEW. D. Einhorn, *Ausgewählte Predigten und Reden*, ed. Kaufmann Kohler (New York, 1881), pp. 315 ff.
WE MUST MOURN ON TISHA B'AV. L. Philippson, *loc. cit.*, p. 276.
FOR A REVIVAL OF HANUKAH. S. Szantó, M. Silberstein, *Verhandlungen zu Augsburg, op. cit.*, pp. 226 ff.

CHAPTER IX

THE PERSONAL LIFE

1. Circumcision

THE FRANKFORT CASE. S. A. Trier, *op. cit.*, p. XI f.
THE EXTERNAL CONDITION OF ACCEPTANCE. N. M. Adler, *ibid.*, p. 10.
HOW TO TREAT THE UNCIRCUMCISED JEW. S. D. Luzzatto, *ibid.*, p. 75.
A BARBARIC RITE. A. Geiger, letter to Zunz, dated March 19, 1845. *Nach-*

gelassene Schriften, vol. V, p. 181 f. Translation from David Philipson, *op. cit.,* p. 136.

THE VIENNA CASE. M. Engel, *Verhandlungen . . . zu Leipzig, op. cit.,* pp. 92 ff.

RESOLUTION OF THE AUGSBURG SYNOD. Translation from David Philipson, p. 320.

2. *Dietary Laws*

FOR A MODIFICATION OF KASHRUT. M. Creizenach, *op. cit.,* vol. II, pp. 42 ff.

KASHRUT—OFFENSE AND PENALTY. French Consistory, *Archives Israél-ites,* vol. I (1840), pp. 67 ff.

3. *Marriage*

THE CEREMONY. *Sulamith,* 3rd year, vol. I, pp. 294 ff.

ONE OR TWO WEDDING RINGS? J. Aub, *Verhandlungen . . . zu Augsburg., op. cit.,* pp. 30 ff.

MODERN MARRIAGE. *Ibid.,* pp. 256 ff. *passim.*

MIXED MARRIAGE. *Protokolle etc.* (Brunswick, 1844), pp. 6 ff.

DIVORCE. *Protokolle der Rabbiner-Conferenz abgehalten zu Philadelphia* (Nov. 3-6, 1869), New York, 1870, p. 88.

4. *Mourning Practices*

RABBINIC DEBATE. *Protokolle der dritten etc.* (Breslau), *op. cit.,* pp. 280 ff.

5. *Home Observance*

ONLY A MIRACLE CAN SAVE US. M. Creizenach, *op. cit.,* vols. III/IV, pp. 54 ff.

CHAPTER X

THE COMMUNITY

1. *The Rabbinic Office*

THE DIGNITY OF THE RABBINATE. S. Holdheim, *IA,* vol. I, pp. 179 ff.

"DOCTOR" OR RABBI? Peter Beer, *AZJ,* vol. III (1839), p. 496 ff.

IT IS HARD TO BE A RABBI. A. Geiger, *Nachg. Schriften,* vol. I, pp. 501 ff.

NEEDED: A RABBINIC COLLEGE. L. Philippson, *AZJ,* vol. I (1837), pp. 349 ff.

2. *The Public Oath*

Protokolle etc., op. cit. (Brunswick, 1844), pp. 33 ff.

3. *Apostates*

LETTERS ON LEAVING JUDAISM. A. Geiger, *Nachg. Schriften,* vol. I, pp. 230 ff.

4. Jewish Education

GOALS OF JEWISH EDUCATION. D. Einhorn, *Inaugural Sermon* (preached in Baltimore, 1855; published in English, 1905), p. 15 f.

PRIVATE INSTRUCTION OR RELIGIOUS SCHOOL? Abr. Geiger, *Nachg. Schriften, loc. cit.,* p. 349 f.

THE TEACHER'S DILEMMA. M. Creizenach, *loc. cit.,* pp. 58 ff. *passim.*

TEACHING CEREMONIES, BIBLE, AND HEBREW. Abr. Geiger, *loc. cit.,* pp. 324 ff.

NEEDED: A REVIVAL OF HEBREW. L. Herzfeld, *AZJ, Beiblatt,* vol. II, (1839), p. 15 f.

A PROGRAM FOR JEWISH EDUCATION. Resolutions of the Leipzig Synod; from the translation by D. Philipson, *op. cit.,* p. 299 f.

5. The Status of Women

THE SERVICE IS FOR WOMEN ALSO. A. Chorin, *Theol. Gut., op. cit.,* p. 47.

NO SPIRITUAL MINORITY. A. Geiger, *WZJT,* vol. III. (1837), pp. 1 ff. Translation from D. Philipson, *op. cit.,* p. 473.

FOR TOTAL EQUALITY. Report to the Breslau Conference, *Protokolle etc.,* pp. 263 ff.

6. For the Sake of Heaven

DISCOURAGEMENT. Orly Terquem, *Archives Israélites,* vol. II. (1841), p. 769 (The article was written under a pseudonym, but the identity of the author is not in doubt).

A REFORMER RECANTS. A. Chorin, in *Eleh divre ha-berith, op. cit.,* p. 98.

THE ETHICAL WILL OF AN ORTHODOX LEADER. Moses Sofer, in Kobler, *op. cit.,* p. 91.

REFORM IS UNNECESSARY. Israel Deutsch, *ibid.,* p. 96.

YET WILL I SPEAK. A. Kohn, *Nachg. Schriften,* ed. Jos. Kobak (Lemberg, 1856), p. 125 f.

I WRITE FOR TOMORROW. S. L. Steinheim, *Die Offenbarung nach dem Lehrbegriff der Synagoge, ein Schiboleth* (Frankfort, 1835), p. XVI.

WE MUST REFORM OURSELVES. L. Zunz, letter to Geiger (May 4, 1845), in Geiger, *Nachgel. Schriften, op. cit.,* vol. V, p. 184.

7. A Guide for Reform Judaism

TORAT HAYIM. L. Stein, *op. cit.,* pp. 463 ff.

Index

When a name occurs more than once, an asterisk indicates the page on which that person's biographical notation may be found.

275